EUROPEAN THOUGHT IN THE EIGHTEENTH CENTURY

European Thought

IN THE

Eighteenth Century

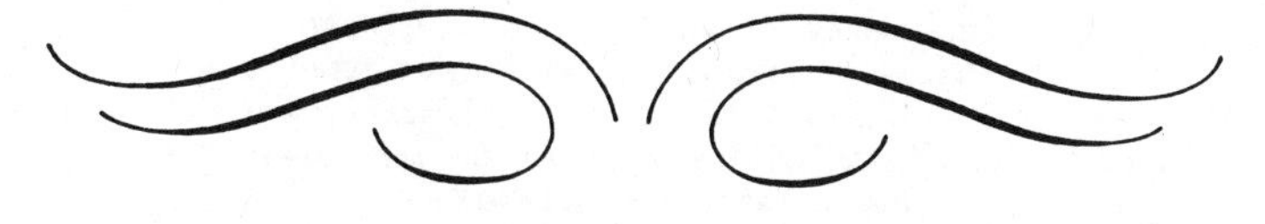

FROM MONTESQUIEU TO LESSING

BY

Paul Hazard

Meridian Books

THE WORLD PUBLISHING COMPANY

CLEVELAND AND NEW YORK

A MERIDIAN BOOK

PUBLISHED BY THE WORLD PUBLISHING COMPANY
2231 WEST 110TH STREET, CLEVELAND 2, OHIO
THIS TRANSLATION FROM THE FRENCH, *La Pensée Européenne au XVIIIème Siècle: De Montesquieu à Lessing* (BOIVIN: PARIS, 1946), WAS MADE BY J. LEWIS MAY.
FIRST MERIDIAN PRINTING AUGUST 1963.

REPRINTED BY ARRANGEMENT WITH HOLLIS & CARTER.
LIBRARY OF CONGRESS CATALOG CARD NUMBER: 54-6569
PRINTED IN THE UNITED STATES OF AMERICA. MWP 863

SUMMARY OF CONTENTS

Part II

THE CITY OF MEN

Chapter IX. Ideas and Manners p. 249

Social types of the day; the Adventurer. Love of travel engenders the cosmopolitan. The tendency grows stronger, and up starts the Adventurer; Cagliostro and Casanova, p. 249. Woman. From the pursuit of pleasure and sensuous delights we must logically ascribe the apotheosis of Woman, Queen of the Age: the *Temple de Gnide,* the *Voyage à Paphos*, the *Congresso di Citera*, *Angola.* Mistresses; all, kings, grandees, even philosophers, have them. Paris sets the tune; Europe follows suit, p. 254. Women take part in the intellectual movement; their rôle; Voltaire and Mme du Châtelet; the salons, Mrs. Montagu in London, others elsewhere, especially Mme du Deffand in Paris, p. 257. The Man of Letters; he lives by his calling now, which means the increase of his social dignity. Emancipated from the patronage of the great the man of letters is the leader of public opinion, p. 259. The Bourgeois; a new class comes into being; the Bourgeois tends to supplant the Nobleman, whose social worth is now contested. He puts up a poor defence, p. 263. Personal merit henceforth the sole title to social advancement, p. 264. Between the dethroned nobility and the uneducated proletariat comes the new class whose patent rests on the idea of freedom and on power based on property, p. 266. The Freemason; representing the spirit of the age, he repudiates austerity, preaches and practises concord, calls for political freedom, declares war on despots and on privilege, and stands forth as the apostle of Deism, p. 267. Originating in England, Freemasonry rapidly spreads all over Europe. Despite the condemnation of the Church, kings and nobles join the movement, p. 269. The Philosopher; a new pattern of humanity. His essential character. The spirit of enquiry, controlled by reason, put at the service of mankind, p. 271. Victory near at hand; England, France and Switzerland very much to the fore; the Latin countries lag behind, but the Northern countries and their sovereigns lead the way for the rest, p. 274. "The face of Europe almost completely changed in the last fifty years", says Voltaire, p. 276.

Part III

DISAGGREGATION

Book I

Chapter I. "Becoming" p. 279

Seeds of decay within the philosophic doctrine itself; triple causes which were to lead to its defeat. The philosophers' primary error regarding Nature clearly brought to light by Kant, who in his *Critique of Pure Reason,* by reducing all problems to the nature of knowledge, reinstated the soul in its due place, p. 279. On the other hand, the heart had not relinquished its rights; the Abbé Prevost and *Manon Lescaut,* Richardson and *Pamela,* Rousseau and *la Nouvelle Héloïse,* Goethe and *Werther,* Bernardin de Saint-Pierre and the *Études de la Nature,* all foretell the appearance of the Man of Feeling, p. 280. The lack of unity and coherence in the doctrine of the philosophers and their divergent views regarding Deism is the major cause of their failure, p. 282. Such are the phases in the history of the philosophy of Enlightenment, p. 283.

Chapter II. Nature and Reason p. 284

Contradictions which defeat the attempt of the philosophers to identify Nature and Reason; lack of any precise definition of the concept of Nature. Voltaire's criticism, p. 285. Empiricism itself by confining knowledge to the perception of sense-data denies any right to postulate the existence of anything external to the mind, such as Nature. Criticism of Knowledge; Berkeley in his *Dialogues between Hylas and Philonous* and his *Siris*, or investigations into the nature of tar-water deduces from the denial of an external world, the existence of a Mind, which is God, p. 287. Enquiries designed to determine whether sensation is purely subjective or whether it corresponds to something external to us; theories of Molineux, Locke and Berkeley confirmed by the experiments of Cheseldon and Hilmer, p. 290. Condillac in his essay in refutation of Berkeley begins with empiricism and ends with a belief in the spiritual, p. 292. Hume complains that the Deists picture their Supreme Being as a kind of Superman, p. 294. According to him causality is merely succession in time; his pure pyrrhonism, p. 296. Contradiction between the notion of evidence as defined by the empiricists, with empiricism itself: the said notion derives from Descartes. The influence of Descartes still active and running parallel, though in the opposite direction to Locke's, is fostered by Fontenelle, the Abbé Terrasson, Mairan; by Père André and the Jesuits who are won over in time, and by materialists like La Mettrie who do not forget the animal-machines, p. 297. The age is equally taken with Locke's empiricism and Descartes' rationalism, mutually contradictory though they are, p. 300. The influence of Leibniz still persists: d'Alembert, Diderot, Buffon pay tribute to his genius which brings about the victorious reaction of metaphysics over the spirit of the times, p. 303. The influence of Spinoza, feeble to begin with, progressively increases and his metaphysical pantheism is absorbed in the philosophy of the *Aufklärer*, p. 305. All these divers elements, Empiricism, Cartesianism, Leibnizianism and Spinozaism, more or less harmoniously mingled, introduce a number of incoherences into the theory of knowledge which must wait for Kant to adjust them, p. 307.

Chapter III. NATURE AND GOODNESS: OPTIMISM p. 309

The problem of evil transferred from the religious to the philosophical, p. 309. Leibniz diminishes the importance of physical ill, denies the existence of metaphysical evil and explains moral evil as the necessary condition for a greater good, p. 311. Pope, trusting in the infinite Wisdom, declares that all is for the best, p. 313. Haller, arriving at the same conclusions, exalts the importance of fulfilling one's duty and submitting to the divine plan, p. 314. Hence the genesis of *Optimism*. A competition organized in 1759 by the Berlin Academy for the best definition of the doctrine, p. 316. That same year the Lisbon earthquake creates consternation in the philosophers' camp. The *Poème sur le désastre de Lisbonne* throws a light on the evolution of Voltaire's ideas which find their expression in *Candide*, a sparkling satire on the foolish simplicity of the Optimists, p. 316. Optimism, now discredited, lives on as the object of irony and rancour, p. 322. Kant, at first a disciple of Leibniz, later proclaims the philosophical bankruptcy of his master, p. 325. Rousseau defends Nature and blames mankind to whom he is to propose the remedy set forth in the *Contrat Social*, p. 324.

Chapter IV. NATURAL POLITICS AND ENLIGHTENED DESPOTISM p. 325

Naïve conception of a policy founded on virtue. If only philosophers could rule the country! p. 325. No easy matter to set up the reign of Reason among men, p. 326. Grimm's melancholy avowal, when his illusions disappear, p. 327. Kings and philosophers coquet together; reciprocal advances. A reconciliation between the two powers looked for in enlightened despotism, p. 328. No settlement possible between the absolute and the liberal forms of government. Even the most enlightened of despots aim solely at establishing the over-all supremacy of the State. Frederick II, Maria Theresa, Joseph II, Catherine II, and the rest, with the support of their ministers, act solely in the interests of the State. These realistic politicians are enthusiastically belauded by the philosophers who believe they have found new allies, p. 329. Frederick II is their particular favourite because of his love of letters and his philosophical antagonism to the Church, p. 333. All the same, the philosophers are a little uneasy about these royal allies of theirs. They thought they were using the kings, whereas the truth was that the kings were using them, p. 333.

Chapter V. Nature and Freedom: Laws are Necessary Relations deriving from the Nature of Things p. 335

No easy matter to set up a morality based on Nature on the ruins of one based on Dogma; the morality of self-interest and the morality of pleasure both equally deceptive, p. 335. The confusion in men's consciences proved by the numerous attempts to set up a new Ethic. Hutcheson founds one on Instinct, Lévesque de Pouilly on a particular state of the brain-fibres, Hume on public approval or disapproval, Adam Smith on sympathy. Bentham, Oswald and Reid give a host of definitions of what morality is, all different, all incomplete, p. 336. Where the partisans of Natural Morality make their initial mistake. Their postulate belied by the facts, p. 339. Vauvenargues; his pathetic destiny; the morality of heroism; his Stoical ideal; no morality but that which aims at the loftiest and most arduous, p. 340. Freedom or Determinism? Though divided in opinion, the tendency of the times, on the whole, inclines to the latter, p. 343. Montesquieu in a quandary. His definition of laws as being " the relations which necessarily arise from the nature of things " would make a fatalist of him, were it not that he denied that blind fate could produce intelligent beings and affirmed that fate as he conceived it was rational, thus, despite his protests to the contrary, approximating to Spinoza and the Stoics, p. 345. His subtlest arguments only avail to show how perplexed he was and how powerless to reconcile fatalism and progress, p. 349.

Book II

Chapter I. Sentiment; Uneasiness; Potencia Sensitiva en el Ombre p. 353

Causes had been preparing out of sight for the arrival of the Man of Feeling, when the Man of Reason had had his day, p. 353. From the scientific observation of the various forms of life men fell to meditating upon them and finally to admiring them. Linnaeus and Buffon reveal the immensity of Nature, but they reveal its beauty, too, p. 354. The principle of anarchical revolt of which we become aware in the writings of such men as Byron, Shelley and Stendhal is traceable to some eighteenth-century ideas, p. 356. Attempts to discover a principle other than Reason to explain how Beauty is recognized and created, p. 357. Unsatisfactory nature of the old rational conceptions of Beauty, the newer definitions lay stress on its objective and relative character and declare that it is born of the passions, p. 358. Winckelmann and his *Histoire de l'art chez les anciens :* in the new way of looking at it, art is regarded as a phenomenon of life governed by the general laws of evolution, p. 361. First Locke and then Condillac expound their theories as to the psychology of desire. The latter of them makes *ennui*, that is to say the dread of it, the universal incentive; and Helvetius has it that passion is at the root of all poetry. So now we are well into the realm of Romanticism, p. 362.

Chapter II. The Feelings: The Primitive and the Civilized p. 364

Civilization *ad nauseam*; too much of it excites the resolve to escape from it. Recourse to the marvellous and the exotic, p. 364. The Noble Savage; the Baron de la Hontan's Adario, p. 365. Others, better informed on the matter of Nature unadorned set their hopes upon the future, confident of the progress of mankind, p. 367. Primitivism *versus* Civilization, p. 371. Voltaire's witty and mordant defence of the latter in his *le Mondain* and *Défense du Mondain*. Endless controversies concerning the opposing theories of decadence and progress, p. 373. Warring ideologies seen in the economic world in the conflict between two major systems—the Mercantilism, formerly preached by Colbert, and Physiocracy based on the rich productivity of the soil, p. 374. Spread of this latter doctrine in Europe. Louis XV's economic experiment in regard to the free circulation of grain; the miscalculations of Terray and Turgot. Downfall of Physiocracy, p. 376. Adam Smith in his *Wealth of Nations* now proclaims that the supreme source of riches resides in Labour. The industrial era about to begin, p. 377.

Chapter III. Diderot p. 378

Diderot, a synthesis of the Man of Feeling and the Man of Reason. All the contrasts imaginable combined in the incomparable richness of his genius, p. 378. His ruling faculty: Denis the Philosopher; his belief in Science based on Experiment; his hesitations on the question of morals. His determinism would exclude merit and demerit; calls for political freedom, state-education and technical training; his enquiries into the nature of Beauty; his anti-clericalism which results from his passing from Deism to atheism; his materialism a mixture of Epicurus and Maupertuis; overflowing with ideas he is always unwilling to relinquish one side for the benefit of another; the affirmative at the expense of the negative. He is the herald of the age of enlightenment, p. 380. He is also the prophet of the *Sturm und Drang*, the initiator of European Romanticism; his imagination supplies what his eye does not see, and pictures create for him his concept of Nature; his ever-lively sensitiveness is constantly pitting the Man of Feeling in him against the Man of Reason; he is an atheist yet he is deeply moved by the ceremonies of Catholic worship; a materialist he believes in the sovereignty of the mind; a fatalist, yet he believes in free-will when it comes to choosing a wife; he is a tyrant-hater, yet he is full of admiration for Catherine II; he professes a code of self-interest, but in practice he is swayed by his feelings; he is a professed aesthete, but he proclaims the emotional power of art with an enthusiasm that borders on the lyrical eloquence of our romantics, p. 383. His conception of Nature as complex as it is contradictory, p. 387. For Diderot, Nature is, first and foremost, instinct, these intense individual powers which enable man to regain his primitive freedom and to cast off the trammels of civilization. Diderot paves the way for Rousseau, and for the attitude towards life of the coming generation, p. 389.

Book III

Chapter I. The Various Deisms: Bolingbroke and Pope p. 393

Deism is not a religion because it takes on as many shapes as it has professors, p. 393. Bolingbroke and Pope, p. 394. Bolingbroke initiates Pope into philosophic thinking. His teaching, p. 395. Pope the poetical interpreter of Bolingbroke's philosophy; *The Essay on Man*, 1733–1734, a profession of faith of the

CONCLUSION

PREFACE

THERE is scarcely a chapter in this book but deals with some deep, conscience-stirring problem; scarcely a chapter but records some movement whose repercussions have persisted down to our own day. Not that it all began in 1715. We ourselves have shown in a previous work that the first symptoms of the great moral and intellectual crisis that was to come about in Europe were discernible as far back as the year 1680. Other writers in their turn have pointed out the various by-paths by which the Renaissance and its ideas came to link up with the eighteenth century.[1] However, it was from 1715 onwards that there became apparent an effervescence and a diffusion of ideas so remarkable in its nature, so far-reaching in its extent as to be without parallel in history. Ideas that had been slowly maturing out of sight suddenly burst forth into the light of day; theories that had hitherto been confined to an exclusive intellectual *élite* became the property of the many; notions that had scarcely dared to show themselves now came boldly forward and challenged the world at large. Rich and weighty as were the legacies bequeathed to us by old Greece and Rome, by the Middle Ages and by the Renaissance, the fact remains that it is the eighteenth century of which we are the direct and lineal descendants.

We do not propose to trace the interrelations and mutual bearings of ideas, or to draw conclusions regarding their influence one upon another. That task we leave to others. Nor is it our intention to play the prophet-in-retrospect, still less the doctrinaire, and least of all the partisan. Our sole concern is with the facts themselves, the facts, not as they should have been, nor as

[1]M. Rossi, *Alle fonti del deismo e del materialismo moderni,* Firenze, 1942.—R. Lenoble, *Mersenne, ou la naissance du mécanisme,* 1943.—R. Pintard, *Le libertinage érudit dans la première moitié du XVIIe siècle,* 1943.

they might have been, but as they were. Such is our one and only preoccupation. No obligation has weighed with us so imperiously as that of displaying the facts in the fullest light of objective truth. We have had no dearer aim than to be undeviatingly faithful to history.

The scene, as we beheld it, was more or less as follows: first there were the critics in full cry, filling the air with their vociferations. It was the chorus of the new generation upbraiding their predecessors for saddling them with so ill-conceived a social order, an order which was the child of illusion and the parent of ill. What had the long process of time resulted in? Disaster. Why, they asked, was this? Thereupon, they openly preferred a charge the like of which for sheer audacity had never before been heard of. Now, the culprit was dragged into open court, and behold, the culprit was Christ! It was more than a reformation that the eighteenth century demanded, it was the total overthrow of the Cross, the utter repudiation of the belief that man had ever received a direct communication from God; of the belief, in other words, in Revelation. What the critics were determined to destroy, was the religious interpretation of life. That is why we call Part I of our work, *Christianity on Trial.*

But these bold men would do more than destroy; they would build up something new. The light of reason, they declared, should dispel the great masses of darkness that enshrouded the earth. They would rediscover Nature's plan. Once they had done that, all they would have to do would be to conform to it, and so restore to the human race its long-lost birthright of happiness. They would set up a new law, a new moral standard, and it should have nothing to do with divine law; the new moral code should be quite unfettered by theology. In the new political structure there were to be "subjects" no more; only "citizens". And so that no children of theirs should ever slip back into the bad old ways, they would bring them up on an entirely new system. Then, indeed, it would be heaven upon earth. In the beautiful bright buildings they would erect, all would be well with the generations of the future; no need for them to seek life's meaning, its happiness, its grandeur otherwhere than in themselves alone. We propose to accompany these innovators; we shall watch them at work, and examine the ground-plan and general lay-out of this city of theirs, the *City of Men.*

However, we must beware of assuming that these ideas retained in the later stages of their development all their original purity, all the clear-cut logic of an abstraction, of a theorem. The generations, as they came and went, never bequeathed to their successors anything but the derelict shell of a building. What they erected always fell in before they were able to complete it. Other ideologists kept arriving in their wake, shoving them out of the way, as they themselves had done to the people they found on the site. So, in their turn, these newcomers moved on like the rest, leaving behind them, not the order they had dreamed of, but confusion worse confounded. We shall have to deal with some of the most clear-headed thinkers the world has ever seen, yet they too, for all their clarity of vision, left behind in their system, luminous as it was, some hidden defects which time brought to light and which in the end were fated to destroy it. Instead of taking a general bird's-eye view of the philosophy of the period we shall rather make it our task to detect and bring to light the flaws that finally spelt its undoing. We shall take account not only of the manner in which a school of ideas essays to establish itself but also of the remorseless flux of things which eventually carries it away. This, the third portion of our work, we entitle *Disaggregation.*

In order to limit our field of investigation—no one could complain that it was too restricted already—we have confined our attention to one particular class or order of minds. If we refer to such writers as the Abbé Prévost with his *Manon Lescaut*, to Richardson with his *Pamela* and his *Clarissa*, to Goethe and his *Werther*, this is merely to point a contrast; we have not studied them. We have, indeed, deliberately by-passed the portrayers of the Sensitive Soul, and all that tumultuous stream of sentiment which flows throughout the eighteenth century. We finish our present survey with the Philosophers and the Rationalists. Arid, matter-of-fact spirits those, who, by the very aridity of their nature, brought about, by way of reaction, the unsealing of the wells of passion and of mysticism. But they were combative also, brooking no ideas that conflicted with their own; unvisited, too, by any love of forest, sea or mountain; cold, pitiless intellects, they failed to attain those lofty peaks to which Spinoza, Bayle, Fénelon, Bossuet, Leibniz won their way. They were but pale shadows of those soaring geniuses. Not but what they too were geniuses in their way and front-line actors in the drama of ideas. Certainly, they were not the sort of men passively to acquiesce in the state of affairs as they found it. They were men of mettle and they dared high things. They were obsessed to a degree which we of today can hardly imagine by the great, fundamental problems of life. Their worldly affairs, amusements, pastimes, even the squandering of their own intellectual energies seemed to them of small importance compared with those age-old riddles. What is Truth? What is Justice? What is Life? Importunate voices, they were never silenced. Always, the same questions arose. If by chance at evening they seemed to have given them their *quietus*, back again they returned with the morning.

It were well worth while to study the other collateral branch of the intellectual family, the restless hearts, the faltering wills, the yearning spirits; worth while to contemplate the slaves of desire, the victims of love, earthly or divine; to give heed to their petitions, their appeals; to contemplate their transports, their ecstasies, with them to discover the treasures of the sequestered life, with them to behold the suns that glitter on the fields of night. To complete our survey of the eighteenth century, we ought to record the birth and development of the Man of Feeling, to track him right down to the French Revolution. On that enterprise we have already embarked. One day, perchance, we shall complete it. One day, *si vis suppeditat*, as the Romans used to say.

PART ONE

CHRISTIANITY ON TRIAL

I

THE UBIQUITOUS CRITIC

ASMODEUS had gained his freedom, and now you ran across him everywhere. He tilted up the roofs of houses to find out what the people were about inside. He roamed the streets and button-holed the passers-by; he poked his nose into churches to see if he could find out the sort of things people believed—that, indeed, was his favourite occupation. However, he did not express his views with the fulminating fury, the sombre ferocity of a Pierre Bayle. No; he frisked and frolicked about like the whimsical antic, the light-hearted jester, he really was.

The seventeenth century went out in an atmosphere of unbelief; the eighteenth came in on a wave of irony. The old school of satire was by no means dead, and Horace and Juvenal now came in for a new lease of life. But soon the thing went far beyond that; it exceeded all limits. Even love stories must have their dash of satire, and satirical comedies, lampoons, epigrams, pamphlets, broadsides swarmed like ants. It was rare fun, and when the supply of writers fell short, the caricaturists filled the gap. And here is another sign of the times. In London, a very learned man, John Arbuthnot by name, gathered some of the leading intellectuals of the day about him, and together they founded one of the queerest sodalities ever heard of. They called it the Scriblerus Club, and its object was to throw ridicule on every kind of literary ineptitude and incompetence. It seemed to give notice to the Europe of 1713 that the spirit of criticism was abroad in the world.

Three tracks furrowed this ruffled sea; to begin with, there was burlesque. In less than no time *Télémaque* was mercilessly parodied. If, in the *Iliad*, there is a specially heart-rending scene, a scene which mirrors the purest love and tenderness, it is that in which Andromache takes her last farewell of Hector. She comes to him with tears in her eyes and, taking him by the hand, pleads pitifully with him, beseeching him by all his different names: "Thy rashness", she tells him, "will be thy undoing. Hast thou no pity for thy little son, no compassion for poor helpless me?" But alas, antiquity was revered no more, nor indeed was anything else, and these are the words in which Hector makes answer to her sorrowing plaint:

> Mon Dieu! que vous savez bien braire!
> Mais quand vous brairiez mieux encore,
> Un roc est moins ferme qu'Hector,
> Et de vos pleurs il se soucie
> Comme en hiver d'une roupie. . . .[1]

The taste for the mock-heroic spread far and wide and became one of the leading fashions of the day. The *modus operandi* was to exalt the trivial, and ridicule the noble. The filching of a lock of hair, or the unseemly remarks of a pet parrot belonging to a company of nuns, or the inane utterances of a swaggering student seemed to offer subjects good enough to parody the Epic Muse, and to make this sort of mockery pass as the soul of wit.

It was about this time, too, that some very innocent-looking foreign visitors arrived on the scene. They pretended to be looking at Europe, and things European, as something quite new and unfamiliar, and, in so doing, laid bare its numerous anomalies, and exposed its defects and vices. A Turkish enquirer was the first to try his hand at the game; then came a Siamese, and both of them paved the way for Montesquieu's Persians. It was in the year 1721 that these latter appeared, and people went into ecstasies about them. Ah, what wit! How their remarks went home, when, leaving aside their tales of the harem for the nonce, they declared, these seeming innocents, how amazed they were at the things they saw. Their trick was to put things "back to fore", and, by virtue of this simple process, the French mode of life was summarily undermined, and its

[1]Good gracious me, how loud you bray; but bray you now and every day, firm as a rock is Hector bold, and for your tears as little cares as he would heed a snivelling cold. Marivaux, *Homère travesti, ou l'Iliade en vers burlesques*, 1717.

habits and customs, which had passed unquestioned because everyone had got used to them, prejudices (sometimes justified by the necessity for compromise imposed on a social order which, unable to reach perfection, had to make the best of what it could get) were now shown up for what they really were, and that is, just prejudices, and nothing more. Institutions, bereft of the prestige which tradition had conferred upon them, robbed of the protection which had shielded them so long, were now revealed in all their naked decrepitude. The veil of reverence was torn asunder, and behind it was nought but a mass of illogicalities and absurdities. All this the Persians performed with so skilful a blend of cunning and simplicity, with such bland and cheerful effrontery, with such unblushing impudence, that you were completely taken in, and before you knew where you were, you were joining in the fun. He was a dull dog who did not become their accomplice. It was their energy, their astounding insight, the frank reports they gave of what they saw, their sure eye for detail, that excited admiration. It was as if they had pulled down somebody's house with such admirable skill that the owner of it himself was compelled to compliment them on their amazing dexterity.

The departure of the Persians was the cue for Oliver Goldsmith to take a Chinaman out of his screen and parade him up and down London. Lun Chi Altangi, citizen of the world, in due course reported to his friends at home what he thought about it all. He was particularly ironical at the expense of those fine gentlemen who were as much concerned for their wigs as Samson was for his hair. And the fine ladies, so painted and bedizened that they had really two distinct faces, one fair and false for the daytime, the other wrinkled and ugly for the night! He told of the false jades who laid siege to him, and of one in particular who came to offer him her heart, and went off with his watch. Then, growing bolder, he insinuated among these pleasant and amusing sketches, a few etchings limned in darker ink, and treating of subjects of more serious import. Look at those flags hung up in the roof of St. Paul's Cathedral; bits of tattered silk which, when new, would have fetched no more than a few Chinese coppers, and are now worth nothing at all. People will have it that in losing them the French sustained a great blow to their prestige, and that the English added greatly to theirs when they captured them. Are we then to suppose that the honour of the nations of Europe resides in a few pieces of stuff riddled with bullet-holes? Look at that magnificent turnout driving down the street with such a clatter; it belongs to a noble lord, the descendant of a kitchen-maid espoused by one of his ancestors, and of a stable-lad, on whom the said kitchen-maid secretly bestowed her favours. From the former, he inherited his taste for gormandizing, and strong liquor; from the latter his love of horses. And that's the sort of individual they call a nobleman!

The Chinaman does three turns, and then exits into the wings. In 1767, a Huron comes on the scene; he lands in the bay of the Rance, scandalizes the Prior de Kerkabon and his sister, says he is going to marry anyone he likes, gets mixed up with the Huguenots and the Jansenists, and causes a great commotion at Versailles, all because he is so very, very innocent; because, having never been taught anything, he has a perfectly open mind; because his understanding, never having been warped by erroneous teaching, is still sound and unprejudiced; because, like Usbek, Rica, Rhedi, and Lun Chi Altangi he insists that he is seeing things for the first time as they really are. But the Huron becomes civilized, he joins the army, and behold him, at once a philosopher, a warrior, and a bore. Then it is Spain's turn to look about for a foreigner to introduce to the public; Spain chose an African. Gazel Ben Aly was a Moroccan who studied Madrid and the provinces. He had a friend called Ben Belly, to whom he wrote a number of letters describing Spain and the manners and the customs of its people. At the same time he pointed out the causes of its grandeur and decay, and alluded to some remedies that were already beginning to have good effect. These were the *Cartas Marruecas* by José Cadalso, which appeared towards the latter half of the century. But these Señores only came on intermittently, and, by way of filling up the intervals, there were many motley figures, Turks, Chinamen, savages from far-off lands, Peruvians, Siamese, Iroquois Indians, all of whom joined merrily in the Critic's Carnival.

Finally, there was a third mode of approach, a third order of critics. These were travellers, too; but imaginary ones, travellers who never left home but, nevertheless, discovered marvellous countries that put Europe completely in the shade. There was the Empire of Cantahar; the Island of Women Warriors; a nation in Central Africa, whose inhabitants were just as numerous, just as civilized as the Chinese; there was the City of the Philadelphoi; there was the Republic of the Agoians. Endless praise was bestowed on the virtues of these marvellously sensible, marvellously happy, but non-existent peoples. Old Utopias were brought back into circulation: Domingo Gonsales came to life again, to fling himself at the moon. New Utopias were invented: Nicolas Klimius made his way into the underworld and found himself among a wise and enlightened people called the Potuans. Then there was the land of the Magpies, that icy region whose inhabitants begin to melt whenever a sunbeam strikes them. Besides all these, there were the Acephaloi who talked with mouths in the middle of their stomachs. There were the Bostankis, whose hearts were seated in the right thigh. Wild flights of fancy, but not so wild as to lose grip of the main purpose, which was to show how irrational life was in England, in Germany, in France, in the United Provinces; in fact, in all the so-called civilized countries. What a fine thing life would be if only people would make up their minds to listen to reason!

From 1726 onwards, the influence of a certain past-master in this particular line began to assert itself on these multifarious Utopias. The past-master in question was Jonathan Swift. The fact that children have made *Gulliver's Travels* one of their favourite story-books has somewhat diminished the formidable significance of that work.

Swift, however, takes a firm grip on the human creature; he reduces him to the dimensions of a midget; he magnifies him to the proportions of a giant. He plants him in countries where all the ordinary conditions of life are completely reversed. He is not content with giving us the finest lessons in relativity there have ever been; with sinister zeal, which becomes devastating as he warms to his task, he attacks everything we were ever taught to believe, to revere, or to love. Statesmen, what of them? A pack of ignorant blockheads, of conceited malefactors. Kings bestow decorations, ribands blue, black or red, on the champion performers with the skipping rope; rival parties are at each other's throats because they can't agree whether a boiled egg should be opened at the big or the little end. And the scientists? Madmen, all of them! At the Lagrado Academy, one of them is trying to extract sunlight from cucumbers and bottle it up for winter use; another is busy building houses and starting with the roof; another, a blind man, is manufacturing colours; another is devising a method for using cobwebs as a substitute for silk. And the Philosophers? A lot of numskulls grinding away *in vacuo*; nothing is too absurd, too outrageous, to be put forward by one or another of them. Gulliver visits the kingdom of Luggnagg and encounters a race of immortal beings who go by the name of Straldbruggs. Oh, hideous and repulsive immortality! There are families in which children are born with a stain on their foreheads. This betokens that they are predestined to live for ever. At thirty, they begin to grow despondent; at eighty, they are oppressed with all the infirmities that age is heir to, and tortured with the thoughts of the further progressive decay which they know awaits them. At ninety, all their teeth and hair have completely disappeared; so has their taste for food; so has their memory. At two hundred, at five hundred, they are hideous wrecks, despised and shunned, horrible to look on, ghastlier than ghouls, helpless and hopeless. And so Swift makes existence itself an odious thing. In the land of horses, a tribe of evil-smelling beasts live in a state of slavery; they are known as Yahoos. These Yahoos have long hair hanging down over the face and neck; their chests, backs and forefeet are covered with a hairy hide; on their chins they have little goatee beards. They can lie down, and sit, or stand up on their hind legs; they run, jump, and climb trees by means of their claws. The females are somewhat smaller than the males, their breasts hang down between their forefeet and touch the ground. These repulsive Yahoos are human beings. When you have got to the end of *Gulliver's Travels* you feel inclined to alter its title and give it the name of one of the books belonging to the library of Glumdalclitch, the young giantess of Brobdingnag, and to call it, *A Treatise on Human Weakness*.

And so Gulliver's descendants, both on the right and wrong side of the blanket, pullulate in such numbers as almost to constitute a new breed of critics—the embittered, the misfits, the maladjusted, or the mere dreamers. They will display to their contemporaries, in deserts transformed into a flowering paradise, in islands where El Dorado lies concealed, on the shores of Groenkaof, in the Archipelago of Mangahour, for which you will search in vain on your map, a race of men and women who enjoy a superior kind of government, a purer religious faith, and all the boons of liberty, equality and general well-being. Wherefore, when all these good things might be ours for the asking, do we go on dragging out such a miserable existence? Because of our vices. And whence come our vices? They are due solely to our having wandered so long, and so far, on the wrong path.

Yes; this was *la critique universelle*, universal criticism, right enough! It got to work in every field, literature, morals, politics, philosophy; it was the heart and soul of the contentious age. I know of no other period when it boasted more illustrious practitioners, when it was so widely active, and when, for all its careless airs, it was more acid.

Nevertheless, it was no radical transformation of our being that it demanded of us; it made no attack on the eternal egoism which the moralists of the seventeenth century had so sternly condemned; it did not require us to change our nature, and become saints or gods. There were two ingredients in the psychological make-up of these would-be reformers; one was wrath, the other was hope. Even Jonathan Swift, sombre though his outlook was, did not fail to let us glimpse a patch of blue amid the clouds. True, he declared that he loathed the animal called man, and told us that the story of his travels was constructed on this basis of misanthropy. But, now and again, he takes it into his head to say something a little less discouraging; he declared that the modicum of reason which, somehow or other, had found its way inside us, might possibly grow and develop; that politics might become a matter of common sense, and be put on a business-like footing. And he gave it as his opinion that whoever could make two ears of corn, or two blades of grass, to grow upon a spot of ground where only one grew before, would deserve better of mankind, and do more essential service to his country, than the whole race of politicians put together. If we could rid ourselves of our besetting sin, that is to say of pride, we should not be so much of a laughing-stock to others and a good deal less miserable ourselves. But we have magnified our existing miseries, and manufactured fresh ones. Who can say whether a new and wiser outlook on things, a little plain and homely common sense, a conception of life better adapted to our nature—who can say whether these things might not prove a sovereign remedy for all our afflictions? We have not applied them, but they are always available. This was a signal for the others to put down the soft pedal a little. Their pessimism did not cover the whole universe; it did not apply to our condition as a whole. They certainly found fault with the existing state of affairs, but then, it wasn't past mending. What they were opposed to was the social structure that was in force when they came into the world. But that might be done away with, and a new one be put in its place. Then all might be well.

Their critical theories were always backed up by something concrete, something definite, by way of illustration. In 1728, John Gay, who was not himself a giant, but who numbered among his acquaintance such giants as Arbuthnot, Pope and Swift, brought out a play which he entitled *The Beggars' Opera*. At a first glance, it seemed harmless enough, just something to amuse. The London Italian Opera had rather got on his nerves; and he made fun of those fashionable singers with their elaborate trills and *coloratura*, their sentimental mouthings, their silly plots, so unsuited to the rugged British nature. He decided to burlesque them, to hold them up to ridicule, so he brought on a gang of thieves, cutpurses, women of the town, and a notorious highwayman, all of whom were intended to take the place of the kings and queens, the tender maidens, the heavy fathers and strictly respectable duennas of the real thing. Every typical operatic situation, the passionate protestations, the duets in the moonlight, the paternal maledictions, the melodious death scenes—all were made to figure in this drama of low life; while, for the musical part, there were the popular ballads of the day, old, old songs, and the ditties that were whistled and hummed in all the purlieus of Soho. In this manner, the artificialities, the swelling phrases, the affectations of this nonsensical Italian rubbish, so unworthy of the sturdy British character, were held up to derision.

But there was more in it than just that. The gang's activities, inspired by the resourceful Peachum, receiver of stolen goods, who allotted the rôles, planned the conspiracies and shared out the booty, who looked after his men and got them out of prison if they were unlucky enough to be nabbed, just as freely as he gave them the rough side of his tongue if they didn't obey orders —this whole thing was designed to hold a mirror up to the body politic, with its ministers distributing among their followers what they had taken from the public, for there's law among highwaymen and honour among thieves. The aristocracy came in for it still more heavily. Looking at the thing as a whole, how did Peachum, as we have described him, and Mrs. Peachum, his spouse, with her sharp and ready tongue, her pithy sayings, her popular wisdom; their daughter Polly, the fairest jewel of the company, and the most remunerative; the pickpockets in their tavern rendezvous; the prostitutes reeking of gin—how did they differ, all these folk, from the fine gentlemen and noble dames that frequented the Court, lived in splendid houses, drove abroad in magnificent carriages, and always took the wall side of the pavement? Whatever difference there was, was wholly external, their feelings were the same, their habits were the same, and so, when circumstances invited, were their misdeeds. These belles and dandies, these fine ladies and gentlemen, what did they do but look after their own selfish interests, and get as much enjoyment out of life as they possibly could? They talked a lot about their word of honour, but they would break it for a song, if it suited them. They prated about their virtues; but weren't they eaten out with vice? What of their boasted integrity? Didn't they cheat at cards? Weren't they always on the look-out for some innocent ninny whom they could fleece, and feather their own nests with the spoils? Sharks, that's what they were. They might look as proud and haughty as they liked, but the fact is, it would be hard to say whether the noble lord copies the rapscallion, or whether it's the other way about. If it came to the point, if one had to choose between them, the rogues would take the palm, for at any rate they were no hypocrites; they got the wherewithal to live without all that elaborate fuss. Hard and untiring workers, full of pluck, never afraid of risking life and liberty; ready not only to help, but to die for, a friend, strictly loyal to their own code of honour, these "practical philosophers" make it their aim to bring about an equitable distribution of the world's wealth, and to redress the injustices of fortune.

Now skip a few years. Take a very different country and a very different literary form. Well, the same social unrest is there. Parini, the son of a Lombardy working man, became an *abbé* and a tutor, and so found himself rubbing shoulders with the aristocracy. He examined them critically, and found them wanting. In 1768, he brought out his *Il Mattino*, following it up a little later with *Il Mezzogiorno*. They were masterpieces, both of them. He takes a young nobleman, and describes just an hour or two, no more, of his life; from the time he gets up, which he does reluctantly, until noon. He does nothing but pamper and coddle himself. He lounges about, never doing anything that is the least bit of good. He sips his coffee from a cup of priceless porcelain; he babbles away idly to the professors who come to teach him dancing, singing, and the French tongue. His tailor calls for his money, and doesn't get it; he spends no end of time before his looking-glass, while his hairdresser—who keeps getting the rough side of his tongue—applies the curling-tongs and the powder-puff. Then he goes off to see some married woman, with whom he is carrying on a flirtation under her husband's very nose. He curls a supercilious lip, or pretends to, at the daintiest dishes set before him; he lets his tongue wag at random, and lays down the law on things he knows nothing about. He is a conceited and ill-natured fop, and if people don't get out of the way of his carriage, he runs them down. Is there anything at all to be said in his favour? What has he done for his country? Nothing! He never drew his sword in her defence as his ancestors did. The only sword he carries is the toy one he wears with his Court dress. Of his name, his rank and his privileges, he is thoroughly unworthy. Parini doesn't leave a rag on him; he jeers at him, trounces him, and sometimes, in a fury of indignation, denounces him with curses, not loud but deep; but no shouting, nothing declamatory.

His poetry is full of feeling and unsurpassed in vigour; yet every now and then a note of wistfulness and hope steals in:

> Forse vero non è, ma un giorno è fama
> Che fur gli nomini eguali, e ignoti uomi
> Fur Plebi e Nobiltade . . .

—"Maybe 'tis not true, but tradition declares there once was a time when men were all equal, when Plebs and Patricians were words never heard of . . ."

And so to the end of the century, till we come to Figaro. So it goes on, and all over Europe. Criticism ends on a note of yearning. There's something they need, something they must have. What is it they seek, these heart-hungry wanderers? What are they railing about? Why do they insist on turning everything inside out? How is it that nothing escapes them, neither the majesty of the law, nor the sanctity of religion. What is it they deem they ought to have, yet have not got? The answer is—Happiness!

II

HAPPINESS

Oh Happiness! Our Being's End and Aim!
Good. Pleasure. Ease. Content. Whate'er thy Name!

WE shall often be hearing them, these invocations; or would incantations be the better word? Time and again we shall have them, revised, analysed, defined. Pope in his *Essay on Man* brings them in as by a trumpet call, as well as any others that could possibly be pressed into the service. No one in those days recked aught of what the jealous gods might do, the gods who grow wroth when they hear man uttering wild and whirling words. On the contrary, they loudly proclaimed that they wanted their share of happiness, and, what is more, that they intended to have it, nay, that they had got it already. *Réflexions sur le Bonheur*, *Épître sur le Bonheur*, *Sur la Vie Heureuse*, *Système du vrai Bonheur*, *Essai sur le Bonheur*, *Della felicità*, *L'arte di essere felici*, *Discorso sulla felicità*, *Die Glückseligkeit*, *Versuch über die Kunst stets frölich zu sein*, *Ueber die menschliche Glückseligkeit*, *Of Happiness*: that is what, in divers tongues, they made so bold as to inscribe on their title pages, and seeing that the discovery they had made, after profiting individuals was to profit the race as well, they enlarged its claims accordingly: *Traité de la Société civile et du moyen de se rendre heureux en contribuant au bonheur des personnes avec qui on vit*, *Des causes du bonheur public*, *De la Félicité publique*, *Della publica felicità Ragionamenti . . . riguardanti la pubblica felicità*, *La felicità pubblica*, *Riflessioni sulla pubblica felicità*, *Of National Felicity*. So that the best works on the subject might be readily accessible, they brought together in a single series a number of books to which they gave the title, *Le Temple de Bonheur*. On the Hill of Happiness, on Mount Pleasant, rose up the beauteous Temple;

at the doorway stood Joy bidding humanity delay no longer, but come and join in life's great festival. Then the critics vied with each other in a more specialized field. It took the form of pointing out that, of all the verities in existence, the only important ones were those that helped to make us happy. Similarly of the arts, and of philosophy itself, if these things were of any good to us at all their sole use was to point out the effective means to happiness; in short, man had but one moral duty, and that was to live a happy life. The Quest for Happiness was sung by the poets, it was the Grail of the modern world. Helvetius, having decided that he would become the Apollo of France, took counsel of Voltaire. Voltaire told him that to write great verse, a necessary preliminary was to have a great subject. Accordingly he looked about him and could find no worthier theme than this: his own happiness and the happiness of the human race. The time was at hand when Oromaze, the god of righteousness, was to end his long struggle by winning a decisive victory over Ariman, the god of evil. Oromaze himself proclaims his triumph:

"Hell is no more; 'tis Heaven now on earth!"

The Quest for Happiness; novelists as well as poets took it for their theme. In 1759, Samuel Johnson, that level-headed, sober-minded man, set his Rasselas to the task, Rasselas the son of the Emperor of Abyssinia. Rasselas, agreeably to his country's laws, was confined, till the time should come for him to ascend the throne, in a remote valley entirely cut off from communication with the rest of the world. Everything he could possibly require was provided for him there, and yet life seemed to him an intolerable burden. He could not endure his prison; things were all too perfect there. So he resolved to escape, and escape he did, and thereafter visited many states and cities. He went to Cairo, where East meets West, face to face, and where you may see life in all its motley variety. Nor did he omit to make his way into the Pyramids, thinking that haply there the Ancients had hidden the key to their wisdom. And all the time he kept repeating, but in tones that faltered ever more and more, "Surely happiness is somewhere to be found!" In 1766, Wieland called his Agathon into being, and he wandered far and wide in divers parts of ancient Greece, questioning everybody, learned and unlearned, harlots and eremites: "Happiness, tell me, I pray you, have you discovered it? Where is happiness?"

Some fell a-dreaming. On the far side of the line, between the fortieth and fiftieth degree of latitude, lay a visionary kingdom. Leliopolis, its capital, was built all of a variegated stone, as fair as marble. Its houses, in the wintertime, were carpeted and hung with rich stuffs, and in summer with webs lighter and more gaily tinted than the muslins and calicoes of India, while the woodwork was coated with a varnish more lustrous than any that China could provide. The country round about was rich and well populated, the fields were cultivated with as much care as we bestow on our gardens, and yielded the most plenteous harvests to be seen in all the world. Mountains of diamonds were to be found there, and countless precious stones, rubies, emeralds, topaz; the rivers flowed along on beds of mingled gold and sand, and beneath the sea lay hidden quantities of pearl, of amber and of coral. Never were trees so green, nor lawns, nor meadows. The very hedgerows were filled with bells and flowerets of a thousand hues, and the air was laden with their scent. The vegetables and the fruits were unsurpassed, the wines delicious to the taste; and springs of the purest crystal abounded. A sky serene and clear, a temperate clime, more genial, less fickle than ours—all these things made these fortunate people worthy of that envied title, "The Happy Folk".[1]

Men roamed in imagination the whole world over. Off they set, in the wake of Robinson Crusoe, over unknown seas, courting adventure and braving the perils of the deep. A storm would spring up and send the vessel to the bottom, but the shipwrecked mariner never failed to reach the shore of a land in which Nature had always obligingly supplied a fertile valley abounding in venison and fruits of various kinds. He had a female companion with him, or if he had not, he managed to light upon one. The couple then proceeded to found a society so wise, so eminently enlightened as to make this old Europe of ours blush for shame.

All this took place in the Isle of Felsenburg, somewhere or other in Utopia; or in some other island still more difficult of access. Its name was *Die glückseligste Insul auf der ganzen Welt*,

[1][Marquis de Lassay], *Relation du royaume des Féliciens, peuples qui habitent dans les Terres Australes* . . ., 1727.

oder das Land der Zufriedenheit: The Happiest Island in all the world, or the Land of Contentment. Everyone, learned or unlearned, initiates or laymen, young folk, women, old men, all were possessed with the same longing. In Warsaw, the Collège des Nobles, in order to impress parents with their high educational standards, introduced ten lecturers to the public, ten beardless youths who discoursed on "Man's Happiness Here Below". In the Paris salons, Happiness was now the "ticket". Theatre-goers could go and see *l'Heureux*, the Happy Man, a philosophical play in three acts, in prose. There was an *Ordre de la Félicité* among the secret societies, and at its meetings they sang such songs as this:

L'île de la Félicité
N'est pas une chimère;
C'est où règne la volupté
Et de l'amour la mère;
Frères, courons, parcourons
Tous les flots de Cythère,
Et nous la trouverons.[1]

"Happiness", wrote Mme de Puisieux, giving some character-sketches of her contemporaries, "is a ball which we chase when it rolls in front of us, and kick along when it stops. . . . One must be very tired indeed to give up the pursuit, and let the ball run on." But, if Montesquieu has the rights of it, no one ever did tire: "Monsieur de Maupertuis, who has all his life believed, and may perhaps have proved, that he was never happy, has just brought out a little book all about Happiness."

There were some *idées fixes* by which people were positively obsessed in those days. They were forever being taken up anew. People insisted on returning to them again and again, to the same old formulas, the same old demonstrations, as though they were never sure of having said enough by way of explaining and establishing their pet ideas. Here we may see a favourite attitude of the times; here we may observe one of its fieriest enthusiasms at work. Wars were always going on; the war

[1]The Island of Happiness is no chimæra; 'tis where pleasure reigns, and it is the mother of love. Brothers, up let us hasten, let us range o'er all the waters of Cythera, and we shall find it.

of the Spanish Succession, of the Austrian Succession, the Seven Years' War; war in the Near East, and, yes, war in the New World, too. From time to time, plague or famine laid waste a number of provinces, and there was suffering everywhere, as there always had been. Nevertheless, the European intellectuals would insist that they were living in the best possible of worlds. The gospel of optimism was the major plank in their platform.[1]

It is the old, old story of perpetual illusion. . . . No, there *were* times of despair; dismal times, when men did not dare give utterance to their hope of better things, lest it should sound like a mockery; times when pain and suffering so completely possessed them, body and soul, that they hardly dared believe in better days to come; times when it seemed to them as if the sum total of the world's burden of sorrow rested on them alone. And there were ages of faith, ages when men, realizing that their afflictions in this world were irremediable, put their trust in a world to come, where all their wrongs would be righted, and all their sorrows healed. All their hopes were on eternity.

Happiness, as conceived by the eighteenth-century rationalists, had characteristics peculiarly its own. Happiness was a thing for the Here and Now. "Today", "Forthwith"—these were the words insisted on. "Tomorrow" was not soon enough for them. Tomorrow might add its quota, its contribution, and help to carry on the good work, but today, not tomorrow, was the time for making a start. Happiness was not something freely bestowed, it was something you had to win by your own exertions. And there must be no trace of the tragic in its composition: *Beruhigung der Menschen.* Let men disquiet themselves no more. A truce to troubles, forebodings, anxieties. Be of good cheer; you are in a delightful meadow surrounded by shady groves and watered by silvery streams; it is as lovely as the Garden of Eden, yet you see it not. An exquisite perfume exhales from its flowers, it delights you not. Gleaming lilies, luscious fruits are there before your eyes, you heed them not. If you approach a bank of roses, you contrive to be scratched by the thorns; if you cross the grassy mead, it is to chase a fleeing serpent. And so you sigh, and make moan, and protest that all the world's against you, that it were better had you

[1]For the optimism of Leibniz and Pope, see Part Three of this work, Chap. III.

never been born. All this is but wilful folly, and you yourself are the cause of all your ills.[1]—Or maybe you are given to calling up a spectre, a terrifying goddess; she is robed in black, her skin is furrowed with countless wrinkles, her hue is deathly pale, her glance fills you with dread, her hands are armed with whips and scorpions. Hark, she speaks and you listen to her voice. She bids you turn away from the allurements of a deceiving world. Joy, she tells you, falls not to the lot of mortal man. You are born to suffer and to be accursed; every creature under the sun is bound to suffer. And so you ask to be allowed to die. But know you not who it is that speaks to you in those words? Know you not that it is Superstition, the child of Discontent, in whose train there follow Fear and Sorrow? The earth is too fair a place for Providence to have made it the abode of Misery and Pain. To turn away from the good things which the author of the Universe has set before you is to give proof of ignorance and perversity.[2]

All this has nothing in common with the joy of the mystics, whose aim is nothing less than the bliss of merging into the Divine Essence and becoming one with God; nothing in common with the joy that filled the heart of Fénelon when, betaking himself in thought to his Heavenly Father, he felt that his soul was safer and more simple than the soul of a little child. Nor did it resemble the tranquil joy of Bossuet, quietly content to be guided by dogma and the Church, and sure of finding himself one day among the elect who stand at God's right hand; nothing in common with the happiness of the righteous who keep the commandments and look for an everlasting reward in the world to come; nothing in common with those simple souls who lose themselves in prayer; the Beatitudes are nought to them.

Ah, those Beatitudes, sweet foretaste of Heaven—these new teachers who had come and supplanted the masters of old, what recked they of them? What they wanted was happiness on earth, and they wanted it now. What they had in mind was a practical happiness, not an ideal one. They wanted to make the most of what limited measure of well-being was here and now attainable, not to go vainly striving for some ideal state of perfection beyond their reach. What they aimed at was a

[1] I. P. Uz, *Lyrische Gedichte*, 1740. *Versuch über die Kunst stets frölich zu sein.*
[2] S. Johnson, *The Rambler*, No. 44, 18th Aug. 1750.

modest degree of contentment, their ideal was the Golden Mean, which forbade them to grasp at too much, on pain of losing all. They were the people who had made up their minds to enjoy contentedly whatever good the passing day might bring. Or you might regard it as a matter of arithmetic—so much on the debit side, no doubt; but then, so much on the credit side, too. And the credit side wins. You can prove the thing by mathematics. First add up the advantages of life; then tot up the ills you can't avoid. Subtract the lesser from the greater. You'll find the figures show a profit. On the one side put down all the good points multiplied by their intensity. Do the same on the other side for the bad ones. If by the end of the day, you find you have had thirty-four degrees of pleasure and twenty-four of pain, your affairs are in a good posture, and you should rest content.[1]

It was happiness made to measure, so to speak. Let us take a glance at the author of *les Lettres Persanes* as he surveys himself in the mirror, availing ourselves, not so much of the *Essay on Happiness*, the *Essai sur le Bonheur*, which, of course, everyone who aspired to be in the fashion was bound to write those days, but rather of the reflections he set down in his private notebooks. Let us see how he managed to make life the signal success which, in his case, it was. Well, said Montesquieu, in the first place, I'm going to plant my feet firmly on the ground. I'm not going to aim at the blissful state of the angels, so I shan't cry because I don't get it. Never mind the absolute, the relative is good enough for me. Thus much being granted, I am bound to say that I think happiness is largely a matter of temperament, and as far as that goes, I think mine is a pretty even one. "There are some people who try to keep well by continually taking purgatives, or being bled. For my part, my one rule is to eat sparingly when I've been eating too much, to sleep extra long if I've been up till the small hours, and not to bring trouble on myself by worrying over-much about things, by too much work, too much play, or too much loafing." He is at his ease in all circumstances; one of those people who salute with like serenity the dawn which ushers in their waking hours, and the night which suspends them. When he says he loves the country best, that does not mean that he detests Paris. He has resources for his happiness on his

[1]Wollaston, *Religion of Nature Delineated*, 1722.

estate, where he has only the trees to look upon, as he has in the capital, where human beings are as numerous as the sands of the sea. But this sort of happiness must be sparingly handled, as sparingly as thrifty folk eke out their savings. Just as many a mickle makes a muckle, so the brief moments of pleasure will mount up in the aggregate to a considerable fortune. Don't let us make too much of our troubles, but regard them rather as reminders of our pleasures. You can't make a hermit go without food but you inspire him with a longing for his roots and herbs. Moreover, we should recognize that even our ills, provided they are not too grievous, have a certain charm about them, while the graver ones, painful though they be, at least preserve us from boredom. What, in a word, we ought to do, is so to look at things as to realize how far more they are for us than against us. Let us adapt ourselves to life, for life, you may depend upon it, will not adapt itself to us. We are people taking part in a game that will go on as long as we do. The player who knows his book holds his hand when the cards are against him, but goes all out when his luck turns, and scores the winning trick. Your indifferent player always comes off second-best.

A cut-and-dried sort of happiness, that? Yet in those days, how many there were with the same sort of outlook. They made a sort of compound of various ingredients which was to serve them instead of happiness pure and unalloyed. Pleasure was rehabilitated and brought back from exile. Why had pleasure been under a cloud all this time? Why had it been sent to Coventry? Wasn't it part of our nature? Was it not pleasure that gave life its charm? Only fanatics could find any satisfaction in self-denial, in mortifying the flesh. Gaiety made gods of us; austerity, devils.[1]

> Sollt' auch ich durch Gram und Leid
> Meinen Leib verzehren,
> Und des Lebens Fröhligkeit
> Weil ich lebe, entbehren?

—Why should I, I too, wear away this body of mine with pain and sorrow? Why should I, in my lifetime, deprive myself of life's good things?[2] Nay Death, even Death, should be divested

[1]Frederick II to Voltaire, Remusberg, 27th Sept. 1737.
[2]Hagedorn, *Die Jugend*, 1730.

of that terrible aspect which it commonly presents. Those terribly mournful deathbed farewells are really contemptible because of the solemn mummery with which they are attended. Men who are really great have faced death with a smile on their lips.[1]

One of the things they included in their recipe was good health. No more praying that our physical ailments might redound to our moral edification. The thing now was not to get ill at all. Then, of course, one must have a respectable balance at the bank. All the material advantages of civilization. Comfort was not yet the vogue, still, people were beginning to attach more and more importance to the conveniences of life.

Some of the recipes were decidedly prosaic. This, for example, is what the Marquis d'Argens recommends: "Real happiness consists of three things: First, not having any crime on the conscience. Secondly, being able to rest content in the station to which God has called us, and in which we have to abide. Thirdly, a clean bill of health." This is how Mme du Châtelet puts the matter: "If you would be happy, get rid of your prejudices, live virtuously, have tastes and passions, be open to illusion, for most of our pleasures we owe to illusions, and woe betide those who lose them. We should begin by impressing on ourselves that we have one thing and one thing only to do in this life, and that is to enjoy agreeable feelings and sensations." Sometimes, obscurely enough by the general run, but more clearly by the thoughtful, another line was taken. They wanted to find out what hidden reason it was that made people entertain ideas so different from those which their fathers had held. There was the idea that we were part of a universal Order, an Order which intended all creatures to be happy; if they were not to be happy, why were they given life at all?

Legions of worlds glitter in the spheres assigned to them; and in those ethereal spaces, where stars without number move in their appointed orbits, all is obedient to a single Order. To conform to this Order, everything that exists was made; it rules alike the gentle zephyr and the raging tempest; it binds everything that exists with its chain, from the tiniest insect to man himself.

Our first law is the well-being of the whole creation. Happy shall I

[1] A. F. B. Deslandes, *Réflexions sur les grands hommes qui sont morts en plaisantant*, 1712.

be if I never impair, by any fault of my own, the Universal Good, to maintain and contribute to which is the sole object of my existence.[1]

Clearly ideas were taking a new direction. To begin with, it was all over now with aspiring to the Absolute. Nevertheless, it was hoped that the change-over would take place quietly, without any breach of the peace. It was pretended, nay, it was seriously believed that the cup was not filled with gall, or that, anyhow, the gall was not bitter. They put "the moral system of the world at a certain point, far below that of ideal perfection (for we are made capable of conceiving what we are incapable of attaining), but however sufficient upon the whole to constitute a state easy and happy, or at the worst tolerable."[2]

Lo! at a stroke Heaven was brought down to Earth. Between the two, there was henceforth no difference, not even a difference in kind. Supposing that the notion of a future life was conceivable, was it conceivable that that life was to be purchased by pain? Was it credible that the Maker of all things had ordained that happiness in this world and happiness in the next were to be obtained by diametrically opposite means? Was it common sense to suppose that to attain to happiness in the next world we had to start by making ourselves miserable in this? It was difficult to believe that God would indulge in the strange jest of depriving us of happiness while we were alive, to bestow it on us when we were dead. The present life, and the future life, if there was one, did not differ in kind. Nor, to acquire the greatest happiness that man in his earthly state was capable of enjoying, were the means any different from those which were to bring him to life eternal, if there was one. There was no break, no contradiction. If there was a paradise hereafter, our life would continue to be what it was here; the same, in its immortal state.[3]

Philosophy should be given a practical turn. Henceforth its object, its sole object, should be the quest for happiness. There is in nature something that is even more universal than what is termed natural intelligence, native sense; something even more evenly distributed, something which is as clear and obvious

[1]Uz, *Lyrische Gedichte*, 1749. *Die Glückseligheit.* French translation by Huber, *Choix de poésies allemandes*, 1760, Tome II, *Ode de M. Utz, La Félicité.*

[2]Bolingbroke, *A Letter on the Spirit of Patriotism*, 1737.

[3]Maupertuis, *Essai de philosophie morale*, 1749.

to the dullest, as it is to the acutest understanding, and that is the desire for happiness. Would it be extravagant to suggest that it is this which should guide us in forming our rules of conduct, and enlighten us as to the truths we ought to believe. If I try to form any clear idea as to the nature of God, as to my own nature, or as to how the world began and how it will end, my mind is in a state of confusion, nor do any of the various religious sects do anything to relieve it. If, in this uniform obscurity, this abysmal darkness, I encounter a system which proves to be the only one that fulfils my desires, am I not bound to recognize it as the true one? Am I not forced to conclude that a system which procures me happiness cannot possibly deceive me?[1]

The upshot was that happiness became a right, something to which we were entitled, an idea that superseded the idea of duty. Inasmuch as it was the aim and object of all intelligent beings, the centre on which all their activities were focused; inasmuch as it was the primary object of desire; inasmuch as the statement "I want to be happy" was the first article of a code far older than any written law, than any religious creed, people now gave up asking themselves whether they deserved happiness; they asked whether they were getting the happiness to which they were entitled. The question now was not, "Am I a good man?" It was, "Am I a happy man?"

Those who took a different view were regarded as reactionaries. Young Vauvenargues, who was a Stoic, who wept and went into transports over Plutarch, who tried to cultivate virtue for virtue's sake, and heroism because it was beautiful, was regarded by his friend and cousin, the headstrong Mirabeau, as completely off the lines. Vauvenargues went wandering about here, there, and everywhere, whereas what he ought to have done was to form some definite plan for getting the one thing needful, the thing we all ought to aim at; that is to say, happiness. The Princess of Cleves who, though mutually loving and beloved, refused the happiness that was offered her and fled into the wilderness to escape from the man who would have made her happy in her own despite, would, in the eyes of an eighteenth-century woman, have done wrong. A completely erroneous method had been applied to history. Those learned men who had endeavoured to discover what nation had been the most

[1]Maupertuis, *op. cit.*

religious, the most temperate, the most warlike, had mistaken their goal. What they ought to have set themselves to ascertain was which nation had been the happiest. The Egyptians were not a happy people, nor were the Greeks, for all their high civilization; nor were the Romans, in spite of their imperial power; nor was Europe as a whole, under the Christian régime. To remedy the chronic sufferings of the people, to do some good to their own generation, what the historians should have done was to ask themselves two questions. The first was, How many days in a year, or how many hours in a day, can a man work without feeling the strain, without making himself miserable? Then, How many days in a year, or how many hours in a day must a man work in order to obtain what is necessary to enable him to live in some degree of comfort? Briefly, "there exists in all states of life an irresistible force of attraction which leads men to seek the best possible conditions, and there it is that we should look for that physical revelation by whose infallible signs all lawgivers should be guided". That pronouncement, of which the Marquis de Chasteleux delivered himself in 1772, in his treatise *De la félicité publique, ou Considérations sur le sort des hommes dans les différentes époques de l'histoire*—"Concerning the public weal, or Reflections on the fortunes of the human race in divers periods of History"—was charged with significance, a significance which became more and more apparent as time went on.

Everyone had been on a false trail, with the possible exception of those *avant-couriers* of the eighteenth century who had flourished under Louis XIV. Hence the bitter judgments, the everlasting reproaches, the accusations of broken promises, of downright treason. Hence the present clamour for happiness, hence the firm conviction that better times were just round the corner, and that now, thanks to reason, to sound sense and to the general spread of education, all would be well.

III

REASON AND KNOWLEDGE

IN the eyes of the religiously minded, reason was a divine spark, a particle of truth vouchsafed to mortals until the time should come when, having passed through the gates of the tomb, they would see God face to face. But in the eyes of the newest school of thinkers all such ideas were the vain imaginings of a day that was over and done with.

As was the case when it came to defining happiness, so here, too, European thinkers began on a note of humility, which, however, was soon to be followed by one of triumph. Nevertheless, its opening proclamation gave notice of a surrender, a renunciation. It confessed that the substance, the underlying reality of things was beyond their apprehension, necessarily hidden from their scrutiny. Long enough, they said, have men invented systems that have crumbled to pieces one by one. Long enough have they presented us with keys to the great enigma which one after another have proved but vain illusions. How mad to think that they could penetrate a barrier which none has ever passed, or ever will. *Usquehuc venies et non procedes amplius:* thus far shalt thou come, and no farther. You lack the power to fare beyond a certain distance. Halt, then, at the limit assigned. No one has ever passed beyond it; no one ever will. Keep that in mind, and whatsoever you do acquire within the permitted limits will be sure and stable. Reason is like a monarch who, when he comes to power, determines to disregard those provinces which he feels he cannot rule effectively and to concentrate on those which he is sure he can control. Scepticism, the age-old enemy, arises from over-reaching ambition, from the attempt to grasp what our limited powers deny us. This vaulting ambition, when it falls and crashes, leaves only ruin in its train.

But thanks to restraint, to moderation, which is only wisdom under another name, Pyrrhonism will be no more.

But what manner of thing is this reason thus confined? To begin with there is nothing innate in its character. It germinates and grows to maturity simultaneously with the mind. It merges with that inward process which, working on the data supplied by the senses, is the origin of our abstract ideas, and adapts itself to our several faculties. Then follows a brief examination into the process of deduction. Deduction is merely a process of unfolding, of explication; it makes no addition to our knowledge, since that knowledge is wholly implicit in the initial sense-datum. But it is on its power of discrimination, of differentiation, that particular emphasis is laid. Truth is the state of agreement or disagreement which we say exists in regard to ideas. For the most part we fail to recognize the relation between them because we lack a middle term. Take two buildings, each at a considerable distance from the other. It is impossible for us to state with accuracy how far they resemble and how far they differ from each other. But that we can find out if we apply first to one and then to the other a measuring rod, for by that means we establish a relationship between the two which we were incapable of perceiving with the unaided eye. Something like this is the part played by reason. When it encounters anything that is doubtful or obscure, it sets to work. It examines, and weighs, and collates, and compares, it applies a common measure, it sifts the facts again and again, and finally it delivers its verdict. There is no higher faculty than reason, for to the reason it belongs to disentangle the true from the false. On the reasoning faculty all science and all philosophy depend.

There was no particular advantage, it was thought, in arguing about what this faculty was and what it was not, about its essence, but the very greatest advantage on the other hand in watching it at work, in studying its methods and its results. It examined the facts which the senses recorded, and as the facts were presented in what seemed at first an inextricable tangle, it addressed itself to the task of unravelling the various threads and reducing them to order. It made no attempt to interpret them, it hazarded no hypothesis concerning them, its business was to take them purely and simply as they were. Its favourite method was the analytical. Instead of starting from *a priori* notions as was the old-fashioned way, what it resolved to get at was the downright, stark reality, instead of mere word-spinning which only brought you back to where you started from. Analysis made it possible to distinguish the various strands of which a complex fact was composed. The next step was to make a systematic list of them. That completed the first stage. The second consisted in comparing them and ascertaining what bearing they had one upon another, and from these observations deducing the laws which controlled them.

No easy or rapid task. However, reason was in a position to examine and re-examine as often as she liked whatever might elude her to begin with; she could make things operate over and over again so as to study them more closely and check the accuracy of her previous findings, and all this was made possible by virtue of a new process of which the metaphysicians were unaware, but by which she set the greatest store, and that process was experiment. Experiment made all the difference between a hypothetical conclusion and a definite result. Experiment was the guarantor, the assurance against error, the safeguard against the fallibility of our perceptions, the carelessness of our observations or the vagaries of our imagination, in short against the various intellectual limitations under which previous generations of enquirers had laboured. Experiment was to be the beneficent power which was destined to bring the temples of falsehood to destruction. The hero of *Bijoux indiscrets*, Mangogul, much as he may be taken up with amusements which, *certes*, have little enough to do with philosophy, is, nevertheless, an enthusiastic votary of reason. In this connexion, Diderot causes him to dream a symbolic dream in which his enthusiasm for the experimental method, now promoted to the ranks of the tutelary deities, is abundantly, indeed overwhelmingly, displayed. Mangogul falls asleep and dreams that he has been borne away by a hippogriff to some strange sort of building that rests on no visible foundations. Its pillars ascend into the viewless distance. The people that crowd about its entrance are bloated or flaccid, with no muscles, as weak as water and almost all of them deformed. Pushing his way through, he found himself near a dais surmounted by a canopy made of gossamer. Seated upon it was an aged man with a white beard who was blowing soap-bubbles through a reed; just the sort of work on which the theorizers employ themselves. But lo! far away in the distance a child comes into view. Slowly, slowly he draws near, and the nearer he comes the longer and bigger grow his legs. And as he waxes in stature he takes on a variety of different shapes. Then he begins looking at the sky through a telescope, estimates by means of a pendulum the velocity of falling bodies, and, with the aid of a tube filled with mercury, calculates the weight of the atmosphere. He grows to a giant's size; his head touches the sky, his feet descend into the abyss, and his outstretched arms extend from pole to pole. In his right hand, he brandishes a torch whose gleams light up the waste of waters and penetrate even into the bowels of the earth. His name is Experiment. He draws near to the ancient building. Its pillars totter, its roof caves in, its floor gapes asunder. It falls with a terrible roar and its ruins crash down into the darkness.

Reason is self-sufficing. Whoso possesses reason and uses it aright, never goes astray: *neque decipitur ratio, neque decipit unquam.* Reason treads infallibly the road to Truth. Reason needs not Authority, of which she is, practically speaking, the precise antithesis, Authority being the fountain-head of Error. Reason recks not of Tradition; nor does she concern herself either with the Ancient or the Modern school. Every aberration comes of believing blindly in things without investigating them in the light of reason. Hard by the Portico of Hypotheses which Diderot imagined, we find the Temple of Ignorance, pictured by Pietro Verri.[1] Ignorance dwells in a tumble-down ruin of Gothic design, over whose principal entrance is depicted an enormous mouth, yawning prodigiously. The vast building is crowded with people, feckless, babbling creatures, stupid dunderheads who don't even know the name of the goddess, nor where their own quarters are supposed to be. The walls are covered with hideous pictures representing shipwrecks, civil wars, death and sterility. On a lofty platform a gaunt and aged woman keeps on repeating, over and over again, like someone preaching a sermon, "Young folk, young folk, hark ye to my words, put not your trust in yourselves. What you feel within you is but vain illusion. Put your trust rather in the Ancients and be assured that everything they did was done aright." At the same time, a decrepit old man, summoning up all his remaining

[1]Pietro Verri, *Il Tempio dell'Ignoranza*, in *Il Caffè*, 10th June, 1764.

strength, cries in a loud voice saying, "Young folk! Young folk! Reason is but a cheating fancy. If ye would know the false from the true, give heed to what the multitude believe. Reason is a cheating fancy!"—Iconography, driving home the same sort of ideas, depicts Experiment making short work of theories, and Ignorance proclaiming faith in the past, deference to ancient precepts, obedience to the ideas of bigotry, and opposition to the free exercise of individual judgment.

If, however, any person has misgivings concerning the validity of his own intellectual processes, one thing suffices to reassure him, and that is the world-wide uniformity of the reasoning faculty, which is the same the world over. It betrays no exceptions. Travellers in distant lands who claim to have discovered irreconcilable differences in the various habits, modes of behaviour of our species refer to what are in reality merely superficial divergences, to non-essential characteristics; or their accuracy of observation is at fault; or else, they are simply lying. Whatever has not been at all times and everywhere—*semper et ubique*—is irrational. The criterion of Truth is extension in time and space. The rationalists had plenty of quarrels to pick with the enthusiasts, their particular foes, and one of the most inveterate was this: they trusted, those fanatical folk, to their own emotions, they let themselves be guided by their own individual and personal sentiments; the result was that their ideas and their conduct issued in chaos. From the most civilized people in the world, down to the Hurons of Lake Michigan, to the most miserable Hottentots, to the last link between man and brute, North, South, East and West, Nature speaks with one voice, the voice of Reason.

The crowning confirmation of its value was its beneficial character. Because it seeks to perfect the arts and sciences, by which our comforts and conveniences are immeasurably increased; because, more unerringly than sensation itself, it tells us what our pleasures are really worth, so indicating those we should eschew and those we should enjoy; because misfortune arises from lack of knowledge or faulty judgment, because it supplies the one and corrects the other, reason will fulfil all the broken promises of the past and bring us happiness and prosperity. Reason will be our salvation. Reason, said Dumarsais, would be for the philosopher, what grace was for St. Augustine. Reason will enlighten every man that cometh into the world, for Reason herself is light.

Light, or rather let us use the plural and say "lights", for it was not a single ray but a sheaf of them which played on the great tracts of darkness that still hung over the earth. The word was a magical one for the people of those days and they were never tired of repeating it, and some others as well which we shall come across in due time. How sweet and pleasant they were in the eyes of the sages, these lights which they themselves had kindled! How beautiful, aye, and how strong! How the superstitious, the deceivers, and the wicked shrank away from them! At last they were shining forth, emanating from the majestic laws of Reason. They went side by side with Philosophy, or followed in her train, Philosophy that was pressing forward with a giant's strides. Enlightened indeed were the children of the age; and the delectable metaphor reappeared with countless variations. They were torches; they were the lamp which illumined the way for them in all they did and thought; they were the dawn of good augury; they were the Sun, constant, steady, unfailing. Mankind had erred hitherto because they had been plunged in darkness, because they had lived enveloped in the shadows, in the mists of ignorance which had hidden the true path from their sight. Their eyes had been covered with a bandage. Their fathers and their forefathers had been blind, but they, they would be the Children of Light.

It mattered little that the image was as old as the world itself; that, maybe, it had come into being when the sons of Adam, terrified at the darkness, took fresh heart when they beheld the first streaks of dawn. Little cared these people that theology had made use of it long before them: "I am the Light of the World, and he that followeth me walketh not in darkness." They appropriated it, they took it for their own, as though they had been the first to discover it. Light—such was the device inscribed upon their banners. And so, for the first time, an epoch gave itself a name of its own choosing. Thus began the Age of Light, the Aufklärung.

Was ist Aufklärung? Such was the question Kant asked himself when, the years having rolled on, he thought the time had come for him to look back a little and take stock of things.

His answer was that it marked a growing-up stage in man's development, a determination to put away childish things. If he had remained so long in leading-strings, that was his own fault. He had never had courage enough to use his reason. He had always relied on some external authority to tell him what to think. But now it was different; he had begun to think for himself: *Sapere aude*. Vast numbers of people never really grow up because they are too lazy, or too timid to think for themselves, so other people find it easy to get the upper hand of them. If I have got a book that tells me what to think, a mentor who lays down my moral code, a doctor who prescribes to me what food I should eat and what exercise I ought to take, what need have I to worry my head about such things? When you've got someone at hand to do your thinking for you, why take on that irksome task yourself? That the vast majority of people should be afraid of assuming the responsibilities of manhood is just what their guardians want, and their first concern is to blunt the intelligence of their flock. They tell these perpetual children all the perils they would incur if they attempted to walk alone. This dependence eventually becomes a sort of second nature to them which in the long run they come to like and find it no easy matter to shake off. All the same, some people anyhow are attracted to the gospel of enlightenment. Here and there a bold spirit breaks away and sets an example to the rest. But their influence is necessarily gradual. A sudden revolution may overthrow a despotism, put an end to some particular form of oppression and still have no lasting effect; a reform, if it is to take deep and lasting root, must be the outcome of a slow and steady process of evolution. Freedom is the breath of life to it, freedom in the best and truest of all the many senses which the word has come to bear, the freedom, namely, to make free and unhampered use of our reason. But at this point some protesting voices make themselves heard: says the officer to his men, "Don't argue, do what you're told"; the financier, "Don't argue; pay the money"; the churchman, "Don't argue; believe". The truth is that in some cases certain limitations are inevitable, but these, far from hindering the Aufklärung, promote it. If freedom of thought and freedom of speech are rightly untrammelled in the case of the cultured and learned few, they are no less rightly curtailed in the case of functionaries who in the performance of their official duties must abstain from questioning the why and the wherefore of them. It would be an extremely dangerous thing if an officer on active service, when receiving a command from his superior, were to begin discussing its expedience, or if a religious instructor, when explaining the Creed to his catechumens, were to draw their attention to the things which the Creed omitted. The various parts of the social machine should be allowed to run on smoothly without any sudden interference with their mechanism. Nevertheless, the drivers of the machine should, as thinking beings, be accessible to fresh ideas, ideas leading to the increase of freedom and the progressive relaxation of control. There are, in fact, two distinct planes; first, the practical plane, the plane of routine activities which for the time being must be allowed to go on as they are, without any sudden interruption; secondly, there is the plane of reason, of the mind, where a process of evolution is ever at work, a process which, when the time is ripe, will have its effect on action. The rôle of the mind, of the reason, is continuous, it never stops.

The sphere of freedom, of emancipation, lies open before us; we have not yet reached it, but we shall persevere, for we are on the right road.[1]

Such, as it was anxious to appear to the world at large, that is to say, in its loftiest and most ideal aspect, was the Aufklärung.

A number of circumstances in the intellectual history of the times contributed to confirm its ascendancy. To begin with, there was the influence of Bayle; then, the discomfiture of Vico; there was Wolff's success, and there was Locke's resounding triumph.

Bayle was anything but a spent force. To refute him was still regarded as a meritorious act of piety. Half a century, nay, three-quarters of a century after his death, the attacks on him were as virulent as they had been at the very beginning of the fray, so clearly did he appear even now as the most redoubtable warrior in the ranks of scepticism. His Dictionary still occupied the most conspicuous place in all the libraries. It was for ever being reprinted and translated. Whether in the big unabridged edition, or in extracts and résumés, it was appealed to when a campaign was on foot to dethrone Authority and set up private

[1]E. Kant, *Beantwortung der Frage; Was ist Aufklärung?* 1784.

judgment in its place. His more direct disciples enlarged on the main theme of this antagonist of religion, the theme that religion and truth are irreconcilable and that there is no necessary connexion between morality and religion. Again and again they returned to the argument that there was nothing to show that Christians were any better than unbelievers, and that a republic of atheists might well be at once more virtuous and less selfish than a republic of Catholics or Protestants. Not one of his favourite dialectical weapons but was pressed into the service again and again. There was the argument, for example, that when we came up against something we could not explain in the light of reason, our only way out of the dilemma was to fall back on religion, with the result that anything, no matter how absurd, might claim to be accepted as an article of faith. "If Holy Writ declared that Chaos existed, if Tohu-Bohu was made a part of the canon, we believe it, with the liveliest faith. Of course in saying this we have only the fallacious light of reason to guide us."[1] The pupil lets himself go more than the master, but the master's teaching is unmistakable, all the same. Often his main stream of thought is split up into separate channels. One might be the matter of the comets; another, Spinoza, or history, or the Bible, but Bayle is at the back of them all, Bayle is the guiding spirit.

If this statement is in need of a little qualification, we might say that a time there *was* when enthusiasm for him cooled off a little. But then it must be borne in mind that what seemed to reach the very limit of audacity round about the year 1700 was looked upon as comparatively harmless fifty years later. There was therefore less incentive then to have recourse to a weapon that time had considerably blunted. Since the days when Bayle criticized David in an article of his *Dictionnaire*, David had come in for a good many more criticisms, and had got used to them. Moreover, the later disciples, though they held that a sceptical attitude was all very well to start with, considered that something definite and practical should follow; a doctrine which your full-blown Pyrrhonist would never entertain for a moment. Between the *Dictionnaire historique et critique* and the *Encyclopédie*, between the recording of human errors and the recording of human achievements in the field of knowledge, lies an interval

[1]Voltaire, *Le Philosophe ignorant. Tout est-il éternel?*

of time in which we may discern the successive stages of a gradual evolutionary process which eventually put Pierre Bayle quite out of date.

If only Italy had lent an ear to Giambattista Vico; if only, as at the time of the Renaissance, she had assumed the leadership of Europe, our intellectual history would have had a very different tale to tell. Our eighteenth-century ancestors would not have believed that everything that was clear was necessarily true. On the contrary they would have looked on clarity as a defect rather than a virtue in the matter of human reason. If an idea is clear, it means that it is finished, rounded off, over and done with. They would have given pride of place in the hierarchy of faculties, not to reason, but to the imagination. Reason, a late-comer on the scene, certainly achieved one thing pretty thoroughly, it dried up the springs of the soul and our ancestors might have looked back with regretful longings on the Edens they had lost. They would not have been so eager to turn a searchlight on to the surface of the earth, knowing, as they would have done, that the secret of things was to be sought far down in the dark recesses and abysm of time. Never would they have believed that we were heading straight for a better future. On the contrary, they would have known that the peoples of the earth are a prey to constant vicissitudes, now emerging slowly and painfully out of a state of barbarism along the road to civilization, whereto attaining, they relapse once more into barbarism. All their ideas, their whole intellectual attitude would have been fundamentally changed.

One cannot but admire the courage, the resolution of this strangely original genius who, undeterred by temporary defeat, remained as determined as ever to direct the prevailing ideas of his times into a totally different channel. Ill health had kept him away from the schools, but a single imperious glance had enabled him to measure the intellectual poverty of teachers who were for ever repeating what they had learned by rote, without ever troubling to think for themselves. Thus he had escaped the influence of scholasticism which at that time had still no lack of devotees. Then, the force of his own personality had prevented him from being unduly influenced by the fashionable ideas of the day, such as those of Descartes for example. In his view, that doctrine had blunted the edge of intellectual endeavour by teaching people to make light of mental application, of improving their minds, of extending their knowledge, by teaching them to undervalue such things as patience and perseverance and encouraging them to rely rather on their own personal intuition. All this had encouraged our natural sloth, the great idea now being to get hold of as much knowledge as possible, in the shortest possible time, and with the least possible effort. He had managed to swing clear of Locke and his ideas, just then newly arrived from London and the very latest intellectual novelty of the day. Nor was his character warped or impaired by subservience, by servility to the great, by straitened circumstances or by indifferent success in his profession. In conditions of the direst poverty he had gone on with his labours, diligently exploring the most multifarious avenues of research, till at last, deeming that he had sufficiently cleared the ground, he brought out his book, the purpose of which was nothing less than to lay down the principles of an entirely new science of humanity, the nature of the different peoples, human rights and the laws which governed the evolution of the human race: *Principi d'una Scienza Nuova intorno all natura delle nazioni, per li quali si ritrovano altri principi del diritto delle genti.* That was the year 1725. There emerged from it all the grandiose idea that the subject and the object of knowledge consisted in the history that each and every people creates unconsciously by living it, and consciously when they regard it as the mirror of our species in the process of becoming. In his view, history was reality in process of being lived. Moreover, it was the evidence, the sum total of the signs and tokens we leave behind us and which, before passing into the realm of memory, are modalities of our existence. History, he held, consists of every building of whatever kind, from the cave-man's pile of stones, to the most finished product of civilization; of every language that had ever been spoken or committed to writing; all the institutions that had ever been set up; all habits, customs, laws. Nothing did Vico touch but he turned it into gold. Language was no more to be regarded as an abstract science of words, but as a series of inscriptions which it behoved us to decipher in case we might discover there some hidden gleams of our bygone states of mind and spirit. Poetry was not a mere matter of verbal manipulation, not mere technical skill in the handling of one's material and subduing it to one's purpose, a process in which success was to be measured by the conformity of the result to the laws of reason, it was the fine flower of a pure and spontaneous outpouring of the soul, a primal loveliness of which later ages had lost the secret. The *Iliad* and the *Odyssey* were not just tales cunningly strung together by some old blind bard, containing many strangely beautiful things, but also many defects, which latter were to be ascribed to the uncouthness of a barbarous age. No; they were rather one of those voices which had once been ours, one of our own modes of being, caught as it were upon the wing and preserved to us of the present day. The new science consisted no more of geometry or physics; it was the deciphering and interpretation of all those signs and tokens which, in the aggregate, made up the record of human life and evolution.

In vain did Giambattista Vico appeal to his learned compatriots in Naples, and to that eminent critic Jean Leclerc whose *Gazette de Hollande* was a European organ of criticism, an organ which had the power to make or to mar a writer's reputation. Europe turned a deaf ear, Italy being particularly indifferent. Yet Vico had bestowed on her one of her great titles of nobility when he pointed out how Latin betrayed evidences of an autochthonous civilization, *De antiquissima Italorum sapientia*, a *sapientia* the sole and rightful attribute of a race worthy to become again what it once had been. It was not until later that his appeal was heard and answered. For the moment it awakened no echo; no converts, no disciples followed in his train. His ideas bore no practical results and even his own folk turned their backs on him.

Christian Wolff was a very professorial personage, very much on his dignity. To see that, you have only to look at his portrait, the imposing wig, the neck encircled by the multiple folds of an ample cravat, the protruding eyes telling of too much reading, too much writing, the pompous self-assurance of the pedagogue who was clearly on the best of terms with himself. He had a teaching post at Halle university. He had started there in 1706 with mathematics, and there was always something of the mathematician about him. Later, he became a professed philosopher. It was in 1712 that he published his first important work, *Vernünftige Gedanken von den Kräften des menschlichen Verstandes, und seinen richtigen Gebrauch in Erkenntniss der Weisheit*—"Plain ideas concerning the powers of the human understanding and on its proper function in the recognition of wisdom." From then on, he "professed" without intermission, reproducing in his various publications the subject-matter of his lectures. Sixty-seven works appeared between 1703 and 1753, some of them in several volumes, not a few of them quartos. Year by year about his professorial chair, within the halo of his brilliant reputation, he collected his proselytes around him. He had become the intellectual leader of Germany.

He was quite agreeable to being looked on as the pupil of Leibniz, provided always that the word was not interpreted too narrowly, provided, that is to say, that he was not regarded as the mere mouthpiece of a man greater than himself, provided it was recognized that he had corrected, improved, transformed an inheritance of which he had made himself something far more than a custodian or trustee. *Philosophia Leibnitia-Wolffiana* was a joint work, of which he, Wolff, was the more important contributor. Leibniz had given him a start, whence he had soared aloft on more ambitious wing, alone.

Very soon he proceeded to cast the splendidly optimistic ideas of the author of *Theodicea* into a systematic mould. He reduced them to a series of categorical statements, to something closely resembling a dogma. In his view, the subject-matter of philosophy was the science of the possible and the whole of the possible. So he proceeded to shut up the possible in a number of different hermetically sealed compartments, packing it in with such care that not a particle of it was spilled. He defined them in each case and his definitions were as firm and rigid as prison walls. "The sciences", his admiring translator Formey explains, "cannot properly be so-called unless they arise from a number of truths firmly interlocked to the exclusion of all possible error. M. de Wolff has devoted his life to putting into true scientific shape the incondite mass of philosophic ideas which, till he set to work on them, were more like an untidy heap of building material than a building proper." Ah, that fine rectilinear draught-board of his which he took for a mirror. All that exists was caught and shut up, without a chance of escape, in those compartments of his:

ideas and his rational philosophy done into German for the commonalty, into Latin for the learned, he flooded first his own country and then the neighbouring ones. True, the course of his career had been interrupted by one rather disagreeable incident. At Halle, on the 12th July, 1721, he had delivered a lecture on the subject of the morals of the Chinese, taking for his text a theme which familiarity should have rendered inoffensive enough, and that was the lofty ethical character of the teaching of Confucius; which teaching conduced to righteousness, not as the result of some revelation from on high, but of a perfectly human wisdom based on reason. At once the pietists on the teaching staff, his colleagues and foes sounded the alarm. The affair, which stirred the university to its depths, was brought to the notice of Frederick William, his King and Governor. The story runs that someone about the Court had given out that M. Wolff was preaching the doctrine of predestination, of fatalism and that meant that His Majesty's soldiers were just so many machines, and therefore, if they deserted, it was wrong to punish them. Whereupon, the King, it was reported, flew into a mighty rage, and gave orders that Herr Wolff was to be sent out of the country. If, after the expiration of twenty-four hours, he was still in Halle, he was to be hanged forthwith. But the tide turned. Frederick II succeeded to the throne. Wolff was recalled to his city and his university and reinstated in his professorial Chair, where he had little more to do than meditate with complacency on his own importance, which he continued to do until his death in 1754. A mighty reputation; which the winds dispersed. They called him The Sage, the name of philosopher not being good enough for him. Whole nations admired him. France admitted him to honorary membership of the Académie des Sciences, the highest distinction they had to bestow. The English had a number of his works translated, convincing evidence of the esteem in which they held him, coming as it did from a nation who considered themselves unrivalled in the sphere of thought and philosophy. The Italians were prompt to recognize his merit and had been among the first to commend his books, not only in Rome, but throughout the schools of Italy. His Majesty the King of Naples went the length of issuing letters patent making compulsory the adoption of Wolff's system in all the universities of his dominions. The countries of the North had given him anything but a chilly reception; Russia made him professor emeritus of the Imperial Academy, while the other countries of those regions bestowed on him marks of the highest honour. This mighty fluttering of wings soon died away, and now, if you would seek the epitaph of Christian Wolff, you should look for it in books about the history of philosophy. But is he dead? Do we still catch echoes of his voice in the writings of some of his successors?

He always proclaimed himself an adherent of real and definite religion. He had refuted Spinoza, and Locke, and Bayle. He had inveighed against the English and their revolting free-thinking ideas, as he had against the ever-increasing encroachments of deism, materialism and scepticism among the French. Some two hours before his death, feeling that his last moments were approaching, he bared his head and, summoning up what little strength remained to him, he clasped his hands together and said, "Jesus, my Redeemer, help and strengthen me in this my hour of need." This certainly suggested a sound Christian belief in prayer and hope; but in his innermost soul, a Christian he was not. Morality, in his view, was purely an affair of reason; faith was an exercise of the reason, and reason stopped short at believing in miracles; and, in the last resort, God was a product of human reason. Such is the light in which subsequent generations came to look on Christian Wolff.

When we come to John Locke, we are filled with amazement. At first, his supremacy seemed unchallenged, and unchallengeable. His *Essay concerning Human Understanding* originally appeared in 1690 and it claimed to direct the current of human thought into a new channel. Until Kant came on the scene this Essay remained the philosopher's *vade mecum*, his bedside book. What Helvetius asserted in the book entitled, *De l'homme, Analogie de mes opinions avec celle de Locke*, holds good for the vast majority: You can count on your fingers the people who have not read, thumbed and admired him. The multitude of his followers is innumerable. I can call to mind no thinker who exerted a profounder influence on the minds of his contemporaries than did he. He quitted schools and universities, learned societies and academies, to talk to the world at large. He had become one of the indispensable "properties" of the fashionable intelligentsia of the day. Pope tells of a young Englishwoman who was sitting for her portrait and wanted to be seen holding a big book in her hand, that big book being the collected works of John Locke; while Goldsmith informs us that French dandies, not content with creating an impression by the elegance and refinement of their attire, were anxious to have their minds adorned as well, adorned by Locke. Destouches, in his comedy *La fausse Agnès*, introduces us to a young girl who feigned madness in order to escape the attentions of a suitor she did not love. Later on she gives convincing evidence of her sanity by expounding the ideas about knowledge as they are set forth by Locke in the *Essay*. Often, a quotation, an allusion, a reminiscence, not from one of the major works but from one of the comparatively unfamiliar ones, shows how people kept him, ready to be drawn on at a moment's notice, in the storehouse of their memory, a piece of gold to be displayed for just one dazzling moment, "to point a moral or adorn a tale".

Few indeed are the writers who devote themselves to the things that matter and to these alone; to religion, morals, politics, education, and who on their treatment of those important topics leave the indelible hall-mark of their genius. Such a one was John Locke and now we of today are realizing that he revolutionized literature itself, and that, not only because he dealt a death-blow to the old standard manuals of grammar and rhetoric by showing that the art of writing was not a mere matter of applying rules and obeying precepts, but much rather of reproducing ideas working in the inner consciousness: not only that, but also because he allotted to impression, to sensation an importance hitherto denied them. I owe nothing to Nature, said Sterne to Suard, who had a vague suspicion that this queer specimen of an Englishman was making fun of him; I owe everything to a long and careful study of certain great books: the Old and the New Testaments, and Locke whom I began to read in my youth and have gone on reading ever since. Thus Locke is at the fountain-head of the sort of literature which deals in the reactions, coherent or incoherent, of the Ego to the phenomena which affect it; we may call it the literature of impression, of sensation.

Now, where shall we look for the source of an influence as extensive as it is profound. Whence comes this apparently universal movement? Locke foreshadowed how the age would regard the problem of being. To him must be ascribed the formal recognition and renunciation of the Unknowable; from him proceeds the imperial edict *De coercendo intra fines imperio.* To him we owe the *dictum* that we have no need of things we cannot make use of. The sailor has no need to go exploring the ocean bed; all he needs is to chart the reefs, currents and harbours. To him, too, wherever he got it from, belongs the idea that there is nothing that is innate in the mind; that our abstract ideas, our reason itself, are derived from the sensations the mind records and its reactions thereto. His, again, is the idea that knowledge is solely the relation between the data which we apprehend in our mind and that truth is merely the consonancy of that relation. He, too, is responsible for bringing man down to the human level. He stands at the well-head of empiricism.

The torch-bearers were marching on. Truth should be dragged from its hiding places into the light of day. They gave themselves a proud title; they called themselves Alethophils, that is to say, Friends of Truth. On a medal representing the figure of Minerva, they blazoned their device, *Sapere aude*, "Dare to know". On they came, "their glance was frank and free"[1]:

> Et ce qu'avait produit l'ignorance grossière,
> Disparaît au grand jour d'un siècle de lumière.[2]

[1]Wieland, *Die Natur der Dinge*, Erstes Buch, lines 77 & 78.

[2]The shades of ignorance, of intellectual night
Will fade and flee before the coming light. Chabanon, *Sur le sort de la poésie . . .*, 1764.

IV

THE GOD OF THE CHRISTIANS IMPEACHED

UNFORTUNATELY for them, the position was already occupied. These greatly daring people found themselves face to face with a conception of life which, for eighteen hundred years, had formed the warp and woof of European civilization. When men came into the world, Christianity was there to greet them; it moulded and guided them through life; it shed its consecrating grace over the principal events of their earthly career; and Death itself it transformed into a release from bondage. Whenever they raised their eyes aloft they beheld on church and temple the Cross that had crowned the Hill of Calvary. Religion was so deeply interfused with their spirit that it seemed part of the very substance of their being. It claimed them, body and soul, and brooked no divided allegiance. He who is not with Me is against Me.

There, then, stood the Christian faith, present and active, and the newcomers collided with a shock against this age-old bastion of belief. According to Christian teaching, life was but a state of transition, of preparation, the difficult road which leads to Heaven; whereas, it was on the present, on the here and now, that those others staked all their hopes of happiness and prosperity. Christianity taught that our own unaided reason might take us a certain distance along the road of knowledge, but that when, sooner or later, we found ourselves face to face with some mystery which our reason was powerless to solve, we should put our trust in a higher wisdom, which, while it helped and supported us in our present state, would one day enable us to pierce the veil which hung between the eye of the flesh and Perfect Truth. Their adversaries, on the other hand, put all their reliance on human reason. Christianity taught that the human race lay under a curse, a curse that was traceable even in the noblest of the species, and that even our loftiest aspirations were marred by a hideous taint of sin. We had therefore to admit this original sin, which had cost us our liberty, but from which we could be washed clean if we made ourselves worthy to respond to the divine appeal. Not so, the others. They declined to believe in any such curse, in any kind of original stain. The appeal of the Christian was to authority and tradition. The answer he got was that authority was a usurpation and tradition a delusion. Thus began a conflict the like of which had never before been witnessed. The era of vague discontents, of local rebellions, of heresies and schisms, so much dead wood that could be cut away to preserve the life of the tree—those times were past. Now it was a case of striking at the roots of the tree itself. It was not a matter of an isolated revolt, here or there, of the insurgence of an individual, or a group, of a controversy between rival theologians; it was nothing short of an attempt to achieve the total defeat, the complete annihilation of religion that was now the object of the campaign, backed by a firm determination to see it through. The onslaught took place in the open, in broad daylight, for the multitude to see, for the multitude to applaud. This conflict it is, a conflict in which both sides were resolved to fight to the bitter end, that lends such poignancy to the history of the times.

It must not be supposed, however, that the battle was one between pure Christianity on the one side, and pure philosophy on the other. There were Pharisees and profaners of the Temple in the Christian camp; the sort of rich, influential people who thought any kind of change unnecessary, since the world as it was suited them so admirably. There were those stubborn, pig-headed mediocrities who would charge blindly at a thing and lay about them at random rather than try to understand the point at issue. Then there were those spurious devotees who think to ensure their salvation by the punctual performance of external practices and were shocked if anyone dared to speak slightingly of some perfectly patent superstition. Christians in name, these, but with more of the pagan in them than the gentiles and idolaters. Folk who knew not charity.

On the other hand, in the opposing camp, there were people

so destitute of religious feeling that they could not understand—they were indeed constitutionally incapable of understanding—the yearning in the hearts of those who lift up their voices to Heaven, or the solace that comes to those who pray. Having, themselves, no need of religion, they mocked and derided those who had: Christianity, they would have it, was so gross, so palpable, so glaring an imposture that they could not imagine how it had started, still less how it had lasted so long. It was a conspiracy concocted between two tyrannical powers, who agreed to share the spoils; the Monarchy was one, the Priesthood was the other. Christianity had left a trail of crime and falsehood all along the track of history. All the ills with which we are afflicted would disappear the day that Christianity was done away with. Excesses which the Church had tolerated, and sometimes encouraged, were represented as being the very substance of Christian belief. The Faith, in their account of it, was a code of *credenda* for the use of the ignorant and the weak-minded. It meant believing, not in what seemed to be true, but in what seemed to be false. For the God of Israel, Abraham and Jacob, they substituted "a superstitious veneration for human nature".[1] *Human nature vindicated.*[2] As if our sufferings had come about, not from our human state, but from the religion which had aimed at unfolding the meaning and the glory of it; as if they came from Christ.

But notwithstanding the welter and confusion of a struggle that was always fierce and often bitter, despite all the arguments that were aimed at the wrong mark, attacks and rejoinders both wide of the target; despite the ill-temper and the violence, the misconceptions, the irrelevancies, we may, none the less, discern the vital question at issue—shall Europe be Christian, or shall it not?

Such was the atmosphere in which the case was opened; a case the like of which had never yet been heard of, for it was God, God Himself, who was the prisoner at the Bar; the God of the Protestants and the God of the Catholics. For the former, however, there were some extenuating circumstances; he was considered more amenable to reason, less averse to the light.

[1]Grimm, *Correspondance littéraire,* III, p. 449, Dec. 1757.
[2]Thomas Chubb, *Human Nature Vindicated,* London, 1726.

But on the whole, there was no very definite line between Geneva and Rome, between St. Augustine and Calvin. Both had a common origin, both believed in Revelation.

It was, says a critic, as if a rumour, originating one knew not where, had at length grown too persistent to be ignored any longer. The rumour was to the effect that God, having departed secretly during the night, was about to cross the frontiers of the world and to abandon humanity. We must bear in mind that at that time God was being put on trial. The affair was, in the intellectual order, nothing less than the *cause célèbre* of the time and it stirred men's feelings to a degree which it is difficult to imagine. Everyone, readers and writers alike, was anxious to know whether there was a God to take care of his immortal soul, or whether there was no God and no immortal soul for him to take care of. That was the problem for the general run of men; did they live in a world governed by a beneficent intelligence, or in a world governed by blind and inexorable force? This was a problem that heated men's minds, a problem that was discussed everywhere, in books, in the pulpit, in drawing-rooms, at the dinner-table, when the servants had left the room. We can no more imagine a philosopher ignorant of, or neglecting, this question than we can a philosopher of the present day unaware of, or neglecting, the quantum theory.[1] Picturesquely put, but perfectly correct, so long as we clearly understand that the God who was on trial was the God of the Christians.

This *cause célèbre* was the main topic of letters that were exchanged from one end of Europe to the other. It was talked of in the press; it formed the theme of poetical epistles, odes and dithyrambs, and of those little rhyming jingles wherewith a prose writer will sometimes give a little variety to his compositions. It was discussed in Court circles by kings and queens, at the Hermitage, Richmond, which Caroline of Anspach had adorned with the busts of Wollaston, Clarke, Locke and Newton, and where Bishop Butler used to appear to lecture from six to seven of an evening on the truths of religion; at Rheinsberg and at Potsdam; at the Court of King Stanislas Augustus; at St. Petersburg, in the presence of Catherine of Russia. They spoke of its latest developments in the salons where Mme de Tencin,

[1] *The Heavenly City of the Eighteenth Century Philosophers*, by Carl L. Becker. New Haven, Yale University Press, 1932.

Mme du Deffand, Mlle de Lespinasse directed the course of the conversation. It was alluded to at academic gatherings; it began all over again in the offices of the Encyclopaedia in Paris. In Berlin, amid clouds of tobacco smoke and the clink of glasses, knots of students, all on fire to learn what the final verdict was to be, sat smoking and drinking, and talked of nothing else. Scientists in their laboratories had their eyes glued to their microscopes, hoping that nature would favour them with some fresh piece of evidence they could add to the *dossier*. People who travelled abroad kept looking about them for some fresh way of settling the matter. On one occasion, Diderot was staying with his friend Holbach at the latter's country house. They had eaten well and the wine had flowed freely; there was a lot of laughter and merriment, a good deal of rather broad jesting and clowning. Then, as though everything that wasn't connected with the big issue was merely an interlude, a diversion, the talk gradually veered round to "things that are not matters of indifference". "General sensibility, the formation of the sentient being, its unity, the origin of animals, their length of life, and all the questions allied thereto—these things and the like are not matters of indifference. Nor is it of no consequence whether or not we deny or affirm the existence of a Supreme Intelligence."[1]

On the side of the prosecution, there was always an atmosphere of bitterness and rancour; always the insistence that it was time, and more than time, that a power which had grown in influence and importance over a period of so many years, so many generations, should be required to render an account of what it had done. The God of the Christians had had all the power in his hands, and he had made ill use of it. In him, man had put all his trust, and that trust had been abused. Man in obedience to his authority had embarked on an experiment, and the experiment had proved disastrous. Wherefore, it was asked, was Christ so sad and sombre? "If it wasn't for religion we should all be a bit more cheerful."[2] Why wasn't his kingdom of this world? "Far from opposing man's attachment to earthly things, religion should encourage it."[3] Why were we told to mortify the flesh?

[1]Diderot, *Rêve de d'Alembert,* Édition Tourneux, Vol. II, p. 135.
[2]Diderot, *Entretien avec la Maréchale,* Oeuvres, Éd. Tourneux, Vol. II, p. 514.
[3]Helvetius, *De l'homme,* Section I, Chapter XIII.

Quel triomphe accablant, quelle indigne victoire
Cherchez-vous tristement à remporter sur vous?
Votre esprit éclairé pourra-t-il jamais croire
D'un double testament la chimérique histoire,
Et les songes sacrés de ces mystiques fous
Qui, dévots fainéants, sots et pieux loups-garous
Quittent de vrais plaisirs pour une fausse gloire?
Le plaisir est l'objet, le devoir et le but
De tous les êtres raisonnables. . . .[1]

Reasonable! That, of all things, was precisely what he was not. He was not even consistent. Judged by the light of logic and reason as we understand them, his idea of Providence did not hang together. So said Voltaire, continuing that Epistle in which he sums up his various grievances, the *Épitre à Uranie*:

Je veux aimer ce Dieu, je cherche en lui mon père,
On me montre un tyran que nous devons haïr.
Il créa des humains à lui-même semblables
Afin de les mieux avilir;
Il nous donna des coeurs coupables
Pour avoir droit de nous punir;
Il nous fit aimer le plaisir
Pour mieux nous tourmenter par des maux effroyables,
Qu'un miracle éternel empêche de finir.
Il venait de créer un homme à son image
On l'en voit soudain repentir
Comme si l'ouvrier n'avait pas dû sentir
Les défauts de son propre ouvrage. . . .[2]

Or to sum up all the complaints in one, God has asked us a riddle; he might have told us the answer had he wished, but he

[1]What a crushing triumph, what an ignoble victory are you seeking to gain over yourselves? Can your enlightened minds ever believe the chimerical story of a dual testament and the accursed dreams of those mad mystics who, sluggish psalm-droners and pious were-wolves as they are, abandon real pleasures for a false glory? Pleasure is the object, the duty and the aim of all reasonable folk.

[2]I fain would love this God, I seek in him my father, and what they show me is a tyrant whom we ought to hate. He created human beings in his own image the more easily to degrade them. He gave us sinful hearts in order that he might punish us, he made us fond of pleasure that he might torment us the more with frightful ills which an eternal miracle prevents from ever coming to an end. He created man in his own image and then of a sudden repented as if the workman could not but have been conscious of the defects of his own work.

did not wish. One day, La Condamine made up a riddle and read it out to a number of his friends, who were grouped in a circle round him. To his astonishment they gave him the answer straightway. He had written it himself in big letters on the back of the paper he was reading from. Ah! If God had only done the same! "If God had only treated us like the good and careless La Condamine, we should not have been cudgelling our brains these five or six thousand years. But it's a sorry jest to play off on people to send them to the Mercury of the next world to find out the answer."[1]

So much for the atmosphere: but before we go on to give in broad outline an account of the conflict, let us take a glance at some of the tortured and embittered souls who were among the foremost to give the period its distinctive tone and colour: an Italian, a Frenchman, and a German.

There was nothing so very new about taking up the cudgels in defence of the temporal power against the encroachments of the priesthood. It was in fact the final stage of a protracted quarrel. This was the manner of it.

Pietro Giannone was born in Apulia on the 7th May, 1676. He spent some time studying scholasticism, and then went on to Naples to work at law. Roman law, Canon law, Feudal law; then History; ecclesiastical history; then Philosophy. Starting as a Gassendist, he later became a Cartesian, he had learnt everything there was to learn. He was by no means a bad sort of man. He was honest, straightforward, and a great believer in justice. But he was not at all easy to get on with. He was crotchety, and quarrelsome, and obstinate. And all his life he was the slave of an obsession. It absorbed him. Ecclesiastical people had always tried their hardest to usurp the prerogatives of the civil power, and always without the slightest legal justification. And that was what he, Giannone, was going to make Naples, Italy, aye, and Europe understand. Wherefore, at white heat, working as though he had not a moment to lose, he began to write his *Istoria civile del regno di Napoli.* It came out in the year 1723.

History is scarcely the right name for it, for its author was none too careful about the authenticity of his sources. Also,

[1]Grimm, *Correspondance littéraire,* Vol. VII, p. 119, Sept. 1770.

in his furious anxiety to prove his case, he showed no compunction about appropriating other people's material. Nor could it be called exactly a work of art. It was more like a battering-ram, or that other military engine, the catapult. He made up his mind that people should be under no illusion about him, Giannone. No good going to him for tales of daring, or battles, elaborate descriptions of scenery, archaeological details and things of that sort. He was concerned with one matter, and one only, with man *qua* citizen. By going back the necessary distance into the past, and bringing his researches right down to his own day, he was going to show how one single struggle had been going on in various places throughout the Christian era, the struggle between the successors of Peter and the representatives of Caesar. The Church, always selfish, always ready to profit by human frailty, cajoling the waverers, frightening the sick and dying with the terrors of the hereafter, grabbing money, heaping up riches of every kind, had all along been a traitor to her mission.

The *Istoria civile* moves along on a wave of passion, and its tone is bitter. Repetition, hammering away again and again on the same note, is its main and constant resource: *Politica ecclesiastica, Monaci e beni temporali.* See, shouts Giannone, see how, all along, the monks have striven to increase their temporal power. Over and over again, the same arguments are repeated, and with ever waxing fury. Such vestiges of affection for the Church as sometimes survive among those who take it upon themselves to medicine her against her will, disappear entirely in these diatribes, and Giannone, that champion of the State, fast becomes an iconoclast, drunk with his own frenzy. The way he speaks of sacred images, relics, pilgrimages, aye, and miracles, tells us that. We see it in his hatred for the regular clergy, in his contemptuous references to the Hierarchy, in his irony, the weapon on which he mainly relies for defence against the attacks which he inevitably draws upon himself: Very well, for the sake of a quiet life, he will say in future that the Pope is the lord and master of the whole world, that he is perfectly entitled to use every means—fines, prison, dungeons, banishment, exile—to ensure the eternal salvation of mankind. He will believe that the Papal dominion does not stop at the surface of earth and sea, but that it extends to the nether regions, to Purgatory, and to

Paradise itself, so that even in the celestial abodes, the Angels must perforce submit to it.

Dauntless, indomitable, Pietro Giannone continued to stand his ground. Not without peril, not without unleashing the vengeance of the powers he defied, he went on launching his polemics, resolved to preserve and to spread far and wide his *Istoria civile*, everlastingly defiant, everlastingly on the offensive. He was excommunicated, his works were put on the Index. He then betook himself to Vienna, where the Emperor, because he supported his prerogatives, took him under his protection. But in 1734, Naples ceased to belong to Austria, and the Emperor ceased to take an interest in Giannone. So Giannone took it into his head to go back to Italy. He went to Venice, and was promptly expelled; then he tried Milan, and met the same fate. Finally, he made for Geneva, and there he was well received. The House of Savoy, however, thinking his presence there might lead to a spread of the contagion, baited a trap for him. On the invitation of someone he took for a friend, he visited a certain village in Piedmont, and there, on the very night of his arrival, he was placed under arrest. Clapped into gaol, dragged about from prison to prison, he gave up the ghost at last in the citadel of Turin. That was in 1748.

However, he left behind him a manuscript, as yet unprinted, which revealed everything there was still to be learned about his views and opinions. It was entitled *Il Triregno*, "The Three Kingdoms". There have been three successive kingdoms in the world; the first, an earthly one, for the Hebrew civilization was of the earth earthy. Its religious beliefs involved no idea of the soul's survival, nothing that implied any hope of immortality. Moses promised certain rewards to all who obeyed his law, but they were all material rewards; fertile lands, abundant flocks and herds, health and prosperity. He had never regarded the spirit as something destined to free itself from the grasp of death. The Egyptians it was who had inspired the Greeks, that gifted race, with ideas which these latter had subsequently developed—the Stygian swamps, Acheron, the Elysian Fields. But here, too, in all these elaborations of the original idea, nought was to be found but an imaginary prolongation of earthly conditions. Next, there came the Kingdom of Heaven. The Gospels tell how God sent his Word into the world, so that the Messiah might make known the way whereby men, earthly and mortal as they were, might become Sons of Heaven, and immortal, it being made plain that salvation was to be gained, not so much by what men believed as by the practice of a few quite simple virtues, virtues so plain and simple that a rustic, a peasant, anyone of the humblest capacity, could understand and obey them. Thirdly and lastly, came that abomination of desolation, the Papacy. Men had taken Primitive Christianity and on it had based and erected an edifice completely contrary to its spirit. They had taken upon themselves to interpret the law of right and wrong, and declared things to be lawful or unlawful, just as it suited them. They had deluded the multitude with the idea that they could open or close the gates of Heaven. Profiting by the ignorance of the rulers and the stupidity of their subjects, they had circulated the belief that spiritual benefits might be purchased with material riches, that redemption might be gained at the price of legacies and bequests, and that Paradise was to be had for good, sound cash. So back they had come to the Kingdom of Earth. To regain the Kingdom of Heaven, the Church would have to be swept away.

It was not the first time that one of the humbler clergy had bewailed the wretchedness of his lot and, so doing, incurred the displeasure of his superiors. This is how one of them gave vent to his discontent.

There dwelt at Etrépigny in Champagne a worthy curé, or, if appearances did not lie, at least a moderately worthy one. He came of a well-to-do family that had given several doctors to the Church. He was himself a man of cultivated mind, much given to browsing among the books in his library. Nevertheless, it cannot be denied that he had had frequent disagreements with the lord of the manor of the place, and had studiously avoided commending him in the pulpit. Wherefore the Archbishop of Rheims had remonstrated with him and called upon him to make amends. The Sunday which followed the receipt of the archiepiscopal injunction, the curé mounted the steps of the pulpit and delivered himself as follows: "This is just the sort of thing that the country clergy have to put up with. These grandees, the archbishops, look down on them and pay no heed to them; they have no ears for any but the nobility. Let us then remember the squire of this parish, M. de Cléry, in our prayers. Let us beseech Almighty God to change his heart, and to give him the grace to refrain from robbing orphans." This utterance, as may be well imagined, did not improve the situation, and the unequal strife went on. One report had it that the squire got someone to go and blaze away on a trumpet just outside the church windows of a Sunday, when the curé was preaching. Jean Meslier had his detractors; nevertheless he discharged his duties, said his office punctually and departed, without any further regrettable incident, in 1729.

However, he left behind him three copies of a testament animated by such a vehemence of fury that even now, after the lapse of two hundred years, it is impossible to read it without amazement. The gall of his spirit gushed forth in floods, inexhaustible hatred, undying rancour, a rage all the more bitter because it was impotent. He shouted for a revolt which he, Jean Meslier, had not had the courage to start himself. The cowardice with which he reproaches himself accounts in a measure for the frenzied insults he hurls at God and religion. How he raves and rages as he deplores that he ever allowed himself to be brought up for the Church, that he had assumed all the appearance of an orthodox priest, that he had let himself be trodden upon, and that, when he had cast away every shred of belief, he did not say so, but held his peace. Time and again, he declared, he had been on the point of breaking out, of giving vent to the fury he had pent up within him for a whole lifetime. Fear kept him back; he had been afraid to incur the wrath of the priesthood, to expose himself to the vengeance of tyrants who would never have found tortures cruel enough to punish his temerity.

This testament of the curé Jean Meslier started with that desire for happiness which is common to every human heart. Why had that desire always been frustrated? Because, some people being ambitious to command, others to achieve a reputation for sanctity, two forces had come into being, the one political, the other religious. When these two forces concluded a pact between themselves, man's fate was permanently decided. The kings and the priesthood, playing into each other's hands, had put the seal on their iniquity.

A torrent of passion swept him completely off his feet. All

religions were impostures. They were the source of division, wars, all the troubles of mankind. Therefore, they could not proceed from God. The proofs which the Catholic Church adduced to establish the unique character of her mission were complete fabrications. Therefore, Catholicism did not proceed from God. Its teaching was contrary to nature, since it sanctified pain; and contrary to reason, since it demanded faith. Therefore, it did not proceed from God. It ordered *Te Deums* and thanksgivings to be sung to glorify massacre and butchery, therefore it was not of God. And so on, everlastingly in the same vein. Himself the arch-fanatic, he execrated fanaticism. He was fired by nothing but the desire to curse. The call of the spirit which sounded in the heart of the humblest peasant in his flock, he had never heard. Of the Scriptures he had never known anything save the letter. He had never plumbed the significance of a symbol. We might almost say he had never prayed.

By the same token, it might have been said that it had never occurred to him that the functioning of a power might be called for by some definite social necessity. Away with kings and governors! Away with them all, and as a beginning, start a rising, refuse to pay taxes. Those upstart jacks-in-office, dressed in a little brief authority, away with them! "There comes into my mind, *à propos* of all this, a wish expressed by one who, though not a man of learning, nor possessed of any outstanding qualifications, seemed, so far as one could judge, to be eminently endowed with the sort of commonsense required to form an estimate of the detestable abuses and ceremonies I am here condemning. . . . His wish was that all the great ones of the earth, all the nobles, should be hanged and strangled with the guts of the priests." And as he repeated those horrible words, he invoked those who would some future day be called on to play the part of Brutus and Cassius, of Jacques Clément and Ravaillac.

His own personal misfortunes he laid at the door of God himself. For with him, according to Meslier, lay the ultimate responsibility; or rather with a being in whose existence men erroneously believed. And Jean Meslier proclaimed himself an atheist. This was the climax, the very orgasm of his rage. Drunk with sacrilege, he sobered down again as he reflected that there was now nothing left for him to destroy. And so his heart sank; sadness and depression were heavy upon him. All had turned to ashes in his mouth. Then he committed his last secret, his final confession, to that confidant, so still and silent, to the manuscript which he had written, copied and copied again through days and nights of unremitting toil. It was the last despairing unburdening of the spirit of one who now had nothing before him but the void. "And now let them think, and judge, and say, and do what they will in the world, I shall pay but little heed. Let them settle matters among themselves, let them govern and be governed as they will, be they wise or be they mad, be they good or wicked; whatever they say or do with me after I am dead, concerns me mighty little. Even now, I have almost ceased to heed what happens in the world. The dead, whose company I am now about to join, have no more troubles, and disquiet themselves no more. So I am putting *finis* to all this; even now I am little more than nothing; soon I shall be nothing indeed. . . ."

Nor was this the first time a Lutheran had forsaken his belief and become a freethinker. It happened to another man of those days, Johann Christian Edelmann, and this is how it came about. Edelmann's roots did not strike so far back into the seventeenth century as did Giannone's and Meslier's; he was born in 1698. He decided to take up a sacred calling and went through various schools, finally going to Jena to read theology at the university there. He began preaching and attracted some attention by the vehemence of his attacks on Socinianism. Of his professors, however, he retained the most unflattering recollections. What he had learnt from them wasn't worth a pinch of snuff. He had got nothing from the theologians but a lot of academic verbiage and he had been only too glad to escape from them. There was plenty of time for him to become a pastor. No need to be in such a mighty hurry. He would get to know something of the world first. He therefore decided to do a little teaching. And here he might have found himself on safe and solid ground. He was in every way qualified for the work: learning, will-power and a very alert intelligence, all were his. He was also the kind of man that gets on well in society, and he derived a good deal of amusement from the diversions of the aristocracy, hunting and shooting in the autumn, skating and dancing in the winter, nothing loth to let his admiring gaze linger on some attractive countess, who would favour him with an approving glance in her turn. So he might have gone on comfortably enough. But there was no stability about him; that was his major defect. Then again he had a terribly high opinion of himself.

He happened to come across Gottfried Arnold's *Unpartheysche Kirchen und Ketzer Historie* and it had a great and decisive effect on him: Yes, Gottfried Arnold was right; it was the heretics who possessed the true faith, not the orthodox people. So, farewell, Lutheranism! Farewell, the Churches, all of them! One morning when he was at Dresden he heard a voice that spoke to him saying: Set down the truths that harm not. Obeying this mysterious injunction, he sat him down at his writing table and began on the first of the pamphlets which later on developed into a whole series, under the title of *Unschuldige Wahrheiten;* and their object was to preach indifferentism in the matter of religion.

Truth is not in orthodoxy; where then is truth? Perhaps in pietism; and he became a pietist for a time; he joined the group that went by the name of the Inspired Ones; they met together, prayed awhile, sang hymns about Babylon and its ill-fated inhabitants; flung themselves on their knees, bowed low till their foreheads touched the ground, and waited for inspiration from above. And Johann Christian Edelmann prayed, sang hymns and waited with the most zealous of them. This lasted till he became acquainted with the leader of the group who came along in person to inspect the new recruit. The new recruit somehow did not feel drawn to him. However, truth was still among the heterodox, but not among the Illuminati.

One day, when he was reading the Gospel according to St. John, his eye lighted on the words, Θεὸς ἦν ὁ λόγος. Oh, the joy, the feeling of certitude that filled his bosom as he read those words! God was reason; God is Reason. Reason, to whose appeal he had so far remained deaf, wandering as he had been in superstition, now took firm and lasting hold on him. It seemed as if he had been suddenly rapt aloft to the summit of a high mountain, whence his gaze extended to limitless horizons. He felt like a captive slave who had been lying gagged and bound in a dungeon, and had suddenly been set free, and restored to the light of day, able to look on the light of the sun once more; or as if the gates of the tomb had been opened and the dead brought back to life.

Henceforth he felt he had but a single mission in life and that was to go forth far and wide preaching the Gospel of Reason to the world at large. He flung away his three-cornered hat and wig, he tore off his ruffles and his fine linen bands, he grew a beard and donned a coarse woollen habit. Thus accoutred, he went forth, trudging along the highways, and the people laughed. But there was something, some saying, that he could not get out of his head. It was something Spinoza had said: "God is the indwelling essence of the world". He felt that he ought to improve his acquaintance with Spinoza, whom the theologians described as a miscreant. So he wrote to a friend in Berlin asking him to look out for his works and see if he could pick them up at some sale or other. What an unlooked-for surprise it was for him, and what an unlooked-for joy! The most despicable of men, indeed! Why, he was the only man who had ever given the true explanation of things! Fortified by a perusal of the *Tractatus theologico-politicus*, Edelmann took it upon himself to prove that the Scriptures were false and that Moses was an impostor. Then he published his *Die Göttlichkeit der Vernunft*, The Divine Nature of Reason (1741).

After that, he wrote no more. He had played his part. Ostracized by society, he was looked on as the personification of Evil, as Satan's right-hand man. His books were impounded and burnt; anyone found trying to pass them on was punished by a fine. He went wandering about from place to place in northern Germany, and at last returned to Berlin, where he was suffered to remain on condition that he published nothing more. That was doubtless the unkindest cut of all, and the obscurity in which he was condemned to pass the last years of his life must have been his crowning sorrow.

V

REVEALED RELIGION

RELIGION; revealed religion, that was what stood in the way; that was the major adversary. Once make it clear that, from the nature of the case, there could be no such thing; once make it clear that, in point of historical fact, there *had* been no such thing, then the philosophers could go ahead. What they had to do was to show that, logically, the idea would not bear looking into, and that, historically, the evidence for it was quite untrustworthy.

Revelation comes under the order of the miraculous, and reason will have nothing to do with miracles. Revelation belongs to a supernatural order, but reason admits none but truths on the natural plane. As soon as revelation is examined in the light of reason, it reveals contradictory elements, and what is contradictory cannot be true. The strictly religious element in religion, that is to say religion in the strictest sense of the word, is based on superstition, and superstition must be attacked and eradicated. Every belief must be based on reason; to reason, even the Supreme Being himself is compelled to defer. Such was the burden of the chant that all the hierophants, no matter what their language, were intoning. Look at a map of Europe, you will easily recognize their points of origin. See here:

A mighty uproar; scandal after scandal, each so glaring as to seem unsurpassable; yet surpassed it always was; then a series of inflammatory works, which, however, might have passed unnoticed had it not been for the outburst of protests and indignation which greeted them. Then a stream of people from widely different points of the compass lining up to go in, one after another, to shout defiance to the foe. Such was the spectacle presented by England, where the example had been set a long time since.

In 1715, neither Toland of *Nazarenus* fame nor Collins the freethinker had retired from the fray. But without waiting for their withdrawal, plenty of others threw themselves into the task of giving orthodoxy, and the pillars of the Church, a thorough shaking up. First came Thomas Gordon, and, after him, Wolston, *Wolstoni furor*. This latter was a man of a scholarly turn of mind. He took his degree at Cambridge and decided to go into the Church, but the promise of a brilliant career was nipped in the bud when he flung himself body and soul into the cause of heterodoxy. Then there was Middleton, another Cambridge man, who, having taken his D.D., was appointed librarian to the University. Next came Tindal, an Oxford man this time. Tindal became a Catholic, but reverted to Protestantism, only to pass thence into the ranks of the militant deists. About the same time, another individual began to attract notice, a little man, short and obese, and anything but well bred, and very uncertain in his spelling. He started as a glover, but he gave that up, and became a tallow-chandler. His name was Thomas Chubb. Following him, we have Thomas Morgan, a philalethist, or truth-lover; and Peter Annet, a schoolmaster, who wrote for the crowd. . . . Pamphlets, brochures, learned works—they flooded the market with their aggressive compositions. They were deprived of employment, their writings were banned, they were put in the pillory, flung into gaol.

And every time, it was something fresh that was attacked. Now it was the Church of England, with its prelates and prebends; then it was the Church in general; then it was miracles; then came the Gospel interpretation of the life of Our Lord, which, they said, was merely a concrete example, an object-lesson, of the spiritual life and of the moral resurrection of each individual. But the brunt of the attack was directed against divine mediation. Religion was based either on the moral law, or on the arbitrary will of God. If God conforms to the moral law, he is wise and good; if he obeys his own arbitrary will, he is neither the one nor the other; his distinction between good and evil is determined by mere caprice. On the other hand, if God subjects himself to the moral law, his mediation is superfluous, since man, by his own unaided reason, is capable of distinguishing between right and wrong, and of recognizing the duty of complying with the general moral law. Therefore there is no alternative but to fall back on Natural Religion. Christianity would have a *raison d'être* only on the assumption that God was an irrational, or a maleficent, being.

Attempts to breach the defences were being made on every side. One assailant furiously attacked the veracity of the Old Testament. Another alleged that the words and deeds recorded of Christ were really to be ascribed to St. Paul. Yet another drew attention to the complete similarity he averred he detected between Paganism and the Church of Rome. Still another declared that David, the man after God's own heart, was nothing but an ignoble evil-doer. All alike, however, set up Reason as their guiding light, and rejected Revelation.

Perhaps the most significant of the works composed along these lines was Tindal's *Christianity as old as the Creation, or the Gospel a Republication of the Law of Nature*, which came out in 1730. It could not be otherwise, Tindal maintained. God was perfect, and God had given the world a perfect law which, being perfect, brooked neither addition, diminution nor change. That being so, then, though the Christian ordinance may have served a useful purpose in its early stages as tending to restore a weakened respect for the Law of Nature, it could not add to it anything substantially new, it could be but a repetition of the first and only law. The idea of a revelation was, not to put too fine a point upon it, totally inconceivable. It was dangerous, too, since it inspired all kinds of delusions, superstitions and abuses, from which it was high time we were delivered. That we could only bring about by taking philosophy, instead of religion, as the basis of our education.

At length, about the year 1760, these fires died down; they had, indeed, begun to decline as early as 1740 or thereabouts. About that time a change came over the atmosphere in England. Public opinion took a different and an opposite turn. People began to lose their taste a little for this anti-religious reason. Abroad, however, it suffered no abatement. Voltaire came upon it and he made lavish use of it. Baron von Holbach did much to propagate it by his translations and adaptations. Still more effective was the influence which the English deists came to have on thinkers in Germany, who were indebted to them not so much for direct quotations, for telling passages, irreverent sallies, as for giving them a general forward impulse. Their works were to be found in the libraries of historians and biblical exegetists; professors commended them, and lent them, to their students, whom they urged to read them; they loomed large in the review columns of the learned periodicals. Germans visiting London personally consulted their authors, and effusively acknowledged the debt they owed them. In 1741, Johann Lorenz Schmidt, whose idea it was to rationalize the Bible, brought out a translation of Tindal's *Christianity as old as the Creation.* At that point it may be said the English current of ideas joined the German, not indeed to mingle with it, but to hasten its flow.

The French took a different line. It was not on exegetical studies that they laid the emphasis. For a writer poring over the sacred texts, a writer well up in Hebrew, not to mention Greek, for a writer who had served a strict apprenticeship to Criticism, for a writer whom you might have taken for Richard Simon come to life again—for a writer such as this, you would have looked in vain, or almost in vain. All they did now was to search through other people's books for arguments they considered cogent and telling; a sort of lucky-dip in fact. The public to whom they addressed themselves were not learned folk, but just ordinary people, the man in the street, so to put it; and the authority to which they most generally referred was common sense, sweet reason. In their lively, slap-dash way, they purposely ran up against difficulties, just to show, in the twinkling of an eye, that they were insurmountable. No metaphysical obscurities about them; no long, boring dissertations to put the reader off; no parade of learning; but a well-knit theme, an attractive style, an agreeable mode of treatment.

Then there was their perspicuity, the atmosphere of luminous simplicity which they imparted to everything they touched; and then, beneath all these airy graces, the grave and enduring purpose which always inspired their thoughts. Voltaire, when he got back from England, gave an account of the things that had struck him there. His narrative might have been just another of those many travellers' tales, but a little more penetrating, a little more witty than the general run. But behold, these letters about England took on a philosophic character, discussing such things as religious freedom, religious indifferentism, and, as the author himself put it, that trifling little matter of the immortality of the soul. Montesquieu added still one more to the long list of Roman Histories, but observe that he too makes some particular incident or other an occasion for ascribing to internal causes, rather than to the will of Heaven, the decline and fall of nations. Furthermore, he produced a legal work in which the main subject was Divine Law. Many writers of inferior calibre followed in his wake. Toussaint devoted himself to a study of the manners and morals of his time; but instead of giving a purely objective account of a passing phase of the everlasting comedy, he went out of his way to endeavour to show that morals and religion had no necessary connexion with one another. Helvetius took man, plain man, for his subject, man with no mystery attached to him, and no morrow to look forward to.

In France, the type was more numerous than in any other country, and, apart from some minor points of disagreement, they presented a united front to the common adversary. They included in their ranks a number of people of talent, and a few of genius. Only the slightest signal was needed, as Grimm reports in the *Sermon philosophique* which he delivered on New Year's Day, 1770, only the slightest signal, and Frère Thomas, Frère Grétry, Soeur Necker, Soeur de Lespinasse, Mère Geoffrin would come running to the rescue; and a host of others besides, if need were. Their onward march was marked by resounding combats in which they were always vanquished by public authority, and always acclaimed by public opinion; there was the thesis of the Abbé de Prades, the banning of the Enclyclopaedia, the condemnation of Helvetius's *de l'Esprit*, the Sorbonne's denunciation of *Bélisaire*. "Come, Sir," said Marmontel to the Syndic of the Faculty of Theology, "is it not the spirit of the age, not mine, that you are condemning?" By people at a distance these controversies were followed with that keenness of interest that affairs in France never fail to arouse, and it is undeniable that most people felt that, represented by a race whose most marked characteristic was a passion for clarity, it was, in every case, the Spirit of the Age that *was* at stake.

They invoked the support of all who, in time or space, had ever shown that it was possible to live a good life without knowing anything about revealed religion; or who had ever rebelled against religion, no matter what. They invoked the Chinese, the Egyptians, the Mohammedans. From the Greeks they borrowed the statues of Socrates and Epicurus. To the Romans they went for Lucretius, that true apostle; and Cicero the determinist, Cicero who had had the insight to see that the cult of the gods was the cult of universal reason; and Seneca the philosopher. They resurrected Julian the Apostate, translating his discourse against the Christians. Constantine was accursed in their sight. A wicked Emperor, they called him, a mocker of God and of man. They appealed to the great Italian rationalists with whom, it must be confessed, they were not very well acquainted. They knew their names, however, and those names it was both profitable and impressive to repeat, as being freethinkers who had suffered for the cause, Giordano Bruno, Cardan, Campanella, Pomponazzi, and their successor Vanini. And with these, all their freethinking ancestors; and the English, their neighbours.

And now the *Contras* began again, but singing a different tune. They were *contra* the Jews, a wretched race, the very last people in the world to be entrusted with a sacred mission; *contra* the Pentateuch, which was the work of Esdras and no one else; *contra* the Bible; *contra* miracles and all who testified to them; *contra* the Prophets, who had never foretold the truth, and never really intended to prophesy at all; *contra* Jehovah, cruel, vindictive and unjust. If he had any good in him, he had got it from outside, from other Oriental peoples more civilized than the Jews; *contra* the Evangelists, a lot of poor ignorant fishermen, no more; *contra* the Gospel; *contra* Jesus Christ himself; *contra* the Church and all her dogmas and mysteries, the idea of original sin and its supposed effect on all the sons of Adam; *contra* the Church, its ordinances, the sacraments of Baptism, Confession, Holy Communion, the Mass; *contra* monks and nuns, priests, bishops and the Pope; *contra* Christian morality, the Saints, the Christian virtues, and charity; *contra* Christian civilization; *contra* the Middle Ages, the Gothic era, the Dark Ages; *contra* the Crusades—mere madness!

They made up mock sermons; they invented stories in dubious taste, and more than dubious anecdotes, for a dash of the indecent found a ready place in their armoury. Then, hey presto! Right about turn! Behold them now Fathers of the Church, reproving Christians for not living up to their own standards! Then, to the right about again. See them now mocking and deriding those same standards! When they desist, they leave Christianity without a rag to call its own. They strip it bare of any trace in history save an injurious one, with not a single problematical good point, not so much as the semblance of a virtue.

In Germany, the same goal was reached, but the process was slower, if it be true that we have to wait till 1780 for it to produce its full effects; and more complex, too, if the process was, as it seems to have been, a double one; the one part worldly, and imported from without, the other inward, profound and belonging to the very core of the Lutheran conscience.

The appeal which the Prussian Crown Prince made for the first time to Voltaire in his letter of August, 1736, inviting him to be his guide, philosopher and friend, would seem very remarkable if it was a case by itself. In point of fact, however, as a result of the general ferment, and more particularly in view of Germany's pressing need for rehabilitation, Berlin had already turned its gaze toward the country which stood for everything most advanced in civilization, that is to say, to France. And not Berlin only, but the princes and nobles throughout the country, who now regarded Paris with the same feelings of admiration as those with which their fathers before them had regarded Versailles. Let us call to mind the change that took place in the life of the youthful Wieland. To begin with he was immersed in sentiment, gave himself heart and soul to the things he loved and delighted in, identifying himself with the Swiss school, and learning therefrom the love of Nature and the poetry of the affections. If he then changed his mind, if, turning his back on his former friends, he took the path of intellectual enlightenment, the explanation is that he had been spending much of his time at the Castle of Warthausen whose owner, Count Stadion, had taught him the fashionable attitude of mind, telling him that the thing to do was to think and write as the French people did, if he wanted to be in tune with the tastes of the day. This was how the real Wieland discovered himself, the Wieland *à la Voltaire*.

Sometimes, reading a book by an *Aufklärer*, people seemed to get the impression that they were listening to an echo. All this had been heard in London and Paris before. The German was merely saying it over again. This applied to a work by Michael von Loen, published in the year 1750. This Michael von Loen was the son of a well-to-do merchant and man of the world. Having little faith in translators, von Loen himself made a French version of his book. It appeared in 1751, and was entitled, *The True Religion, unique of its kind, universal in its principles, corrupted by the disputes of theologians, split up into divers sects, restored to unity in Christ.* "Let no one be surprised that I, though not belonging to the Church, am addressing myself to the subject of Religion: it is a subject that affects every Christian, the common weal, and the happiness of all mankind. If I study the history of the most ancient races, I find everywhere ideas that are simple and shared by all, whether they have to do with virtue, or what people call God. God manifests himself through Nature and through Revelation. One single truth unites one with the other. No difference or contradiction can exist between them. If Revelation conflicted with, or differed from, the law of Nature, it would be at variance with truth. Likewise, virtue is of one sole kind and is summed up in a commandment that has never changed: "Thou shalt love the Lord thy God with thy whole heart, and with thy whole soul, and with all thy strength and with all thy mind, and thy neighbour as thyself." There is nothing substantially new in this way of putting things; any deist, whether he dwelt on the banks of the Thames or the banks of the Seine, might have put his signature to it.

But what we have not seen, and could not have seen, is the patient toil of scholars forever poring over the text of the Scriptures, and drifting ever farther and farther away from the orthodox conception of Revelation. How many parsons' sons were there who, having been through the secondary school in their own district, went up to the university, and there, becoming tutors or professors, sought in Biblical exegesis for confirmation or contradiction of their views and beliefs. They knew Hebrew, and not only Hebrew but other Oriental languages; they composed learned dissertations, recondite theses; they produced fat volumes for the edification of their brother specialists; they had no *a priori* prejudice against religion. On the contrary, they regarded it with unvarying respect, indeed with a nostalgic longing, hoping against hope that, notwithstanding the multiplication of sects and the spread of infidelity, reason might yet discover some formula that should bring back at last the long-lost age of unity.

Such was the *Aufklärung* of the German universities. It was at once more scholarly and more temperate than its English counterpart. It accepted indeed some principles of the latter, but disapproved of its violence. It was less irreverent in tone than the French school, whose support, however, it did not decline, though its ironical and mocking tone seemed to have a hollow ring about it. In 1730, Siegmund Jacob Baumgarten was appointed reader in theology at the University of Halle and in 1743 succeeded to the professorship. He gained the ear of his students, not by the charm of his teaching, for his delivery was monotonous, his voice feeble and his lectures difficult to follow, but by reason of a certain dignity in his bearing and the extraordinarily wide range of his scholarship. He took his stand somewhere between pietism and rationalism. Like Wolff, he delighted to pronounce the word "reason", which, he was convinced, offered the true key to real Christianity. "My words", he said, "are intended for those who are at once Christians and men of reason." He lectured on Church History, and subsequently embodied his views in a volume on the subject. And what ought such a history to be but "a narrative based on the texts"? On the text as it actually was, not as one person or another imagined that it ought to be. That was his guiding principle. Though he did not go so far as Gottfried Arnold's avowed predilection for heretics, he at least displayed a constant interest in them. Moreover, he wrote a history of them: "Outline of a history of the religious parties, or various bodies in the service of God, their disputes and divisions, both in and outside Christendom".[1] He dealt with them in two Reviews which he published, *Nachrichten von einer Hallischen Bibliothek* (1748–1751), *Nachrichten von merkwürdigen Bücher* (1752–1758): twenty volumes, all told. And what were these books which he exhumed? Nearly all anti-religious. Of course, he refutes them; of course, he indicates the books that should be read as an antidote to these enemies of religion. All the same, he lives, intellectually speaking, in the closest companionship with those whose avowed purpose it was to destroy it. It was as if he wanted to show how close he could go to the fire without getting burned.

[1] S. J. Baumgarten, *Abris einer Geschichte der Religions Partheyen, oder Gottesdienstlichen Gesellschaften, und der selben Streitigkeiten so wohl als Spaltungen, ausser und in der Christenheit* (1775).

Let us imagine ourselves in the room where his colleague, Christian Benedict Michaelis, is lecturing. He is engaged in expounding the prophet Jeremiah.[1] He says that if you would understand him, the first thing you have to do is to put him back in his own times. The material circumstances prevailing in the prophet's own day throw the necessary light on the prophecies. From that, to regarding prophecies in the light of mere historic fact quite apart from any sort of providential intervention, is no great step: *etenim historia, uti temporum, sic vaticiniorum lux, est qua demta, tenebris et caligine plena sunt omnia.* Or he would comment on the New Testament exactly as he would on Herodotus or Polybius.[2] The New Testament presents a variety of readings which is natural enough seeing that, though the authors of it were unquestionably inspired, its copyists very decidedly were not. Hence a number of mistakes, accidental or deliberate, some of which may be positively misleading. Now, to decide on which reading one is going to choose, one must have a system of some sort to go upon. The readings of the Fathers carry less weight than those of the translators, those of the translators less than the manuscripts. The same rules of criticism which apply to profane authors apply to the authors of the Scriptures.

So said Johann August Ernesti, the Leipzig philologist, eminent Latinist, *Germanorum Cicero*, and almost equally eminent exegetist. To put the matter plainly, a text presents a single, definite meaning, not a number of them. There is no question of an allegorical interpretation, allegory does not enter into it. The thing means precisely what it says, and that depends on usage. For the connexion between a thing and the sign used to denote it is a matter of human arrangement. It is governed by human usage and nothing else. It is a matter of grammar: *nullus alius sensus est nisi grammaticus, eumque grammatici tradunt.* All books, whether divine or human, are to be treated in the same manner: the Scriptures cannot be understood theologically if they have not first been understood grammatically; criticism is a matter of philology, or it is nothing.[3]

[1]*Ch.B. Michaelis S. Theologiae ac Ph. Prof. Halensis prolegomena in Jeremiam,* Halae Magdeburgicae, 4th Ed., 1733.

[2]*D.Ch.B. Michaelis, Tractatio critica De Variis lectionibus Novi Testamenti caute colligendis et dijudicandis*, Halae Magdeburgicae, 1749.

[3]*Io. Augusti Ernesti Institutio Interpretis Novi Testamenti ad usus lectionum,* 1761.

Peculiar people, psychologically, these scholars. They will set a fuse to the most daring ideas apparently unaware or regardless of what they are doing. It is their successors who, in the fullness of time, realize the implications of their legacy. Meanwhile, they themselves still cling to tradition. S. J. Baumgarten had an enquiring, not to say a restless, mind, yet neither his intellectual constitution nor his historical and scientific studies availed to draw him away from revealed religion. His natural tendency to conservatism was confirmed by habit and principle. It was only the extreme advance guard of his intellect that contemplated anything in the way of change or innovation. J. A. Ernesti, while stressing, as we have seen, the paramount importance of applying the most strictly philological methods, also opined, not without a measure of self-contradiction, that its application should not lead us to ignore the divine inspiration of the Scriptures, or the inerrability which necessarily flowed from it. He gives us his idea of the perfect theologian. Him, he declares to be a man that plays two parts at the same time; one of them he shares with the grammarians; the other is peculiar to himself, and is entirely his own affair. Better than anything else he ever said, this utterance displays his resolve to maintain a balance of forces, a poise, which many others regarded as impossible.

This new wave of criticism was following its destined course. Johann David Michaelis was Christian Benedict's son. He became a professor at Göttingen, as his father had been at Halle, only his subject was not theology but philosophy. As a professor of theology he would have been obliged to subscribe to the Augsburg Confession, and that he would not do. Conscientious to a fault, and so independent that he apparently wanted to reconstruct all rules and systems to suit his own ideas; grammarian, linguist, historian, exegetist, he gave a fresh impetus to Oriental studies, while insisting in very definite terms on the measure of science his school demanded. In 1750, we find him producing an introduction to the various books of the New Testament.[1] This he revised and augmented; and sometime during 1787 and 1788 he brought out a fourth edition of it. He said that the inspiration of the New Testament books was of less importance than the authenticity of their text. He held

[1] J. D. Michaelis, *Einleitung in die gottlichen Schriften des Neuen Bundes.*

that if not one of these books was inspired, even if the Apostles and Evangelists had no other resource than the ability to write down what they knew, then, if these books were genuinely authentic and entitled to credence, the Christian religion would still be the true one. We may have our doubts about the inspiration of the New Testament, we may even deny it altogether, yet still be sure that the New Testament is true. Its historical credibility would be unimpaired: a number of people either openly profess these ideas, or hold them privately, and it would be unjust to class such people as unbelievers. The books to be admitted to the canon should be limited to those which can be proved to have been actually written by the Apostles; those and only those. Having laid that down, he divides the books into two separate groups. In the first he puts those which bear the names of the Apostles Matthew, John, Paul, James and Jude. The others were not written by the Apostles but by their assistants or companions, "the others" being the Gospels of St. Mark and St. Luke and the Acts of the Apostles. When he began his studies, he saw no reason for excluding the books of this second group, but—as if we needed some further indication of the destination to which his ideas would inevitably lead him—the deeper he went into the matter, and the more he compared the books of the second group with those of the first, the more rapidly his doubts about them increased. In the third edition of his book he went on setting out the arguments for and against, still uncertain what conclusion he would finally come to. In the fourth, he inclined definitely to the negative. If the works are not authentic, they must be rejected. Neither the authority of the Church, which, he said, would presuppose the power to decide what is heretical, nor any inward stirring of the conscience, nor any considerations of moral advantage, could be brought into the matter. The question was purely a textual, a philological and an historical one. It was wholly a matter of the genuineness of the descent. Johann David Michaelis was thus for discarding the Gospels of St. Luke and St. Mark, and he was sure that in so doing, he was rendering a service to Christianity. This was the line he took: The main arguments advanced by the opponents of religion are directed against the Gospel of St. Luke, though St. Mark, too, is a target for similar attacks. Well then, surrender them both, St. Luke and St. Mark, and you will disarm the objectors, for they will then have no more contradictions to complain of, contradictions which, it must be admitted, are not always very easy to explain.

But now we come to a case in which the very essence of the Christian faith was changed and tampered with, and that by a theologian who thought he was grossly slandered when people told him he was no longer a Christian. Johann Salomo Semler was Baumgarten's favourite pupil, and he, Semler, was always profuse in expressions of grateful admiration for his master. The kinship is unmistakable. Their careers, too, were similar. In 1752, Semler was appointed Professor of Theology at the University of Halle. He was as dauntless as he was brilliant. His powerful voice rings through all the major controversies of his time. In his idea, religion was synonymous with morality. The history of religion was the record of man's moral progress. The inward life, varying in intensity with each individual, a well-spring soaring aloft from the innermost depths of our being, religion is a force spontaneous and free. If you try to direct its course by interference from without, you impair its nature, you impede the free play of its energy. Now what do the dogmatists do? The theologians, how do they set to work? They act on a false principle. They, these gentlemen of limited vision, have pitched upon a particular, limited period of time, a transient phase of history. In a civilization fated to perish, in the Jewish and in the Christian religions, they have insisted on seeing the one and only religion. On values that were purely relative, they have striven to impress the stamp of the absolute. That has been their mistake. They have taken one particular expression of religious feeling, and made of it Religion itself, something sacrosanct and inviolable. They have taken a purely local and transient manifestation and from it deduced an immutable law, which, they declared, was the one and only law applicable to all ages and to all peoples. Of elements whose very nature was fleeting and impermanent they constructed something they intended to endure for all time, one and unchangeable, and their error has lain heavily on the generations that followed. As well might we expect people always to wear clothes fashioned after the pattern of some bygone age, as to expect their spiritual raiment to remain the same in perpetuity. In no long time they would become objects of mirth. The consequences, said Semler, were disastrous. The true spirit of religion, he declared, had been smothered under a heap of rules, ordinances and rites. That innate will to righteousness which is the hidden source of religious faith, they confined in a number of external rites and obsolete observances. What it amounts to is this: the rulers of the Church elevated what was a merely local theological system, a purely local manifestation of religious feeling, and a social organization born of special circumstances, into a universal and everlasting religious system which they claim to be the one and only way to Salvation.

Semler never regarded himself as irreligious; the idea of such a thing never entered his head. His notion of a bad Christian was a theologian of the old school, one of those orthodox people who presumed to exclude from their communion anyone they looked on as a heretic. As if heresy itself was anything more than a temporary phase, a transient manifestation of man's everlasting faith in the Divine Goodness. The real enemies of Christianity were the people who rejected any idea of a revelation, which, however, he held to be an abiding reality. To him, it had been vouchsafed at long last to explain its real nature. Revelation, then, was a message, continually renewed, from God to Man. He explained, from the point of view of the critic, how he thought it should in future be understood. He made a careful study of the New Testament and declared that there was no cogent reason why such and such a text should be included in the canon, or why such and such another should be excluded from it. They, all of them, represented a more or less local and transitory aspect of the faith, an aspect, or phase, which could be historically accounted for. Then he made a similar study of the Old Testament, bringing the most rigorously critical methods to bear, and applying them, as he thought, with a completely open and impartial mind. The conclusion he came to was that the Old Testament was a purely national, that is to say, a purely Jewish, creation, nothing more and nothing less. The books of the Bible had not been written with the purpose of revealing a religion, since they contained statements that conflicted with the truths of eternal revelation, a theme to which he was constantly reverting. The God of the Jews was not the God of Nature; Virtue, as understood by the Jews, was not the Virtue derived from the laws of Nature. The Jews did not believe in the immortality of the soul. That was an idea that came to them later on, as the result of influences from without, after the Babylonian and Persian captivities; it was consequently an error to regard the Bible as the Truth and the Life. It was a reflection, a gleam, and its value was no greater, and no less, than all those other gleams that had shone on the road down the ages, as, for example, in the case of the Pagans, for the Pagans, too, had sent forth a gleam, a gleam from the great light of the Eternal Revelation, and there was true religion among them every time there had been a sound ethic.

VI

CHRISTIAN APOLOGETICS

WHEREVER Christianity made common cause with the State, the State came to its assistance. In Spain in particular, it was extremely difficult to secure, not only the publication, but even the circulation of anti-religious works. Side by side with the royal authority, perhaps even above it, the Inquisition was on the alert. The same in Portugal; on 18th October, 1738, Antonio Jose da Silva was garrotted, and then burnt in an *auto-da-fé* at Lisbon. Again, in 1778, Francisco Manoel do Nascimiento was arrested and imprisoned on a charge of proclaiming his disbelief in the Deluge, and of casting ridicule on the doctrine of Original Sin. He managed to escape before his trial came on, and so avoided the fate that awaited him. In France, to say anything against Divine Right was nothing less than *lèse-majesté*. There, ecclesiastical censorship, the licensing of the printing and selling of books, denunciations by the Bishops and the Assembly of the Clergy, Parliamentary intervention, Royal sanctions, were all part of an attempt to check the rising flood of infidelity. In Italy, where the country was so much split up, conditions varied. Tuscany was easy-going, and permitted the Encyclopaedia to be reprinted there. The Grand Duchy of Parma, very French in character, was by no means rigorous. In Venice, where trade was the important thing, the nature of the merchandise handled was not too closely inspected. Rome, on the other hand, was strict to the last degree, while Piedmont resorted to measures that were not merely restrictive, but violent. In Austria, Maria Theresa was especially alert. In Vienna, the Censorship forbade the circulation of the Index, it being considered that the mere reading of their titles might excite curiosity about books whose existence, they thought, had better remain unsuspected. The more active philosophical propaganda became, the sterner grew the measures for counteracting it. Interdicts, prohibitions increased in frequency and severity even in countries where, to begin with, the authorities had turned a blind eye to what was going on.

In Protestant countries, of course, there was supposed to be complete freedom of speech. However, in Germany this did not prevent Wolff from being deprived of his chair at Halle and from being driven out of Prussia. Edelmann was persecuted, Johann Lorenz Schmidt was flung into prison, Karl Friedrich Bahrdt was deprived of his employment. In theory, Berlin was the most tolerant of cities, extending a welcome to all who had been persecuted and outlawed for preaching irreligion. No sooner, however, did anything political enter into the matter than a complete change came over the situation. So said Lessing, and he is a witness above suspicion: in Berlin, you can deliver yourself of any sort of nonsense about religion; but just put a finger into the political pie, and you'll see how your so-called freedom will turn into serfdom. Even in England, things could be pretty harsh. As late as 1779, Catholics were still excluded from the operation of the Toleration Act.

These things are worth noting as a matter of interest, but be it granted that if Christianity had had only the secular arm to defend herself with, she might have justified some of the accusations that were brought against her.

Since it was in France that philosophy had become a matter of peculiar public interest, so also was it in France that its opponents put up a peculiarly stubborn resistance, and that, on its own chosen ground. At least that was what they endeavoured to do. And sometimes they got a blow well home. They invented a nickname, and a telling one, for their adversaries: they called them the Cacouacs. In 1757, *L'Histoire des Cacouacs* began to be talked of all over Paris. Somewhere, about the forty-eighth degree south, there had lately been discovered a tribe even less known than the Caribbeans. The Cacouacs had a weapon peculiar to themselves: it was a pouch of poison concealed beneath the tongue. Whenever they spoke, no matter how softly, this poison began to flow, then shot out and spread all around. They recognized no authority, declared that all things were relative, and kept on saying the word "Truth" over and over again. They had a tremendous opinion of themselves and thought they had the universe at their feet. Scorning Divine Wisdom, they made Nature their God. By means of slogans and catch-phrases as specious as they were misleading, they were slowly and surely gaining ground, when behold! a race of free men, albeit few in number, declared war upon them. The battle began; the Cacouacs came on with a great deal of fuss and noise. They might have carried all before them had it not been for a terrible weapon which their adversaries had at their disposal, and that was the buzzer. At a given moment they sounded their buzzers, and at the noise, the Cacouacs broke and fled in disorder.

Some of their shafts were peculiarly devastating. "The origin of the Cacouacs, if we may believe their own story,. goes back to the Titans, who attempted to scale the heights of Heaven." The Cacouacs study nature in all things. They erect no temple in her honour, because that would have the appearance of worship, and one of the maxims they inherit from the Titans is that to know is better than to worship. And here is a title for one of their books: "Scheme for a universal religion for the benefit of those who do not need one, in which a Deity is admitted, provided he interferes in nothing." Add to this, all manner of jests, quips, sallies, parodies, and quotations selected for their portentous vacuity, like the "Young man, take and read" of Diderot, and you will get some notion of the style and contents of Jacob Nicolas Moreau's *Avis utile* and his *Nouveau Mémoire pour servir à l'histoire des Cacouacs*. Moreau was a distinct success. Others took their cue from him. The philosophers were furious. They did not mind laughing at others, but that others should laugh at them was beyond endurance. Before long they were put on the stage. Everyone has heard of the comedy, *Les Philosophes*, 1760, and of how Palissot caricatured Grimm, Helvetius, Diderot, Mlle Clairon, and in particular, Jean Jacques Rousseau, who appeared creeping along on all fours, and pulled a lettuce out of his pocket. Less well known is the regular campaign, defence and counter-offensive and the rest of it, that was everywhere going on. Abraham Chaumeix made a dead set at the Encyclopaedia. It was the crusade of his life. Full of dash, and full of determination, he put his finger on the weak spots.

He took off the sort of spirit by which the whole thing was animated. "I did not trouble myself to find out whether M. Diderot had given an accurate account of the manner of weaving stockings, or of the various ways of cutting out a shirt. It sufficed me to consider what sort of an idea the Encyclopaedia gives one of man, of his nature, his aims and his happiness." Or else he started pulling the book *De l'esprit* to pieces, and fine work he found it. Linguet dealt some shrewd blows: *La Philosophie?* "The name means love of wisdom. It is like some coats-of-arms we know of, emblazoned with symbols that have nothing whatever to do with the character of the people who display them. Many a white-livered poltroon has sported a lion on his scutcheon." "Religious fanaticism dyes the soil with blood; philosophic fanaticism robs men of their physical and moral strength."

"The philosophical disputant who discusses and argues, who nicely calculates the rights of this, that and the other power, who holds forth on virtues and vices, is too much of a coward to be able to obey. His heart, withered up by his so-called knowledge, is open to one thing only, and that is fear. Country, honour, duty—these words mean nothing to him. He has examined them, dissected and analysed them in every possible way. He knows many things about them. What he has no idea of is their strength and their sweetness."

The toughest fighter of them all was Fréron. A hard-headed Breton, he was no sooner down, than up he bobbed again, ready to renew the fight. His habit of laying about him left and right, and preferably at the big-wigs, got him into prison, in the Bastille, at Vincennes and at For-l'Évêque. As soon as he was out, hardly giving himself time to take a breath, he started again. He brought out his *Lettres de la Comtesse*, *Lettres sur quelques écrits de ce temps*. They were stopped. Little cared he. In no time he began to issue the *Année littéraire* which, by some manner of means, he managed to keep going till he died. He was far from being a person of no account. He wielded a graceful pen himself, and he knew good writing when he saw it; he had considerable taste, with a penchant for what was new. He recognized the ills that afflicted society, and clamoured for their removal. He availed himself freely of the pleasures life could offer, and he was liberal, not to say extravagant. In short, he was no ordinary personality. The mere sight of a philosopher infuriated him. He had them all down in his writings, not a single one is missing. He stood up to Voltaire himself. "I returned to the ring with the ardour of a man who, when his cowardly opponent has dealt him a foul stroke, finds his courage increased rather than diminished." He knew what he was in for—fierce words, biting epigrams, spiteful strokes, vindictive blows. But it pleased him to invite these reprisals. He had a mission to fulfil. It never seemed to dawn on the philosophers that they were substituting trouble, bitterness and despair for the consolations of the Christian faith, but he, Fréron, would denounce their error. He would show them that they were mad if they thought that a people which shakes off a sacred yoke would long endure a human one. "Never was there an age more fertile than ours in seditious writers, in writers who, following the example of the poet Linière, concentrate all their powers on attacking the Godhead. They style themselves the apostles of humanity, never realizing that it ill befits a citizen, that it is to do a grave disservice to mankind, to rob them of the only hopes which offer them some mitigation of this life's ills; they do not understand that they are upsetting the social order, inciting the poor against the rich, the weak against the strong, and putting arms into millions of hands hitherto restrained from violence by their moral and religious sense quite as much as by the law. This contemptible attack on religion, moreover, is a mark of weakness rather than of strength. People would not be so ready to attack religion in what they say and in what they write, if they were not secretly afraid of it. All those writers in prose or verse who flesh their satire on religion are like nervous travellers who are ever in fear of robbers, and sing with all the force of their lungs to hide their trepidation."

To the anti-philosophers, it looked as if someone had carelessly set fire to the old dwelling when trying to improve the lighting.

If we were to take it into our heads to revive a certain fanciful idea that was rather popular in those days, and describe a battle of the books, with pages whirling about in the air in all directions, tomes of all shapes and sizes hurtling violently into one another, it would not be so extravagant as it might seem, because that, in very truth, was pretty much what was actually happening.

Never had there been such a spate of books against religion; never had there been such a spate of books in its defence. There would have been enough, and to spare, to furnish whole libraries withal. In the contemporary press, only one department of literature was more abundantly represented than the assailants of Christianity, and that was its defenders.

The Ancients were invoked by the attackers in support of materialism. The apologists refuted them. While the assailants called on the freethinkers of the world to help them, the defenders appealed to the illustrious champions of the Faith. Bossuet's mighty voice pealed forth anew, calling man back to the Lord. Was it the Bible that was attacked? Dom Calmet spent his whole life defending it. It was alleged, was it, that Moses was not the author of the Pentateuch? It is true, replied Astruc, the learned Astruc, that the book appears to reveal traces of different origin; true that, according to one tradition, God is called Eloim, and according to another, Jehovah; and quite possibly there were still others, but all these difficulties disappear as soon as we realize that Moses worked on several records which all, so to put it, converged on him. A favourite mode of attack was to allege that all the spiritual element in the Jewish tradition was imported from other oriental religions. It was then the turn of the apologists to show that the great myths, cults and mysteries of Paganism were but spurious imitations of the stories, customs and traditions of the Hebrews. Some critics tried to discredit the traditional account of the Church's original foundation, and, indeed, tradition in general. So, behold, the *Histoire ecclésiastique* of the Abbé Fleury, all the thirty-six volumes of which Alfieri used to say he had read in his young days. The Lutherans came out with their *Institutionum Historiae ecclesiasticae antiquioris et recentioris Libri IV* (1726), a work of some note, by J. L. von Mosheim, Toland's antagonist. The philosophers borrowed their destructive arguments from collections of heretical works, so other opposition collections were brought out, in order that the believers might be still further fortified in their creed. One of these compilations was the *Delectus argumentorum et Syllabus Scriptorum qui veritatem religionis christianae . . . asseruerunt* (1725). Heresy sought to extend its influence by way of the universities. That had to be countered; hence university sermons, dissertations, theses, to bring back the students to the orthodox fold.

Whatever move one side made, the other made a move to counter it. Down with the Socinians! Confusion to the deists! Exterminate the atheists! Locke was at the root of all the trouble. He was a philosopher, was he? Then philosophy would teach him a lesson. Geometrical demonstrations are the ruling fashion, are they? Well, then, we will give a geometrical proof of the truth of the Christian religion. So we have article against article, letter against letter, dictionary against dictionary, satire against satire. *Le Philosophe chrétien; La Religion vengée*. . . .

The first thing the defenders did was to strengthen their own position, to overhaul the traditional arguments, and so, as we may say, to put their own house in order. They re-read the Fathers of the Church and the great theologians of old. They mustered all their internal resources. To strike at the root of the evil, wrote Mgr. de FitzJames, the Bishop of Soissons, to Montesquieu on 29th September, 1750, "we must think seriously about reviving theological studies, now completely neglected, and try to ensure that our clergy are well up in theology and able to defend their religion. The Christian religion is so beautiful that I do not think anyone could really know it without loving it. People who make blasphemous remarks about it simply do not know what it is. If only we could call back from the shades such men as Bossuet, Pascal, Nicole and Fénelon! Merely to ponder on their teaching, to contemplate their personalities, would do more good than any number of formal ecclesiastical condemnations."

So the apologists went on, speaking the language of the schools to such as could still understand it; to those who could not, they used a different idiom. Reason? Well, why not? Are reason and religion mutually exclusive? Not at all. The Church has always regarded them as allies. We can only know things according to the idea we have of them, and the accuracy of our judgment depends on the clarity of our ideas. Well, that may be. Nevertheless, there is a domain to which our ideas, limited and often faulty as they are, cannot attain. That no one denies. God cannot deceive us; every deist would freely grant that. Well, then, since God has revealed certain truths which would otherwise have remained beyond our reach, we must perforce believe them. Belief in mysteries, then, cannot be said to be contrary to reason; reason, indeed, enjoins upon us submission to Divine authority. Thus speaks one of the most fertile apologists of the times, the Abbé Bergier, who begs his readers to remember St. Paul's *rationabile obsequium*.[1]

The facts, and why not? Apologists must not stay wrapped in silence. Nor must they attempt to coerce. Persuasion, charity, gentleness—these should be their weapons, for there is no true religion save that which is voluntary, and no human power can storm the impenetrable fortress of freedom. The apologist, then, must lend an attentive ear to the arguments of his opponents, and meet them on their own ground. Another writer adopts the same attitude, to wit the Abbé Houtteville, whose *La religion chrétienne prouvée par les faits*, first published in 1722, was reprinted again and again during the remainder of the century. He took care to establish, in strict accordance with the rules of historical investigation, the authenticity of the facts adduced; then he went on to show that the miracles recorded in Holy Writ and described by eyewitnesses or contemporary writers whose honesty and accuracy were beyond all question, considered in the light of subsequent events, and recognized even by persons who would have much preferred to deny them, bore upon them the marks of incontestable credibility. Whether or not they contradicted the laws of Nature, they had to be admitted. Moreover, that contradiction, that seeming contradiction, was merely due to the limitation of our vision, and disappeared in the light of the Divine Wisdom which could comprehend the manner in which all things are linked together, one with another, and, out of seeming diversity, create unity.

Facts; reason. But there is another force, also. It is born of reason; it takes note of the facts, and then soars aloft into the empyrean of emotion and exaltation. Then are the beauties of Nature made manifest to our eyes. Interlocking forces, all obeying a single order, a harmony which embraces the infinitely great and the infinitely small, a beauty diffused over all created things, animate or inanimate—do not all these things move us to give thanks from our hearts to God who made them? Let us, then, lift up our voices in praise to God. It is not enough for us merely to acknowledge his presence. Therefore let the

[1] *Apologie de la religion chrétienne*, 1769; chap. V. See, by the same author, *Le déisme réfuté par lui-même*, 1765.

heart, together with the mind, give utterance to the feelings which move it. So Derham in England and, very soon, Nieuwentydt in Holland, raised their voices in thanksgiving, in outpourings of the spirit, in lyrical effusions. That was the first signal. It was immediately hailed by those who were looking out for it. Far and wide, it was flashed abroad and soon there was scarcely a country in Europe which, in its own tongue, did not take up the strain and sing "The Heavens proclaim the glory of the Lord, and the firmament sheweth his handiwork." The name of the song might vary, but the sentiment was everywhere the same. It is not incumbent upon us to give details of these effusions here, since we are limiting our considerations to the intellectual sphere; but it was from observation and reasoning that these sentiments proceeded, and the apologists made the most of them. From goodness and beauty they derived an argument for truth. As far back as 1741, Père André, in his *Traité sur le Beau*, had enunciated an idea which, fostered out of sight by a few little-known writers, gradually, under the impulse of events, came to maturity, and at last blossomed forth triumphantly in the *Génie du Christianisme*: "We have spoken of God as it behoves a Christian philosopher to speak of him: we have proved his existence, explained his nature, described his ways, constantly bringing out the very close accord of religion and faith with God the Sovereign Lord of all. First, pondering on God in his essence, we have seen that there is nothing mightier, nothing more marvellous, nothing more terrible than God as he manifests himself to our sight. Then, considering more closely how God works in regard to ourselves, we have seen how there is nothing better, nothing more lovable than this same spectacle of the Divine. It was less difficult for us to behold it than to explain it."

The Anglican apologists put all their heart and soul into the matter. Berkeley descended into the lists, and taunted the "minute philosophers", the pigmy breed, who imagined they were so profound.[1] The anti-God party were going too far, and they were going too fast. Swift told them they might attack Christianity, but they could not abolish it; a whole army of

[1] *Alciphron, Or the minute Philosopher; in seven Dialogues, containing an Apology for the Christian Religion, against those who are called Freethinkers,* London, 1732.

people declared it was an imposture, that it was not worthy of serious examination, that it was an object of derision, something to laugh at, and to laugh at it would be an appropriate return for all the years it had spent robbing the world of pleasure; well, this was no reason for abandoning it, but rather for rehabilitating it and presenting it as it really was. It was the fashion to laugh at good Christians, to put them out of countenance, to make them look foolish. They should be furnished with fresh arguments suited to the times, with fresh courage, and their confidence in the truths of their religion should be restored. Now that the trial was in progress, the verdict would follow as a matter of course. This was not a mere metaphor, for it actually occurred to one of the defendants, Bishop Sherlock, to stage a trial in proper legal form, with judge, jury, foreman; the sort of thing to be seen any day in London and the provinces, except that the witnesses who were put into the box were those who had testified to the resurrection of Christ.[1]

Judge: Gentlemen of the Jury, I have laid before you the Substance of what has been said on both Sides. You are now to consider of it, and to give your Verdict.

The Jury consulted together, and the Foreman rose up.

Foreman: My Lord, we are ready to give our Verdict.

Judge: Are you all agreed?

Jury: Yes.

Judge: Who shall speak for you?

Jury: Our Foreman.

Judge: What say you? Are the Apostles guilty of giving false Evidence in the Case of the Resurrection of Jesus, or not guilty?

Foreman: Not guilty.

Among the exegetists, theologians, historians, and preachers of the day, two men stand out in conspicuous relief. One of them, Warburton, Bishop of Gloucester, was a singular personality; forceful, rugged, an omnivorous reader, a tremendous worker and a redoubtable controversialist. Before taking orders, he had studied law, and he always retained a taste for legal hair-splitting. Very much the man of his times, he had been prompt to consult Locke on the new philosophy, and Bayle on scepticism. A great lover of paradox, he practised it in a manner peculiarly

[1]*The Trial of the Witnesses of the Resurrection of Jesus,* London, 1729.

his own; he pretended to yield the whole case to his opponents, and then, just as they were congratulating themselves on their victory, he would take them unawares and smite them where they least expected it. For example, in his *Alliance between Church and State* (1736): The Church is a body apart; it has no claims on the State. The State is a body apart and has no claims on the Church. At such an auspicious exordium, the dissentients could hardly have failed to rejoice, and the philosophers must have felt that they had discovered a new friend, and what is more, a friend in the ranks of the clergy. But then he went on, Religion has need of the State and the State of Religion, if it, the State, is to maintain its true character. It would be intolerable that its servants should deny the very principles on which its stability depended, such as the natural and essential distinction between good and evil. It was within its rights in requiring an assurance on such a point as that. Neither power was in any way inferior to the other, but there was an indissoluble alliance between them. And Warburton ended by declaring for a state religion based on the fundamental ordinances of the law of Nature and the law of Man.

More striking still was the work he published some two years later, *The Divine Legation of Moses*. Everyone will agree that when a wise lawgiver sets about establishing a religion and a civil government, he does not go to work haphazard; he is guided by reason and he has his definite aims. An ordinary religion, if it is to endure, must include belief in a future life. An ordinary state, if society is to subsist in a normal fashion, must adhere to the doctrine of reward and punishment. But neither belief in a future state nor the doctrine of reward and punishment is to be found in the law of Moses. What follows, if we grant that Moses was an able lawgiver, as he undoubtedly was? That he took as his foundation, not just ordinary values such as might suffice for a purely humanistic religion, but values that were exceptional, superhuman, divine. Whatever may be said in theory about the validity of Warburton's arguments, there is no doubt about their practical effect, as Voltaire's replies abundantly testify.

A very different sort of person was Joseph Butler who, though born a Presbyterian, died an Anglican bishop, and, starting as a dissenter, finished up a sound churchman. It was not ambition that prompted him, for he was plain and simple in his habits, avoiding luxury and display. His sole aim in life was the pursuit of truth and the practice of the Christian virtues. Nature, reason—these were his starting points, and since Locke's ideas had given rise to a general disinclination to accept anything that was beyond the grasp of the human intelligence, he reared his argument on a purely empirical basis. Hence his popular appeal, his influence, and the immense success of his book: *The Analogy of Religion, Natural and Revealed, to the Constitution and Course of Nature* (1736).

He declared the most perfect manifestation of truth to be that which is revealed by demonstrative evidence; but he observed that in the affairs of our ordinary, everyday life, it was not on positive evidence that we relied, but on probability, which proceeded by a series of degrees, from the very lowest presumption to the highest moral certainty. It is supposable that there may be fog in England on any given day in January next; probable, that there will be on some day of the month; and there is a moral certainty that there will be in some part or other of the winter. A man's having observed the ebb and flow of the tide today, affords some sort of presumption, though the lowest imaginable, that it may happen again tomorrow; but the observation of this event for so many days, and months, and ages together, as it has been observed by mankind, gives us a full assurance that it will. Probable evidence, in its very nature, affords but an imperfect kind of information; and it is to be considered as relative only to beings of limited capacity. For nothing which is the possible object of knowledge, whether past, present or future, can be probable to an infinite intelligence, but to us, probability is the very guide of life.

It likewise establishes the soundness of natural religion. The passing from a known to an unknown state; that, stated in its simplest terms, is belief in the immortality of the soul. Now is not this idea of passing over, of transition, consonant with the processes of nature, as we see them going on before our eyes? Just as the chrysalis changes into the butterfly, just as creeping things become winged ones, as silkworms pierce the cocoon, as chicks break the egg-shell, to undergo the most remarkable transformations; so, by analogy, it is probable that after we have died in the flesh, we shall live again in a new life.

Religion causes us to fear the pains which will constitute the punishment for our wrongdoings, and to hope for the joys that are to be the reward of virtue; well, just as intemperance over a given period of time causes us to pass from a flourishing into a miserable state of health; and just as our good conduct procures us in the end both health and strength, so it is possible, probable, morally certain, that our offences against the Creator will be followed by retribution, whereas if we duly observe the moral law, joy will be our recompense.

As to revealed religion—which only differs from natural religion in that it satisfies our native longing for what is firm and definite—one of the great stumbling-blocks for the non-Christian is the mediation of Jesus Christ. Yet, is not mediation but another of the factors which govern our lives and which we acknowledge with gratitude? All created beings come into the world through the instrumentality of others, by whom they are nourished and protected; and the satisfaction of our several needs we owe to others. Therefore, the coming of a mediator between God and man, the coming of Christ, who became incarnate for us, to cleanse us from our sins, may, on this analogy, be expected and believed.

It was a persuasive voice, and it was pleasing to religious people because it made them feel that they were not so outmoded and backward after all; that they might feel, as everyone wants to feel, level with the times. But it was a voice that startled the unbelievers because it echoed some of the things which they themselves were saying. It was a line of argument based on a method recognized as the only sound one, observation tested by experiment. Joseph Butler, Bishop of Durham, had the satisfaction of giving ordinary people a kind of philosophic status. The lien established on Truth seemed so powerful, that deism was constrained to acknowledge defeat.

One catches a glimpse here of something new, something of which no record is to be found in history, and that something is what, to employ the language of the times, we may call "enlightened Christianity"; a movement, European in scope, and aiming at freeing religion from the accretions which had accumulated about it, and at presenting a creed so liberal in doctrine that no one in future could accuse it of obscurantism, so transparently clear in its moral teaching that no one henceforth could deny its practical efficiency. Nothing tentative here, but the firm guarantee that the principles which had upheld civilization for eighteen hundred years were valid still, and would always remain so.

Anyone who attempted, however roughly, to sketch the outlines of this great endeavour, would remind himself first of all of those thinkers who considered that Aristotelianism belonged to another era, and accepted Descartes, though the preceding generation would have none of him; accepted him, and drew on him for arguments in support of the immateriality of the soul; Christian thinkers, who read and admired Locke, rejecting indeed his agnosticism, but turning to good account the psychological treasures he had brought to light. He would cite men of Science, and those the most eminent, men such as Père Boscovitch at Ragusa, Haller and Bonnet in Switzerland, Réaumur in Paris, Euler in Germany, who showed that the experimental method, far from leading to unbelief, tended to support the doctrine of finality. He would call to mind those moralists who reminded the wielder of the royal power that his prerogatives required of him the fulfilment of duties more exacting and more onerous than any the philosophers had ever demanded of him. Such, for example, was the pious Muratori, whose profound absorption in his studies never led him to overlook the realities of life, and who, when assailed by doubts, as he sometimes was, found refuge in his *Credo*. Those who wield the powers of government should have no other preoccupation than the welfare of the State; they should in all things obey the law of God which forbids the commission of evil, and commands them to strive for the good of all, even of their enemies: do unto others that which you would have them do unto you. For the best cure for human ills lies not in a multiplicity of ideological treatises, but in charity; and the one rule proclaimed by the deists, love ye one another, came not from them, but from Christ. And he would call back from the shadows the ghosts of priests and bishops who taught their flocks the virtues of toleration, and condemned superstition; and he would bear in memory all the saints to whom the eighteenth century had given birth. He would not forget the work of the religious orders. Let us instance a certain Jesuit who for upwards of forty years was a professor at the *Collège Louis le Grand* and a contributor to the *Mémoires de Trévoux*. Reading him, we shall learn that Locke was the first man of his day to attempt to explain the working of the human understanding, refusing to have anything to do with theories that were not based on facts; in which respect, his philosophy, compared with the systems of Descartes and Malebranche, is like a history as compared with a romance. Père Buffier's philosophy was the philosophy of common sense. It was sufficiently sound to be adopted and developed later on by the Scottish philosopher, Thomas Reid. His ideas concerning social life were neither timid nor retrograde. That men are born equal is a cardinal principle that must never be lost sight of. Functions differ, as for example those of ruler and subject, but men are equal. On the whole, Père Buffier's idea was to follow that light of the human understanding which was the least suspect.

Or shall we take a Benedictine as an illustration? It is difficult not to nourish a soft spot in one's heart for Père Feijoo, so guileless, so straightforward, so sturdy was he. A freeman of the Republic of Letters, that is what he called himself, and the name becomes him. Spain's intellectual backwardness was a favourite theme with the philosophers at the beginning of the century, but this same Feijoo it was who, from his monk's cell, called upon it to look alive. He was not lacking in the critical spirit. Indeed, he never let slip a chance of displaying it. People say the tenth wave is the biggest. Well, look and see. It is nothing of the sort. The thing is just a popular error. Then people will have it that the heliotrope always turns to the sun. It does not. They tell you not to eat too soon after drinking chocolate. Just another common delusion that won't bear examination. Take no notice of hearsay; stick to what is definitely proved. A man of encyclopaedic knowledge, Feijoo was theologian, historian, man of letters, and scientist. He was an admirer of Bacon and Newton, who ranked in his eyes as the oracles of experimental truth. Descartes he regarded as a genius, a rash one but a genius all the same, and he would break a lance in his support whenever occasion offered. As a reformer, he did not hesitate to impeach those members of the nobility who showed themselves unworthy of their privileges, nor to inveigh against the long drawn out procedure of the courts of Justice, nor to protest against the use of torture. As a citizen of the world, he was all in favour of intercommunication among the nations, of the abolition of party spirit, and he longed for the establishment of universal peace. And inasmuch as he was animated by all these ideas, he was profoundly Christian. He considered that it was to degrade religion to encourage belief in unauthenticated miracles, or the practice of childish observances, or to associate it so much with the past. It was not the Church's dogmas that dwarfed the intellect and hindered the march of Science; it was the usurping authorities, spurious Aristotelianism, for example, that had paralysed the Spanish mind, and even now, in the middle of the eighteenth century, was doing its best to keep it under its benumbing spell. For century upon century, the Philosophers, as they were called, had cudgelled their brains over the works of Aristotle. What misdirected zeal! Far better had it been if they had devoted themselves to the study of Nature. Whoso is content to talk of things in the manner and terminology of the Schoolmen is but playing the game of the ignoble Cacus who cunningly lured Hercules into his cave so as to render his weapons useless by blinding him with the smoke which he vomited. For his part, he had no intention of falling into any such trap. He would rid Catholicism of the contraband which had been smuggled into the Temple. Feijoo was equally at home in the traditional and in the modern worlds. To integrate the New into the Old, the modern into the traditional; to disembarrass the teacher from the lumber of the schools, to encourage the observation of facts, to emphasize the merits of Bacon and Newton; to arouse the Portuguese from their complacency, to accustom them to criticism, and to thinking for themselves; to stimulate them, to incite them to recover their place in the intellectual life of Europe, a mighty task indeed, and it was undertaken by the author of the *Verdadeiro Método de Estudar* (1746–1747), Père Luis Antonio Verney, a Franciscan. His successors were also ecclesiastics, viz., Oratorians.

If we wanted to call up the man who was perhaps the most typical representative of this "enlightened Catholicism" it would be on a priest that our choice would certainly light, one Antonio Genovesi, and this because of the firm position he took up at the very outset. Of what that position was, the following will give an idea: Thinkers who attack the Christian religion do not really understand what they are attacking; they therefore take a distorted view of it. To refute them, what is needed is one who knows it from within, who practises it steadfastly and shows forth its spirit. And then he sets to work. First, he makes himself thoroughly acquainted with the writers and thinkers who have opposed revealed religion. He quotes them when occasion requires and his pages are constant reminders of them. The Christian apologists, too, he has read, every single one of them. All the problems to which the age gave rise, and to which it was incessantly returning, he had considered frankly and freely; such things as the origin of ideas, natural law, rationalism, empiricism, optimism. He proved himself a doughty champion of Christianity by reason of his thorough familiarity with the arguments of his adversaries, and his no less thorough knowledge of the cause he was defending. He championed it also by his life.

He had been an Aristotelian in his young days, an able disputant *pro et contra*. He was ordained in 1736, and came to Naples the following year. At that time Mgr. Galiani was busy reforming the scheme of studies and he took sides with the reformers. He was a Cartesian, and he was familiar with the ideas of John Locke, and to some extent concurred with them. He was professor, first of metaphysics, subsequently of ethics at the university, and in 1743 he published his *Elementa Metaphysicae*, an epoch-making event. He never ceased to employ the means best calculated to influence men's minds, and that was to get at them when they were young. He was for ever impressing on them that they should never content themselves with passively accepting what was told them, however imposing the authority. Belief in anything should be the outcome of rational enquiry. Belief was not to be confounded with bigotry; bigotry only served to smother the inward fire. Catholicism had nothing to fear from modern philosophy, which it refuted when in error, and profited by when it was not. As regard politics, things began all over again, but with a livelier *tempo*. Genovesi helped to divert men's minds to another centre of interest. It was one of capital importance for Naples and for Europe generally. The important thing now was not so much defining the theory of a state, or going back to the theocratic origins of civil government, or consolidating the structure of constituted authority, as of asserting the rights of the subject and of demanding the reforms necessary to secure the welfare and happiness of the subject on a sure and satisfactory foundation. Feudalism lay heavily on the Neapolitan territory, but a sort of understanding was arrived at between the ruling prince and his subjects, a coalition set up against the intermediate power, which was hostile to the interests of both. Genovesi was among the most ardent supporters of this agreement. However, his ideas meant trouble for him, and he was denounced at Rome. He did not get the chair of theology which he had coveted, but he kept within the bounds of orthodoxy. There was nothing of the ascetic about him. He was a well set up figure of a man, and by no means objected to a glass of sound Salernian. But at heart he was a thorough Christian and a most loyal practitioner of the greatest of all the Christian virtues, that is to say, of charity. A favourite saying of his was, "I adore the Gospel, for it is made of love. How sweet to the ear that word is, and how happy would be the lives of all of us if they were ruled by love, and love alone."

Nor must we omit to note the way in which Christian thought, as well as philosophical ideas, was handed on from one country to another. One of the most curious instances is afforded by the influence of the *Scuole pie*, the Italian Piarists, on various European countries; an influence sometimes direct, sometimes transmitted by foreigners coming to complete or continue their studies in Rome. Their novel ideas spread to Hungary, South Germany, Austria and her possessions, as well as to Poland. When, about the middle of the century, this last-named country began to modernize herself in her turn, and felt the time had come to reorganize her educational system, a Piarist, Père Konarski, with signal liberal-mindedness, recommended the study of Bacon, Gassendi, Descartes, Malebranche, Locke and Genovesi. *Sapere aude*—that, as we have seen, was the motto adopted by the new school whose aim it was to make the quest for truth the sole preoccupation of their lives. King Stanislas Augustus ordered a medal to be struck bearing the head of Konarski and the words *Sapere auso* round the rim.

Let us picture to ourselves the various workers in the vineyard, let us imagine all the bustle and flutter of black robes, white

VII

THE GROWTH OF UNBELIEF; JANSENISM; THE EXPULSION OF THE JESUITS

OH, for another Bossuet, another Fénelon! They came not; nor yet another Pascal. Père Gerdil, and he a Cardinal, controverted Locke, but what could he do to stem the tide? What did Crousaz avail against Pope? John Leland defended the Old and New Testaments, and Revelation, but despite it all, Hume had the laugh of them. They were fine stout fellows, these champions of religion, but they were not geniuses, and geniuses were what was needed.

Often enough, and with the best intentions in the world, they were tedious and long-winded; their lengthy prefaces, their pedantic dissertations, their massive periods, were not suited to the popular taste. They argued in the style of their grandsires, and their audience paid no heed. Or else, trying their best to be up to date, they made themselves ridiculous. The Abbé Pellegrin thought he had hit the mark when he set some of the great Christian verities to popular airs of the day. Then, Astro-theology, Physico-theology, Hydro-theology—not very satisfying things, these. Lesser thought he had done something that would last, with his Insecto-theology. God, he said, so ordered things that the most harmful insects belonged to the least fertile species. He pointed out that insects had their uses because in some countries they served as food. St. John would have died of hunger in the wilderness had it not been for the grasshoppers there. Insects have a theological significance, since they were the means whereby God punished the guilty, a scourge the more terrifying because there is no means of warding it off; they have also a juridical connexion since they it was that punished adulterers, the ancient laws ordaining that such offenders should be exposed naked on an ant-heap, or delivered over to be stung by a swarm of bees. Nay, more than that. . . .

The Anti-Cacouacs were not very brilliant performers on the buzzer, but the Cacouacs were past-masters with it. Men like Guenée and Nonnotte, highly respectable persons though they were, became mere laughing-stocks. However much we may try to make of Fréron's meritorious qualities, there is no forgetting the mischievous epigram which Voltaire attached to his name:

> L'autre jour, au fond d'un vallon,
> Un serpent mordit Jean Fréron;
> Que pensez-vous qu'il arriva?
> Ce fut le serpent qui creva.[1]

Jean Jacques Lefranc, Marquis de Pompignan, a worthy magistrate, and a far from successful man of letters, made a fierce attack on the philosophers in the speech he delivered before the Académie Française on the occasion of his reception into that body. Voltaire took him by the scruff of the neck and never let him go. Lefranc de Pompignan thenceforward became his everlasting butt; and inspired another epigram:

> Savez-vous pourquoi Jérémie
> A tant pleuré pendant sa vie?
> C'est qu'en prophète il prévoyait
> Qu'un jour Lefranc le traduirait.[2]

Epistles, satires, attacks constantly renewed, weighed crushingly upon the unhappy victim. At last it came to this: he dared not show his face out of doors. Voltaire had extinguished Lefranc de Pompignan.

The unwritten portion of the life intellectual, the conversations, the whispered asides, the allusions, the witticisms passed from lip to lip—there was no controlling this sort of thing.

[1] The other day, down in a valley, a serpent stung Jean Fréron; what do you think happened? Why it was the serpent that died!

[2] Do you know why Jeremiah wept such a lot all his life? The reason is that, being a prophet, he foresaw that one day Lefranc would translate him.

Philosophy was abroad in the world, everywhere, in clubs, assemblies, in cafés, at tea-tables—how was anybody to get a hold on it? It was in the air, it seeped in no matter where. Policemen mingled casually with the crowd, among the people strolling and chatting beneath the trees at the Palais Royal, or in the Luxembourg Gardens. Whenever they heard anything against religion, down it went in their notebooks. Godless talk everywhere, and from all sorts of people, abbés included! Impossible to deal with such a host of blasphemers. Nicolas Boindin, a man of letters and a member of the Académie des Inscriptions, was usually "at home" at the Café Procope, and was a recognized freethinker there. He had a jargon all his own, and a plentiful assortment of nick-names. Liberty he called Jeanneton, Religion was Jacotte, and God M. de l'Être. "May I venture to ask", said a detective who was listening, "who this M. de l'Être may be who so often misbehaves himself, and with whom you seem to have so much fault to find?" "Yes, Monsieur; he's a police spy." Even a speech in a play might sound suspicious. Ought the people who applauded to be sent to prison? Even such a well-known book as *Télémaque* might be used for philosophical propaganda; was *Télémaque* to be publicly burnt? All this sort of thing created an atmosphere which, in the long run, reacted on the Christians themselves. Sometimes a travelling salesman called and delivered for spot cash a manuscript bearing some such title as *Historical Dissertation on the Apocalypse, and the other books of the New Testament,* or *A Critical and Historical Essay on the three most famous impostors, Moses, Jesus and Mahomet; A few of Jean Meslier's Opinions; Last Will and Testament of Jean Meslier; The Materiality of the Soul,* and so on and so forth. In France there was a secret society with which Fréret, Mirabaud, and Dumarsais were pretty closely mixed up, and which had France for its field of operations, with its dealers in manuscripts, contractors, copyists, travelling salesmen. As for its *clientèle*, they were upper- and middle-class people, ecclesiastics, in Paris, and in the provinces, too; a paying but illicit trade; a clever way of influencing opinion at all levels. This sort of merchandise took the place of books which it might have been too risky to print, and it included, on occasion, quite recent works within its scope. In August, 1755, Grimm makes his foreign correspondents' mouths water by telling them that manuscript copies of M. de Voltaire's *La Pucelle* were becoming far more plentiful, and that it was possible to get fourteen *cantos* for anything from five to ten louis.

And the books themselves; no one, seeing the weight of public opinion against him, ever effectively interfered with their printing and circulation. Such and such a book, having failed to pass the censor, could not get a licence from the book syndicate. Never mind; printed it was, all the same, by secret presses, little portable outfits that were easily concealed. They were sold in the theatres, places of amusement, even within precincts belonging to the king, or the royal family, or to the religious orders. Sometimes the manuscript would get across the frontier and reach London, Liège, Bouillon, Cologne, Geneva, Yverdon and other places; or, better still, Holland, where there were printing-plants expressly engaged in the production of prohibited works. Once printed and bound, it would start on the reverse journey again. It was commonly said that the stricter the ban on a book, the more likely it was to find buyers. Apropos of Toussaint's *Les Moeurs* the *Correspondance littéraire* remarked, "The magistrate, in ordering this book to be burned, has, as always, made people the more curious to read it." D'Alembert, writing to Frederick II on 10th June, 1770, said, "I know nothing whatever about the *Essai sur les Préjugés* which Your Majesty has been at pains to refute; I understand, however, that the book in question showed itself in Paris, and was sold for a very high price there. But a book has only to touch on certain questions and to attack certain people to fetch an altogether fantastic price, and that as a direct consequence of the measures taken by the authorities to suppress it, measures which often confer on the author a reputation far beyond his literary deserts." The most striking instance is the *Histoire philosophique et politique des établissements et du commerce des Européens dans les deux Indes*, the author of which was the Abbé Raynal. Banned in France, put on the Index, torn to pieces and burnt, as impious, blasphemous, calculated to stir up rebellion against the sovereign authority, and to subvert the basic principles of civil government, the book went through twenty authorized editions, not to mention numerous pirated ones. It was issued in instalments, and procured for its author something resembling an apotheosis. A moralist, Denesle, making a study of the *Préjugés du public*, will have it that a duly licensed book has little chance of selling, whereas if only it lacks the words "By permission" on the fly-leaf, it will go like hot cakes. All that had to be done was to get five or six book-pedlars, looking very apprehensive, to introduce it with a great show of secrecy into the various houses, and to ask ten times as much for it as it was really worth.

Pietro Verri lived in Milan; Alessandro Verri lived in Rome. The two brothers kept up a lively correspondence, never failing to report anything new in the book world, especially when the new book happened to be a forbidden one. This is how such books were got through. In the case of Milan, they come via Switzerland, through booksellers in Tuscany and Parma, and this, thanks to the complicity of a messenger who comes ostensibly with the edifying *Histoire ecclésiastique* of the blameless Fleury, but also, tucked in as packing between the several volumes, plenty of incendiary pamphlets. As to what happens in Rome, this is what Alessandro tells Pietro. "I haven't had the *Encyclopédie* yet, but it's now only about twelve miles from Rome. This is how I managed. I got it as far as Cività Vecchia and from there, when opportunity served, to the outskirts of Rome. From there, in a Cardinal's carriage, it will come along unchallenged. That is what I have done with all the books that have come to me from London" (29th December, 1770).

In 1764, in Venice, the precautionary measures were considerably tightened up. No bookseller was allowed to open a consignment of books from abroad except in the presence of an official appointed by the State. The problem was, therefore, how to hoodwink the police. Books coming from Germany were unpacked at Padua; there they were done up in small parcels, put on boats and brought down to Brenta. Sometimes they were sent by post. Finally, they finished their journey at the bookshops in St. Mark's Square. When the books came by sea, someone went aboard the boats that ply between the ships and the harbour and contrived to effect a substitution. The banned books were taken out and some harmless ones put in their place. Sometimes the goods were booked to a place farther on, but somehow or other the trick was worked. The directions were not too rigidly insisted on. The goods remained at Venice instead of continuing their journey. Diplomatic immunity also played a part. We know what the books were, from the reports of the police officers who were detailed to seize them, and who, in spite of every attempt to circumvent them, did succeed. They were books by Locke, Collins, Mandeville, Bolingbroke, Hume, Bayle, the Marquis d'Argens, Helvetius and the Baron d'Holbach; Rousseau's *Émile* and *Le Contrat Social*; Voltaire's *La Pucelle, Questions sur l'Encyclopédie, L'Ingénu*—not to mention works of an improper character; there were plenty of those.

New barriers meant finding new ways round them. Even in that least penetrable of countries, Spain, heterodox ideas managed to get in, sometimes in the most unforeseeable manner: a personal acquaintance with some foreign writer whom you got to know on a journey; an apparently harmless correspondence enough into which a few tell-tale phrases find their way; a review of some book which, while pretending to refute its ideas with great indignation, begins by describing them in the minutest detail; and all this quite apart from the contraband trade. One of the many booksellers who encouraged the circulation of these books—like Gabriel Cramer of Geneva, Marc Michel Rey of Amsterdam—François Grasset of Lausanne wrote to Jean Jacques Rousseau on 8th April, 1765, "I am sure you will be very surprised, my honoured compatriot, when I tell you that I saw your *Émile*, in quarto form, publicly consigned to the flames in Madrid. It took place in the principal Dominican church one Sunday, after High Mass, in the presence of a whole crowd of gaping imbeciles. The immediate consequence was that a number of Spanish grandees and foreign ambassadors began trying to get hold of a copy regardless of cost, arranging for it to be sent them by post."

The government authorities themselves took part in evading their own regulations. The King of France appointed Malesherbes Controller of the Book Trade. Malesherbes had some very pronounced ideas of his own about the matter. Personally, he considered it a great advantage to the State for writers to have complete freedom of expression. In any case, what was the good of trying to enforce a law when the country as a whole was determined to evade it? Quite so; but then why put Malesherbes in charge of a department whose official business it was to prevent the printing and circulation of prohibited books? The King of France was the protector of Religion and Madame de Pompadour of Philosophy. The King objected to

Piron's election to the Academy, but he did not object to consoling him with a pension. Then suddenly, measures of such savage cruelty were put in motion that everyone with any sense of right and wrong was aghast at them. Giannone was flung into prison, Calas was broken on the wheel. Then the storm died down again, no more was done, and those things were forgotten. It was the poor and defenceless who were attacked, but the Baron d'Holbach kept open house and made open profession of his atheism. A warrant was issued for the arrest of Rousseau, but his friends were given ample time to warn him, and he ample time to disappear. He started off, and on his way ran into a number of police officers. They just saluted him. Voltaire's anti-religious works were banned; but his friend Damilaville, chief clerk at the revenue office, whose duty it was to put the Controller-General's seal on letters and parcels, took care that they got about. And he was but one of many. The manuscripts of the atheist Naigeon were the rankest poison, that was notorious, yet he sent them, without the slightest interference, to his brother, who was *contrôleur des livres* at Sedan; from there, they made their way to Liège, and from Liège to Amsterdam. How, in common logic, are we to account for the fact that Van Swieten, the favourite counsellor of that devoutest of ladies, Maria Theresa, used his utmost endeavours to get exemption from the Austrian censorship for books which she was most anxious to condemn. How came that same Maria Theresa to choose for her husband a hidebound freemason, François Étienne, Duc de Lorraine, when Freemasonry was expressly condemned by Rome? How came it that the see of Liège was occupied by another "adept", Bishop Delbrück, who used his influence to protect philosophers in general, and in particular Pierre Rousseau, editor of that *Journal encyclopédique* which was such a bastion of irreligion in the Austrian dominions? The *Journal* was condemned by the Faculty of Theology at Louvain, and suppressed on 27th April, 1759. Pierre Rousseau was banished from the country. He then took up his abode at Bouillon and founded the *Journal de Bouillon*, which was the same paper under another name, and he was subsidized by that same Imperial Majesty who had expelled him; a secret alliance between the State and the philosophers against the Church, of which, nevertheless, the State was the official defender.

Prohibition, if prohibition there was to be, might have been strict and regular in its application; as it was, the official net had so wide a mesh that there was precious little difficulty in getting through. Fits of fanatical severity alternated with spells of anarchy. Owing to all these permissions, exemptions, exceptions, and what not, no one knew where he stood. People held their ground, and their resistance paid. There was a prevailing idea that life ought to be a pleasant sort of business. There was a flood of freedom, of independence very partially held in check by a very imperfect dam. No sooner were the cracks repaired than they appeared again, still wider. The world was out of joint, full of anomalies. The nobility clung jealously to their privileges, yet they carried on a flirtation with the philosophers who denounced them. The shadiest of adventurers, no matter how notorious a character, had the *entrée* to the courts of princes. The Assembly of the Church of France refused to pay the tax and insisted on the voluntary contribution of which the Church itself fixed the amount, and so rebelled against the very authority which it did not hesitate to invoke against the unbelievers. The French Calvinists were still persecuted, hounded down, and excluded from any share in the civil government. It took three-quarters of a century to bring about, first a mitigation, and at last the abolition of, these long-standing repressive measures. However, those measures became a dead letter when it was a question of recalling absentee abbots to their abbeys, of preventing the episcopate from being recruited almost entirely from the aristocracy, and of denouncing those unsatisfactory priests whose unedifying conduct and unsound beliefs made them a public scandal. The theologians were, very properly, unyielding in the matter of dogma. Nevertheless, fashionable preachers preferred not to say too much about dogma, but talked in a vague way about morality, a morality so much akin to natural morality that it no longer scared anybody. A similar weakening in matters of doctrine was observable in the reformed Church. Leaving aside the solvent effects of pietism on orthodox belief, since that is not in our province, we may nevertheless make mention of the rationalizing tendencies of the leaders of Lutheranism. It may also be added that French Calvinism, while making a valiant fight against persecution, did yield ground a little on one or two doctrinal points, and that even some Genevan pastors had to give way a little in a few of their ideas, to avoid having to admit some of the extremer consequences of a Socinianism to which the philosophers would have been only too happy to see them committed.

The psychological effect of these compromises is admirably described by Paul Valéry in his comments on *Les Lettres Persanes*. The restrictions imposed by civil order always weigh oppressively on the individual. Disorder, however, makes him long for the police, or death. These are the two extremes in which human nature is ill at ease. What he desires is one of those agreeable epochs which combine the maximum of freedom with the minimum of restraint. Such an epoch generally occurs when any given social order is drawing to an end. Then, just before order comes to an end and disorder begins, there is a delightful interval. When the particular relationship existing between the governing power and the persons governed has yielded all the good it can, it is then possible to enjoy the initial relaxation of the system. The institutions of government are still there; they are still grand and imposing. But, though no visible change can be noticed in them, they are in fact no more than a presence, an impressive presence. They have yielded all the good that was in them; insensibly their future has disappeared. They are venerable no longer, or at any rate they are no more than that. Criticism and indifference wear them down and leave them with no influence in prospect. From the body social the morrow gently fades away. . . .[1]

It was all over; Port Royal had been destroyed, and nothing more would be heard of Jansenism. But, on 8th September, 1713, the Bull *Unigenitus* condemned no less than a hundred and one propositions in a book which had appeared originally in 1671 under the title of *Morale de l'Évangile*, and which had been several times reprinted under a different title, *Réflexions morales*. The author was Père Quesnel, a priest of the Oratory. The propositions in question were declared to be heretical. This was a signal for the whole controversy to be started all over again, and this was how it was that, now and for many a year to come, Jansenism was, in varying degrees, to trouble the religious conscience of Europe.

[1]Paul Valéry, *Préface aux Lettres Persanes*, in *Variété*, II, 1930.

It flourished at Utrecht, where it found an apostle in the person of one Gabriel Duparc de Bellegarde. By his published works, by his letters, and by the influence of his personality he made the place a stronghold and a centre of activity for heresy. It had its branches in the Low Countries, at the Court of Vienna, where Van Swieten was its mouthpiece; in Spain, where a body of men, learned in Canon law and supporters of the Monarchy, welcomed it as an ally; in Portugal; at the Collegium Germanicum in Rome; at Naples; in Lombardy and Tuscany. Scipione de' Ricci, who was appointed Bishop of Pistoia in 1780, expressed pleasure at receiving some propagandist pamphlets sent him by his friend Bellegarde, and he adopted, for use in his diocese, a catechism strongly flavoured with Jansenism. He drew up a number of pastoral letters of the same complexion, openly expressed his admiration of Père Quesnel's work, gave his patronage to certain printing presses producing pamphlets inspired with his ideas, gave his countenance to a Florentine periodical called *Gli Annali Ecclesiastici* which carried on the traditions of the *Nouvelles Ecclésiastiques*, till the climax came when ninety of the propositions set forth by the Synod he summoned in September, 1786, were condemned by the Papacy.

As for what happened in France, it is generally known that the King gave orders for the Bull to be respected and that Parliament viewed with favour all who disregarded it. We all know how the Bishops were divided among themselves and how religious dissensions were the result. We know about the *Convulsionnaires* and all that went on at the tomb of the deacon Pâris in the Saint-Médard graveyard, and how the graveyard was closed to the public, and all about those alleged miracles, and how nuns gave themselves to be trodden underfoot, beaten with wooden logs, crushed beneath planks, and suffered crucifixion, in order to give conspicuous and convincing proof of their Jansenist beliefs. We have heard how the faithful who wished to receive the Sacraments were required to produce a permit, a *billet de confession* signed by a priest who subscribed to the Bull, and how such priests were prosecuted by Parliament. We know about the long struggle which ensued between Parliament and the King, and how Parliament was worsted. How the public was split into two opposing parties, how bitter was the struggle between them, how profoundly emotions were stirred, and how fierce was the anger that prevailed in men's hearts.

Nor were the consequences that followed any less clearly marked. Doctrinal questions of the most delicate nature were dragged forth, as it were, into the market place, and anyone, no matter how uninstructed, considered himself qualified to pronounce whether the propositions condemned by the Bull were to be found in Père Quesnel's book or not. People as obstinate as mules, any Tom, Dick or Harry, even a serving-wench, would have died for their opinion about nice shades of meaning, minute differences in interpretation, things completely beyond their comprehension.[1] The secular arm was called upon to intervene in matters of religion and it did so in such a high-handed, arbitrary manner as to forfeit all its credit. The hierarchy, too, came under fire. Why should the Pope be obeyed more than the bishops? Were not the bishops the direct successors of the Apostles? Why should bishops carry more weight than the clergy? Weren't they, too, ministers of the Gospel? And why the clergy any more than the faithful? Were they not members of the Christian community, and could not they have their say? The lower clergy were egged on to criticize their bishops, and the temporal was exalted above the spiritual. All this, of course, was highly gratifying to the rationalists, who lost no time in making the most of such a fine opportunity for scoring off their opponents.

There can be no doubt that Jansenism inwardly sapped at the religious structure which it aimed to defend. "Jansenist ideas and behaviour had shaken the layman's respect for ecclesiastical authority. The Church, which should have presented an unbroken and united front to the philosophers, had breaches within itself, and the devout pilgrims who, with the little manual of 1767 in their hands, made the pilgrimage from Paris to les Champs, as though they were making the Stations of the Cross, little suspected that this Port Royal religion, whose supreme liturgical rites they were celebrating, had become, quite unwittingly, the pinfold of Voltaire and Diderot, whose very names they abhorred."[2]

[1] *Journal* de l'avocat Barbier, year 1729.

[2] Georges Goyau, *Histoire religieuse,* in *l'Histoire de la nation française,* published by G. Hanotaux, Vol. VI, *La fin de l'Église d'Ancien Régime,* p. 481.

But it may be, too, that when its last flames had flickered out and it remained no more than a lifeless cinder, there disappeared from the public conscience an element of stern, unyielding austerity which the philosophers well knew represented the hard core of opposition to the relaxations which it was their aim to introduce.

The expulsion of the Jesuits evoked the greatest surprise, for they still appeared to be a very influential body. The Jesuit Fathers were wealthy, and they were numerous. All over Catholic Europe, their schools were attended by the children of the upper classes. They were the spiritual directors of kings and queens; they had missions in China, their influence was predominant in the South American colonies of Spain and Portugal. Then, in a year or two, the whole structure came to the ground. It was like some brutal drama hastening to its ruthless close.

The charges brought against them were so old, so old and so often repeated, that one would have thought they had been worn threadbare. Still people went on saying that their moral ideas were too easy-going, that they were always ready to gloss things over, that their subtle casuistry was the very thing for making the sinner easy in his mind; that their God, conceding grace to such as did not ask it, finding something or other to palliate every fault, was weak and partial. They were told they were so much wrapped up in the things of this world, that they forgot all about the next. But it all sounded like some old song that had been sung, and sung to death, long ago; sung by their foes the Jansenists, and the Jansenists were now no more. Then, about the middle of the century, the old complaints cropped up again, the old reproaches, and flew more thickly than ever. They took on an angry and threatening tone. Whatever the Jesuits did was interpreted to their discredit, and their errors were not merely errors, they were crimes. A great wave of hostile opinion reared itself against them, and swept them away.

It was from Lisbon that the first signal went up, and it was given by Sebastian Joseph de Carvalho e Mello who, in 1759, was Count d'Oyeras, in 1770, Marquis de Pombal. He had been *Chargé d'Affaires* in London, and Ambassador in Vienna. In 1750 King Joseph, shortly after his accession, called him to office and he began to exercise his powers in a way that soon became dictatorial. His object was nothing less than the country's complete reform, the substitution of discipline for disorder, and of prosperity for destitution. And it must be done without delay. No haggling about how it was to be done, whether his measures were legal or moral. So far as he was concerned, those words were meaningless. He swept away everything calculated to interfere with the absolute authority of the State, or to detract in the slightest degree from its sovereign power. He came up against the Jesuits, and he straightway joined battle with them. He called all his strategy into play, making the most of their more vulnerable points, fomenting the envy and hatred which their activities had provoked. He struck wherever he saw a chance of dealing a telling blow. At last came the final and decisive phase. In 1750, he forbade them to continue as confessors to the royal family, and banished them from the Court. In 1758, he inhibited them from preaching, or hearing confessions anywhere within the realm. On the 3rd September, that same year, an attempt was made on the life of the King, Joseph I. Pombal accused the Jesuits of being concerned in the plot, arrested ten of them and imprisoned three. On the 19th January, 1759, the Jesuit Fathers were placed under house-arrest, and their property was confiscated. On the 17th September, a hundred and three Jesuits set sail from Lisbon under a deportation order. On the 5th October, a decree was issued, bearing date 3rd September, making their banishment perpetual and forbidding them, under pain of death, to settle anywhere in the Portuguese dominions. Among the Jesuits charged with complicity in the plot against the King was a certain Père Malagrida. The minister had had a bone to pick with him in the Colonies, from which he had been recalled, and then again, later on, in Portugal. In the prison cell in which Père Malagrida was confined two manuscripts were found in his writing. One was a life of St. Anne, the other was concerned with Antichrist. The result was that he was brought before the Inquisition on a charge of heresy. He was condemned, and died at the stake at four o'clock in the morning of the 21st September, 1761. One would take it that the Count d'Oyeras needed the flames of this *auto-da-fé* to proclaim his triumph to Europe.

In France, too, the Jesuits were far from popular. They themselves were responsible for setting light to the fires that had been preparing, and this in two ways. Père Berruyer, in 1728, brought out a work entitled *Histoire du Peuple de Dieu*, which gave an unwelcome shock to public opinion. In 1753, he published a second part, which was condemned by the ecclesiastical authorities. A third part, which appeared in 1758, met with no better fate. Père Berruyer began by asserting that the Scriptures, even when translated, are obscure; that they did not represent a complete and coherent story; that there were doubtful passages in them which needed clearing up, and that the bare narrative ought to be enriched with moral and political commentaries, as had been done in the case of profane history. In short, the Bible, the Gospel, the Apostles' story even, were lacking in continuity and in attractiveness of presentation. This ought to be put right. His idea was that the several parts should be linked up so as to form one single whole. It should be so arranged that the several characters in the drama should carry on the action right up to the final *dénouement* and that they should meditate, speak and act as in real life. Their deeds were to be portrayed, not merely recorded. Their utterances would be heard, and their inmost feelings made manifest. This precious enterprise its author pursued with an intrepidity, a complacency, a self-assurance and a blindness, that rendered him impervious to criticism.

Although Père Berruyer had been publicly disowned by his superiors, the whole Order was involved in the scandal. Its enemies were quick to avail themselves of the incident to declare that the Jesuits, not content with whittling down the moral law, were now for profaning the Scriptures themselves. That, it was alleged, was precisely what they wanted to do. If they had maintained a strictly uncompromising attitude in regard to religion; if they had proclaimed to a frivolous and corrupt generation the existence of a God in three Persons, a God who became incarnate in the womb of a Virgin to die on the cross of infamy; if they had preached the Gospel in its entirety, then the world they loved, the world whose smiles and support they courted, would have slipped away from them. And so they presented to that world a Christ without the Crown of Thorns, a Christ without a Cross. The Jesuits were but deists in another garb.[1]

[1]*Lettres théologiques, dans lesquelles l'Écriture Sainte, la tradition et la foi de l'Église sont vengées contre le système impie et socinien des PP. Berruyer et Hardouin, Jêsuites. Ouvrage posthume de M. l'Abbé Gaultier. . . .* 1756; tome III, pp. 359 *et seq.*

When Père La Valette, visitor-general and prefect apostolic, met with disaster over his colonial enterprises and his establishments in Martinique, and when, endeavouring to settle with the Marseilles merchants in kind, his goods were seized by the British blockading force; when the Jesuits, in spite of the fact that they had been found liable by the consular court at Marseilles, refused to pay, and appealed to Parliament; when they produced their constitutions, and Parliament set to work to examine them, it was all over with the Order. On the 3rd July, 1761, the Advocate-General of the Parliament of Paris, Joly de Fleury, in his speech for the prosecution, submitted that the existence of the Order constituted a danger to the State. The same thing happened in divers provincial Parliaments. The *Compte rendu des constitutions des Jésuites*, by M. Louis René de Caradeuc de La Chalotais, the King's Procurator General in the Parlement de Bretagne, was a particular success. Its main argument was that the Jesuits swore absolute obedience to the Pope, even in matters temporal; that the Pope delegated his powers to the General of the Order, and that, in consequence, the Order was in conflict with the State, with its laws, indeed, with its very being. It would have to be put down; the most pressing need being to deprive it of the education of the young. It was further represented that they served no useful purpose, that they were a growing menace because of their increasing numbers; that they were a hindrance to the secular clergy, to the *curés* and curates who had to bear the burden and the heat of the day. Now, the Jesuits are the aristocracy of all the religious Orders. To strike at them, is to strike at all the rest. Several decrees were issued, directed against a Society "inadmissible from its very nature, in any well-regulated State". On the 18th November, the King of France decreed its expulsion from his most Christian Realm.

Soon it was His Most Catholic Majesty's turn to take action. He had not precisely fallen out with Rome, but there was a certain tension between them, by reason of his determination to insist on the prerogatives of the Spanish crown, and thus it was that Rome's most valuable servants the Jesuits ceased to be in favour. There, too, they were the sole Order to be attacked. There, too, as much as possible was made of the hostility of the other Orders towards them; and there, too, their total overthrow was resolved upon. In 1766, a popular rising known as the *émeute des chapeaux*, the hat riots, caused grave alarm to the King, Charles III, who forthwith quitted Madrid. The riot suppressed, the next thing was to discover the ringleaders. Well, what more natural than to put the whole thing down to the Jesuits? Proofs may have been lacking, but what matter? Did not the whole world know that it was they who had poisoned the public mind in the battle of the pamphlets that had gone before? That was the pretext put forward; how to act on it was a problem of some difficulty. To do so was no easy matter, in the very country in which the Society had been born, and to which it was still attached by innumerable ties. There might well be trouble ahead. The civil authorities received in due course a sealed missive to be opened, in the case of Madrid, on the night of the 31st March, but, in the provinces, on the night of the 1st April, 1767. The packet contained orders to occupy, with the support of an armed force, the various Jesuit houses; to convene the Fathers, and to recite to them the order of banishment signed by the King. Within twenty-four hours, they were to be sent to a certain fixed assembly-point, and thence to a port from which they would set sail, never to return. These instructions were carried out so promptly and effectively that all the two hundred Jesuits domiciled in the city were on the road well before sunrise.

What had really brought about the overthrow of the Jesuits was, to begin with, the *Zeitgeist*, the spirit of the times, the age of philosophy, of "enlightenment". Among the philosophers who evinced surprise and delight at an event they had so little expected or openly hoped for, perhaps the most outspoken of all was d'Alembert in an account he gave of the affair, which he entitled *Sur la destruction des Jésuites en France* (1765). He described it as an occurrence worthy to figure among the outstanding events of an age which itself would prove a landmark in the history of the human mind. It would rank, he said, with such things as earthquakes, wars, broken alliances, attempted assassinations of kings and the like. It was, he declared, an event with a first claim on our attention. The Order towered above all the rest because of the pre-eminent place held by its members in the departments of Science and Art, as well as by reason of their exemplary conduct and moral behaviour; because, also, of the skill with which they contrived to adapt the moral law to the failings of humanity.

The Order had reached its zenith under the reign of Louis XIV. Now, it had fallen from its high estate because it had sought to dominate the world, and nothing so shocks the thoughtful mind as to see those people who are supposed to have renounced the world, doing their best to gain dominion over it. La Chalotais puts it well: "The monastic spirit is the plague of governments. Of all those animated by it, the Jesuits are the most pernicious, because they are the most powerful. We've got to get rid of them first, if we want to do away with the rest of the obnoxious breed." Bring down the leaders of the herd and the rest will disperse and go straggling through the wood. In this way, the other communities would be brought down in their turn. Reflecting, as he did, on the insignificance of the causes that were alleged to have produced this prodigious result, bearing in mind that the storm had sprung up in a country which, of all others, was most closely attached to its priests and its monks; remembering, too, that it was a decaying and discredited sect which, against all expectation, had brought off an enterprise which had baffled men like Arnauld, Pascal and Nicole, surely d'Alembert was right when he assigned the real credit for the achievement to Philosophy. Philosophy it was that struck the decisive blow at the Jesuits; the Jansenists were but tools in the matter.

Next to Philosophy, the power that discomfited the Jesuits was the State. The State was becoming completely secularized, and was both instinctively and deliberately unwilling to acquiesce in the existence of any power, whether its sanctions were higher than, or equal to, its own, a power over which it could exercise no control. The Bourbons were most implacably opposed to them because, ruling over the most Catholic of monarchies, they felt it the more necessary to break with these agents of Rome. Frederick II gave asylum to the Jesuits because, his country being Protestant, he had nothing to fear from them; but Joseph, co-Regent with his mother Maria Theresa of the Austrian Empire, would have readily expelled them, if we are to place any reliance on some of his confidences to Choiseul: "As regards the Jesuits and your plans for getting rid of them, you have my complete approval. Don't count too much on my mother. A close attachment to the Jesuits is hereditary in the Habsburg family; Clement XIV has proof of that. However, you have a friend in Kaunitz, and he does what he likes with the Empress.

He is entirely with you, and so is the Marquis de Pombal, so far as suppressing the Jesuits is concerned, and he is not a man to do things by halves. Choiseul, I know these people as well as anybody knows them; I know all about their consistent plotting, their efforts to spread darkness over the world, to dictate to Europe and to create trouble from Finistère to the North Sea. In Germany, they are the lofty intellectuals; in France they are Academicians; in Spain and Portugal, Grandees; in Paraguay, Kings. . . . Anyhow, that's how things were, Choiseul, but I've an idea that a change is not far off."

The Order had been expelled from the Republic of Venice, from the Grand Duchy of Parma, from the Kingdom of the Two Sicilies; after some vain attempts at resistance, the Company of Jesus was suppressed on the 21st July, 1773, by the Bull *Dominus ac Redemptor*.

Vainly, in this Bull, did Clement XIV appeal to all the inhabitants of Christendom to restore peace to the Church; vainly did he call attention to the determined attacks the common enemy was trying to press home. Confusion reigned in the ranks of the faithful. While their leaders were loudly deploring the progress of irreligion, the philosophers were as loudly acclaiming it. The dyke had been breached, and the flood-waters of impiety were rising.

Had they, the philosophers who now took over the direction of men's minds, had they indeed ripped out Christianity from their hearts? Had the old faith, even in the height of their rebellion, no words to whisper to them? Had they not, hitherto, weighed all their problems in the light of the Christian faith, and never apart from it? Did not the very fierceness of their attack betoken the presence within them of some stubborn force that still remained unconquered?

Be that as it may, they believed that they had shaken off the yoke. What the historian of ideas must, in the first place, put down to their account is the immense effort they made to transform into a non-Christian Europe the Christian Europe that confronted them. What he would next have to consider is the nature of the substitute they proposed to put in its place.

PART TWO

THE CITY OF MEN

I

NATURAL RELIGION

THE City of Men should be built on simple lines. The first thing to be done was to clear the site of the miscellaneous jumble of buildings that encumbered it. Even the old foundations would have to go, for nothing really satisfactory had ever been erected on them. Once the ground was cleared and levelled, honest, sensible buildings would be put up. The new builders would in no way be bound by the past, nor would they waste their time trying to put right this or that detail of the old structures. That would take too long. Their work would be to plan a kind of building thoroughly suited to the needs of people who would now cease to live in Babel, and cease to hope for the attainment of some problematical heaven.

A single word sufficed to put heart into the daring ones who were making ready to begin the task; yet another talisman, in addition to those with which we are already familiar, Reason and Knowledge. That new, that magic word was Nature. To it they ascribed a virtue more potent than any, since Nature was the source of Knowledge and the touchstone of Reason. Nature was wise, and Nature was kindly. Let man but render a willing ear to Nature, and never more would he go astray. All he had to do was to obey her kindly mandate.

So, as a first step, Religion should be based on Nature; not only because religion, properly understood, was but an emanation of Nature, but also because it would be one with that instinct which Nature implants in us, enabling us by its means to distinguish truth from falsehood and good from evil; and yet again because, instead of teaching us to look on our earthly life as a time of trial, it would conform to Nature, whose aim it is not to make trial of us, but to make us happy. Long since, its coming had been foretold by the prophets, and slowly but surely, out of sight, far underground, and unsuspected by the mass of mankind, it had been making ready. And now, behold, it was coming forth into the light of day. It was not so much the substance of it, as its arrogance, its audacity, and its eagerness to proselytize that made it seem so startling a prodigy.

God was to remain, but a God so remote, so watered down, so pallid that his presence imposed no constraint on the City of Men. He would neither visit them with his wrath, nor bedazzle them with his glory. Deism and theism required no act of faith. The process involved was a purely intellectual one, culminating in one simple and satisfying conclusion, namely that God exists. We have but to glance at Creation as a whole to recognize how admirably it works. But we cannot imagine effects without a cause; therefore we must take it that a primary cause exists. A clock implies the existence of a clockmaker. Well, we have before us what we may compare to a well-regulated clock; therefore there must be somewhere the skilful craftsman who made it and who keeps it in order. That craftsman is God.

What was it that led God to create the world out of nothing? The question is an embarrassing one. But it would be still more embarrassing to have to suppose that the world came into existence by chance, that it works by chance, and that it exists for no special purpose. It would be tantamount to saying that reasoning beings were created without the intervention of reason. Let us be sensible, and prefer the difficult to the absurd. Let us accept the theory of final causes. A makeshift conclusion, which still does duty.

Deism had recourse to a sort of filtering process. If we strain off whatever strikes us as superstitious in the Church of Rome, in the reformed Church, and in every other church and sect, what remains at the conclusion of the process will be God; a God whom we know not, and whom we cannot know. Hardly anything has been left to him save the bare fact of his existence. Of all the possible adjectives, he was awarded the one which was at once the most honourable and the most vague; he was called the Supreme Being.

What is the good of sacraments, of religious rites, of churches, temples and mosques? The Isle of Reason shall have a beauty all its own, a beauty that can dispense with domes and towers.

What good are priests and pastors? There is but one way to worship God, and that is to worship him inwardly, with heart and mind and soul. To acknowledge in a general sort of way a primary and Supreme Being; to lift up our hearts to him from time to time; to abstain from whatever is deemed dishonourable in the land in which we dwell, to fulfil certain prescribed social duties—these are the essential things; anything else is merely supererogatory. There is no need for pious observances. Such things do but distract the mind from the true object of worship. Taken up with listening to sermons, people forget all about helping their neighbour. Orgon's sole companion was his daughter Philothée. He fell into a faint. His daughter made him inhale some *eau des Carmes*. It failed to revive him. As, however, it was nearly time for church, Philothée commended her father to God, snatched up her wimple and her prayer-book, and hurried away to the Grands Augustins. The service was long; solemn Benediction. Orgon died, there being no one to succour him. Philothée, however, was firmly convinced that the bells she heard were the voice of God bidding her come, and that she was performing a deed of heroism in obeying the call of Heaven rather than the promptings of her heart. Thus it was that she made to God the generous sacrifice of her father's life, believing that her act was the more meritorious by reason of the pain it cost her.[1] Toussaint the deist, who tells that story, thinks that all will be well, that men will all devote themselves to virtuous deeds, as soon as Philothée gives up crossing herself.

No more, now, of those pictures of the Son of God nailed to the Cross, of angelic hosts, of the saints in glory. The old custom, when the faithful used to gather round the Crib at Christmas time, to shout aloud their Alleluias at Easter—all that was a thing of the past. Little children were forbidden to think of God as one who had a body like theirs, with arms to draw them to him, or with hands to bless them. If they were not to make little idolaters of them, children's teachers should be forbidden to make any allusion, or to use any expression, that might lead their pupils to think that the Supreme Being could in any way be represented or portrayed. There is a story about a certain deacon named Photin, a learned man who, once upon

[1]Toussaint, *Les Mœurs,* 1748, *Discours préliminaire sur la vertu.*

a time, went to visit the Fathers of the Desert. There, in their midst, he found a holy monk whose name was Serapion. This monk lived a life of great austerity, and his conduct was without reproach. Howbeit, he was wont to picture God to himself in the shape of a mortal. Photin remonstrated with Serapion, and with such effect as to convince him of his error. Then he departed and continued his journey. But now, Serapion, whenever he tried to say his prayers, was filled with profound despair. "Alas!" he cried, "what sorrow is mine! Behold they have taken my God from me, and now to whom shall I turn?" Poor Serapion; for all those longings, for all those tears of his, the deists would have had not a grain of compassion. Rather would their scorn have been his portion.

They hoped that the idea of an ever-living God which they thus preserved would win them a Catholicity vaster than any which Catholicism itself had ever attained. They argued that, because the Christian religion had started at a comparatively recent date, and because it had only been promulgated among a minority of the peoples of the earth, it laboured under a twofold limitation. Deism, on the other hand, drew its adherents from the whole expanse of Time and Space. We claim (they gave out) that our religion is as old as the world. We say that it was the religion of Adam, of Seth, and of Noah. Li, Changti and Tien worshipped by the peoples of the East; Birmah, the father of Brama, worshipped by the tribes of the Ganges; the Great One called Oromasius by the ancient Persians; Plato's Demiurge; the great and beneficent Jupiter, whom the Roman Senate invoked when giving the law to three-quarters of the known earth—all these are but different adumbrations of one and the same God, of the Supreme Being.[1] Even were there living beings on the stars of the Milky Way, they, too, would be deists.

"Last night, I was meditating, absorbed in the contemplation of Nature. I was filled with wonder at its immensity, at the stars in their courses, at the mutual interaction of those countless orbs, one upon another, which people look upon unmoved. And I marvelled still more at the Mind which governs the whole mighty scheme. A man must be blind, I said to myself, not to be dazzled by such a spectacle, a fool not to acknowledge its

[1]Voltaire, *Les Adorateurs, ou les louanges de Dieu*, 1769.

Author, a madman not to adore him. What tribute of adoration can I pay him? Must it not be the same, wherever it is offered? Whatever thinking being inhabits the Milky Way owes him the like homage. The light shines for Sirius, even as it shines for us."[1]

No one now will be beyond the pale; no one will henceforth be damned. Every human creature has a share in this universal religion. The Americans shared in it, lost though they were in their undiscovered continent; so likewise did the pagans, every pagan of goodwill who lived before the Christian revelation.

What sort of a part did the atheists play, side by side with the deists?

In the first place we ought to include among the supporters of atheism some descendants of the freethinkers. There was, for example, a certain "little hump-backed abbé called Méhégan who, when the celebrated Boindin had to quit the Café Procope, where he had made more or less open profession of his atheism, thought he would step into his shoes and carry on the good work. Not content with giving expression to his views by word of mouth, he wrote a book—and pretty badly written it was—entitled *Zoroastre,* in which he made a clean sweep of revelation, and set up naturalism in its stead. This little book landed him in the Bastille for more than a year."[2] Or again, there was that Piedmontese who was at war with everyone, himself included, and who, his own country being too hot for him, made his way to England, where he struck up an acquaintance with Thomas Morgan, and afterwards crossed over to Holland, and finally died without leaving enough to defray his funeral expenses. According to Alberto Radicati di Passerano, first a Catholic, then a Calvinist, then a deist and finally an atheist, there is no such thing as Justice in this world, there is no such thing as eternal life. The idea of a beginning and the idea of an end are alike untenable; death is but the dissolution of one's constituent elements, which Nature uses to produce new forms of life. It is nothing to be afraid of, and if a man is unhappy, he can always kill himself.

The general background against which these extremists stood

[1]Voltaire, *Questions sur l'Encyclopédie,* article *Religion,* 1771.

[2]Grimm, *Correspondance littéraire,* II, p. 218, 1754.

out gradually became less strongly contrasted with their negations. The atheist was no longer held to be an unmitigated criminal. He was graciously allowed some extenuating qualities. It was thought that he might quite possibly be the victim of a delusion, and that he erred in good faith. In point of fact, people told themselves, there were two kinds of atheists, two distinct brands. There were the vicious and immoral sort, who were against religion because it condemned their mode of life. These, of course, were the bad ones. But were there not other atheists, quite distinct from these, of quite another kidney? Were there not some worthy and respectable atheists, who loved whatsoever was good, commendable and fair? They loved their fellow men, they were good members of society, and, if they had acquired some regrettable notions, it was really their native good sense that was at the root of it all; that was the real explanation. They had been suckled on superstition at their nurse's breast, and ever since then they had mistaken religion for superstition. It was to be deplored, but it was understandable. After all, it was easier to get an atheist on to the right road than an enthusiast, or a fanatic.

A good many of those who underwrote Bayle's paradox were careful to say, in the atheist's favour, that, though he was no doubt in the wrong, he was not, on that account, to be put at the bottom of the human ladder. Moreover, was not the name frequently misapplied? Was it not used to vilify some highly respectable philosophers whose sole fault lay in their attempt to rid the general run of people of some of their misapprehensions? Had it not been applied to some of the greatest thinkers? To Socrates, for example? Vanini was burnt for his atheism, when the truth was he was not an atheist at all.

Admitting that prolonged meditation combined with profound study, moral rectitude, as well as the resolve to get free of all prejudice, may lead an outstanding genius to atheism; or, if you prefer to have it so, admitting that atheism is the black spot on the minds of certain intellectuals; bearing in mind, too, that an atheist, M. de Wolmar, was the first of his kind to figure as a hero, and an engaging one, of romance, as he did in *La Nouvelle Héloïse*, the most famous novel of the century—bearing all this in mind, must we not conclude that such indulgent sentiments, following as they did upon the uncompromising severity of the time immediately preceding, are to be regarded as a premonitory symptom of an imminent modification in the general attitude of mind? And now for the second symptom.

There was a tendency, a drift, towards philosophic materialism. Mind was wholly distinct from matter. That was an established fact. Yet two men attacked it. One of them was Locke, who was anxious to remain a Christian; the other was Voltaire, who adhered firmly to his deism. There have been cases of ideas being twisted, and even completely misinterpreted, and then, from that very distortion, deriving their subsequent success. Here is an idea that eluded its inventor and put him in an unwelcome position: though designed to illustrate the omnipotence of God, its real effect was to confound mind and matter, and to prove, to the satisfaction of a whole school of philosophers, the unsoundness of what they termed the soul-hypothesis.

Locke had retained his Puritan conscience. He took the Gospel as his rule of faith, and was greatly distressed when he found himself numbered among the unbelievers. But, engrossed as he was with defining the narrow limits of the knowable, he demonstrated with almost wearisome insistence how impossible it is to attain the certitudes to which we aspire.

"*We have the ideas of a* square, *a* circle, *and* equality; *and yet, perhaps, shall never be able to find a circle equal to a square, and certainly know that it is so. We have the ideas of* matter *and* thinking, *but possibly shall never be able to know whether any mere material being thinks or no; it being impossible for us, by the contemplation of our own ideas, without revelation, to discover whether Omnipotency has not given to some systems of matter, fitly disposed, a power to perceive and think, or else joined and fixed to matter, so disposed, a thinking immaterial substance. . . .*"[1]

Voltaire dwelt on this passage when he devoted to the incomparable Locke the thirteenth of his *Lettres Philosophiques*. He made a great point of it, giving it, however, a certain lightness of touch, so as not to collide too violently with the theologians who are so thoroughly convinced of the spiritual nature of the soul that they would burn, if they could, the body of anyone who doubted it. That is how he put it when he spoke in confidence to his friends. When he wrote with an eye on the

[1]*Essay concerning Human Understanding,* Book IV, Chap. III.

public, he expressed himself a little more cautiously, but his attitude was hardly less decided:

Locke, having disposed of the theory of innate ideas . . . goes on to consider the extent, or rather the néant, *the nothingness of human knowledge. It is in this chapter that he ventures, with due modesty, to remark: "We shall, perhaps, never be able to say whether a purely material being thinks or not."*

Thereupon the theologians, and religious folk generally, sounded the alarm.

It was loudly protested that Locke was aiming at dethroning religion. In reality, however, religion did not come into the matter at all; the question was a purely philosophical one and had nothing whatever to do with faith or revelation. All that had to be done was to consider quite calmly, without animus of any sort, whether there was anything contradictory in saying: matter can think and God can endow matter with the power of thought.

A dozen, a score of times, Voltaire harked back to this same idea. It was a way he had. He embellished it, bespangled it and gave it a resonance, a carrying power, it had not hitherto possessed. But before Voltaire, as soon in fact as the *Essay concerning Human Understanding* made its appearance, both those who accepted, and those who rejected the idea had been greatly exercised about it. Edward Stillingfleet, Bishop of Worcester, gave utterance to a vehement protest, to which Locke replied. Coste, his translator, gives the gist of what he said. "M. Locke stated yet again that there is no necessary contradiction in supposing that God's power, which is unlimited, might go to the length of endowing matter with the faculty of thought; that was all." Bayle, who looked upon it as his duty to squeeze from every formula its last drop of meaning, asked to be informed what this one really meant. "This theory of M. Locke's would have us straightway admit that there is only one substance and that this substance is allied by one of its attributes to extent, and by the other to thought. Once that is granted, there will be no longer any reason to assume that, because a substance can think, it is therefore necessarily immaterial." Collins and Toland were quick to exploit the implications of this argument, which was all the more telling in that it had been advanced by the opposing side. Leibniz grieved to see natural religion sensibly weakening: many people held that body and soul were one;

some said the same of God; Locke and his school are asking whether the soul may not be material, and therefore mortal. Clarke, in his reply to Leibniz, had made the position perfectly clear: Yes, there were passages in Locke's writings that might lead one to suspect that he questioned the immateriality of the soul; but on that point, only a few materialists agreed with him, the only things they *did* agree with in his writings being his errors. The idea had been extant for well nigh half a century and had already been widely discussed and commented upon, when Voltaire brought it into fresh prominence, holding it to be a thing so plain and luminous as at once to dispose of a difficulty long thought to be insoluble: "My letter to Locke simply amounts to this: human reason is powerless to demonstrate that it is impossible for God to endow matter with the power of thought, a proposition which, I imagine, is as true as this one: triangles whose heights and bases are equal are equal to one another."[1]

And now, those who denied the spiritual nature of the soul considered that the matter was settled, and that it was Voltaire's argument that had settled it. Why then go on clinging to the idea of a dual substance? Locke has said, and rightly said, that the soul may be material.

And now for a move towards scientific materialism. All life, say the scientists, manifests itself through matter and through matter alone. Thus do the scientists come to the support of these enterprising philosophers, on whom, however, they look a little superciliously. They regarded them a little scornfully, as being people who were satisfied with mere verbiage. They pretended, these philosophers, to deal with facts and nothing but facts, yet when it came to the point, they made the whole business a mere matter of word-spinning. These learned scientists, on the other hand, spoke as observers who kept their eyes on Nature, on the living thing, and knew precisely what it was. If they kept on turning out book after book on the question whether or not animals had souls, it was because they thought that the supporters of the spiritual theory supplied them with a valuable argument: organic creatures can exist without souls, and yet live quite satisfactorily. Epicurus and his system, with its atoms and its

[1]Voltaire to M. de La Condamine, 22nd June, 1734.

combination of atoms; those innumerable throws of the dice which at last combined in such a manner as to produce the world—all this was still dear to their minds. Nevertheless, these various theories did not seem altogether able to account for the phenomenon of life. They required to be overhauled, brought up to date. And that was what several somewhat eccentric gentlemen decided to do. One of them was that retired diplomat, Benoît de Maillet, who had been Consul in Egypt, Ambassador in Abyssinia, Consul at Leghorn, Inspector of the French establishments in the Levant and on the coast of Barbary. In 1748, he brought out a book which he called, *Telliamed, ou Entretiens d'un philosophe indien avec un missionnaire français sur la diminution de la mer, la formation de la terre, l'origine de l'homme*, etc. . . . Memories of the East, the Land of Wonders and Sages; the old, traditional attraction of imaginary tales of imaginary travel, echoes of Fontenelle and his *Entretiens*, the desire to find the key to some enigma of the day, such as how it was that sea-shells came to be found on the tops of mountains; truths very unsubstantiated, a collection of very naïve beliefs. . . . The sea's boundaries are not fixed, the sea is receding; its expanse is contracting; that is proved by actual measurement. Moreover, soundings no less accurate reveal that the sea's bottom has mountains and valleys just like the earth; the sea-shells found on the tops of mountains are clear evidence of that. It therefore follows that the story of the Deluge is a mere gloss, a fanciful account of a scientifically established fact and needs no divine intervention to account for it. Therefore, this planet of ours has been formed by a gradual process of evolution through the ages, and was not created *ex abrupto*. Matter itself is indestructible, but it assumes a variety of forms, as is shown by the Solar System, which can only be described as unchanging in a purely relative sense. There are stars which have disappeared, and others which have taken their place. The ultimate fate of this earth of ours is uncertain; possibly it will eventually be turned to a cinder. Perhaps life originally came from the sea. The existence of mermaids and mermen points in that direction.

In the beginning, there was but a confused conglomeration of seeds, which took on definite form and character after fertilization. Earth and water, air and fire began to increase, rocks and minerals to reveal themselves; mountains and peaks slowly took shape, vegetation began to appear. Nature continually renewed those attempts of hers, which finally resulted in the production of man. Such was the origin of life on our planet, as described by Robinet in his *Considérations philosophiques de la gradation naturelle des formes de l'être* which was published in 1768. Grandiose visions, these, and Robinet added that the patterns we find on fossils, the stones which resemble a finger, or an ear, or a shin-bone, or a heart, are just Nature's experiments, the various parts she made and discarded as, imperfectly but patiently, she pieced together the tentative pattern of Man.

Then there was Hartley, the country doctor. He upheld revelation, and invented a theology of his own, from which the idea of eternal punishment was excluded. Also, he declared that the faculty of thought originated in the spinal marrow, and that the soul was material.

Then came Priestley. He was a deist, one of the "enlightened Christianity" school. The soul is material; and why be afraid of that? All the more reason to admire the Supreme Being, who could endow matter with the power of thought.

Then Maupertuis; and then, most clamorous of them all, La Mettrie. Materialism, he shouted with all the force of his lungs, materialism is the way to salvation, materialism is the truth. We must start with Nature, a power devoid of knowledge and of feeling, as blind when she bestows life as when she takes it away. How does she go about her work? Does she create seeds of every species which are scattered throughout the universe till at last they meet together? Or does she proceed by way of an evolutionary process, the early generations imperfect or monstrous, those alone surviving in whom no essential organ is lacking? What is undeniable is that all our anatomical and physiological experiments go to show that, what we are pleased to call the soul is nothing but an appanage of the body. Its manifestations are, in fact, determined by the different states of the body; it is affected by illness, it is soothed by opium, it is excited by coffee or wine, hunger makes it cruel and savage, it has its successive periods of growth, maturity and decay; it changes as it grows old, and it varies according to climate. In short, it has no existence apart from matter; it *is* matter. It is a vague term, without any definite meaning behind it; a word by which we denote the thinking part of us. Thought is merely a property of organic matter, like electricity, or the faculty of motion, or impenetrability, or extent. Its study is a branch of natural history, *Histoire naturelle* of the soul (1745). There is nothing in man to differentiate him from the purely mechanical character of all other living things; *L'homme machine* (1747). Being a machine made to feel, to think, to know good from bad, as you know blue from yellow; in a word, to be born with an understanding, and a sure moral instinct, all this has nothing more out-of-the-way about it than being a monkey, or a parrot, or in knowing the things you like. Or, if you prefer it, man is a plant, for plants, too, are machines: *L'homme plante* (1748): "Anyone who looked on man as a plant was no more uncomplimentary to that noble species than he who regarded him as a mere machine. Man grows in the womb by a process of vegetation; his body runs down and is wound up again like a watch, either by its own recuperative power, which often works satisfactorily, or by the skill of people who understand it, not in this instance watch-and-clock-makers, but biochemists." And we must needs be fatalists: "We are no more committing a crime when we obey our primitive instincts, than the Nile is committing a crime with its floods, or the sea with its ravages." Nay, we ought rather to be pleased: "Do you know why I still retain some respect for mankind? It is because I seriously look on them as machines. If I did not, I know but few whom I should regard as very desirable companions. Materialism is the cure for misanthropy."

The audacious La Mettrie having created scandal upon scandal, ended by taking refuge with Frederick II. "The King's Atheist in Ordinary", Voltaire called him. There was more matter in him than in the general run of men. He was enormously fat, bloated and pot-bellied, and a chronic glutton. On the 11th November, 1758, his machine broke down. Indigestion was the trouble.

And now, Atheism for the Many was set forth in a host of books. One of them calls for special mention, *Le Système de la Nature* (1770) of which *Le Bon Sens, ou idées naturelles opposées aux idées surnaturelles* (1772) was an abridgment. There was a professed atheist who was read by all manner of folk, learned and unlearned, duchesses and ladies' maids, and his name was Paul Thiry, Baron d'Holbach. He was really a German, and was born at Hildesheim. He came to Paris to pursue his studies, and in Paris he remained. A fine town-house, first-rate dinner-parties twice a week, a charming place in the country, he was well equipped for the campaign. Many Europeans of note were entertained by him, with great hospitality, at his house in the rue Royale Saint-Honoré, or at the Château de Grandval. It must not be supposed that the Baron was a genius, or that there was anything strikingly original about his ideas; he appropriated them from others right and left. His prose was as stodgy as dough, and when he attempted the grand style, the result was mere bombast. Nor was he by any means a paragon of amiability. He was full of whims and fancies, blowing now hot and now cold. Diderot knew him intimately, and here are some of the things he said about him: he was a gay satyr, had rather a biting tongue; he was off-handed, crotchety, self-willed; he had an uncertain temper, which his friends sometimes found a little trying, but he was kind-hearted and liked to do a good turn; he was quick to take offence and was rather a trial to those about him. However, if he was ill-tempered one day, he would be all smiles the next, usually, that is to say, though not invariably. He attracted and he repelled. But he was rich and he was sociable, and he held a place of his own in the best society. He was active and industrious, and he considered that his one great mission in life was to discredit religion and, if he could, to destroy it.

Never were the enemies of Christianity satisfied with reviling it, never could they fling mud enough. To the host of anti-religious books which had already appeared, he now added some others grossly attacking the clergy and specially designed for mob consumption: *Le Tableau des Saints*, *De l'imposture sacerdotale*, *Les Prêtres démasqués*, *De la cruauté religieuse*, *l'Enfer détruit*. So many were they that it is no easy matter even to list them, nor is it possible to say with certainty how much of the total output was his own, and how much the work of his various coadjutors. If there was a book of any sort, ancient or modern, no matter what, that he thought would serve his purpose, he would have it translated. If there was any old manuscript that could possibly help his anti-religious campaign, he would unearth it. For example, there was the manuscript which the late M. Boulanger left behind him. *L'Antiquité dévoilée par ses usages* was its title, and it purported to prove that our religious scruples all arose from the haunting terror which the Deluge bequeathed to its scanty survivors. He it was who ran the workshop, the foundry, which poured forth a flood of propaganda so crude, so fierce, that even the brethren grew weary of it. They took him at last to be a friar turned atheist.

There were others, too, who kept the campaign going; a little group, despised and humble no longer, but holding their heads high, and not at all backward in demanding a place in society, for they claimed to be sages and would have it that a sage is better than a god. Boulanger, Naigeon, Charles François Dupuis, Sylvain Maréchal, Jérôme Lalande, to name the most prominent, have all a sort of family likeness between them; they are all afflicted with the same monomania. Naigeon, Diderot's successor, the Baron d'Holbach's literary ghost, collected together in his *Recueil philosophique ou Mélanges de pièces sur la religion et la morale* (1770) everything of any note that might be held to tell against religion, a sort of atheist's breviary. Sylvain Maréchal aspired to be a French Lucretius, and put his attack on religion into verse:

Il n'est point de vertu si l'on admet les dieux.[1]

He compiled what he called a *Dictionnaire des Athées*, or Unbelievers' Directory, in which he lays claim to some very unexpected personalities, including Abeilard, Zoroaster, Berkeley, Boccaccio, Gregory Nazianzen, Jurieu, Wolff the philosopher, and Young the poet. Whole nations figure in it, English, Brazilian, Chilean, and Americans in general. It was the work of a maniac pure and simple. And the *Discours préliminaire*, puffed up with pompousness, bursting with conceit, would be of just as little account did it not afford us an idea of that fierce intellectual ferment whose beginning and development we have already witnessed. An atheist is just a natural man, a man who, aware of the limitations of the knowable, cannot see how his necessarily restricted knowledge can enable him to reach up to God. He is one who, with no desires beyond his happiness here and now, needs no God to help him to attain it. "The question whether there is a God in Heaven or not, no more

[1]If the gods exist, then virtue doesn't.

concerns him than the question whether or not there is animal life on the moon." Having decided that the whole Christian civilization is founded on error, he naturally desires the complete elimination of that error. "The utter destruction of a long-standing and imposing error, which affects everything in existence, which distorts everything, virtue itself included, which is a pitfall for the weak, a lever for the strong and a barrier to genius—the utter destruction of such a gigantic error would change the face of the world."

Much cry and little wool, all that! Pilati, a contemporary, declared that nowhere in the world was there so much atheism and deism as in Italy. Even if the recorded expression of Italian thought did not give him the lie, the way in which he confuses deists with atheists would suffice to invalidate his statement. In England, the progress of psychology, far from issuing in the negation of religion, tended to encourage it. In France, Helvetius declared that the theologians had so misused the word materialist that it had come to be a synonym for an enlightened mind, and indicated those eminent writers whose works were most eagerly devoured. This was merely scoring a debating point. Everybody knows the story about Hume, how, when he returned to Paris as Secretary to the Embassy, he did not believe there were any atheists, because he had never seen one. "There are eighteen of us round this table", said his host; "fifteen of them are atheists; the other three don't know what to think." But his host was the Baron d'Holbach. The whole object of the German *Aufklärer* was to establish, not atheism, far from it, but "*eine vernünftige Erkenntniss Gottes*", a rational knowledge of God.

Though people no longer clamoured for these ungodly ones to be burnt at the stake, their books were still regarded with horror. When La Mettrie dedicated his *Homme Machine* to the learned Haller, the latter took it as an insult and, in May, 1749, addressed a solemn protest to the *Journal des Savants*: "The anonymous author of *L'Homme Machine* having dedicated to me a work as dangerous as it is unsound, I feel that I owe it to God, to religion and to myself to make the following statement, which I beg those who are responsible for the *Journal des Savants* to insert in their columns: I declare that the book in question is completely alien to my sentiments. I regard its dedication to myself as an outrage, exceeding in cruelty all those which its anonymous author has inflicted on so many worthy people, and I beg the members of the public to be assured that I have never had anything to do with the author of *L'Homme Machine*, that I do not know him, that he is in no way a friend of mine, and that I should look upon any consonance of views between us as one of the most unmitigated calamities that could possibly befall me." Haller was a religious person; not so d'Alembert, Frederick II and Voltaire; yet they all refuted *Le Système de la Nature*.

Against the atheists, the deists piled argument upon argument, contesting their conclusions, one after another. Experiment shows, said the atheists, that when portions of matter which we had supposed to be inert and inanimate are combined in a certain way, they become active and endowed with life and intelligence: that is false, say the deists. Matter and motion suffice to explain everything. Not so. Matter is eternal and necessary. It is not. When you say you are going to prove that there is no God, that matter acts of itself, by eternal necessity, you are bound to prove it as clearly as you would a proposition in Euclid, otherwise all your theories are but founded on a peradventure. What a foundation for a thing which concerns mankind more deeply than any other imaginable.[1]

But the atheists did not give in. They had the same scorn for deism as the deists had for Christianity. "A materialist once said to me that a deist was the sort of man who was not weak enough to be a Christian and not strong enough to be an atheist."[2] Some excitable female philosopher is said to have declared that Voltaire, being a deist, was necessarily a bigot. What did they mean, these feeble creatures, these "final cause" apostles, by a religion without mystery? Surely, that was a contradiction in terms. And how prevaricating to go on worshipping a God, of whom, on their own confession, they were unable to form the slightest conception. The difference between the God of the deist, the optimist, the enthusiast and the God of the devout, the credulous and the zealot was entirely a matter of feeling and temperament. From deism to superstition is never more than

[1]Voltaire, *Dictionnaire philosophique*, article *Athée, Athéisme*; article *Dieu*.

[2]Le P. Bonhomme, *L'anti-Uranie, ou le déisme comparé au christianisme*, 1763.

a step.[1] Of the deist, as of everyone else who professes a religion, we might appropriately say, *Ecce homo;* whereas the real man, the man who never bends the knee to anyone, in other words the atheist, we should greet with an *Ecce vir.*[2]

Thus did these *quondam* allies, who once thought to make common cause against a common foe, call each other over the coals, and in no honeyed terms. It now began to be borne in upon them more and more clearly, that their ideas were fundamentally divergent.

Taking it on the whole, the eighteenth century was deistic rather than atheistic; but, however unwillingly, it was compelled to make room for an atheism which taxed it with the same sort of timidity as that with which the deists had taxed the Christians.

[1]Baron d'Holbach, *Le Bon Sens, ou idées naturelles opposées aux idées surnaturelles,* 111.
[2]Sylvain Maréchal, *Dictionnaire des athées,* An. VIII, *Discours préliminaire.*

II

NATURAL SCIENCE

SCIENCE, the Science *par excellence*, was the Science of Nature; and so Natural History was given pride of place. Geometry came second.

True, many people continued to delight in mathematics, which they held to be the finest of all intellectual exercises, the clearest, the most vigorous, and the most methodical. Europe was far from being confronted by any sudden dearth of mathematicians. There were always plenty of people like that M. de Lagny of whom the following story is told. M. de Lagny was on his death-bed; the people round him whispered to him words of the utmost tenderness, but not a syllable could they get from him in reply. Then M. de Maupertuis appeared on the scene and said that *he* would persuade him to say something. "M. de Lagny", he said, "what is the square of twelve?" "A hundred and forty-four", answered the dying man in a faint voice, and never spoke another word.

Nevertheless, geometry lost the supremacy it had at one time enjoyed, because people came to the very definite conclusion that it added nothing to the stock of knowledge. All it did was to develop, to add, by deduction on deduction, to principles already securely established. Thus it had no contact with reality. Seeing that in real life there is no such thing as surface without depth, length without breadth, nor anything answering to the definition of position without magnitude, nor anything exhibiting the theoretic regularity which geometry assigns to things, what we learn from geometry would appear to be no more than a dream expressed in a number of equations. The idea of explaining creation in terms of motion and extension was the purest moonshine. It was M. Descartes who started it, and M. Descartes had had his day.

At the moment, it was Newton's turn. Newton had enlisted mathematics in the service of Natural Science. Because he started, not from abstractions, not from axioms, but from actual fact to arrive at further facts, duly authenticated; because, for the laws of Nature he had gone to Nature herself, the rising generation had made him one of their heroes. He had emerged from the era of mists and shadows and was now expounded to the most incredulous. Disciples in various seats of learning, erudite professors, commented on his works, which seemed inexhaustible in their content. He was made accessible to the general public by various people, by Voltaire for one, in his lucid French; while Algarotti served him up in a popular Italian version: *eccovi il Neutonianismo per le Signore.* His fame spread steadily. Scientists who were sent to Peru in 1735, and to Tornea in 1736, to verify his earth measurements returned with their verdict. They had put the matter to the practical test and Newton was found to be perfectly correct. He had his backers even at the old Sorbonne. The schools, jealous guardians of ideas, which they are slow to adopt, but, adopted, stubbornly maintain—even the schools gave Newton the *entrée.* "The force of gravitation is creating more of a stir in Holland and England today, than Descartes and his vortices ever did in France. Barristers neglect the Bar, clerics their theological exercises, all for the sake of finding out about the Law of Gravitation."[1]

Galileo, though he did not attain these heights, had at all events some amends made to him, something to console him. In 1737, with circumstances of great solemnity, his ashes were transferred to Santa Croce, the Florentine church in which Italy pays tribute to her illustrious dead. But there was yet another name, a name that stood for a science less abstract, less remote, and, if one may so put it, more "natural" than mathematics, or physics, and that was the name of Bacon. The precursor, the sage of sages, the foe of empty hypotheses, the master mind, he who had brought back the rule of reason, charted the ways, disposed of difficulties, and made clear the work that still remained to be done, the greatest and most universal of philosophers; the genius of empiricism incarnate. When Bacon declared in simple terms, and not without a touch of pathos, that formal logic was more apt to confirm and perpetuate error than to discover truth;

[1]Le marquis d'Argens, *La philosophie du Bon Sens,* 1746. *Réflexion III,* par. 20.

that the syllogism fettered the mind and did not get to the reality of things, when he went on to declare that we should not blindly trust what previous thinkers, however great, had laid down, that there should be no worshipping of idols, that we should change our working methods, practise careful observation and have recourse to experiment—when he said all this, he was sowing the seed of ideas which, a hundred years or so after the *Novum Organum*, germinated and, springing up, brought forth a harvest that covered the face of Europe. *Aphorismi de interpretatione naturae et regno hominis.*

You only had to give a cursory glance around you to see signs of an unmistakable effervescence. Everywhere the *curiosi* were getting down to work. Here is someone starting a butterfly collection; here is someone else getting together an album of every kind of plant. Here is yet another ordering prisms to be sent him from somewhere abroad so that he may split up the rays of light; or, maybe, a telescope to enable him to discern the ring of Saturn. If you wanted to give pleasure to your lady-love, you would send her some rare insects to add to the curiosities in her treasure-table. If you wanted to get a reputation for learning, it was no bad idea to publish an account of some natural history collection. If you went abroad, you would be sure to take with you plenty of boxes, nets, scissors, magnifying glasses and so on. In addition to pictures, Gersaint now has sea-shells for sale. The upper ten, the aristocracy, lead the way. Let them do it; what does it matter? is the comment. If they've got to be fleeced, better be fleeced by a chemist than a shark. Science, at least, will benefit. Even royalty catch the infection. Louis XV has his collections. The Dauphin takes up a course of physics, George III interests himself in Botany, John V in astronomical research; Victor Amadeus III goes through the Abbé Nollet's experiments with Gerdil. Outside the Abbé Nollet's front-door, in the rue du Mouton, near La Grève, where he teaches experimental physics, duchesses who want to be galvanized keep driving up in their carriages. The middle classes are also in the fashion, and the young folk, too. The Abbé Pluche shows them *Le Spectacle de la Nature,* a collection of objects calculated to stimulate their curiosity and train their understanding.

If one probes a little farther to find out the deeper causes of all the excitement, one soon realizes how serious was the nature of the work which the fashionable people merely took up to pass the time. The journals give so much space to reviews of books about science that it resembles a positive inundation. Books on physics, botany, medicine come along in ever-growing numbers. But, owing to the rapid progress in their departments of knowledge, they are soon out of date, and need to be replaced by new ones. And replaced they are. To this huge multitude of books, this mass of printed matter, all announcing some new discovery, the Academies fling wide their gates: the Berlin Academy, the St. Petersburg Academy, founded in 1725; the Stockholm Academy, founded 1739; the Royal Society of Copenhagen, founded 1745, while such respectable dowagers as the Institute of Bologna, the Paris Académie des Sciences, the Royal Society of London, maintain their traditions, each of them making it a point of honour to associate foreigners with their labours. It was a thing to be proud of, and much sought for, to have one's work discussed and criticized by these tribunals. In 1746, Voltaire, who had written a *Dissertation sur les changements arrivés dans notre globe et sur les pétrifications ou'on prétend en être encore les témoignages*, sent an Italian version of it to the Bologna Institute and an English one to the Royal Society, London. He even thought of putting it into Latin and sending it to the Academy of St. Petersburg. In 1773, the latter had presented some works to the Lisbon Academy. Its president at that time was the aged Count d'Ericeira, who, many years before, had translated Boileau. The Count gratefully acknowledged the gift in a speech full of flowery and highly decorative phrases. He brought in the Queen of Sheba, the Sibyl of the East, who, from the frozen North, had sent, writ on leaves of gold, the works of her Academicians; but he brought in Bacon, too, and, that subtlest of men, René Descartes, who had succeeded in wedding algebra to geometry. Newton, too, he mentioned, England's greatest philosopher, who had proved all that it was possible to prove in Natural Philosophy, and whose teaching was very rightly respected. So we had the latest ideas in Science and Philosophy decked out with all the old familiar rhetorical flourishes.

The movement had a twofold character. To begin with, there was the desire to expand, to reach out, a desire which led these seekers to transcend the boundaries of their province, their kingdom, their continent, or whatever it might be, so that, bit by bit, they might bring the whole of creation beneath their purview. Here are some of their works: *Catalogus plantarum quibus consitus est Patavii amoenissimus hortus; Flora Noribergensis; Botanicon parisiense; Hortus uplandicus; Flora lapponica; Historia naturalis curiosa regni Poloniae; The Natural History of England; Flora cochinchinensis*. . . . As there was a presentiment that there were unknown lands still to be discovered, ships which set sail on voyages of exploration took naturalists with them, and they in due time returned to Europe bringing specimens of flora and fauna which men had never even dreamt of. The farther afield they ranged the more did the numbers of animal and vegetable species multiply, so overwhelmingly, in fact, that they defied enumeration. The list of today would be hopelessly out of date tomorrow. This ever-swelling tide carried away all landmarks. The bewildering immensity of the ocean of life surpassed anything that had ever been conceived. At the same time, there was a pull in the contrary direction, a tendency towards concentration. The most eager of these enquiring minds shut themselves up within four walls and would have all this teeming life to come to them. Their labours had an atmosphere of mystery about them. They cut up and dissected. They peered down microscopes, shook up strange-looking substances in glass bottles. Thus did the expert of the laboratory come into being. Ill-equipped these laboratories may have been, often lacking the simplest of instruments; and ill-equipped the workers, rarely troubling to doff their velvet coats or even to roll back their lace sleeves, yet it was men such as these who began the long epic of experimental science.

Then there followed, one after another, in majestic procession, a series of names of which each one is associated with some striking achievement. In astronomy, there are the Cassini, a dynasty in themselves; in geology, Jean Gottlob Lehman and Horace Benedict de Saussure; in botany, Charles de Linné (Linnaeus) and the first of the five Jussieus. Entomology gives us René Antoine Ferchault de Réaumur and Charles Bonnet; physics, William Jacob S'Gravesande, Leonard Euler, Alessandro Volta; physiology, Hermann Boerhave, Friedrich Hoffmann, Albrecht von Haller, Gaspar Friedrich Wolff, Lazaro Spallanzani,

Georg Ernst Stahl, Joseph Priestley, Charles Guillaume Scheele. Often it would be wrong to limit them to any one single department; everything was being discovered at once. Let us call up, since we cannot have them all, just two of these legendary figures: Galvani, stimulating the muscular reflexes of a dead frog; Lavoisier, grave and handsome, behind an array of test-tubes and retorts.

They belonged to a variety of countries, there being scarcely one that did not delegate one of its distinguished sons to bear a hand in the great work. To put it more correctly, they were a nation to themselves, one among all the rest, a nation whose subjects went on with their labours even though wars might be raging all around them. Even when communications were almost entirely cut off, they managed to get through to one another. They checked each other's work, compared results, and exchanged congratulations. Such was the ideal Republic of Learning.

But it was not such an easy matter. Ambitions aimed too far, too high. People talked a lot about "slowly and surely", "little by little", and all that sort of thing, but they went off with such a bound, so blithely, so light-heartedly that they seemed to be borne along on the wings of the wind. They launched out on the most extravagant undertakings. Take, for example, the plan started by the newly formed Académie de Bordeaux in 1759. It was nothing more nor less than a History of the Earth, of all the changes it had undergone by reason of earthquakes, floods and any other causes, with a full and accurate account of the developments of sea and land, of the formation and disappearance of islands, of rivers, mountains, valleys, lakes, gulfs, straits, capes, and all the changes that have affected them, as well as of the works of man, whereby the face of the earth has been transformed. All the material was to be sent to M. de Montesquieu, President of the Parliament of Guyenne, who was to pay the carriage on it. Did he have much to disburse? Not much; the plan fell through!

Wonders were not now in request; yet it was no easy matter to avoid having recourse to the marvellous in order to explain some things, especially in the early days, before, that is to say, Science had got into its stride. Theories, hypotheses, too, were at a discount. All the same they were a very present help in time of need, when no explanation was available. The plague was raging in Marseilles and all over Provence. Now what exactly *was* this plague, and what caused it to spread? It was not contagious; it would have been stupid to say it was. Oh, yes; it *was* contagious, but only as an epidemic is contagious, and this is caused by under-nourishment. Or it could be spread by sores, by urine, by sweat, and, consequently, by a mattress, by clothing, by anything, in fact, which had been in contact with a case. But what was it, exactly? What was its nature? It consisted of miasmata, of particles of sea-fans, of antimony, of tiny little worms which, in the morning, swim like fish, at noon fly like birds, and die off at night; it was caused by insects so microscopic that they make their way in through the tiniest openings in the skin, especially in winter, when they feel the cold. What was the cure? Coffee? Drinking plenty of water? Drinking acids, as the old-fashioned doctors used to prescribe? Viper-grass tea, with a few drops of lemon-juice or spirits of sulphur added? Or what about tincture of gold? Or an emetic? Or a cordial? A purgative? A sudorific? For the buboes, plasters, or a piece of caustic kept in place for several hours. Lyons, Montpellier, Paris, Zurich, London, all squabbled together about the proper treatment. Meanwhile the victims went on dying.

It took more than damning words to get rid of the doctrinaire mentality. The first thing tackled was the most difficult, and that was the problem of generation. How did living organisms come into being? Before all the evidence had been accumulated, evidence based on observation, theories were formed only to be immediately contradicted and superseded by other theories. Soon complete confusion prevailed. Endless discussions went on about these rival theories. It looked as if Science had run off the track and come to a dead end.

It happened that sometimes an error, by its very flagrancy, attracted general attention. In 1748, John Tuberville Needham, an English physiologist, had seen life spontaneously generate before his very eyes. He shall tell his own story. We will listen while he describes his experiments, the precautions he took to ensure accuracy, and the marvellous results he obtained. "I took a quantity of Mutton-Gravy hot from the Fire, and shut it up in a Phial, clos'd up with a Cork so well masticated that my Precautions amounted to as much as if I had sealed my Phial hermetically. I thus effectually excluded the exterior Air, that it might not be said my moving Bodies drew their Origin from Insects, or Eggs floating in the Atmosphere. I would not instil any Water lest, without giving it as intense a Degree of Heat, it might be thought these Productions were convey'd through that Element. . . . I neglected no Precaution, even as far as to heat violently in hot Ashes the Body of the Phial; that if anything existed, even in that little Portion of Air which filled up the Neck, it might be destroyed, and lose its productive Faculty. Nothing therefore could answer my Purpose of excluding every Objection, better than hot roast-Meat Gravy secur'd in this manner and exposed for some Days to the Summer-Heat: and as I was determined not to open it till I might reasonably conclude, whether, by its own Principles, it was productive of any thing, I allow'd sufficient Time for that Purpose to this pure unmix'd Quintessence, if I may so call it, of an animal Body. . . . My Phial swarm'd with Life, and microscopical Animals of most Dimensions, from some of the largest I had ever seen, to some of the least." Splendid! But it was all wrong. It took years to examine Needham's theory, to check it, to refute it and to show that what he took to be fermentation of life was caused by germs, which, in spite of all the measures he had taken to exclude them, had come in from outside. So, again, it was "Halt! Mark time! About turn!"

The ups and downs which the history of ideas presents to our astonished eyes, the unexpected relationships, victories which turn out to be defeats, reverses that bear unexpected fruit, all are here seen at the very climax of their activity. Botanists, imbued with the scientific spirit, were bent on formulating a system of plant-classification based on objective observation, and, following in Tournefort's track, Linnaeus considered he had succeeded in his task when he wrote the *Systema naturae*, which came out in 1735. "I am the first to introduce the system of classifying plants according to their natural characteristics." At the same time, these botanizers, like the rest of the scientists, and like the philosophers, their real if unacknowledged masters, wanted to fit the universe and all its products into a sort of preconceived scheme or pattern. They conjured up something they called The Great Ladder of Creation, on which not a rung was missing. You passed from one step to another by gradations so slight as to be almost imperceptible; but the gradations were there, nevertheless. Discontinuity was excluded *a priori*. Nowhere could there be a void. Nowhere was there any gap between the gradations of a series, or between one series and another, between animal and vegetable, vegetable and mineral; and there was a viewless link connecting mankind with beings above them, that is to say, with the angels. At the highest point, detached from all the rest, and the only one to be so, was God. At all costs, every compartment must be occupied. If, at the moment, you could not see what was in any given one, be patient, it would appear plainly enough one day. Thus we find that the very people who proclaimed themselves liegemen to the Fact are, willy-nilly, subjecting the Fact to the *A priori*.

To get away from the doctrine of the fixity of things, and to substitute for it the theory of continuous evolution required a prolonged and strenuous effort. However, there was no gainsaying that under the influence of exotic climatic conditions, some animals and some vegetables had undergone a change. Nor could the evidence of the palaeontologists regarding the discovery of the remains of extinct creatures in the lower geological *strata*, be set aside. Then there were the physiologists with their examples of the degeneration, or hybridization, of species.

But it was not all plain sailing. Maupertuis was described by some as a crank. People who went to see him reported with astonishment that his house was a positive menagerie, filled with all sorts of animals, which didn't make it any the cleaner. Also, they said, he indulged in the strange pastime of mating animals of different species. La Mettrie they thought crankier still. He said that some of the earliest species had been very imperfect; some, he said, had had no oesophagus, some no intestines, and that the only animals to survive had been those furnished with all the essential organs, and only the hardiest of those. An immense weight of ignorance and prejudice had to be dispelled before Lamarck and his theories about the transformation of species began to come into view.

Hard and long was the task, and many the set-backs; but there were also moments of triumph and joy. It would be a very imperfect record of the times that left the thrills of excitement and victory out of account.

Oh, most marvellous, most wondrous world of insects! Behold, Charles Bonnet, observing the habits of the green fly, makes the most astounding discoveries! He discovers, in fact, that they propagate, without any intervention on the part of the male, by parthenogenesis. And then the no less wondrous world of plants! Here Abraham Trembley, observing the shoots of certain aquatic plants, notices that they extend, push out horns or arms, draw back, and even move from their places. Can they possibly be animals? He cuts up the polyps into several parts, and each part becomes a fresh polyp. They are propagated by cuttings, therefore they must be plants. But wait! That cannot be so. These polyps lay hold of tiny worms, take them into their mouths, then into the cavity of their bodies, and there digest them. Therefore, they must be animals. No, that won't do; they must be both plant and animal together.[1]

Réaumur tries a few of Trembley's experiments. "I must confess that the first time I saw two polyps gradually forming from one I had cut in half, I could hardly believe my eyes. It is a thing I should never get used to, though I saw it hundreds and hundreds of times." Then came an experiment with fresh-water worms of the kind called *naiades,* as well as with ordinary earthworms. These were cut up into pieces, and in every case the pieces came to life. Spallanzani cut off the horns and even the heads of snails; the horns reappeared, and the heads grew again. He next tried water-salamanders, red-blooded creatures, and cut away their feet. The feet reappeared. It was the age of miracles come again; but, this time, miracles of the natural order. Plants breathed. No one now spoke of the air as one of the four simple elements. It was composed of different gases, which, before very long, scientists would be able to separate. From Philadelphia, in the New World, came the news that a man called Franklin, Benjamin Franklin, had discovered the secret of lightning. He had, as people put it, captured the celestial fluid, filched it from the gods. "I am tired of telling about wonders."[2]

[1]Abraham Trembley, *Mémoire pour servir à l'histoire d'un genre de Polypes d'eau douce . . .,* 1744.

[2]Charles Bonnet, *Considérations sur les corps organisés,* 1762, Chap. XI.

But already the reward had come. Knowledge was power. If you want to make Nature serve you, you must learn her secrets. Matter was man's slave now. A good thing people had given up worrying their heads about first principles, and essences, and substances. A lot of good that was, when you could make things do what you wanted them to do, make them serve your purpose. From this altered mode of approach, manifold benefits resulted. Solid benefits, too, and derived from sciences which, on the face of things, were little likely to yield them. "The discoveries of the scientists are the triumphs of the human race."[1] "Man is not weak."[2] His strength would wax greater from day to day.

Science would lend worth and beauty to life. Now it was that there appeared on the scene, enwreathed with a new and unfamiliar aureole, one who had the power of setting Nature to rights when she went astray, one who could cure the ills that flesh is heir to; and that man was the doctor. Theatre-goers might go on laughing at Diafoirus as of old, but Boerhave of Leyden, Tronchin of Geneva, Bordeu of Paris, who, all three of them, had European reputations, were living examples of the newly mastered power. Everybody took a lively interest in long discussions about inoculation; and at last smallpox was conquered. "Everything gives way to the great art of the healer", said La Mettrie, who, for once in a way, forgot to fling mud at his colleagues. "The doctor is the one philosopher who deserves well of his country. He comes, like Helen's brothers, when the storms of life are upon us. The magic, the wonder of the thing! The mere sight of him restores our calm, brings peace to the troubled mind and breeds fresh hope in the breasts of helpless mortality. He gives notice of life and death even as the astronomer foretells an eclipse."[3] Yes, he is your true, your one and only philosopher, for "he, and he alone, has seen and noted the phenomena. He has seen the human machine in calmness and in frenzy, whole or maimed, peaceful or raving, now dim, now enlightened, dull or noisy, listless or active, alive or dead."[4]

[1] Joseph Landon, *Réflexions de Mademoiselle X, comédienne française,* 1750, page 54.
[2] S. Johnson, *Rasselas,* 1759, Chapter XIII.
[3] La Mettrie, *Dedication of L'Homme Machine,* 1748.
[4] Diderot, *Encyclopédie,* article *Locke.*

On the 14th February, 1750, Buffon himself recorded the success of his *Histoire Naturelle*. Three volumes of it had been published the year before. "The first edition, large as it was, sold out in six weeks, a second and a third impression are in preparation and will shortly appear. The book has been translated into German, English and Dutch. . . ." Buffon may not have been the greatest genius of his day, but he was certainly the most typical. To him we are indebted for another *Discours de la Méthode*. He called it *De la manière de traiter l'histoire naturelle*. In that work he deposed mathematics from its pride of place. What, he said, the mind of man now required much more urgently than geometrical demonstration, was a real and accurate acquaintance with the facts. There is a hint of revolt in the following passage:

There are truths of various kinds, and most people give first place to the truths of mathematics. These truths, however, relate to definitions, and these again are concerned with propositions that are simple, indeed, but abstract; and all truths in this category are but consequences deduced from these definitions, but still abstract. We have enunciated propositions, combined them in every possible way, and the sum-total of these combinations constitutes the science of mathematics. There is therefore nothing in that science but what we ourselves have put there. The truths of physical science, on the other hand, have nothing of this arbitrary character, they are quite independent of ourselves. Instead of being based on propositions of our own devising, they rest wholly on facts. In mathematics we advance an hypothesis and reason upon it; in physics we take a fact and reason upon it. In the abstract sciences we proceed from one definition to another, in physical science we proceed from one observed fact to another. In the one case we have abstract proof; in the other we have concrete certitude.

He came near to paradox in his anxiety to put man at the centre of the universe. He was not in love with the system of plant-classification proposed by Linnaeus. His own method, which was not confined to plants but embraced the whole of Creation, proceeded from a different starting point. Suppose that someone who awakes from sleep has completely forgotten all that he ever knew. Imagine him in a situation where beasts, birds, fishes, rocks—everything, come before his eyes as complete novelties. At first, he will be utterly bewildered; everything will be hopelessly confused; he will be unable to distinguish one thing from another. But soon he will notice a difference between animate and inanimate matter. In the former he will notice a difference between animals and plants; hence the great primary division, namely, the division between the animal, vegetable and mineral kingdoms. As he contemplates the animals, our observer will soon discern three distinct species, those of earth, air and water; hence the division into beasts, birds and fishes. The quadrupeds he will classify according to the nearness of their relation to himself. In the front rank he will put the horse, the dog and the ox. The list of the more familiar animals completed, he will turn his attention to others which always haunt the same regions, as, for example, hares, deer and other wild creatures. Only after all this is done will his curiosity prompt him to interest himself in those that dwell in foreign lands, such as elephants, dromedaries, and so forth. Putting together like with like, separating those which differ, judging resemblances and differences by taking man as the standard of comparison; and so to present man with a portrait of nature by furnishing him with a complete description of the whole natural world, such was his ambitious design.

His *Histoire de la Terre* and *Les Époques de la Nature* helped to bring about the substitution of an evolutionary for a static conception of things. He showed that it was impossible to get down to that bedrock reality which he aimed at mastering as a whole and in its parts, otherwise than by observing how it had developed in its earlier stages and by noting the various modifications it had undergone. He started with the wild confusion of the earthly scene—peaks, ravines, plains, seas, marshes, rivers, caves, gulfs, volcanoes, mountains, rocks riven and shattered, whole tracts of land swallowed up—and then, thanks to geology, he went on to penetrate into the bowels of the earth. In the light of the age-long action of fire, and of the great watercourses, he had discovered the key to the enigma. He had, as he expressed it in his own sonorous phrase, searched deep into the archives of the world and set up milestones along the everlasting highway of Time.

Everything, even his mistakes, seemed to concur in making a symbolic figure of him. For he did make mistakes sometimes. He made one when he looked into the microscope that Needham lent him, though it was a better one than any he had himself. His preparations had been faulty and his results wrongly interpreted.

He had come to think it beneath him to concern himself with minor details. Opposed though he was to theoretic systems, he was greatly wrapt up in the theory of matrices and moulds, which he long and ardently upheld. But if he erred, it was against his better judgment, from neglecting to observe the rule which he himself was constantly harping upon. Fallible, then, though he was, it was he himself who bequeathed to posterity the means which enabled it to convict him of error.

He symbolized hard work, that long, enduring patience, that infinite capacity for taking pains, which came to be regarded as synonymous with genius. Time, that precious gift, which others squandered on futilities, on pleasure, on occupations extraneous to the task in hand, he devoted wholly to his work, *Le Jardin du Roi, L'Histoire Naturelle*. The temptation to live an easy-going, care-free existence he had put aside; he eschewed social distractions and foreign travel—he was only a few months in Italy, and in England he stayed just long enough to serve his apprenticeship to Science. And so, master of his fate, his feelings, his character, his powers, thoroughly disciplined and tempered like the finest steel, he calmly and resolutely devoted his all to the task before him. Fixed times for rising, for meals, for bodily exercise, were observed with the strictest regularity. He was like the man that never rests, because he knows his work is never done.

He symbolized the stern morality of Science, the consciousness of its exacting law. He symbolized the hopes to which Science gives birth. "Let us continue to add to our experience and avoid all theorizing, at least until we have thoroughly mastered the facts. We shall find out easily enough some day where to put our material, and even if we are not lucky enough to complete the building, we shall at least have the satisfaction of knowing that our foundations have been well and truly laid. And, perhaps—who knows?—we may have progressed beyond all our expectations with the superstructure."[1]

There was no eventide of life for him; as his years advanced, he entered into a sort of glorious Valhalla. His defects, a somewhat materialistic outlook on things, a cunning way he had of getting the people he wanted to work for him, his taste for the "lightly come and lightly go" in his love-affairs—all his

[1]Buffon, Preface to the translation of *La statique des végétaux,* by Hales, 1735.

shortcomings were, so to speak, faded out in a cloud of incense. One of the forty Immortals of the Académie française, Perpetual Treasurer of the Académie des Sciences, Member of the Academies of London, Edinburgh, Berlin, St. Petersburg, Florence, Philadelphia, Boston, be-crowned, flattered, cosseted, he might see in his gardens, the monument his son erected in his glorious honour, and his own statue in his beloved Jardin du Roi. Montbard began to rival Ferney as a place of pilgrimage. Prince Henry of Prussia came in person to call on this very illustrious personage, and afterwards made him a present of a china dinner-service adorned with a pattern of swans. Jean Jacques Rousseau went down on his knees and kissed the threshold of his doorway. People wrote poetry about him, celebrating him as the spirit of Creation, the genius sublime. Madame Necker called him the man of all the ages; Catherine of Russia, in an autograph letter, told him that Newton had made the first step forward, and he the second. When people had been all round the thirteen terraces, when they had seen the work room, so austere and bare, in which the great task had been brought to completion, and when at last they turned their gaze upon the author, they would have seen a man of stately mien, a handsome, impassive countenance, young-looking for all his eight and seventy years. Houdon, in the bust he carved of him, may give an idea of his gravity, his lofty bearing, but he gives us none of his flashing eyes, his black eyebrows contrasting so strangely with his beautiful white hair. He resembled man as he himself had portrayed him, tall, stately, upright, commanding, his august countenance turned heavenward and instinct with that dignity which was his distinguishing characteristic.

What labour, what toil, what endless controversies, all to establish the plain and simple truth that, in matters of science, we must always begin with the most minute examination of the facts. Precisely. Time and again that truth had been driven home; time and again it would be driven home in the future. Claude Bernard was but a return to Bacon. It was as though the tide came up every century, generation after generation, to submerge again the islands that the previous age had brought to light; and so, every time, they had to be charted anew at an immense expenditure of toil and talent.

III

LAW

HASTE, then, to work! Garner in the fruits of the ground won by Grotius, Pufendorf, Cumberland, Leibniz and Gravina. Let all Europe, nay, all the world, understand, at long last, that there is but one law, one original law, whence all others have their source, and that law is the Law of Nature. Haste, and give the lie to those who, even now, attack it; nay, turn back behind you and deal a blow at that unholy Hobbes, who would have had us believe that force was the ruling factor in human affairs. Let us press on with our work of definition and development, so that all the miscellaneous acquisitions we have made may be sorted out and put into proper scientific order; and let us, so far as in us lies, put our theories into practice. The teaching of Natural Law spread swiftly all over Europe. A chair of Natural Law was founded at the Collège Royal in 1771. The curtain had rung down now on the inventors and discoverers. The time had come for the professors to have their chance. So now we shall have monographs, records of researches, long and wordy explanations by the specialists; not, on the face of it, a very exhilarating prospect. On the face of it; but, in point of fact, a movement was on foot which was to go to the very heart of things, a movement which ran parallel with all the other movements of the time, and not seldom dominated them. The object of this movement was to divorce law from religion. Henceforth law should have no concern with religion, except in so far as religion was compatible with reason.

1730. Johann Gottlieb Heinecke, *Elementa juris naturae et gentium*.

A very learned man was this Johann Gottlieb Heinecke, in Latin, Heineccius. He quitted the university of Halle only to return to it, for nowhere else did he find himself so thoroughly at home. He was a first-rate lawyer and a sound classic to boot. He wanted his own pupils, and students generally, to have a manual that would set the seal on the union of Natural Law and legal science; for jurisprudence would be worth nothing were it not imbued with the spirit of Natural Law. What, indeed, is jurisprudence if not Natural Law, as it affects mankind? So we have the following definition: "Natural Law is the sum-total of the laws which God has made known to the human race through the agency of right reason. Regarded as a science, natural jurisprudence is the practical way of ascertaining the will of the Supreme Lawgiver as manifested by right reason, and of applying it on all due occasions."

1740–1748. Johann Christian Wolff, *Jus naturae methodo scientifica pertractatum.*

Johann Christian Wolff throws himself into the movement, and henceforth there will be no holding him back. His task it was to be to enshrine Natural Law in a logical system, and to integrate it into the grand pattern of Truth and Life.

Man is made up of soul and body. Just as our whole organic mechanism aims at the preservation of the body, so does the reason tend to spiritual perfection. Hence our actions take on an intrinsic character of good or ill; whatever contributes to this perfection is good, whatever hinders it is evil. Such is the edict of Nature's law, based as it is on the essential nature of men and things. "Since Nature, which is always the close ally of Truth, does not brook contradiction, which is Truth's inveterate foe, the only sound rule for determining our human actions is to see to it that they are directed towards the same ends as those of Nature." That being granted, let us now consider the matter of law. In order that we may be able to fulfil these natural obligations, we must be free to do whatever is necessary to that end. We must be free to make use of things, or not; to act or not, as we may see fit. The incorporation of people into a social order gives birth to obligations other than those which affect the individual. In this way we have laws which are classified as individual, social or national. And Wolff accomplishes the *tour de force* of deriving all particular cases from these premises. He goes into detail, he instances a landed estate, the rights which it confers, and the obligations it entails. He deals with bequests, contracts, informal agreements; with the rights and duties appertaining to the married state, to parents and their children, with international law, and with human rights. Contemplating the logical perfection of his exposition, Formey, one of his admirers, is lost in wonder. "Nature would have man as healthy as possible, both in mind and body. Reason says the same thing. If we imagine a man in whom Nature and Reason always work in absolute harmony, that man would be perfect. Such is the main principle on which M. Wolff's arguments are based and never did philosopher boast a greater abundance of ideas, or present them with greater lucidity." Nevertheless, something was lacking to jurisprudence even now, though Wolff laboured to such good effect that he brought it very near to perfection. It was now like a machine which only needed to have its several parts adjusted in order to make it work. Someone else was to arise who, while making full use of Wolff's ideas, would correct such minor imperfections as might have escaped his notice. Perhaps the day would come when this system, developed to the full, would take its stand on the ruins of its predecessors, and serve as a guide to all the lawyers of the future.

1740. Fr. H. Strube of Piermont, *Recherches nouvelles de l'origine et des fondements du droit de la nature.*

Away back in 1732, Frédéric Henri Strube of Piermont noticed that neither authors nor professors could agree on a definition of the laws of Nature. So, relying on what he personally thought about the matter, he came out with his *Recherches de l'origine et des fondements du droit de la nature.* And now, he thought, here is the secret of the whole matter.

The most ancient among the philosophers gave the name natural law to the eternal and immutable order of creation. The Roman lawyers saw in it the directions given by nature to the whole animal kingdom. Moralists for the most part regarded them as rules dictated by reason, and limited them to man alone. But no; that would not do. In reality they were something very different. Every created being can only have been made for his or her conservation; a similar line of reasoning compels him to think also of conserving his fellows. Therefore every man must needs conserve himself and also those with whom he is united. In short, he must ensure the continuity of the human race. That is the first, the only, principle of the law of Nature.

But reason, which is wholly concerned with the relationship of ideas, is not calculated to enable us to recognize what the laws are designed to teach us. The will, another of our faculties, is equally incapable of doing so. There remains passion, passion which is really the active principle of the soul. Passion carries with it a force that ensures fulfilment. It is passion that brings us to obey the laws of Nature.

1742. François Richer d'Aube, *Essai sur les principes du droit et de la morale.*

Now it is the turn of M. d'Aube, a law-officer of the Crown by profession, and a nephew by marriage of Fontenelle's: Natural Law, which has on it the mark of eternity and universality, needs no one to interpret it, for it is graven on the hearts of all. Man is a material being; therefore he strives to preserve himself; man is a spiritual being, therefore he strives to be happy. Nature, with God behind it, God the Sovereign Ruler of the Universe, is the inspirer of this law, which makes for the welfare of society.

1748. J. J. Burlamaqui, *Principes du droit naturel.*

Dauntless, a great talker, mathematically precise, very critical, much more of a dogmatist than he himself suspected, Jean Jacques Burlamaqui, professor of Natural and Civil Law at Geneva, was a great hand at definitions. He defined man, seeing that the idea of law, especially Natural Law, is related to the nature of man. He defined happiness, whereunto all men naturally aspire. He defined the understanding, which, in its nature, is unerring, and carries with it the power to recognize truth, and to distinguish the true from the false. He defined evidence, against which human passions are powerless to prevail. He defined reason, which always carries with it the idea of perfection. He defined virtue. Thus liberally equipped, he addressed himself to the idea of law:

We understand by a law of Nature, a law imposed by God on all men, a law which they are able to read for themselves and interpret by the light of their own unaided reason, duly bearing in mind their nature and condition.

Natural Law is the aggregate, the sum-total of all these laws.

Finally, natural jurisprudence is the art of ascertaining the laws of Nature, of developing them, and applying them to human conduct.

Further, Natural Law is:

Everything which the reason recognizes with certainty as a sure and direct short cut to happiness, and approves as such.

"A law imposed on all men by God": Does this imply that Burlamaqui still retained some vestige of belief in Divine Law? Let us examine the position: God being the author of the nature of things, and of our constitution, it follows that, if as a result of the said nature and constitution, we are logically led to a certain conclusion and to act in accordance therewith, the Creator's intention is sufficiently manifest, and we can be no longer in any doubt regarding his will. The voice of Reason is therefore the voice of God. God being Reason, and Reason being human reason, obedience is not demanded of us by God in the sense that we can only obey the command of a superior by preliminary adherence to the principle that inspired that command. In short, God is re-absorbed into Reason, and Reason into Nature, and what used to be called Divine Law is now but a law prescribed by Nature and Reason. Of Divine Law no trace must be left; we must needs embrace the definition laid down in the Encyclopaedia under the heading Law:

Law in the general sense is human reason, governing as it does all the peoples of the earth; the political and civil laws of each nation can only represent the said human reason in its application to various particular cases.

1757. Martin Hubner, *Essai sur l'histoire du droit naturel.*

What a splendid thing it would be to be able to prove that Natural Law had been engraven on men's hearts all the world over, to the utmost limits of the earth, and from the very beginning of time! How good to be able to go back to the primeval state of Nature, and so to base on actual experimental data the theory on which the said law reposes. We may therefore imagine the excitement that was aroused by the news that a wild girl had been discovered in the woods of Champagne, and a wild man in the forests of Hanover. They could be questioned, and Nature's answers, plain and unadorned, could be recorded. Drama and fiction made up whatever these persons failed to supply. In Marivaux's comedy *La Dispute*, the main idea is to discover how inconstancy came into the world. Who started it? Man or woman? One of the characters in the play is to decide the matter. "The world and its earliest love-affairs will be brought before us as they were in their primeval simplicity, or rather as they must have been." The prince's father, who was a philosopher, gave orders that four infants, while still in the cradle, were to be taken to some lonely spot and there kept from all contact with the rest of the world. These infants, two boys and two girls, were brought up apart and never set eyes on one another. At length they grew up, and the time came to release them from their confinement, and to let them see each other. "What they do, how they comport themselves will be like a page from the world's primeval story." But Marivaux comes to no decision, and we shall never know on which side inconstancy began, for what it all comes to is that neither sex can justly blame the other, virtues and vices being evenly distributed between them. But Beaurieu, in his novel *L'Élève de la Nature* (1766), took a bolder line. A man had prevailed on his wife to agree that if they had more than six children, those above that number should be set apart and used in order to bring to light the secrets of Nature. They had seven, as it turned out, so the seventh and last (a boy) was shut up in a cage and cut off from all contact with the outer world. Food was passed in to him by means of a revolving hatch. The cage was taken away and put on a desert island. Not until he was twenty did the hero of the tale begin to make contact with his fellow men. He was a kind-hearted, sensible fellow. He became in due course the father of a family, and the family proved to be a model of all that a family should be.

Literature did not come into it. But what could be done, and it would be for the first time, was to outline the history of Natural Law. It was a Dane, one Martin Hubner, who tried his hand at the task. Oh, how he delighted to deliver himself of those familiar stock-phrases! I have argued from the point of view of a man who has nothing to guide him but the light of his own reason. I apply the name Natural Law to the system or *corpus* of obligatory rules which pure reason prescribes for us as indicating the sure road to happiness. The idea of Natural Law is incontestably relative to man's nature; that is to say it is consonant with his essence. Man desires happiness, all his acts are directed with a view to his happiness, but to satisfy this longing, by which he is incessantly pricked on, to achieve the aim for which he is so constantly striving, he must necessarily have regard to the means by which he is to attain his end. Hence man must needs have certain rules, and those rules, which govern our conduct, which are the means which lead to the happiness of man, we call Natural Law. Man's own nature was, it might be said, the initial propounder of Natural Law. Then he searched deep into the past for the great ones in whom this teaching office had been made incarnate. There was that worthy scribe to whom we owe the history of the time before the Deluge and who gave us a very concise summary of these Natural Laws, and that was Moses. Then there were the Chinese, and the Greeks. And that Montesquieu of the ancient world, he to whom we owe the formal recognition of Natural Law, to wit Socrates. Among the Romans, notwithstanding their overweening, quasi-fanatical political ideas, there were two, Cicero and Seneca. Epictetus, too, he mentioned, and Marcus Aurelius. There was a notable falling-off in the Middle Ages, but what could one expect from a period so barbarous and uncouth? The Renaissance, however, put us back on the right track again, and so we come to Grotius, Pufendorf, Cumberland, Wolff, Barbeyrac, Burlamaqui. The English and the Danes were won over. In Germany things went almost too fast. That vast Empire, with its many provinces, was simply gorged with universities, if we may so express it, and in practically every one of them there was a chair of Natural Law. There were such hosts of Essays, Epitomes, Systems that it was impossible to keep count of them. They would have stocked a whole library, if anyone had thought it worth while to spend time and money getting them together. People least given to reflection there, often fell back on this theme when they could find nothing else to employ their pen withal. Natural Law had undoubtedly encountered some opponents: unbelievers like Spinoza; heretics like Bayle, Mandeville and Bolingbroke; but their writings availed little or nothing against acknowledged verities.

1783–1788. Gaetano Filangieri, *Della Scienza della Legislazione.*

Goethe speaks of Gaetano Filangieri, whom he met in Naples, and who introduced him to an author named J. B. Vico, in memorable terms of praise: "He belongs to a group of young men worthy of all esteem, who do not fail to keep in view the happiness of mankind and a sound conception of liberty. From his general style of behaviour, you would recognize the soldier, the chivalrous gentleman, and the well-bred man of the world. His aristocratic bearing, however, is softened by an aura of delicate moral sensibility which, imbuing his person as a whole, radiates with great charm, not only from what he says, but from his whole personality." Benedetto Croce calls him an apostle of the New Gospel, the Gospel of Reason.

With the *Scienza della Legislazione,* law finally loses its historical and factual character, and becomes an ideology, which, as soon as it enters into the sphere of actual practice, will bring about a complete revolution in the lives of men. Looking at it through the historian's eyes, one sees only a welter of hopeless confusion, only a medley of laws set forth by the lawgivers of various nations, and at various times. But only reduce it all to a system, to a science, and you will see how simple it will prove to be, and how beneficent. "O Nature, simple and infallible, the more I study thy plan, the more I abhor the plans of men; the more I strive to follow thy ways, the more it delights me to turn my back on theirs."

We must start with sound definitions, and, by a concatenation of propositions, we shall arrive at a true notion of law, civil, criminal, political, and religious; at true definitions of education, of the family and of property. In the dim forest where "our barbarous forefathers" were content to dwell and have their being, "the Wise Lawgiver" will drive roads that will lead us straight to justice and to happiness. Princes shall hear his voice and obey his counsel: "To the ministers of truth, to the peace-loving philosophers, this sacred office belongs." Selfish interests shall yield to a love for all mankind; a sense of equity shall sweep away all wrongs; the documents of ages past shall be destroyed, together with all their commentaries and glosses; past decisions shall be invoked no more; litigants, advocates, judges—all shall become disciples of Natural Law, and the world shall win through to salvation. As he uttered these words, Gaetano Filangieri felt his heart burn within him; felt himself swept on by a vehement wave of passion. He preached and he catechized unweariedly. When he contemplated the errors of the past, he felt sick at heart, and of that he made no secret; but then, he is uplifted, and filled with joy, when he glimpses all the progress that the future has in store. And then it is not alone his mind that speaks, it is his heart also.

All the same, whence and wherefore all this disorder, this confusion in the sphere of law? It arose from the treachery of the lawgivers, from folly and selfishness, and all manner of shortcomings, in the faithless guardians of a sacred trust. Well, maybe; nevertheless this seems to have been spoken a little sweepingly. Montesquieu's greatness lay in his resolve to gain those lofty peaks whence he could look down and discern order in disorder, and all his life was one long upward climb towards those commanding heights. There is a hint of nobility about the way in which he enters into possession of his handsome landed estate and still is not content; how he wins a high reputation in his province, and still is not content; how he secures fame throughout the whole of literary Europe on account of his *Lettres Persanes*, and still is not content. So far from seeking repose, he sets forth anew on his unending quest. He has indeed hitched his waggon to a star. He works and works and works, heavens, how he works! He reads and reads and reads —what does he not read! Books of the richest, books of the most thankless kind; books that he loves, books that he finds "cold, dry, savourless, hard". He devours them all, "even, as the story tells us, Saturn swallowed stones". When the time was ripe, he came forth from his study, and, bidding farewell to his beloved Guyenne, his official labours and his country, he went away to study at first hand the working of the several constitutions and the various ways of men. After a while, he returned to France and to La Brède, where he set to work once more, reading and meditating, in order to master all that he had gained from his investigations. When he had got his material into order, when his ideas were thoroughly matured, he began to see, from his commanding heights, what others had only seen through a glass darkly. What stores of knowledge! what a rich understanding; what a measureless abundance of light; what a clear, instinctive, recognition of the subject to select for treatment, what skill in the treatment of it, and what care for style; a self-restraint that never allowed him to lose his bearings; a kind of hallowed egoism which held him immune from anything that might have diverted him from the aim he had in view; a bulwark against the passions, even against the affections, against the desire for vain things, against the lure of the *dolce far niente;* and, finally, the reward: "From here it is that we must look down upon the spectacle of human existence. . . ."

1748. Montesquieu, *L'Esprit des lois.*

Laws, in their widest sense, are the necessary relationships which spring from the nature of things.

He was not unaffected by the restless spirit of the age. Laws of the Romans, Laws of the Franks; Laws of Africa, Laws of Asia, Laws of the New World; Laws that thousands of years ago had governed the lives of men who were still in a state of barbarism, laws which dictate the decisions of the London courts, or the Paris Parliament. The mere thought of their number and diversity fills one with something like despair.

Then a dawning gleam came to light up his excogitations. A law, no matter how arbitrary it may seem, always implies a relationship of some kind. A law is related to the people for whom it is enacted, to the government, to the physical conditions of the country, to its climate, to the quality of the soil, to the mode of life, to the religion of the inhabitants, their wealth, their numbers, their trade, their manners and customs. Laws are mutually inter-related, they are related to the source whence they derive, to the aims and objects of the legislator.

How does this relationship come about? It arises from the nature of a being; it proceeds from a given being to the manifestations of his existence. Given a material world, laws exist adapted to its material nature. In the case of an angel, laws exist adapted to its angelic nature; in the case of an animal, laws exist appropriate to its animal nature. Even the Divine has its laws. God is related to the Universe as its creator and preserver. The laws by which he created it are the laws by which he preserves it. He acts in accordance with these laws because he knows them. He knows them because he made them; he made them because they are of a piece with his power and wisdom.

This connexion is in no way arbitrary; it proceeds from logic and reason. It is the outcome of a primary reason which existed before anything was made. Before intelligent beings actually existed, their existence was possible; relations with justice were therefore possible for them. Passing from the possible to the actual, those relations conformed to the reason which presupposed them. To say there is nothing either just or unjust save what positive laws require or forbid is tantamount to saying that until you drew this circle, its radii were not all equal. It is the same with all laws.

Let us look at those which concern mankind. Man is a physical being; consequently, as such, he is subject to the laws of Nature. But he is also a thinking being; he has a mind. He will therefore have laws appropriate to his intelligence, which is limited, often distorted by passion, a prey to ignorance and error. Such laws will be the laws of religion, which will call him back to his Creator, when he has gone astray from him; moral laws to recall him to his real self when he has misconceived it; political and civil laws to remind him of his duties to society.

With the question of the divine source of law, Montesquieu does not concern himself. He is not a theologian, but a political writer. If he examines the various religions of the world, it is but to assess how much the civil government benefited by them, regardless of whether they had their roots in Heaven or earth. He is aware that there are things in his book that are not to be regarded as wholly true, save from a purely human standpoint. But the insertion of this proviso, the mere fact that he went out of his way to enter this *caveat*, as well as the care he took to point out in the work itself the unhappy consequences that have invariably followed any encroachment by ecclesiastical authority on the temporal sphere—all this is a clear indication of what he had at the back of his mind. He was sanctioning the divorce between Natural Law, and God's Law.

At last he puts down the pen. His work is done. His investigations have guided him to a single solitary principle, the vital, the essential principle from which all the laws of the world proceed.

In practice, however, it was very different. When La Chalotais presented his case against the Jesuits before the Parliament of

Brittany, he declared that he would confront sixty-one institutions and the rules of the religious orders with the principles of Natural Law and afterwards with the actual laws, secular and divine, especially with those operating in France. But to the first-named he made no further reference throughout the whole of his discourse. When Morelly brought out his *Code de la Nature*, in order, he alleged, to comply with the demand of the whole of Europe, which had long been clamouring for an elementary treatise on Natural Law, all that Europe got was just one more literary dissertation. It might have been hoped, seeing all the books that had been written about the theory of law, that something useful, something adopted by the various European courts, something about inheritance say, or contracts, or fiscal matters, or delinquencies might have emerged. But neither Grotius, nor Pufendorf, nor the *Esprit des lois* quoted a single verdict, whether from Le Châtelet in Paris, or the London Old Bailey.[1]

However, beneath all this seething ferment of ideas, which had no visible practical effect, the demand for justice was gathering strength. The Cité, holding that the temporal powers were abusing their strength, were anxious to be able to point to some inalienable birthright belonging to each separate individual, and which of itself protected their rights. It desiderated something operative, something active. The truth is that ideas *were* having their effect on practice. Something practical *was* resulting. There were still countries in Europe where the fires of the Inquisition were blazing. If they were subsequently put out, who will deny that the philosophers played some part in bringing about so desirable a result?

The Slave Trade, which some excused as being a necessary sequel to conquest, an inevitable concomitant of colonization, or because it was advantageous to trade, or merely because it was the customary thing, would find no justification in Nature, which confers an equal dignity on all her children; or in reason, which does not admit that a difference in the colour of their skin should condemn a whole race to suffering and infamy. Thus began a trend of ideas which gradually brought about the abolition of slavery. An anti-slavery literature came into being which began to affect public opinion and this in turn influenced

[1]Voltaire, *Questions sur l'Encyclopédie*, Article *Lois, Esprit des lois.*

the ruling powers. There still linger on in our memory some passages from Chapter V of the fifteenth book of the *Esprit des lois*: "The people in question are black from head to foot and their noses are so flat that it is hardly possible to pity them. One can hardly imagine that God, who is so very wise a being, would have put a righteous soul into so completely black a body." Montesquieu continues, calling Christian charity to his aid: "It is impossible that we should regard such people as human, because, if we looked on them as human, people would begin to think that we ourselves were not Christians." His raillery is but suppressed indignation. "Small-minded folk exaggerate the injustice inflicted on the negroes, because, if it was anything like what they say, wouldn't it have occurred to Europe's rulers, who make so many useless agreements, that they might make a general one between them all to promote the exercise of pity and compassion?" These words of his did not bring the slave traffic at Tripoli to a sudden stop, but they did foreshadow the day when the slave-market would be shut down, the slave-dealers brought to justice, and the slaves themselves set free.

A belligerent group came into being at Milan. It consisted of a number of young men who had got it into their heads that their fathers' ideas were hopelessly reactionary, a notion which crops up, of course, with every fresh generation, but, in this case, the thing was more than a mere battle of words. They were out to *do*, not to talk, and, to make it clear that they meant business, they chose a challenging name for their party; they called themselves the Society *dei Pugni*, the Punch-hards. They started a review of their own, which they called *Il Caffè*, because the editors were supposed to meet and discuss in some imaginary café. The moving spirit of the party was one Pietro Verri, who included among his followers a loutish sort of fellow called Beccaria. This Cesare Beccaria had more time on his hands than he knew what to do with; his father being a leading citizen of the place. To look at him, you would have taken him for more of a loafer than he really was, the sort of individual who might well have spent a completely useless sort of life had it not been for the people he had about him, and for the prevailing temper of the times. Having a vague idea that he would like to figure in some big movement or other, he took to study, reading philosophy, particularly the writers who were the most provocative of ideas, the French philosophers. Their influence, that of his friends, and the general atmosphere of a city where law was much in evidence, roused him from his apathy. To begin with, he wrote on the currency, not yet having found his true line. At length he discovered it, and somewhere between his indolent youth and his barren old age, he produced a masterpiece, *Dei Delitti e delle Pene*, "On Crime and Punishment". The year was 1764.

He duly paid lip-service to the popular illusions of the time: How unfortunate, he said, it was that, from the very beginning, laws had not been based on reason. People were groaning under laws imposed by an ancient conquering race, that is to say, the Romans. The finishing touch was put on them by the arbitrary enactments of a ruler who, in the twelfth century, had his headquarters at Constantinople, and a further incrustation, arising from the obscurantism of the Middle Ages, was the result. The truth was that the whole of the existing structure required to be swept away and a new one set up in its place, one based on Natural Law.

Having delivered himself of that statement, Beccaria had the good sense to confine himself to a sphere with which he was peculiarly familiar, having been visitor to the prisons of Milan. He had thus frequently spoken with people under arrest, listened to what criminals had to say, and had been deeply moved by the various instances of injustice which had come to his notice. Irregularities in procedure, arbitrary judgments, the cruelty of the penal laws, so far, none of these things had been made the subject of a formal indictment. He was now going to see to it that they were. Laws were social in their nature, and social they should remain, in their application, as well as in their essence. Whatever their origin, they were nothing more nor less than the buttress of society. It followed that judgments should be delivered and penalties assessed, with nothing in mind but the welfare of society and in strict accordance with the social importance of the offence. For this purpose, the whole scale of penalties would have to be completely revised.

This being granted, it would be well to prevent people going wrong rather than to punish them after irreparable damage had been wrought. It was an error to treat an accused person, who was himself a member of the body-politic, as though he were a criminal *a priori.* He was one called upon by society to explain his conduct before a group of its selected representatives, who, for their part, should furnish him with full assurances of his moral freedom. Again, it was wrong to adjust the penalty to the intentions of the perpetrator, rather than to the harm actually inflicted. Finally, it was an error to mistake harshness or ferocity for justice. Harshness and ferocity, in the long run, never did anything but harm to the common weal. There was one method of criminal investigation that was peculiarly iniquitous, and that was the infliction of torture. As its application was carried out in secret, it had not even the advantage of being a deterrent, which, perhaps, is the real object of all punishment. If a criminal was strong enough to bear the pain, he might get off scot-free. If he was innocent, he might in his agony confess to a crime he had never committed. This was criminal folly, a crime in itself, and to be repudiated by any state with any pretensions to call itself civilized.

Beccaria's treatise on Crime and Punishment did not put an end to torture then and there, but its effect was that torture dropped out of future codes of criminal justice, and finally disappeared altogether. There was scarcely a line in his book which did not have an effect on the minds of the legislature, and so, in due course, on the law.

IV

MORALS

HERE was the great test, and it was freely acknowledged to be so. Just as we know a tree by the fruits thereof, so a philosophy is judged by the good that flows from it. Now that the Christian system had been definitely abandoned, something had to be found to take its place, something loftier and purer. Failing that, the whole scheme would turn out a fiasco.

As for the Stoic philosophy, Stoic morality, we had had enough of that. We respected Zeno, but we preferred Epicurus. Seneca, too, we admired, because he was opposed to despotism, but he was too austere a counsellor to be our guide to happiness. The worldly, fashionable code had no appeal for us either. In the precepts which Mme de Lambert addressed to her son and daughter, in Lord Chesterfield's advice to his son, and in hosts of other letters, treatises and so on, we got only a stale whiff of the seventeenth century. We did not want the "Gentleman" to guide us any more. He was out of date. His qualities were too lightly come by for us to envy them. A good conceit of oneself, easy circumstances, fashionable vices, such was his stock-in-trade. Virtue went for nothing in it; all the "Gentlemen" that ever lived were not worth one good man.

So much for the Gentleman. Now, what about the "Hero"? Of that greatly over-rated personage, too, we have had more than enough. He aggravates, he infuriates us. Make an Aunt Sally of him, we should never have brickbats enough to knock him over. He's got into people's hearts, and they still insist on making a sort of god of him. However, we've got to get rid of him somehow, and that will be one of our most urgent tasks. This much vaunted hero, so called, this puffed-up, reckless dare-devil, what is he but a destroyer, an infamous robber, a gilded scoundrel? He must always have a stage and an audience to show off to. He must be in the limelight, he must have his halo, but when you look into him you find that he's simply made of ambition; ambition the scourge of mankind. Let the ancients sing his praises as they will. We hold him in abhorrence and that abhorrence shall be passed on to our children, and our children's children for ever and ever. Let us cease to call great those troublesome and turbulent monarchs who spread havoc and destruction over the earth. Let us rather reserve the name for those who have earned renown by adding to the amenities and the charm of life. Those who ravage and lay waste the land—*they* are *your* heroes![1] Down with the statues of men like these, and, in their place, set up memorials of those princes who, reluctantly compelled to lead their armies forth to repel an aggressor, laid down their arms, the victory won, and, putting aside their laurels, went back to the ranks of the philosophers. Such a one was Sethos, whose story was told by the Abbé Terrasson. Destined for the Egyptian throne, then persecuted and banished from his country, Sethos spent his long years of exile in searching out unknown races whom he delivers from the cruellest persecutions and whose lawgiver he becomes. On his way back, he saves, by his bravery, a powerful republic from an enemy at its gates and craves for no reward save that the vanquished should be suffered to depart in peace, though their king, or tyrant, had attacked him. Back at last in his own country, he went out of his way to show kindness to those whom he had reason to look on as foes or rivals.[2] Sethos and his like show how true heroism differs from the false. Theirs is a peace-loving heroism, which should commend itself to every enlightened mind.

Never, to be sure, was there such a busy band of moralists as now; but not of the order that made the human heart their study. It was thought that all there was to know about the human heart was known already, and that there was nothing left to discover. They were moralistic theorizers, not psychologists. They aimed at laying down the principles of our moral conduct, to start with. What had to be done was to refashion the moral code, and to do so in the light of modern knowledge and ideas.

[1]Voltaire to Thiériot, 15th July, 1735.
[2]Abbé Terrasson, *Séthos,* 1731, Preface, xv–xvi.

Diderot summed up the general position with characteristic vigour. "Shall I give you the story of our troubles in a nutshell? Well; here it is. There was once upon a time a natural man inside whom an artificial man was somehow introduced. They were always squabbling, and kept it up all through their lives. Sometimes the natural man got the best of it, sometimes he was floored by the moral and artificial man. Whichever way the struggle went, the unhappy monstrosity was harassed, pummelled, tormented, tortured, in never-ending misery."[1] Put more briefly still, "morality in a good man is but another name for nature".[2]

"Let us look at nature in its earliest stages; our sensations are agreeable or the reverse; they give us pleasure or pain. From this experience we pass on to the abstract notion of harm or benefit. Impressions stamped at an early stage on the soul remain indelible; they torment the wrongdoer and console the upright, and they serve as an example to the legislator.[3] If we fall in with the obvious will of Nature, we shall see that she is kindly disposed, that her desire is to promote the well-being of mankind, and so, in this respect again, it behoves us to obey her law. We went wrong at the very beginning. We took it for granted that man was born wicked, or at least that that was the case after his original sin. This gave rise to a jaundiced moral system, wholly repressive in character. Far from taking this line, we should foster and encourage the instinct which prompts us to seek for happiness, and we should cultivate those mental attributes which help us to attain our goal. *Moral, oder Sittenlehere, oder Anweising zur Glückseligkeit*: Morals, or the Science thereof; or a Handbook of Happiness—such was the slogan of K. Fr. Bahrdt,[4] and in those words was implicit a total revolution.

The passions are a fact of nature; therefore it would be wrong to try to suppress them; and not only wrong, but impossible. The passions for us are what sap is in plants, they enable us to live. They are as necessary to the life of the soul as our appetites are to the life of the body. We can hardly say that hunger and thirst are not real. The passions, it was said, have a useful

[1]Diderot, *Supplément au voyage de Bougainville,* 1772.

[2]*Encyclopédie,* Article *Leibnizianisme.*

[3]Diderot, *Apologie de l'Abbé de Prades,* Œuvres, I, p. 470.

[4]Carl Friedrich Bahrdt, *Handbuch der Moral für den Bürgerstana.* Halle, 1790, p. 81.

mission to perform, and to prove it, a metaphor was pressed into service which was to do duty again and again, in book after book, with a few variations here and there; this was the gist of it: Just as a pilot dreads a dead calm and whistles for a breeze to get his vessel under way, even though the breeze may freshen to a gale, so do the passions swell the sails of the spirit. True, they may cause us to founder if we don't take care, but the thing is that, without them, we should never be able to sail at all. Morals, which control the passions, are the rudder, the compass and the chart which should enable a man to keep on the course that Nature sets him, the course that will bring him to Felicity. And that was not all. Pleasure itself must be given back its rights. Pleasure is a gift conferred on his creatures by the Supreme Being; in the hierarchy of sensations, it is the one we seek spontaneously, which tells us what to long for and what to shun. In its most potent form it is the sexual instinct, and as this is essentially connected with the reproduction of the species, it is obviously not incompatible with philosophy. "I am a very voluptuous sort of philosopher", remarked Voltaire of himself.

Further than that, Nature, being Reason, has established rational inter-relations between all things. The quality of goodness is the consciousness of these relationships and obedience thereto. Evil implies ignorance of these relations and the consequent failure to obey them. Crime, in its ultimate analysis, is always an error of judgment. The logicians push this idea very far indeed: If a man steals a horse, he steals it because he does not thoroughly realize that the horse belongs to someone else. If he had realized this more completely, he would not have stolen it.

Reason is the world's Great Law. The Supreme Being himself is subject to that Truth which is the theoretic basis of morality; so that morality does not proceed from him, the Supreme Being, but from a power higher still, from Eternal Reason. To conceive the exercise of an infinite power, must we not postulate possibilities independent of that power? To conceive the manifestation of a divine will, must we not postulate wills independent of the divine will? If that were not so, the divine will would have created itself, which is inconceivable. Similarly, if there were not a morality independent of the divinity, there could be no moral attributes appertaining to that divinity.

Nature empirical or rational: morality must be natural or nothing.

The consequences of these principles did not all take the same direction. But if we wanted to instance tendencies that ran parallel, we might mention two data at least that were regarded as established by the great majority of contemporary moralists.

First, the propriety, the lawfulness, of self-love. "There is no such thing as selfless love." "The strong affection for ourselves with which Nature inspires us, tells us our duties to body and soul."[1] "The desire for our own well-being, which is stronger than the desire for life itself, should be to morality what weight is in mechanics."[2] Or, to put it more prosaically, as Mme d'Epinay expressed it in a letter she wrote to the Abbé Galiani on the 29th September, 1769: "The chief thing is to look after number one, is it not?"

That is what observation tells us, and there is no denying it. It has the additional advantage of being within the reach of everyone. Neither Christianity nor Philosophy brought virtue to this earth, doubtless because the wrong reasons were appealed to for making it seem desirable. We have got to begin all over again, and what we have to appeal to, in order to win the co-operation of the multitude, must be something more general and easier to understand than the love of God, or the love of Wisdom, and that is the love of Self.[3]

Now let us be quite clear on this matter; there is no question of an unbridled display of utter selfishness. Reason must control the instinct which prompts us to pursue our own interests; it tells us that our happiness is not the happiness of brute beasts, from which our gifts of understanding sunder us; nor, on the other hand, is it the happiness of the angels, which is beyond our reach. It distinguishes between the various kinds of pleasure; it subordinates them to a law of moderation, and counsels us to abandon them as soon as they threaten to gain the

[1]Toussaint, *Les Mœurs,* 1748, I, 1.

[2]*Il Caffè,* 1764, semestre primo: *La fortuna dei libri.*

[3]Frederick II, *Essai sur l'amour-propre envisagé comme principe de morale,* 1770.

mastery over us. In short, it remains in control. "What is vice, and what is virtue? The former is, I think, no more than the excess, abuse, and misapplication of appetites, desires, and passions, natural and innocent, nay useful and necessary. The latter consists in the moderation and government, in the use and application of those appetites, desires and passions, according to the rules of reason, and therefore often in opposition to their own blind impulse."[1] At this point comes in the second statement, to mark the limits of the first: The pursuit of our own interests must do nothing to prejudice the interests of others. Thus there is no such thing as individual wellbeing apart from the wellbeing of the community.

The Sage

What, in your opinion, are the duties of man?

The Proselyte

To make himself happy. Whence follows the necessity of helping to make others happy, or, in other words, of being virtuous.[2]

Virtue stands for fellowship, sociability. The Baron d'Holbach has defined sociability in this sense of virtue: "Sociability in man is a natural sentiment, fortified by custom and fostered by reason. Nature, by making man a sensitive creature, endowed him at the same time with a love of pleasure and a dread of pain. Society is Nature's work because it is Nature that makes man a social being. . . . Man is sociable because he likes wellbeing and comfort, and is easy in his mind when he feels a sense of security. These feelings are natural; that is to say they flow naturally from the consciousness of a being whose object is self-preservation, who aims at living a happy life, and eagerly embraces the means of doing so. Everything tends to impress on man that the social life is good for him; custom draws him to it and he is unhappy when he feels that he is deprived of the support of his fellows. That is the real origin of sociability."[3] But it is probably d'Alembert who puts the matter most clearly when, in the fourth chapter of his *Éléments de philosophie*, he says:

[1]Bolingbroke, *Letters on the Study and Use of History,* 1752, Letter III.

[2]Diderot, *Introduction aux grands principes*. Œuvres, tome II, p. 85.

[3]D'Holbach, *De la politique naturelle,* 1772. Discours I, *De la sociabilité.*

"The science of morals is perhaps the most complete of all the sciences when we consider the truths of which it is composed, and the manner in which they are linked together. It all rests on one single and incontrovertible fact, and that is the need which men have one of another, and the reciprocal obligations which that need imposes. That much being granted, all the moral laws follow therefrom in orderly and ineluctable sequence. All questions that have to do with morals have a solution ready to hand in the heart of each one of us, a solution which our passions sometimes prevent us from acting upon, but which they never destroy. And the solution of each particular question leads, by one or more branches, to the parent stem, and that, of course, is our own self-interest, which is the basic principle of all moral obligations."

Are not the interests of the individual and the interests of the group sometimes incompatible? Never. At first sight it may seem that loyalty to society calls for renunciations, sacrifices, from the individual, but these always redound in the long run to the advantage of him who consents to them. The complete egoist, the man who thinks only of himself, would reap the suffering consequent upon his self-imposed isolation. The exchange is nicely balanced: to work for others is to work for oneself, and the obligation of each is the obligation of all.

But do not the accounts brought home by travellers and the records of history tell us of remarkable differences in ideas of morality, differences accounted for by differences of soil and climate? In the most distant parts of the earth, there are savages who devour the aged members of their tribe. The Spartans approved and encouraged theft, whereas in Athens, thieves were sent to work as slaves in the mines. In ancient Rome, a man was forbidden to marry his sister; among the Egyptians, he was allowed to marry his father's sister. To this, the reply was that there were differences in regard to the interpretation of certain values, but none at all in the idea of the permitted and the forbidden. Were there, here and there, any isolated cases that withstood the law of general interest which was present to every mind, engraven on every heart?

B—*What is natural law?*
A—*The instinct which gives us a feeling for justice.*

B—*What do you call just and unjust?*

A—*What seems so to the universe as a whole.*[1]

So here again, and not without some trouble, universal fact linked up with universal reason. In short, morality was preparing to become an "experimental science", or "natural psychology". Thereafter, everything became simple, everything was plain. Henceforth, all that had to be done was to obey a few elementary formulas: Do not unto others what you would not have others do to you. Do to others what you would have others do to you. Love God. Be just. Then will the wicked disappear, or very nearly. The only evil-doers left will be a few stubborn ones, a few incorrigibles. Since the good and the wise would be rewarded; since they would be honoured in public demonstrations, they would grow daily more numerous and the whole world would be happy.

The great thing was to win over the general public to the new way of thinking. They were to be acted upon by journals dealing with moral questions, whose circulation would gain ground from day to day; by books which should not be too recondite but such as to appeal to people in general. On the borders of China stretches the wide land of Tibet which is under the spiritual authority of the Grand Lama. To the Grand Lama, the Emperor of China sent an envoy, in the person of an illustrious scholar. The latter, after a sojourn of six months, returned to Peking, bringing with him all manner of curios and treasures, among them a manuscript dating back to the remotest antiquity. It was a moral treatise, which had never been translated because it was written in the language of the ancient Gymnosophists or Brahmins. The learned doctor translated it into Chinese, and from the Chinese it was done into English, to the great profit of Europe, where it rapidly began to circulate.[2] Practical Guide to Wisdom: First, learn all about man, and how far his powers extend; then go on to enquire what personal virtues are capable of bringing real happiness, and what social virtues tend to the same end. By a marvellous coincidence, due allowance being

[1]Voltaire, *Dialogues philosophiques, l'ABC,* 1768. *Quatrième entretien, De la loi naturelle et de la curiosité.*

[2]Dodsley, *The Œconomy of human life, translated from an Indian Manuscript, written by an Ancient Bramin,* Dublin, 1741.

made for a certain difference in phraseology, the counsels enunciated by the Brahmins, or Gymnosophists, long before Christianity appeared on earth, bore a marked resemblance to those advocated by the philosophers of the eighteenth century.

Now catechisms—Why not have philosophy-catechisms for young people? No bad thing to take a leaf out of your opponent's book. If you don't capture the rising generation, you capture nothing at all. So, little catechisms made their appearance, dealing not with Faith this time, but with Reason and Experience. D'Alembert would have liked to see one giving the elements of his philosophy for the use of children. Grimm was not always satisfied with providing his royal clients with stories from the Republic of Letters. Sometimes he had ideas, and he liked to develop them in his *Correspondance littéraire*. Then he would put them aside for a while, taking them up again and toying with them a little later on. He thought things out: Man differs from the animals in his perfectibility. Horses and bears today are just like the horses and bears of three thousand years ago; no better and no worse. Man's progress along the road to perfection is so slow because he is constantly letting himself be drawn away from nature, returning to it again after bitter experience, when the best of his powers have been wasted. It is easy to see why he goes wrong. For one thing, it is a sheer outrage on common sense to teach little children the elements of the Christian religion. Beyond doubt it is in this universal practice that we must look for an explanation of the influence exerted on men's minds by ideas of the most absurd, and often the most dangerous character. In this way, whole nations are steeped in folly. The catechism of humanity should come before the catechism of religion, for the simple reason that one should be a man and a citizen before being a Christian. The first of these catechisms would instruct the young in their rights and duties as members of the human race, the second in their rights and duties as members of society, and in the laws and government of the country to which they belong. Montesquieu would have been the right man for the second; Socrates himself would not have been too great for the first. So saying, Grimm has a try at the task himself. Fifteen short paragraphs seemed to him enough for his *Essai d'un catéchisme pour les enfants* (1755).

Later on, Saint-Lambert also tried his hand, and made a better job of it than Grimm. His *Catéchisme universel* for children of twelve or thirteen contains in essence all the principles of the contemporary moral code:

> Question: *What is man?*
> Answer: *A being possessed of feelings and understanding.*
> Q.: *That being so, what should he do?*
> A.: *Pursue pleasure and eschew pain.*
> Q.: *This desire to obtain pleasure and avoid pain, is this not, in man, what we call self-love?*
> A.: *It is the necessary effect thereof.*
> Q.: *Does self-love exist in all men alike?*
> A.: *It does, because all men aim at self-preservation and at attaining happiness.*
> Q.: *What do you understand by happiness?*
> A.: *A continuous state in which we experience more pleasure than pain.*
> Q.: *What must we do to attain this state?*
> A.: *Cultivate our reason and act in accordance therewith.*
> Q.: *What is reason?*
> A.: *The knowledge of the truths that conduce to our well-being.*
> Q.: *Does not self-love always lead us to discover those truths and to act in accordance with them?*
> A.: *No, because all men do not know how self-love should be practised.*
> Q.: *What do you mean by that?*
> A.: *I mean that some men love themselves rightly and others wrongly.*
> Q.: *Who are those who love themselves aright?*
> A.: *Those who seek to know one another and who do not separate their own happiness from the happiness of others. . . .*

A new morality must needs have new virtues: there were three of them.

Tolerance.—This, to begin with, had been nothing more than a business rule, observed by people engaged in trade. A Turk's money, or an Arab's, has no particular smell about it; nor has a Christian's. Protestants had agitated for it. Protestantism held sway over millions of souls, whole nations adhered to it, and the Catholics would certainly have to display toleration. Bossuet, nevertheless, would have none of it. It was sheer weakness, the giving up of all attempts to save souls that had fallen into error; it was moral cowardice, a poison that was spreading all over Christendom. However, in 1689, Locke had put the stamp of nobility on toleration. It was now gaining ground, and gaining respect. It was also gaining a variety of meanings. It meant intelligence, because it implied an understanding capable of entering into the minds of others. It also meant realizing our own shortcomings. We are all weak, all liable to error; let us then make allowances one for another. It was a social safeguard, because without it men would become like wolves again. It was a first step to love, and something to pray for. A great change came over the view of its constituent elements. Instead of being looked upon as an act of condescension, it became a realization of the numerous different elements which go to the making of an idea, of the different motives which prompt us to act as we do, and a recognition of the degree of truth or justice which may inhere in an opinion we do not share, in a course of action of which we disapprove. When it made a comparison it was not for the purpose of discovering defects but of eliciting virtues.[1] Steadily it gained ground, and made visible progress. Soon, it would spread all over the world; at all events that was what was hoped for. "My friends, when we proclaimed toleration, in some of our seats of learning, and in all our societies, we did a service to nature, we reinstated humanity in its rights, and today there is not one ex-Jesuit or ex-Jansenist who dares to confess his intolerance."[2] After all its toils and prolonged endeavours it scored victories; it set to rights some of life's injustices. In 1781, Joseph II was to issue his Toleration Edict in favour of the Lutherans; in 1787, Louis XVI would reinstate the Calvinists in their civil rights.

Beneficence.—This was something newer still. It was the Abbé de Saint Pierre who, in the year 1725, gave it its name. He considered that the word Charity had had some of the bloom rubbed off it, and that it meant precious little. He wanted a new word, and he coined one. "Ever since I came to see that Christians did not know what the word charity really meant, since they persecuted their opponents, and that heretics claimed

[1]Lessing, *Nathan der Weise,* 1779.

[2]Voltaire, article *Tolérance,* in the *Dictionnaire philosophique* and *Questions sur l'Encyclopédie.*

that they practised charity when they persecuted other heretics, or Catholics themselves. . . . I have been looking out for a word which would clearly remind us that it was our duty to do good to others, and I have found nothing that better conveys what I have in mind than the word beneficence.[1] People may do as they like about using it. I find it clear and unequivocal."

Humanity.—This, too, was a new virtue, for now it was that it attained the plenitude of its significance. It was a virtue peculiarly adapted to the eighteenth-century moralists because it stressed that human condition from which they thought they always had to start, to which they must always return, and which, in consequence, was for them, the all in all.

[1]For the history of the word, see *Dictionnaire de Trévoux,* 1772, article *Bienfaisance.*

V

GOVERNMENT

WHENCE did Machiavelli get the idea that we were compounded of such sorry stuff? Out on this Machiavelli fellow! To the flames with that *Prince* of his! A pernicious book, if ever there was one, inspired throughout with the false maxim that all government should be determined by reasons of State. Every chapter oozes poison. If Europe did not throw overboard these Machiavellian notions, these ravings of a disordered mind, so much the worse for Europe.

But this Florentine quill-driver, wretched fellow, was not the only one to go off the lines. Among the heap of balderdash piled up in the course of the ages, the old ideas about politics are particularly absurd. "The whole world, my dear Aristias, is one huge map of political blunders."[1] Those who had a share in the government, and, more especially, those who had none; the nobility, who were anxious to recover their *raison d'être*; the parliament-men of France; the jurists of Spain; Italian theorizers; English coffee-house philosophers; the pundits of the Club de l'Entresol; ecclesiastics called on to defend, or to denounce, Rome's attitude to matters temporal; writers, historians who were thinking of the morrow as they gazed on the past; even the humble folk in certain towns, if Holberg[2] is to be believed, and if there is any truth in the caricature he has given us showing a tinsmith, who, with his mates the dyer, the wigmaker and the dominie, founded a club which was to reform Europe and make it all like Hamburg—all plunged headlong into discussions about the theory of politics, and to such effect that at

[1]Mably, *Entretiens de Phocion,* 1763, *Troisième Entretien.*

[2]J. Holberg, *Den Politiske Kandestöber.* In *Comédies,* vol. I, Copenhagen, 1824. French trans. *Théâtre Européen, Théâtre danois et suédois,* 1835 and 1891.

last the rulers themselves, catching the infection, busied themselves with reforms, were it but to strengthen the foundations of their own power.

Politics were to be practically synonymous with morality. Virtue was to be their alpha and their omega. There was to be nothing secret about it all; everything was going to be open and above-board. Mutual trust and confidence were to reign between the king and his subjects, between nation and nation. There were not to be two separate codes, one for the ruling class, another for the ruled, but one, and one only, which should be binding on all alike. Prosperity would be the sure reward of a republic's merits; adversity, of its vices. "If your neighbour gains possession of a town, or a province", says Phocion to Aristias, "go you and acquire a new virtue, and you will be mightier than he." Chaos, in this sphere too, would be changed into a science. From Natural Law, which preceded any other sort of law, would flow a few clear, simple rules of universal application.

Ardour, candour, naïveté; magnificent ignorance of the necessities by which the statesman is bound. Soaring flights of eloquence; more and more, bolder and bolder, flow the promises, but nothing real, nothing tangible. The tide is in flood after a long ebb. Add to this an apostolic fervour; enthusiasm that spreads like a contagion, and a ceaseless advance from the abstract to the practical, and finally a fresh drive towards humane government.

The idea of a primitive contract grew fainter, but it did not disappear: one day, weary of enduring the ills of anarchy, individual man had sacrificed a minor portion of his rights in order to set up a ruling power, which power, however, was never anything other than a trust, and the rights thus conferred might be withdrawn if the trustee failed to act in accordance with his obligations.

In the earliest times it was quite possible that the contract was a tacit one; but one which might very well have been set down in writing as soon as civilization provided the means; perhaps a contract which after all must rest in the limbo of ideas, since its practical realization would not be easy to imagine. It would be difficult to picture a number of men, realizing their weakness and their needs, assembling one day on a vast open space and choosing, then and there, the most powerful of their number to be their leader. Be that as it may, and however it came about, the contract was a reality, the contract was there. Such was the view of the majority. "Though society had not its formal beginning from any convention of individuals, actuated by their wants and their fears; yet it is the *sense* of their weakness and imperfection that keeps mankind together; that demonstrates the necessity of this union; and that therefore is the solid and natural foundation, as well as the cement of civil society. And this is what we mean by the original contract of society."[1]

But as the concept of Nature grew in power and extent, so did the desire for political liberty increase, till it became at length one of the dominant notes or features of the age. Inasmuch as no one had been empowered by Nature to lord it over his fellows, freedom was a man's inalienable birthright, a thing engraven on every heart. How good it was to reflect that this freedom was complete and sovereign. Even the restrictions imposed by living in community, even obedience to the law and the slight measure of constraint which the State required—all this was but a voluntary concession freely agreed to, a concession which was in principle nothing but a token of a self-disciplined independence. The nation of the Féliciens was a free and sovereign state, governed solely by laws of their own making.[2] "Every age has its dominant idea; that of our age seems to be Liberty."[3]

The idea of Equality, like a river swollen with many tributaries, was endeavouring to make its way. One ally it had, and that was the instinctive revolt, old as the world itself, against the unjust encroachments of privilege. Equality was painted in glowing colours by visionaries who pictured it as reigning in the blissful times of the Golden Age, or in some Utopia, or in those lands on whose shores only imaginary travellers are privileged to set foot. Some there were who thought they saw it rising again in the New World, in Paraguay, when the Jesuits set apart a tract of land for all the Indians of the *pueblo* to sow and reap; a collective farm, in fact. Equality was invoked to justify the growing part played by women in the social scheme. For both

[1]W. Blackstone, *Commentaries on the Laws of England*, 1765–1769.

[2]*L'heureuse nation*, or *Relation du gouvernement des Féliciens, peuple souverainement libre sous l'Empire absolu de ses lois*, 1792. (Par Lemercier de la Rivière.)

[3]Diderot to Princess Dashoff, 3rd April, 1771.

sexes, equal rights and equal duties. Then, if you liked, you could derive the principle of equality from the natural world. That was precisely what Helvetius did—and great was the scandal he aroused when he set out to prove that at the time of their birth there was no difference between one man and another. It was education, and education alone, that put a different stamp on the various representatives of the species, who, to begin with, were all equal. The idea also sprang from a deeper source, from the basic tendency of the times. Jeremy Bentham, in the wake of several others, crystallized it in the famous phrase, "The greatest happiness of the greatest number". Happiness, and, with it, the administration of public affairs, on which it largely depended, and which henceforth should not be regarded as the prerogative of a select few. Everybody had a right to be happy.

Nevertheless, the idea was not so alluring when it came to be put into practice. The ruling powers were ready enough to admit the principle when it was a matter of levying taxes; ready enough to admit the equality of clergy and nobility in relation to the throne when it was a matter of maintaining or strengthening the royal prerogative; public servants and officials were all on a level when it was a case of getting more work out of them, but when the idea looked as if it were going to imperil their own authority, they, the rulers, strenuously opposed it.

The principle lost something of its force because it at once found itself confronted with a limitation. Political equality—ah, yes; well and good; but social equality? Oh, no; that would never do! Many were the arguments adduced to show that social equality was impracticable, and, worse still, illogical. There could be no such thing as equality, in the strict mathematical sense, among men. That being the case, what was it that our interests and our reason alike demanded? Why, that in order to provide for our mutual happiness, we should rest content with a moral equality, which consists in maintaining everyone in the enjoyment of his rights, in his station, whether inherited or acquired, in his estate, in his home. It was, according to d'Alembert, the height of absurdity to accuse philosophers —at any rate those who were worthy of the name—of preaching equality, for equality is a delusion. Nature, according to the Baron d'Holbach, establishes a necessary and legitimate inequality among its creatures, an inequality based on the immutable aim of

Society, that aim being its own preservation and well-being. Security, according to Filangieri, was intimately bound up with happiness. *Conservazione e tranquillità* are the two words he puts down together in his list of things necessary for perfection, for the ideal. The good man and the rogue cannot be equals; neither can the man of brains and the fool, the brave man and the coward. Men have their moral inequalities, just as they have physical ones, young and old, active and infirm. It would be foolish to attempt to equalize the classes; suffice it that men should be equal before the law and that no privileges should attach to birth. That is the only proper equality.[1]

Some alarm was felt among the conservatives when it became evident that it was no Salentum people had in mind, but Paris or Berlin. Just as from the scientific point of view the world was one vast collection of things, each animal, each plant, each stone occupying its allotted place in a strictly graduated scale of things, which only a mighty cataclysm could conceivably upset, so it appeared that it was only the fixed state of the various classes that ensured what was called the permanence of society. The classes were looked upon as the steps of a ladder, the squares on a chess-board. They kept their place, and anyone who attempted to disturb them would be defying the will of Heaven and impairing the happiness of mankind. Let us take a glance at Voltaire's line of argument, as set forth in the *Dictionnaire philosophique* under the heading, *Égalité*. Yes, all men enjoying the faculties proper to their nature are equal; they are equal when they perform their animal functions and when they exercise their understanding. But they have wants. In order to supply them some degree of organization is called for; for this purpose they subordinate themselves to one another. "It is inevitable, in this imperfect world of ours, that men living in society should be divided into two classes; one, the wealthy, who are the rulers; the other, the poor, who obey. These two main classes are divided into a number of others which themselves are differentiated from one another in various ways."

The fence that could not be got over was property: *the law of*

[1]D'Alembert to Frederick II, 8th June, 1770; Baron d'Holbach, *La politique naturelle,* 1773, paragraph XXXII; Pietro Verri, *Modo di terminare le dispute,* definition of the word *Aquaglianza*; Gaetano Filangieri, *La scienza della Legislazione,* 1783, Book I.

property necessarily excludes equality.[1] True, some bold spirits, riding for a fall, displayed amazement at the sacrosanct character which still invested it. They were indignant at the proposal to change the political state, while leaving the social state unaltered, and foretold that the outcome of it all would be "a terrible and useless revolution."[2] True, that in 1755 Morelly, in his *Code de la Nature*, set forth the principles, and gave a detailed programme, of this social revolution: This ruthless law of property is the mother of all the crimes which inundate the world; it must be done away with. Therefore: "(I) Nothing shall belong to anyone individually as his sole property, except such things as he puts to his personal use, whether for his needs, his pleasure, or his daily work. (II) Every citizen shall be regarded as a public person in that he is to be maintained, that is to say kept and employed, at the public expense. (III) Every citizen shall contribute his share to the common weal, according to his strength, his abilities and his age; and his needs will be estimated accordingly, in conformity with the laws of distribution." Thus it will be all over with that monstrous giant in whose honour so many altars have been raised the world over. It seems as if its feet reached down to the lowest depths and rested on a heap of bones and corpses; it had a thousand heads and countless arms whereof the hands lay hold, some of fragile vessels filled with sands or vapours, others of crowns and sceptres. On its breast is written this one word, several times repeated, *Encore*.[3] It will die, this wicked giant, for men, coming back to Nature once again, will see there is but one sole law, the law of fellowship; one sole vice, greed; one sole stronghold of evil, property. And further it is true that a little later on, in 1776, Mably, in his treatise *de la Législation*, exhorts us to adopt "that happy community of property" which will be the remedy for all the ills that issued from Pandora's box. Equality should be the corner stone of private, as it is of social life, but that it ceases to be when property gets a foothold. "I have no hesitation in regarding this ill-omened property system as the source and origin of the inequality in wealth and social conditions and, therefore, of all

[1]Lemercier de la Rivière, *L'ordre naturel et essentiel des sociétés politiques,* 1767.

[2]Dom Deschamps, *Le vrai système, ou le mot de l'énigme,* published by Jean Thomas and F. Venturi, 1939.

[3]*Naufrage des Iles flottantes, ou Basiliade du célèbre Pilpaï, poème héroïque traduit de l'indien par Mr. M.,* 1753 (attributed to Morelly).

the ills that are." "Do you know the fountain-head of all the ills that afflict mankind? Property!"

And it is also true that in England as well there were some faint tendencies in the same direction. In 1775, one Thomas Spence, a second-hand bookseller by trade, read, before the members of the Philosophical Society, a paper entitled *The Real Rights of Man.* This marked the beginning of an adventurous and revolutionary career which lasted until 1814. His aim was to reorganize society on a new basis, making each parish a nuclear cell or unit of egalitarianism. In 1780, William Ogilvie, professor of Latin and Greek, humanist and numismatist, came out with *An Essay on the Right of Property in Land.* In it he gave a philosophic account of the principles of an agrarian law designed to give every individual a share in the soil. Still, with these exceptions, few in number, vague and tentative in substance, early forerunners of the Communism to come, the eighteenth century gave, generally speaking, emphatic expression to its belief in the moral right to possess property. Under natural conditions, man is necessary to man; man must needs have associates; he makes a pact with society; society guarantees his wellbeing; he guarantees society its permanence. And permanence demands inequality, which prevails, and will always prevail, among men. "Never let us exclaim against inequality, which was always necessary, and is the indispensable condition of our happiness."[1] So much for property in general. And now for landed property in particular, as looked at by the physiocrats. At first, there was one universal society, but as men continued to multiply, the free and spontaneous fruits of the earth became insufficient to support them and they were compelled to become tillers of the soil. From the obligation to cultivate the land came the obligation to share it, and thus it was that property first came into being.[2]

The thing is well and firmly established, do not let us meddle with it, whether it be capital, chattels or land that is in question. Let us accept the resulting inequality, let us not tamper with the foundations of the edifice that shelters us, lest it come tumbling about our ears. Leave those egalitarian ideas to the day-dreamers. Let us cherish liberty, for that *is* within our reach, and cherish it

[1]D'Holbach, *op. cit.*

[2]Lemercier de la Rivière, *op. cit.*

with an ardour all the greater so that we may be able to concentrate all our efforts on obtaining it.

We were to be free to think what we liked, and to say what we liked, in speech or in writing; free to choose our religion according to our conscience—Catholic, Protestant, Buddhist, Moslem, or what you will. Judges would treat the guilty with complete impartiality; all alike, nobles or commoners, rich or poor. No matter who he was, a man's personal dignity was duly protected. A man should be free to go where he wanted, to stop at home or to go abroad, and the latter without let or hindrance. Freedom of the seas, freedom of trade and industry—all these various freedoms were merged harmoniously in a single whole—the Liberal State.

Shame upon despots and despotism! As a direct attack was not feasible, they vented their indignation on antiquity. Thomas Gordon, that fire-eater, set the example in his historical, critical and political dissertations on Tacitus, in which he thundered anathema at Julius Caesar, Augustus, the wicked emperors, against everyone, in fact, who had robbed the people of their sacred birthright, Liberty. The oriental despots came in for their condemnation—all of them arbitrary, absolute and steeped in evil; the tyrants of Turkey, Mongolia, Japan and Persia. One might go to any lengths one liked in vilifying these eastern despotisms: there was not a hint of anything like honour, greatness or glory about them; not so much as a spark of magnanimity. Their sole weapon was fear. Knowledge was a dangerous thing, emulation a curse, talent of any kind was smothered. The ruler, the chief prisoner in his own palace, became a bigger imbecile every day in his seraglio, delegating his functions to his vizir so that he might be free to wallow in his stupid passions. Vice triumphed, the country was ruined and became like a desert. Yes; despotism spelt death.

Well, then, what was to be put in its place? Republic, oligarchy, monarchy? Whatever it might seem, the choice was not really a matter of such terrible importance. Each had its advantages; and each its drawbacks. The best republic was one which, by reason of its stable laws and uniform government, was most like a good monarchy. The best monarchy was one in which power was no more arbitrary than it was in a republic. Wieland's Agathon, having had experience of the different nations of which Greece consisted, had no liking for the sort of democracy which was really a tyranny in disguise, nor for an aristocracy whose power depended on the complete subjection of the people. Nor did he care for the kind of mixture for which the political alchemists who made it claimed that it was a most satisfactory compound of the most contradictory elements. On the whole he favoured a monarchy. He considered it unlikely that there would be a succession of bad kings, and one good one would be enough to repair all the damage of his predecessors. Such was the prevailing view of the matter. However, a complimentary bow was vouchsafed to the republican system, concerning which it was said that its natural climate was antiquity, and that it was eminently adapted to smaller states. That said, the vote went for a monarchy, for which the general run of people still had a warm spot in their hearts.

The great thing was that a government should be so constituted that no one of its elements should dominate the rest. It did not signify what form of government it was so long as a proper balance prevented the authorities from abusing their powers, and the people from defying them. It should be a machine so well-contrived that the brakes went on automatically the moment one of its parts looked like getting out of hand; the controls coming into operation the moment danger threatened. Thus a modicum of authority was dispensed to those who had never before had any—to the subjects; and a great deal more than a modicum was withdrawn from those who had hitherto had a lot of it—from the kings. These latter were especially mistrusted because of their readiness to encroach upon and abuse the rights of others, and because they were always prone to acts of violence. For these reasons they were bereft of all but the shadow of their former might, and reduced to the level of overseers. They were judged fittingly to have discharged their office if, instead of governing others, they so comported themselves as to create the least possible need for others to govern *them*. Adjudicating between the different departments of State, but themselves adjudicated upon whenever they came into conflict with one or other of those departments, they had to surrender the Sword and the Scales of Justice. All that remained to them was the Sceptre, which their fellow-citizens had condescended to leave in their hands, by way of a final *solatium*.

Now there was in the world a liberal State which held its own, which flourished and which, at a stroke, had attained to prosperity and power, and that was England. Thus England came to be regarded as the ideal of States. How admirable, it was said, was her constitution, with its provision for the separation of the executive, the legislative and the judicial branches of the government. England was of the same opinion. Some wealthy Maecenas or other founded a chair of Civil Law at Oxford so that a certain learned jurist, William Blackstone by name, might expound, in the light of reason and of history, what an excellent constitution that of his country was. This view of the matter was entertained by Europe as a whole. People who visited the island returned home full of its political merits, such men as Béat de Muralt, the Abbé Prévost, the Abbé Leblanc, Voltaire; nor must we forget the Genevan advocate, M. de Lorme, who wrote a whole volume so that Europe should be fully informed about this unrivalled constitution: Liberty, which, on the Continent, was a dream rather than a reality, had made its home on the shores of the Atlantic Ocean, and it was there that she had raised her citadel. Even the glories of early Rome grew pale in comparison with hers. London was putting Rome in the shade. Thanks to England, Liberty had revealed her secret to mankind. Montesquieu fixed for all time this fateful moment in the history of ideas. Everybody is familiar with the passage in the *Esprit des lois* in which he demonstrated that the best form of government was that which offered the maximum of freedom and the maximum of security, in which the powers of the several departments mutually limited and controlled one another. He held up England as the model of such a State, England which was the very mirror of liberty, and explained how the marvellous virtues of the English Constitution reacting in their turn on the nation that had created it, produced men of strong character and steadfast purpose, of alert, enquiring, vigilant minds, passionate and indomitable in spirit, whose qualities had won them the sovereignty of the seas, the leadership in trade and commerce and endowed them with originality of mind and a virile perfection in the sphere of arts and letters.

A State is a moral entity. Just as one individual finds himself in contact with other individuals with whom he not only has to bear, as with people possessed of rights as valid as his own, but whom he must regard as necessary to him, so also the State finds itself in the midst of other States with which it must needs establish such relations as are indicated by a due application of Natural Law. The rules which have guided foreign relations in the past, and which claim to guide them still, are obsolete; no religious system, such as Christianity; no traditional idea, such as that of an Empire gathering a whole group of European nations beneath its aegis; no separate grouping of nations between two great rival houses; no fine dream such as that of one great and universal monarchy, can take the place of the principles that have now at last been brought to light. "The several nations being made up of men who are free by nature and who, before the establishment of civil Societies, dwelt together under natural conditions, these same nations, or sovereign states, should be regarded as so many free individuals dwelling one with another under natural conditions."[1]

Natural Law, then, postulates a Society of Nations, larger than any regional groups, but not differing from them in kind. This major Society rests on a single, uniform pact; its members have united together for their mutual advantage and profit, and are therefore bound to observe the said pact. Nations who broke it would merely be bringing disaster on themselves. People living in a village, a town, or a province have rights and duties in respect of their neighbours. So also have they rights and duties in respect of the inhabitants of Europe, and of the world as a whole; for "the Universal Society of the human race being a thing of nature, that is to say a necessary consequence of the nature of man, all men, whatever their condition, are bound to foster it and to carry out the duties which it imposes on them. They cannot evade this obligation by forming a separate association of their own. When, then, they unite in a group to form a State, a nation apart, they may quite properly enter into engagements in respect to that group and its members, but this in no way dispenses them from discharging their obligations in regard to mankind as a whole."[2]

To be sure, the coming into being of the different nations,

[1]Emmerich de Vattel, *Le Droit des gens, ou Principes de la loi naturelle appliquée aux affaires des nations et des souverains,* 1768, Préliminaires.

[2]*Ibid.*

involving the creation of new and conflicting interests, had brought about clashes far graver than those which had arisen between separate individuals; it had brought about war, unending war. A river of blood flowed all across the great page of history. And the more powerful and determined any one of these groups became, the more readily it resorted to force to impose its will; hence wars of religion, which had flung the nations of Europe at each other's throats, one by one, or all together; wars of conquest, that had set Europe against Asia and against Africa as well. The thought of all these endless massacres filled one's heart with sadness, loathing and despair.

However, the evil was not incurable; and it was particularly fitting that the enlightened age should undertake to mitigate, to diminish and finally to banish it altogether from the face of the earth. War, like every other evil, was the outcome of error; once that error was removed, war would automatically disappear, or nearly so. The various nations would have a truer idea of their own interests. They now had a better grasp of things, traced effects back to their real cause, and had got a clear idea of the origin of their age-long enmity. Never again would they be led astray by the prejudices which had armed brother against brother. The dawn of universal peace was at hand.

Leibniz was an old and tired man when he read the *Projet pour rendre la paix perpétuelle en Europe*, "The Plan for bringing about lasting peace in Europe," by the Abbé de Saint Pierre.[1]

A lasting peace in Europe! That was what he himself had striven for; that was one of his cherished but ineffectual dreams. The Abbé's scheme was not so far removed from his own ideas. From his youth onward he had devoted his attention to law, and particularly to international law. Well, then, how stood the matter? The fact was that what was wanting was the will; if only mankind had the will, they could free themselves from a multitude of ills. But what sovereign, what minister even, had ever condescended to hear what he had to say? The aim of bringing the Spanish kingdom under the royal house of France had meant fifty years of war; it looked as if the aim of getting it back again was going to account for fifty more. All previous

[1]*Œuvres* de Leibniz, Édition Foucher de Careil, 1862. Tome IV: *Observations sur le projet d'une paix perpétuelle de M. l'abbé de Saint Pierre, revu d'après la manuscrit de la bibliothèque royale de Hanovre.*

attempts had failed, his own included. At one time, a system of international law had been agreed upon among the countries of Latin Christendom, and the lawyers had based their arguments upon it. The Popes were regarded as the spiritual, the Emperors as the temporal, heads of the Christian world. But then came the Reformation, and completely changed the face of things. An irreparable rift had resulted. Then again the lack of unity within the Empire was due, not to the Emperor's having too much power, it was due to his having too little. Leibniz, whose death was drawing near, came to the conclusion that some sinister fate was always interposing between man and the attainment of his happiness.

But the Abbé de Saint Pierre did not lose heart. Right up to the day of his death in 1743, he pursued his great design.[1] With a mind beset by the cruelties, the massacres, the raging fires, the deeds of violence for which war is answerable, grieving at the devastation which weighed so heavily on the countries of Europe, he set himself to try and find out whether the establishment of lasting peace was, after all, a thing so utterly out of the question. What of a pact, which would be but the everlasting covenant in modern form, if certain conditions were fulfilled? These are the conditions: There shall be maintained from now onwards a permanent Union between the sovereigns of Europe, including the Czar, the Grand Turk and the Berber chiefs. The main function of the Union shall be to preserve order and tranquillity. Each State shall retain its sovereign rights, and the Union's sole function shall be to settle any disputes that may arise between them. No territory within the Union shall suffer dismemberment. No one prince shall rule over two States. The sovereigns, both those who through their plenipotentiaries now signify their adherence to the Union, as well as those who sign hereafter, shall be deemed, by virtue of the said signatures, to have renounced, for themselves and their successors, all claims they might believe themselves to have, against any of the other contracting States. No members of the Union shall enter into any treaty among themselves, save with the consent of a majority of three-fourths of the total voting strength of the Union, and then only on

[1]Abbé de Saint Pierre, *Mémoire pour rendre la paix perpétuelle en Europe,* Cologne, 1712. *Projet pour rendre la paix perpétuelle en Europe,* Utrecht, 1713. *Projet de paix perpétuel entre les Souverains chrétiens,* Utrecht, 1717.

condition that it is concluded in the city of Peace; and thereafter, the Union shall hold itself responsible for ensuring that the obligations mutually undertaken are duly carried out. Those who fail to fulfil their obligations shall be declared enemies of the Union. The city of Peace shall be free and neutral, whether it be Utrecht, or Geneva, or Cologne, or Aix-la-Chapelle. The enemies of the Union, if there remain any such when all attempts at mediation or conciliation, and all orders of the Court of Arbitration, have proved ineffective, shall be dealt with by a force composed of troops of the different nations serving under the command of a leader appointed by a majority of votes. No one State shall keep a larger body of troops under arms than any other State, the number of troops to be so maintained shall be duly determined. Thus did the Abbé de Saint Pierre make provision for the future, even considering such details as the selection and transport of the plenipotentiaries, rules of procedure for the assembly, office administration, the amount of the contribution to be demanded of each member State.

Quite out of date were those formal approaches, those learned epistles composed with scholarly care; gone the days of suggestion, of caution and hesitation; the days when things were left for time to mature. Abandoned now were the tactics which Leibniz had adopted for bringing about lasting peace and the reconciliation of the churches, even as Leibniz himself had been abandoned. All he now did was to advise the Abbé de Saint Pierre to look up precedents and make sure of his history. But the Abbé de Saint Pierre was not going to bother himself with a lot of precautions. He was going straight ahead, with his head well up. The principle was plain enough; Nature wanted man to be happy; international law was the channel which was to bring happiness to mankind. Peace was bound to flow from international law properly understood; it would take but a little logic to indicate the infallible means of ensuring it in perpetuity.

Because they were fruit which, slowly ripening, had at last come to maturity; because they represented a process of simplification which made politics a matter of logic; because they responded to some of the deeper chords in our nature, these ideas became dominant in the European mind. Having won over the more thoughtful among the people of the Old World, they gave Liberty to the New.

Two hundred years or so after the Abbé de Saint Pierre had campaigned so strenuously for his Plan, that very plan was taken up once more. The league of nations, the assembly of delegates, the city of Peace, all these things were brought from dreamland and turned into realities. The only difference was that the force which was to serve the great cause of maintaining peace was never brought into being.

In the several countries internally these ideas brought about a change in the terms of the political proposition. It was now no longer a question of the sovereign's power in relation to a still higher authority, such as the Church, or the Empire, but between rulers and ruled.

The very word "subject" took on a different shade of meaning; to be exact, there were subjects no longer, but "citizens".

Then, again, there was the word "sovereign". England herself found it necessary to define the nature of the bonds which subjected, not indeed the nation to the king, but the king to the nation. This was what Bolingbroke did when, sound conservative and Tory leader though he was, he published, in 1749, his *Letters on the Spirit of Patriotism*. To put life into his party, and to defend the hereditary character of the British monarchy, he stressed the liberal doctrine. He explained that the institution of monarchy reposed on common law and on the public interest; it derived from two laws instituted by the Creator, the law of reason, which is universal, and the law of the particular régime to which any given State has voluntarily subjected itself. It is because any break or interruption in the operation of this latter would involve the risk of troubles and disorders that the royal power is handed on from father to son. Hereditary monarchy persists merely because it is the best kind of monarchy. Nevertheless, he who wields the royal power can only earn the respect due to his office in so far as he earns the esteem, the trust and the affection of those whom he is called upon to govern. Thus the kingly power is "the free gift of liberty, which finds therein its surest guarantee." There can be no patriot kings save those who identify themselves with the interests of their country, and accept the conditions their country imposes on them.

In countries where these ideas were stubbornly opposed, the

result was revolution. There was the American Revolution; a colony towards which the Mother Country refused to apply the principles and ideas which she herself had proclaimed, became the United States. When, in 1774, Boston rose in revolt, and thus started the American War of Independence; when, on the 4th July, 1776, the thirteen colonies proclaimed their independence, when the famous Declaration was drawn up affirming that governments could only be founded on the authority freely accorded to them by the governed; when England was obliged to give in, and to put her signature to the Treaty of Versailles; when the Convention of Philadelphia drew up the constitution which was adopted on the 17th September, 1787, something of capital importance, not only in the history of ideas, but in the history of world politics, was recorded. Drawn to the Old World by ties of kinship, and by memories of those valiant souls who, over thousands of miles of ocean, had come thither to found a New England; by ties of language, culture and religion; by the ideas she had borrowed from Locke and Montesquieu to help her build her constitution, the Republic of the Star-spangled Banner still remained a part of Europe, but a part lopped off and separate. She was the same, yet not the same. She was proud of her independence and always ready to proclaim it; yet there was one link she would not break and that was a moral link. It was to Europe she turned when threatened with the loss of her dearest possession, the possession of which eighteenth-century Europe had taught her the price, and that possession was her Liberty.

Then there was France's revolution, France where theories found their most powerful expression, but where the actual practical world would have nothing to do with the new school of thought. Here is an Order in Council promulgated by Louis XV in December, 1770: "We hold our crown from God alone, and the power to make laws belongs to us absolutely, and to us alone." Thus says the Declaration of the Rights of Man, as Man and Citizen; it was adopted in August, 1789, and put at the head of the Constitution of 1791: "Men are born free and equal before the law.—Social distinctions can only depend on common usefulness.—The aim of every political association is the conservation of the natural and indefeasible rights of man; these rights are liberty, the right to hold property and to resist

Education, then, has three objects: it trains the minds of the young, and adorns them with such knowledge as they are capable of assimilating; and it aspires to crown its work by making good Christians of them. Latin, with a modicum of Greek, should continue to be, as it always has been, the main ingredient. If Charles Rollin had been writing his book in Latin, how much more at home he would have felt. He himself made no boast of it, but it was a fact that he wrote more easily in Latin than he did in French. But of course he had his pupils to bear in mind, and not all of them by any means were to become professors and declaimers of Ciceronian eloquence. So he decided to fall back on French, and to illustrate what he had to say with examples drawn from French writers. He was devotedly attached to the good old rhetoric which you acquire from observing the precepts of the Ancients and modelling your style on theirs to the best of your ability; fine, flowing rhetorical periods, which you build up according to a recognized and established system, which system he proceeds to expound. When he stresses the importance of reading and getting at the heart of such and such an author, it is not because he thinks you may make some new discovery or find yourself participating in some startling intellectual adventure; all he wants is to hold up models for you to imitate, no matter to what category they belong, from the ordinary, everyday level to the loftiest heights of the sublime. The master, when occasion arises, will duly point out to his students how the author, in his exordium, sets himself to gain the sympathy of his audience; he will remark on the clarity, the conciseness of the treatment, on the author's air of sincerity, on the hidden purpose and the subtlety of it all; for art's secrets are seldom known except to Masters of Arts. Ideas count for much less than form, and he says quite frankly the expression of an idea is just a mere verbal exercise: "*Pensée* is a very vague and general kind of word. It has a number of different meanings, just like the Latin *sententia*. It is clear that what we are here considering are the thoughts that enter into works of an intellectual character and form their principal ornament." So too in poetry; what beauties to cull in Virgil or Ovid, what passages of sublime loveliness to be learnt by heart! No doubt it is in the profane writers that these treasures occur, and some over-rigid pedagogues would have us avoid them, but are we to be stricter than the Fathers of the Church? They did not hesitate to search and study them as models of style. Just as the thought, the idea, was no more than an adornment of the discourse, so we read poetry in order to find out how epithets are to be employed, how emphasis is obtained, how a long speech is dealt with; but as for the poetry of the thing, of the real poetic feeling not a word do we hear.

Charles Rollin is no dryasdust. Indeed, it would have been no bad thing if he had been a little more so. He is not imperious, but just amiably authoritative. If you could have heard him, you would have got the idea that whatever he was talking about at the time was something of immense importance and calling for particular attention. Speaking about a train of reasoning and the proof towards which it is directed, "Here", he declared, "is the most vital, I may call it the indispensable, part of the speaker's art. It is the very basis of it, and upon it we may say everything else depends." On the subject of Fables he says, "There is scarcely anything which is more commonly employed in the sphere of *Belles Lettres* than what I am here speaking about, nothing worthier of study, nothing more bristling with difficulties." He is himself so thoroughly convinced of the truth of what he is saying, that he convinces his reader, too; and that is the remarkable thing about him. Nowhere could you find a more accomplished advocate. Yet his tone was authoritative, too, and, while championing the glories of an age that was past, he did not omit to correct the backslidings of the present. His subject-matter? The classics, the humanities, and practically nothing else. The guiding spirit? The inspiration? The desire to hand on an intangible treasure. For his pupils as individuals he had no thought. Their rôle was a purely passive one, their task was simply one of imitation. In their hearts, minds and souls there was to be nothing but the traditional values which their master had planted there.

Not that he left the class just as he found it. Now and then, he half-opens a window, or sets a door ajar. He thinks a great deal of Locke, though Locke "had his own peculiar ideas about things, which one could not always adopt. Moreover, he seemed to be very inadequately acquainted with Greek, as well as with polite letters, which he esteemed far below their proper value." Then, in the views he expressed about heroic warriors and despots, Charles Rollin found himself at one with the philosophers. He insisted that if pupils have duties towards their tutors, so have tutors towards their pupils; on this he laid great stress. But when we remember the date of his work, and all the clamour and clashes of those times, we cannot resist the impression that the people he was really addressing were the gentlemen of a bygone day, of a seventeenth century that just held its own, as an eddy flowing back against the main stream.

The times demanded a change. People pointed out the defects in the education they themselves received and which they still saw given to their sons. They alleged that when a youngster left school, he knew nothing, or next to nothing. He mumbled a few words of Latin and fewer still of Greek. He'd got Pibrac's quatrains by heart, and La Fontaine's fables, which he understood amiss, and the Catechism, which he didn't understand at all. Then he went on to an Academy where he was taught riding, dancing, fencing, music. Of geometry he knew but the simplest rudiments, and he couldn't even subtract correctly. He completed his education in the world at large, in a manner always superficial, and often egregiously foolish. Perhaps, instead of going to school, he was given a tutor, a person half-pedagogue and half-lackey. In that case his ignorance was greater and his character more unsatisfactory than ever. His tutor schooled him in envy and spitefulness, which he called emulation and vivacity; and taught him to look on money as the most precious thing in the world, impressing on him that it is better to be a rich rogue than an honest pauper. They have strange ideas, these people, of setting a boy to work. "They dictate a long passage to him, which it takes him anything up to three hours to put into Latin, and this the tutor finds highly convenient. The boy makes no complaint about the length of his task, particularly if the tutor does not come down on him too heavily for his numerous mistakes. He takes things very easily; sticks in a line or two, knocks off for a bit, adds two or three more, and then starts fooling about. After a while he returns to his job, then munches an apple or something, goes off to talk to one of the servants, comes back, plays the fool, starts boxing with his fellow-pupil, and at last, after all these interruptions, gets to the final word. If he has been lucky enough to do a line or two without a mistake, someone hurries off to tell his father what a wonder he is; his howlers merely excite a laugh. Finally, when the fair copy is displayed, the proud father deludes himself with the idea that it is the unaided work of the hand that wrote it. Seeing his child going through the same mill as he himself went through, he seems to grow young again and to be back once more in his early days."[1]

Supposing, however, that, without going to an Academy, and thereafter into the social world, the young man enters a University; there fresh troubles will await him. He has to take down things from dictation without any idea of what they are all about. They steep him in scholasticism, which overloads the memory without training the judgment. They ask him the sort of questions they used to put in the Middle Ages: Parrot darling, *quotuplex causa*? Parrot darling, *quotuplex idea*?[2] Out of a hundred possible answers, the master insists that one and only one is correct, and he insists not only on getting that answer, but on getting it in a certain form of words, and none other. This is flying in the face of common sense. Really, at this time of day, in the eighteenth century, you can't call a man a Master of Arts when all he knows is the Latin Grammar and the rules of the syllogism *in baroco*. If it be true that intellectual enlightenment has increased these past two hundred years and that we are "enlighten'd beyond the hopes and imaginations of former times",[3] it is likewise true that what is habitually taught in schools, colleges and universities will have to be revised from top to bottom. That demand became more persistent every day, and the upshot was that certain definite reforms were insisted upon and adopted.

The curriculum would have to be radically changed, for a start. What we must always bear in mind to begin with is that the subjects of study were drawn up in an age when they had to be adapted exclusively to the needs of future clerks in Holy Orders. They were enlarged so as to meet the requirements of candidates for the teaching profession, which was regarded as more or less the same thing as the Church: but now, these

[1] J. P. de Crousaz, *Nouvelles Maximes sur l'éducation des enfants,* 1718.

[2] *Idem, Traité de l'éducation des enfants,* Lausanne, 1722.

[3] An age "enlighten'd beyond the hopes and imaginations of former times". William Worthington, *An Essay on the Scheme and Conduct, Procedure and Extent of Man's Redemption,* 1743.

bodies formed but a small minority of the total population. The system, moreover, was maintained chiefly for the benefit of pupils destined to occupy high social positions, men of wealth, the leisured classes. But were they the only people in the world? Anyhow, even the children of the nobility and gentry ought to be taught a craft of some sort. That would keep them clear of a multitude of vices and preserve them from pride, idleness and loose-living. Anyhow, the vast majority of men are compelled to earn their own living; we should see to it that they are taught betimes to address themselves to what Joseph Priestley calls the *business of active life*.[1]

That being so, far less time would have to be spent on Latin. What, in the practical affairs of life, was the good of Latin? Possibly it might not be necessary to do away with it altogether; but be that as it may, the taste for studying Latin was certainly on the decline. If it was to be retained, then, for goodness' sake, find some simpler and quicker way of teaching it. Don't go on throwing away seven whole years, which for most youngsters are seven years of toil and misery, all for the sake of learning a dead language. Far better spend the time learning the language of the country you live in. History, of course, must have its place; not ancient history so much as the political history of Europe, which people who are destined for public life find they know so little of, when they come to take up their duties. Learning history means learning geography. And of course it would never do to neglect the sciences, particularly natural science, along with mathematics and physics. As regards foreign languages the position was not so clear. Some were for a course of moral philosophy, starting with Grotius and Pufendorf; and natural law. Some people thought so much of the practical side that they were all for apprenticing the pupil to a mechanical trade of some kind. Better a youth should know how his shoes are made than be able to reel off yards of Aristotle. Why not have various sets of tools in the school itself, and, outside it, workshops of different kinds, with people to explain how the several machines are run—weaving, printing, watch and clock making, and so on?

[1]Joseph Priestley, *An essay on a course of liberal education, or civil and active life*. First published in 1764. Grimm, *Correspondance littéraire*, May, 1762. Œuvres, Vol. V, p. 81.

There would have to be a radical change in the way teachers tackle their work. *Methodus erudiendae juventutis naturalis*, so Basedow put it in 1752, by way of prelude to his work of reform.[1] It being understood, once more, that there is nothing innate in the mind, and that the mind is developed by the impact upon it of sensations which are gradually transformed into abstract ideas, education should follow the lines of progressive psychological development; it should keep pace with it step by step. Instead of being something applied from without, with a rigour more or less disguised, on a mind which is gradually forming, it should conform to and keep pace with the inward evolution of the mind. The consequences of such a method would be incalculable. The infant would be an object of interest from its very cradle. Its parents, instead of handing it over to the servants to look after, and taking no notice of it themselves, because it had not yet arrived at the age of reason, would tend and watch over it so as to direct and foster its development. The father will, by his own example, teach it good manners; and before the child has any idea of the meaning of the word virtue, he will plant seeds of goodness in the child which time will bring to maturity. Nor will the mother's part be any less important. Hers it will be to show the child what a sweet and gracious thing this quality of virtue is. Thus both will be playing their part as educators, before the time for regular schooling begins.

Then the child's bodily welfare has to be considered. The clothes it wears by day and night—important matters these. Still more important is the sort of food it has to eat. We know too many little girls who are allowed to stuff themselves with sweets, too many young gentlemen who pile rich sauces on to everything they eat, and learn too soon to drink more than is good for them; we've often seen them with attacks of indigestion curing themselves with remedies worse than the disease. They should drink what they require at meals, but never a drop between them. They should stick to good plain, nourishing food, and eschew dishes with juices that drain the cerebral glands. They should have their meals with their parents, except when the latter are entertaining company. The child's

[1] *Pro summis in Philosophia honoribus rite consequendis inusitatam eamdemque optimam honestioris juventutis erudiendae methodum . . . publice predicandam dabit Johannes Bernardus Basedow.* Kiliae, 1752. *Caput II*: *Methodus erudiendae juventutis naturalis*.

body must be kept under careful observation. Its muscles will acquire agility and strength by physical exercise. We shall have no more of those little weaklings who don't know what to do with their hands and feet. If fathers teach their boys to rough it a little they will see them put on strength every day. These are Locke's ideas on the matter, and from England they found their way to other countries. "A learned Englishman, a Mr. Locke, has gone into these matters with a wealth of detail in which I am certainly not going to follow him, at least not in everything. Our French refinement and way of life are by no means adapted to all his rules and all his precepts. Some, however, of the things he says are so excellent that I really must give a general account of them when opportunity offers."[1]

The choice of a tutor must not be left to chance. Many qualities are required of him. He must have a real vocation. He must have not only knowledge, but character. He must know how to temper firmness with discretion. In short, he must be a man of wisdom.

Education must follow a natural course. To that end, all you have to do is to note how knowledge finds its way into a child's mind, and how the adult mind acquires it. "The first thing felt is the first thing known. . . ." Therefore, "the underlying principle of any and every method should be to begin with something that can be apprehended by the senses, and from that to go on cautiously to what may be apprehended by the mind. Proceed from the simple to the complex; and make sure of the facts before trying to discover their cause."[2]

Those old-fashioned schoolmasters, who, say what you like, knew pretty well what they were about, were quite alive to the fact that you don't try and teach a child of six what you would teach a youngster of sixteen, or eighteen, or twenty. Still, they were rather too much inclined to be slaves to rule. What they taught at any given age was fixed by rule. In future, if we are to trust the philosophers, the teacher will follow, step by step, the progress of the growing mind. He will note the awakening of the childish faculties; he will bring into play the ones that are the first to show themselves, curiosity, imitativeness, memory.

[1]Le Père Poncelet, *Principes généraux pour servir à l'éducation des enfants. . . .* 1763. Livre III, Première époque.

[2]La Chalotais, *Essai d'éducation nationale,* 1763.

If natural history is the subject, children should first be taught to distinguish between the different kinds of trees and fruits, the different breeds of birds and insects. If it be physical geography, the thing will be to explain the alternations of day and night, to tell them something about the moon and the stars. If the lesson is about physics, then start with a few striking experiments; if Latin is the subject, don't begin with the syntax. Gently, gradually, pass from the concrete to the abstract.

Education, properly understood, is, and must be, a labour of love. Sarcastic remarks, endless fault-finding, strictness, severity, and the drabness that is born of them, take all the heart out of a child. But now, eagerness to learn, the respect and affection which parents and teachers alike will come to win for themselves, will be the natural concomitants of a well-ordered educational system. Corporal punishment, which used to be so liberally administered, will be abolished, except perhaps in a few very exceptional cases. You can't bang knowledge into children's heads with a stick. The inevitable fruit of violence is resentment or revolt.

Education should make for good citizenship. Instruction is one thing; education is another; and education is by far the more important since, if it is based on sound principles, it turns out good citizens. The same idea keeps cropping up amid the general intellectual ferment. Schools should be the affair of the nation. "The process of forming men is everywhere so closely bound up with the kind of government operating in the particular country concerned, that it is impossible to effect any material change in the prevailing system of public education without altering the structure of the constitution itself."[1] Whatever the government is, such are the schools. Under a despotism, no sort of education is possible. Education should be an integral part of the State for two reasons: it shapes it, and it is shaped by it.

The government was only too anxious to get control of education. The Abbé de Saint Pierre suggested the creation of a permanent Bureau to take charge of it under the direction of the Minister, whose department was to include the national police: or as we should now say, a Secretaryship of State for Education, as a sub-division of the Home Office. We may

[1]Helvetius, *De l'Esprit*, 1758. Discours IV, chap. XVII.

surely detect something more than a mere coincidence in the fact that this same La Chalotais, with whose hostility to the Jesuits we are already acquainted, and who urged that the first thing to do was to take their schools away from them, came out in the year 1763 with an *Essai d'éducation nationale.* The nation's needs must be met by the nation itself. The nation must never let education get into the hands of people whose aims and ideas run counter to those of the country as a whole. The schools have to form good citizens, men capable of serving their country, therefore education should conform to the constitution and laws of the country. At the present time it is steeped in mysticism. What I say is, let it be made to train good citizens. The public good, the country's good name demand that the rising generation should be regularly trained to acquit themselves with credit in whatever profession or occupation may fall to their lot. In his educational treatise, no less than in his indictment of the Jesuits, he was directing his shafts at one and the same thing, and that was what he called "the evils of monasticism".[1] At this same time, in the Protestant countries, rulers, without troubling their heads very much about theories, were doing what the liberals elsewhere had only got as far as proposing to do, they were making education a government department.

To sum it all up, there was not one of the modern school that did not voice his approval of progressive education. There was that question about the breast-feeding of infants. Ought infants to be wrapped in swaddling clothes, or ought they not? Then again, which was the right thing, to send a boy to school and have him brought up with a lot of others, or give him a private tutor? And if the latter, what sort of a man should you choose for so responsible a post? Ought the child to learn some handicraft? If so, what? Was education in the wider sense, that is to say character-building, more important than book-learning? These matters had been discussed and written about times without number. So, too, the question of female education. All these things were awaiting, inviting, inciting a man of genius who would soon be making them burning questions indeed.

[1]La Chalotais, *op. cit.*

VII

THE ENCYCLOPAEDIA

A CRITIC once said that the Encyclopaedia was the supreme event of the age, the acme of all that had preceded it, the centre of any true history of seventeenth-century ideas. From the European standpoint, this is putting it rather high. Nevertheless, it cannot be denied that, conceived as it was on an English model, given permanent shape in Paris, vouchsafed a home in Switzerland and Prussia, shedding its rays over all manner of different countries, reprinted in this one, imitated in that—it cannot, we repeat, be denied that the Encyclopaedia is a typical example of European influence.

Its aim was to be at once learned and popular, a combination of which we of today deny the possibility. It was, then, in the first place, an example of the sort of popularization that was so characteristic of the age of enlightenment. Just as, in the realm of ideas, the spirit of the times aimed at popularizing philosophy, so, too, in the realm of knowledge, far from trying to keep the layman at arm's length, it set itself to attract him. The recondite, the esoteric, the abstruse were not to its taste at all. This attitude was shared by the intelligentsia and by the more enlightened middle-classes, who were far more anxious to possess the world than to worry about what it was made of. The true significance of the Encyclopaedia resides in the fact that the eighteenth-century philosophers took possession of a world which, in its essence, was always to remain an enigma to them, and they accepted it on those terms, not troubling their heads about its inward implication. They very wisely confined themselves to collecting facts, and then to putting them into encyclopaedic order.

"Once they have arranged all the material they have got together, they will see the universe take on a recognizable shape;

they will behold a mass of scientific data, of facts duly authenticated, something which man can take hold of, something he can call his own."[1]

"People want to be well-informed about things, but with the least possible trouble to themselves; that is the most notable thing about this age of ours." So remarked one of the editors of the *Mémoires de Trévoux*, writing in August, 1715. What will you? "A Short Cut to Geometry"? "Science without a Master"? "Latin without Tears"? "Grammar made easy"? Whatever you wanted you could always get. A book just out would offer you attractions like this: *Mathematics made easy; a new system enabling you to learn without a master, study or trouble.* The motive of the offer never varied; the way it was worded seldom did. Here, four and thirty years later, is the *Journal des Savants* echoing what the *Mémoires de Trévoux* had said so long before: "People like to know things, but they want to learn quickly, and they don't like hard work. That no doubt accounts for the new 'methods' that come out every day, and for all the short cuts to knowledge we see about." (November, 1749.)

This was no exaggeration. Abridgments met you everywhere. From the too voluminous writer they extracted his essence and gave you the *Thoughts*, the *Reflections* of this person and that. We have *The Essential Bayle, The Essential Montesquieu* and heaven knows how many *Esprits*. "M. de Blainville, a young musician of promise, has just brought out a book which he calls *l'Esprit de l'art musical.* Titles of this sort are all the fashion; we have *l'Esprit des Nations, l'Esprit des Beaux-Arts, l'Esprit de Montaigne, de Fontenelle,* and so on. We have just seen an *Esprit du jour;* and I am almost afraid to mention *l'Esprit des lois*. It looks as if we were out to quintessentialize everything, to put everything through a sieve; we *must* get at the quiddity, the rock-bottom of things."[2]

And the *Handbooks*, the *Vade mecums*! Then, those uniform series they call "Libraries"! and the "Dictionaries"! Anyone writing the history of these latter would have to note the successive changes in their subject-matter; in the days of the Renaissance, dictionaries of the classical languages for the

[1]B. Groethuysen, *L'Encyclopédie.* In *Tableau de la littérature française,* XVII et XVIII siècles, 1939.

[2]Grimm, *Correspondance littéraire,* 24th Sept. 1754. Vol. II, pp. 187–188.

humanists; in the seventeenth century, modern language dictionaries for the gentry; next, dictionaries historical and critical. Soon, another sort of dictionary was in demand: dictionaries of the arts, trade, commerce, geography. But now the great *desideratum* was a dictionary comprising all the others, a dictionary of dictionaries, a dictionary capable of satisfying the prevailing greed for information. A dictionary both universal and handy; that would have been the ideal; but if that couldn't be had, if the thing had to be both bulky and heavy, well, never mind, so long as it was universal; that was the great thing. Ephraim Chambers, more lucky than his predecessors, had managed to cram universal knowledge into a couple of folio volumes, which he called his *Cyclopaedia, or Universal Dictionary of Arts and Sciences*, and which won him reputation, profit and the posthumous glory of a tomb in Westminster Abbey, where he was laid to rest beside the illustrious Englishmen who had earned the gratitude of their country.

Grimm, who had to review all these productions, grumbled as usual. It was positively terrifying to see how these literary middle-men were multiplying, grubs that gnawed away at the literary tree and consumed it to the very roots. And so he grumbled, not realizing the change in matters intellectual that was taking place before his very eyes. Gone was the time when some profound metaphysician or other would shut himself up in his lonely room and seek to discover the secret of being. That task, harder to accomplish than the finding of the philosopher's stone, had been abandoned, or else left to incurable dreamers. It was the world of appearances that men were now setting out to investigate, appearances, which had now come to be regarded as the sole reality. The mariners of old spent all their time and trouble trying to explore the ocean's profoundest depths; today, wiser in their generation, they were content to chart the winds, the reefs, the sea-routes and the havens. The comparison was accurate. But now everyone is to take part in this great and novel adventure; everyone, at all events, is to get the benefit of it. Everyone is to have knowledge within reach of his hand on shelves labelled A, B, C, D, etc. The Encyclopaedia was what the spirit of the age required, and what it purchased.

D'Alembert saw all that plain enough; and Diderot, whom nothing escaped, saw it plainer still. Both recognized that "methods", "rudiments", "epitomes", "complete sets", were all the rage. Dictionaries kept pouring forth in such formidable numbers that they had all they could do to keep pace with them, let alone praise them. They enlarged upon their obvious utility. Making up their minds to swim with the stream, they would help it to its appointed end. To gentlemen of the Court, to Army officers, to people of standing, aye, and to ladies too, to all in fact who wanted to improve their minds, they gave every possible encouragement. They treated the sciences and the arts in a way that called for no preparatory knowledge. They gave what it was essential to know, and nothing else. Also, they did away with learned terminology, so that no one would be handicapped on that score; they translated all the quotations into the vernacular, so that no one should have any more hieroglyphs to puzzle over. They provided a work that would take the place of a library for the ordinary man, no matter what his chosen subject; and for the specialist also, on every subject save his own. A snap of the finger, a few seconds waiting, then, just the time it takes to turn up the required word, and lo! your ignoramus becomes a pundit! Most people know the tale that Voltaire invented by way of illustrating this state of affairs. One night, Louis XV was having supper at the Trianon with some intimate friends. The talk turned upon game-shooting and then upon gunpowder. It soon became obvious that no one had the slightest idea what gunpowder was made of. Mme de Pompadour was just as ignorant about the rouge on her cheeks and the silk stockings on her legs. No matter; the thing was soon remedied. At a sign, the footmen hurried away to fetch the Encyclopaedia. Back they came with it. There, under "powder", "rouge" and "silk-weaving", was all they needed to know. Soon they had all pounced on the volumes of the Encyclopaedia as eagerly as the daughters of Lycomedes flung themselves on the jewels of Ulysses, and in no time they found what they wanted. People who contemplated going to law, found out exactly where they stood legally; the King got to know all about his regal prerogatives. While they were all thus busily turning the pages, the Comte de C . . . said in a voice loud enough for all to hear, "Sire, you are indeed fortunate to have, in your reign, men capable of mastering all the arts, and of handing on their knowledge to posterity. Everything is here, from the way to manufacture a pin, to that of casting and firing your big guns. Everything, from the infinitely small to the infinitely great. . . ."

Europe was going to open a fresh account-book. *Sancti Thomae Aquinatis Summa theologica in qua Ecclesiae catholicae doctrina universa explicatur*. . . . For the philosophers, all that was a thing of the past, over and done with; let it be forgotten! But *Encyclopédie*, or *Dictionnaire raisonné des sciences, des arts et des métiers, par une société de gens de lettres*—that was a different thing, that was the dawn, that was daylight. What had to be done—these imperious gentlemen were always giving their orders—what had to be done, was to make an inventory of things known, and in order to do that properly, to examine everything thoroughly, to turn it inside out and upside down, ruthlessly, no matter what it was. Away with childish things, down with the idols that reason condemned; but honour and glory to the Brave New World!

The children of the age were determined to be free; whatever they did, they would do of their own free will; not at the behest of any royal master; nor would their work bear any resemblance to those official proceedings which move so slowly that they are always a day behind the fair. They would work quite independently of any particular government. They would decline the assistance of an academy of any sort, for academies were, all of them, but narrow-minded cliques. The sole bond between the several collaborators would be the bond of mutual goodwill and regard for the common interest. The children of the age were not out to amuse or entertain, nor were they a pack of *dilettanti*. Therefore there would be nothing that was not up to date in the Encyclopaedia, nothing that was not essential. Everything would be living, actual reality. Things would not only be described and explained, but plates and engravings would picture the various arts and crafts at their ceaseless toil of rearing the fabric of civilization, for the children of the age were going to build a new world, nor were they going to follow Bayle's example and waste time, as he had done, in pointing out, one by one, the various demerits of the old. Their business it was to get together the requisite materials for the building of the New City. And the children of the age would be true to their gods, Reason and Nature. "In these days, when philosophy is advancing with giant strides, subduing to her uses everything she needs; when she speaks in such commanding tones, and we are beginning to cast off the yoke of precedent and example and obey the dictates of reason, we can scarcely discover a single elementary dogmatic work which can be regarded as wholly satisfactory. We find that all these productions are based on man-made ideas and not on the truths of Nature. Even Aristotle, even Plato are looked on a little doubtfully, and the time has come when works which still enjoy the highest reputation will soon be shedding some of their glory, or even be falling into complete neglect, so rapidly is reason progressing." The results achieved were to be no small matter, for, on the one hand, no one could say that the *Dictionnaire universel* was not in every way up to the level of the times, and, on the other, that if all the books in the world were swallowed up in an earthquake and the *Dictionnaire* were the sole survivor, nothing essential would be lost, human knowledge would remain unimpaired.

The notion of their ideal was thus clear before them, namely, to collect all the knowledge there was to be gleaned on the earth's surface, to explain its underlying system to their contemporaries, to hand on their knowledge to the generations to come, so that their great-nephews, by increasing their knowledge, might grow in virtue and contentment. Far from being scared at the amplitude of the task, they were intoxicated at the prospect of harvesting so infinitely rich a vintage. Hence the enthusiasm of the opening stages, the rousing fanfares, the lavish promises, the appeal to those of great name and high repute in the world of literature and science. It was with no idea of personal aggrandizement that Diderot and his coadjutor d'Alembert took their places in the forefront of the undertaking. It was rather that they felt they were leading a crusade, the crusade of philosophy. Hence the thrill of high expectancy that followed the publication of the prospectus in October, 1750, and of the first volume, which appeared on the 1st of July, 1751. Hence, too, the massing of the opposing forces, quick to scent the danger that threatened. Hence, once more, the rapidly deepening sensation which followed the news that publication had been a first, and then a second time suspended; and all those alarms and catastrophes too well known to need re-telling here; and that sorrowful day when Diderot learned that Le Breton, the bookseller, had been secretly mutilating his text. "I am wounded to the quick", he cried. At last, in January 1766, Samuel Fauche of Neuchâtel, by a subterfuge which the European public pretended not to see, but which really deceived nobody, announced that the volumes subsequent to the eighth had been printed off in Switzerland, and were available to subscribers through him.

Possibly, if everything had gone off smoothly, if it had not been for all this hullabaloo, all this bickering, with the ultimate victory, which was only a victory because it did not seem to be one, the Encyclopaedia would not have made the stir it did. Something of the dramatic clings about its history. Its antagonist was the Old Order, both in thought and action; *incipit vita nova.*

A dictionary based on a system, a dictionary which should display the order, the interdependence, the concatenation of all the various departments of human knowledge, would have been regarded as something of a paradox in any other period than the eighteenth century. How was the analytical discontinuity which the alphabetical order of a dictionary necessitated, to be reconciled with the synthesis which was the dream of the age? Chambers had tried his hand; the Encyclopaedia proudly declared it would do better; it would not only try, it would succeed.

But what principle was to guide them in setting out this order of theirs and in displaying the mutual interconnection of its various parts? Were they to take theology as their pattern? By no means. In the classification of the various sciences, theology occupied a very modest space, and even that it was obliged to share. It was divided into two sections. There was natural theology, which derived its knowledge of God solely from human reason, and that did not take it very far. Then there was revealed theology. But this latter was in reality reason applied to the truths of revelation. It might be said that it appertained to history in respect of the dogmas which it taught, and to philosophy in so far as it treated of the consequences deducible from those dogmas. In other words, depending as it did on reason, and being merely a department of history or philosophy, theology bore a strong resemblance to a queen discrowned. No more were the sciences to be ranked in the light of their relation to the science of God.

On the contrary; man henceforth was to be the dominant factor. No room now for the transcendental. The primacy of man, that was the great thing. Sciences were to be ranked in the light of their relation to man's psychological development. Sensations make known to us our own existence, and the existence of our fellow-men. Gradually a social order, morals, and religion are evolved. It is clear that the essentially intellectual concepts of vice and virtue, the principle of law and the necessity for it, the spiritual nature of the soul, the existence of God and the consciousness of our duties towards Him, in a word the truths that are essential to us, are the fruit of mental processes which our sensations arouse and set in motion. Then again, our anxiety to shun pain and to pursue pleasure, the necessity for ensuring our physical wellbeing, teach us to ward off the ills which threaten, and to cure those which afflict us, and invite us individually and collectively to increase the sum-total of our knowledge. First, agriculture, medicine and all the essentially necessary arts are brought into being. Whether in the theoretic or the practical sphere, man is responsible for what he knows and for how he lives. Hence came the principle of interdependence of which it will here suffice to give the heads:

It follows from what has hitherto been said that the different ways in which the mind operates on various objects, and the different uses to which those objects may severally be put, constitute the means primarily offered us for distinguishing, one from another, our several kinds of knowledge. Everything is related to our needs of one sort or another, whether it be an absolute necessity, or something that conduces to our comfort and adds to our pleasure, or something we desire from mere habit or caprice.

D'Alembert, whose words those are, is not content to look at the whole *corpus* of knowledge in the way that Buffon looked on Nature, he does more, he links up with Pope, "The proper study of mankind is man",[1] and with Lessing, "Man's noblest study is man".[2]

[1]Pope, *Essay on Man,* Epistle II.

[2]Lessing, *Œuvres,* Ed. Hempel, XVIII, p. 25.

Might it not be possible, however, to hit on another unifying system still more human—if one may so express it—in character? The progressive development of our sensations and reactions does not proceed without the intervention of circumstances outside our orbit. For the acquisitions which our needs have procured us cannot be represented by a single, even and continuous line. That line may be intersected by obstacles or interrupted by halts. So far from being a straight line, it is much more like a twisting lane, or the tortuous circumvolutions of a maze. Sometimes humanity turns round in a circle, sometimes it harks back again on its tracks. Science encroaches on science; this one forges ahead, this one lags behind. Hence not a few complications, not a little confusion. A guide more clear-sighted, more efficient must be found, and behold, here is one ready to hand. Yesterday, today and tomorrow too, among the Hottentots as among the Parisians, three ruling faculties have been and will be recognized: Memory, Imagination and Reason. Such will be the three divisions of the encyclopaedic order. Memory gives us history, from the Reason proceeds philosophy; from the Imagination come the fine-arts. All these will be further sub-divided in their turn. It is to this view of the matter that the Encyclopaedia will conform, because the fact which it perceives is simpler to grasp than was the progressive development of the human mind. Notes inserted after every word will enable us to attach the leaf to the twig, the twig to the branch, and the branch to the trunk, which would remain the most denuded thing of all, to wit the existence of the human faculties. Thus it was that the two great leaders, the one of European thought, the other of European science, Locke and Bacon, both had their effect in determining the plan, the system, that the Encyclopaedia was to adopt.

"How now! What is this we hear?" people exclaimed when they had read what the *Discours préliminaire* had to tell them; "How now! Are we to understand that knowledge no longer comes from God, and that God's law is not the law of morality?" And yet d'Alembert had assigned a line or two to the subject of the Supreme Being: the union of soul and body as well as the reflections which inevitably occur to us regarding those eternal problems Mind and Matter, alike lead up to the idea of a supreme, all-powerful Intelligence. Nay, more, he had gone the length of referring to the need for a revealed religion to serve as a supplement to natural religion. Although the expression, "a supplement", smacked somewhat of irreverence, although he seemed to imply that the truths imparted by this revealed religion were for popular consumption, and not for the educated, he had some regard for people's feelings, he took care what he said and how he said it. Diderot spoke out more bluntly when he came to the item *Encyclopédie* in the Dictionary. He boldly espoused the ruling principle of the work, and made no apology for putting Man at the very centre of the Universe:

If man, if that thinking and contemplative being, were banished from the surface of the globe, the spectacle at once pathetic and sublime which Nature unfolds would become a silence and a desolation; the Universe is dumb, silence and weariness brood upon the scene, all has become one vast solitude wherein phenomena now unobserved pass by as in a dim, unheeding twilight. The presence of Man it is that gives interest and meaning to the existence of living things, and how better could we record the history thereof than by taking this consideration for our guide? Why not give to man in this work the place which is allotted him in the universal scheme of things? Why not make him the centre round which everything revolves?

In the beginning, God made Heaven and Earth, according to the Bible; and when he had made Heaven and Earth, he made Man. However, when he comes to his dictionary definition of Man, Diderot forgets his Bible and leaves out God:

MAN; NOUN MASC. *A sentient, thinking, intelligent being, moving freely over the earth. He is above all other animals and exercises dominion over them; gregarious in his habits, he has invented various arts and sciences, and has virtues and vices peculiar to his species. He has appointed rulers and made laws for himself, etc.*

The prominent place accorded to the arts and crafts in the Encyclopaedia, and its practice of giving, under the head of each, whether liberal or mechanical, the general principles underlying it, and its essential elements, have sometimes been regarded as a new departure peculiar to the publication in question. Its secondary aim was to furnish, over and above the theoretical explanation of the various items dealt with, rules and directions for their practical application.

To be astonished at such an aim would argue ignorance of

one of the tendencies of the times, a tendency which, more than any other, was to affect the social conditions of the future; it would be to forget those precursors of things to come; Descartes, whose advice was to take concrete form in the Collège Royal and in other buildings intended for public use, spacious assembly halls for workmen and, attached to each hall, a room containing the tools necessary, or convenient, in whatever art or craft was to be taught. Next, Leibniz, who had an idea of a sort of universal exhibition where there were to be amusements of every kind, sports, tight-rope dancing, acrobatic displays, fire-eaters, dancing horses, fireworks and suchlike attractions calculated to draw the crowd. The crowd would then have an opportunity of getting to know something about the progress of the sciences; they would see natural history collections, an anatomical theatre, the camera obscura, experiments carried out in water, in air and *in vacuo*, inventions and machinery of every description. But prior to all this, the *Essay concerning Human Understanding* had given mechanics a place in the sun: It is from machinery, looked down on and despised as it is (the word is regarded with contempt in the world), it is from machinery, I say, operated by unlettered folk that we get the arts so useful to life, arts which are becoming daily more perfect. And dictionaries had made it known by their titles that they would include the arts and sciences within their scope, that they would deal with technology. Already skilled mechanics were constructing *automata*; Vaucanson had exhibited his Flute Player at the Académie des Sciences, which was soon to be followed by the Talking Man, invented by Kempelen Farkas, an Hungarian.

Machines! the marvels that were invented in those days! Weaving machines which did their work so quickly that the spinners could not keep pace with their requirements. Then came spinning machines, which spun at such a rate that the looms were outstripped in their turn. There were machines worked by coal for smelting ore, and, marvel of marvels, there was the steam-engine. In 1733, John Kay invented the shuttle; in 1738, John Wyatt and Lewis Paul patented their weaving machine; in 1761, James Watt began his experiments, and, by 1767, he had achieved his object, taking out his patent the following year. In eighteenth-century Europe, machinery was beginning to oust the workman; and nothing in all the history of our race was ever fraught with weightier consequences.

Thus the Encyclopaedia was coming to be part and parcel of a general movement, lending it dignity and prestige. It purported to instruct its readers in the details of the mechanical arts, a branch of knowledge which the high and dry intellectuals, who looked on metaphysics as the only subject worthy their attention, were either ignorant of, or regarded with disdain. Its various contributors went into shops where things of ordinary, everyday use were sold, and, better than that, into workshops of all kinds, and thus got to know how the bookbinder binds his books, how the carpenter makes his chests, the glass-blower his bottles, and how the miner attacks his coal face. There was one man in particular, the son of a Langres cutler, who kept his eyes very wide open, asking all manner of questions. He went about with draughtsmen, who made copies of everything, from the simplest to the most complicated bits of machinery.

This change of outlook, this interest in technical matters was inevitably attended by a change in the social order. In thus enhancing the importance of the mechanical arts, it followed that the status of the workers themselves was correspondingly raised. The Encyclopaedia throws a revealing light on this readjustment of values, when it enjoins us not to "look down on manual workers, on craftsmen. They are our equals, if not our superiors. Whence, then, your disdain? Possibly from a sort of vague, unconscious antipathy. To begin with, social inequality arose from inequality in physical power. Later on, that inequality was replaced by one of another kind, an inequality based on mental superiority. The mind had turned the tables on physical strength. Your disdain arose from a mistaken view of things. It used to be thought that in practising or even in learning the mechanical arts one lost caste, debasing oneself to the level of things toilsome to acquire, ignoble to dwell upon, difficult to explain, lowering to trade in, as infinite in number as they were negligible in value." "A prejudice which led to the filling of our cities with conceited intellectuals and unprofitable onlookers, and our countryside with petty, ignorant tyrants, idle and supercilious drones." "If it be true that the liberal arts are superior to the mechanical arts by reason of the greater intellectual effort that the former entail, and the difficulty in mastering them, it is no less true that the latter excel the former in usefulness. The man who invented the watch-spring, the balance-wheel, the repeater is no less worthy of respect than those who invented and perfected the science of algebra." Or still more triumphantly, "Put on one side of the scales the tangible fruit of the most exalted sciences and the most honoured of the fine-arts, and then, on the other, put the solid advantages of the mechanical arts, and you will find that the esteem with which they are respectively regarded bears no relation to the advantages derived from them. We shall find that we have praised those who tried to convince us that we were happy, far more highly than those who took practical measures to make us so."

The desire, the determination to be happy, and to be so here and now, came back in this guise and it kept on coming back. All honour to those who contributed to our earthly happiness. Material progress, that was the road to happiness. Empiricism demanded a transference of dignity, and it now passed from the sphere of speculation to the sphere of the practical; from thought to action; from the head to the hand. Diderot, in espousing the cause of the mechanical arts, was true to his doctrine, to the ideas he shared with his brethren, to the philosophy of his age.

The Encyclopaedia had its defects, and they were not a few. That became more and more evident every day. From the very start, its enemies reproached it with borrowing wholesale, and with borrowing without acknowledgment, from previous compilations, periodicals and books, and called it a scissors-and-paste affair. Again, that was true. They blamed it for admitting a number of errors, and not a few downright absurdities. That, too, was true. Its contributors were a motley crowd. Some of them, men of genius, were more ready to promise their help than to give it; then there were a number of obscure quill-drivers who gave what they could, and that was not very much. Hence a striking inequality in the value of the articles. Inequality in ideas as well, for they were frequently contradictory. Diderot, admirable as an inspirer, was not always so satisfactory as a sub-editor, a task that needed more patience than he could boast of. He let through a quantity of repetitions, and failed to detect omissions. As the work progressed, he left things more and more to Élie de Jaucourt, whose main preoccupation was not so much consistency of ideas as always to have enough copy ready to keep the printers going.

But enough of its shortcomings; let us rather see what the Encyclopaedists really did. A good dictionary ought to have some effect on the general course of ideas. Did the Encyclopaedia do that? Now, it might so happen that the article you pitched on was perfectly orthodox, and so, after perusing it, you might feel inclined to say what a certain Italian Abbé named Ziorzi wrote in the year 1779: "For my part, I am far from sharing the view of the people who take the Encyclopaedists for a pack of unbelievers. On the contrary, I should just like them to read the article on Christianity, and a few others of the same kind, and tell me if they did not find religion, not merely treated with respect, but stoutly defended." Yes, but go on a little farther and you will have reason to change your tune. It is true enough that the articles in which ecclesiastical people might expect to find something to fall foul of are all harmless enough, but running through the others, there is always something, a matter cursorily glanced at, or left out altogether, something, at any rate, that betokens clearly enough the writer's hostility to accepted teaching, to anything connected with authority and dogma. Instead of taking things as they are and plainly recording them, the dictionary sets going all manner of doubts and counter-suggestions. That is the first effect to be noted.

The second is all-important: there is no doubt that this dictionary is well-adapted to the City of Men. It helped, so far as it possibly could, to suppress the word divine, and all which it implied, by the word social, and all which that implied. Not that the social sciences, which were still in the tentative stage, reach their full development in the dictionary. The sound theory that, if we are to study humanity, we must start, not with the individual but with the group, finds no place in it. It was not until 1767, in *An Essay on the History of Civil Society*, that Adam Ferguson declared that all the information we possess, the most ancient as well as the most recent, and from whatever part of the globe it came, never presents man save in groups or societies, and that we should take that as our starting point. Thus Ferguson may be regarded as the founder of modern sociology. But at any rate the Encyclopaedia gave liberal space to social sciences; it revealed something of their spirit and gave a rough pre-view of them. The science of man, anthropology, in the modern sense, did not take definite shape in the Encyclopaedia, but it was adumbrated.

But was there another and more secret influence at work? Was the Encyclopaedia a product of Freemasonry? There is no doubt whatever that the Freemasons did contemplate bringing out a complete Dictionary of all the liberal arts and all the useful sciences. Ramsay, the Grand Master of the Order, made an express reference to it in a speech which he delivered on the 31st March, 1737. "A start on the work has already been made in London,[1] but now that our confrères have joined in the undertaking, a few years more may enable us to bring the thing to perfection. Not only will the technical meaning and derivation of the words be given, but the history of each particular art, its broad principles, and its mode of operation will be explained. In this way, all the knowledge of every country will be brought together in a single work." A tutor of the Comte de Reuss, Gensau was his name, also gave out that in 1742 Ramsay told him of a scheme for levying a subscription of ten guineas a head from all the freemasons of Europe, the money to be devoted, in the first place, to printing a universal dictionary in the French language, to include the four liberal arts as well as the historical sciences. But, he added, the material support which would permit of these possibilities becoming certainties is, so far, not forthcoming. The Encyclopaedia was beginning to have its effect. Condemned by a number of publicists, it was formally proscribed by the Church who condemned in any shape or form and no matter where it might appear, the *Spissum opus in plures tomos cujus est titulus Encyclopédie*, on the ground that it contained erroneous doctrine, false, pernicious and scandalous statements, calculated to foster unbelief and to bring religion into contempt. In Tuscany, two editions of it were published, first at Lucca, then at Leghorn, where it obtained the patronage of the Grand Duke Peter Leopold, which was all capital business for the book-trade. It paid so well that the trade contemplated other undertakings on similar lines; there was a positive ferment

[1]The *Cyclopaedia* of Ephraim Chambers is dated 1728, and Chambers was a freemason.

of excitement in the printing world. It was published at Geneva, and, again, a little later, at the same place in handier form. It came out at Berne, Lausanne, and Yverdon. In 1782, Panckoucke started bringing it out in a modified form under the title of *Encyclopédie méthodique*. It shone its rays all over Europe.

VIII

THE WORLD OF LETTERS AND IDEAS

WE have seen the great change that overtook the world of letters when it became the battle ground of ideas. But the City of Men must needs have beauty, too. And what sort of beauty was it that took its fancy?

PSEUDO-CLASSICISM

We are never quite so up-to-date, so novel as we should like to be. That was a truth the eighteenth century did not recognize; but it was affected by it, all the same. When it compared itself with its elder, the seventeenth, its feelings were mixed; a touch of jealousy mingled with a modicum of respect. It claimed to be superior, as it stood so proudly upright, superior in ideas, superior in scientific knowledge. But as regards art and letters, that was another matter, and there it had to acknowledge its inferiority. It paraded all the reasons it had for hating Louis XIV, and then, when it had said its worst, it agreed that Louis still stood erect on his pedestal, with a throng of other statues around him, all of them men of genius.

And so, there was nothing else for it, the new age had to drag along a heavy load of imitations. It obeyed the rules; it argued about them, no doubt, but none the less it obeyed them. It kept to existing forms. It would have liked to discover new ones, but it could not. Some there were who tried to write fables like La Fontaine's, men like Iriarte and Samaniego, Gay and Gellert. Others who attempted dialogues of the dead, after the manner of Fontenelle and Fénelon, men like Gozzi, Frederick II, and many besides. A number vied with one another in inditing Odes with the calculated enthusiasm of a Boileau, a task which Gottsched recommended to the bards of Germany. Finally, there was the Epic. Who was going to revive the glories of the Epic? There was the *Henriqueida* of Xavier de Meneses, Moratin's *La toma de Granada,* the *Hermann* or the *Heinrich der Vögler* of Otto von Schönaich, and a host of others in various lands. M. de Voltaire had set the key with his *La Ligue*, or *Henri le Grand*, as far back as 1723:

Je chante les combats, et ce roi généreux
Qui força les Français à devenir heureux,
Qui dissipa la Ligue et fit trembler l'Ibère,
Qui fut de ses sujets le vainqueur et le père,
Dans Paris subjugué fit adorer ses lois,
Et fut l'amour du monde et l'exemple des rois.

Muse, raconte-moi quelle haine obstinée
Arma contre Henri la France mutinée
Et comment nos ayeux à leur perte courants
Au plus juste des rois préféraient des tyrans. . . .[1]

This had been greeted with applause. The Epic, silent for so long, had recovered its voice, through the merits of that brilliant son of France of whom everyone was so proud.[2]

How many were the comedy writers who tried to surpass Molière, or, if that were too perilous a venture for some, how many tried to copy him! Destouches' *Le Glorieux*, Gresset's *Le Méchant* are but the offspring of *Le Misanthrope* and *L'Avare*, and pallid offspring at that. Holberg had plenty of local types before him, and plenty of dash inside him, to knock off some original comedies. They would have been more original still if he had been less tied down to Plautus and Molière, and not so terribly afraid of sinning against the three unities. Of all the cemeteries where dead plays had gone to sleep the unawakening sleep, the most densely populated was the one allotted to tragedies that were no more, those which had been famous in their day,

[1] I sing of battles, and that generous king who forced the French people to become happy, who dispersed the League and made Iberia tremble, who was both the conqueror and the father of his people. In Paris now subjugated by him he caused his laws to be loved and was the beloved of the world and the pattern of kings. Muse, tell me what stubborn hate it was that set rebellious France in arms against Henry, and how our ancestors rushing to their ruin preferred tyrants to the most just of kings. . . .

[2] *Journal des Savants,* 1724, p. 246.

like Voltaire's *Zaïre*; those that had run for a week or two; and those which had been hissed outright, and straightway honoured with the crown of martyrdom. No epitaph survives upon their graves today other than their long-forgotten names: here lies *Cosroès*, here lies *Aristomène*, here lies *Briseïs*, here lies *Eudoxe*, and here lies *Zarucma*. So many were the tragedies and tragi-comedies that, by 1761, there were enough to fill a dictionary; ah, yes; yet another dictionary! The pan-European competition for the prize-tragedy, which had chosen *Cato* as the subject, now began again, this time with *Mérope*, and this time it was an Italian that carried off the palm. At all events, that was the verdict of his compatriots, when the play was put on at Modena on the 11th June, 1713. They were proud to be able to boast that they had, in the person of Scipione Maffei, a dramatist in the strictly classical tradition. Meanwhile, his fellow-countryman Luigi Riccoboni presented the figure of a living paradox, for, though he was the reputed head of a company of comedians *dell' arte*, he was always lamenting that the Italian theatre had never been properly brought up to date. Outside France, people were bleating the fatuous cry: "Corneille and Racine are out of date!" In France, the cry was "The Classics have had their day!" But did they believe what they said?

At all events they went on as before. They agreed to play the game under existing rules, believing that a few slight changes—a little less love-making here, a little deepening of the tragic colouring there, themes taken from any and every period—that this sort of thing was all that was needed to secure perfection. In these days, when it was no longer the fashion to dwell long and intently over a work, to try to make it as perfect as could be; when the pen raced over the paper with a speed hitherto undreamt of, when an endless stream of books came pouring from the printing-presses, and a feverish unrest replaced the calm of a bygone day, hundreds and hundreds of books were born only to die, books not worth the money it took to bind them. The result is that when one comes to sum up the effects of this projection of the past into a new age, it is difficult not to regard it as a great error, an immense waste of time and talent. Be bold in all things! Yes, but when it came to literature they could not be too cautious. However, we should be giving a wrong impression if we left it at that. The continuance of the classical spirit, the classical outlook, which was beginning to degenerate into pseudo-classicism, is not to be accounted for by the glamour of the great models of antiquity, by the compelling influence of those shining exemplars; nor again is it to be attributed to the unenterprising nature of men who would rather do over and over again what had once proved a success, than start on something new; no, it was something more than that; it sprang from an identity of view, a similarity of outlook, an inward unanimity. It arose from the order which the reason discerns as prevailing throughout the whole of Creation.

Zu Ordnung ward, was ist, eh etwas war, erlesen[1]: There must be a rational spirit of literature, just as there was of law. The classical spirit stood for the relationships which necessarily derive from the nature of the different *genres*, these latter representing, as it were, the hierarchical order imposed by the great concatenation of living things. On this point, philosophy was one with the classical ideal, and both were hostile to the irrational.

Moreover, if it be true that by this time the classical spirit had yielded the best of its fruit so far as France was concerned, and that what it was now giving there was devoid of savour, it was not so in other European fields.

The impressive list of works on the Art of Poetry which repeat, with some not unimportant variations, pretty much what Boileau had said already, would have had little *raison d'être* if it had not been thought that there was something useful in them.

1711: *The Essay on Criticism.*

The rules are Nature still, but Nature methodized. No barren formula that, as the work of Pope himself bears witness.

1729. *Versuch einer Kritischen Dichtkunst*, by Johann Christoph Gottsched.

Gottsched is small beer, and there is little to be said for him in regard to the intrinsic merits of his writings, but, pedant though he was, and very cocksure, and always recommending to the Germans specimens of French drama that were quite unsuited to them; and dangerous, too, if you had let him have his head, Gottsched, nevertheless, supplied one of the needs of the hour; he would have rule, discipline; and that curb, that pruning it was that brought about the blossoming of a later day.

[1]Uz, *Die Glückseligkeit, loc. cit.*

1737. The *Poetica* of Ignazio de Luzan.

More about Greece and Rome and classic Italy; more of Boileau's France, and of rules, still more and more. Yes, but, at the same time, there was war on a literature that had become a mere matter of verbal virtuosity. War on bad taste, on pretentiousness, on preciosity and affectation. Literature must be put back into the melting pot, and the Spanish genius must be purged of all this dross.

Portugal knew well enough that she had dropped behind in the march of ideas. The only remedy she could think of was to revert to her own tradition, and that was bankrupt; or, alternatively, to copy the Italians and their make-believe Arcadia; and that, though intended to rescue poetry from the boudoir and bring it out into the fresh air, had soon degenerated into something like the bleating of lambs in a sheepfold. However, in 1746, there appeared the *Verdadeiro Metodo de Estudar* by Luis Antonio Verney, a work explaining to his countrymen how they should study, and use their brains to better purpose. In 1748, yet another *Ars Poetica*, this time by Francisco Jose Freire. The classic spirit was still to be reckoned with in Portugal.

We should be taking a very shortsighted view of the matter if we concluded that a tendency so persistent was the result of a sort of passive contagion. On the contrary, we seem to hear a cry coming from country after country where the classic spirit had been hitherto inoperative, imploring it to come to the rescue. Slowly but surely it monopolized the field. Once an avenue to freedom for the spirit, it had degenerated into a mere fetish. It now began to look as if it had pushed its conquest too far, as if it had sown the wind and was reaping the whirlwind, as if it had made retaliation inevitable, as if it had left men with no alternative but a literary revolution. It looked, in short, as if the *Aufklärung* had started the *Sturm und Drang*.

There was now not a capital, not even a good-sized provincial town that did not aspire to an academy. England, even England, thought she, too, ought to have a dome of her own, with chairs for forty immortals underneath it. It was a time when language, grammar and spelling were all being overhauled, to see if they could be brought more into line with modern requirements ; a time when, side by side with philosophic criticism, literary criticism sprang up, and became one of the major forces of the day. Protests were frequent against the severity of its judgments. Any upstart, any conceited coxcomb, any little twopenny-halfpenny rhymester could take it on himself to air his views, to say slanderous things about a writer's work, to pick famous authors to pieces. The emptier his skull, the louder he ranted. Yet the only result of these complaints was that a higher dignity was claimed for the critic, investing him with powers not a whit inferior to those of the creative artist. By virtue of his office, if duly performed, the Critic might aspire to an eminence equal to that of the Orator, the Poet, or the Playwright. And it happened that there came on the scene just then some of the greatest critics that ever were, Pope, Voltaire, Lessing. And if these three men won other titles to be held in remembrance, others there were wholly devoted to criticism, men of letters who discharged their office with such distinction that they, too, earned for themselves the reward of undying recollection.

Giuseppe Baretti took it into his head to call himself Aristarco Scannabue, Aristarchus Oxfeller, and his review *La Frusta letteraria,*[1] *The Critic's Lash.* And how he lashed his erring victims, laying on and sparing not, when he got back to Italy again, after a stay in England! He declared war on Arcadia—no more of that—and on those *antiquari* who thought of nothing but the past and gone; war, too, on those conceited charlatans who thought to conceal the poverty of their matter beneath the magnificence of their dedications; war on those bards who wrote long poems about nothing, and on those sonneteers for whom fourteen lines were far too many, seeing how little they had to say. Naturalness, spontaneity, those were the things he wanted, in matter as well as style. Good, honest common sense, that was what he went by. Enough of those out-of-date pedants, of those pettifogging small-fry who, whenever they took anything from tradition, always took the wrong thing. Burning with ardour, revelling in the din of battle, quite happy if he could give as good as he got, he was the type of the Merciless Critic. If he had contented himself with being one of the purveyors to the London Opera, or with giving Italian lessons to My Lady

[1]*La Frusta letteraria,* Oct., 1763–July, 1765.

this, or My Lady that, or with compiling that Italian-English Dictionary of his, which held the field so long, he would have occupied a modest place among the writers who were attempting to climb Parnassus, to employ a metaphor very much in vogue at the time. But brandishing his whip about him right and left, he slashed a way through the crowd and won a place of honour close by Apollo himself.

For the benefit of posterity, Sir Joshua Reynolds painted a portrait of Samuel Johnson: "Squarely built; head well down between the shoulders; massive features; heavy jowl; narrow, wrinkled forehead; thick lips; a questioning, rather grim look about the eyes; a serious, thoughtful, somewhat dour expression generally."[1] Samuel Johnson sits himself down at his desk; he's going to study Milton; how is he going to set about it? He starts with a very accurate biography after a very thorough review of the author's various works. Then he collects his ideas. A great work demands great care; I am about to examine *Paradise Lost* which from the point of view of its design merits the first rank; from that of its execution, the second. By general consent the epic poet is he who merits the highest glory, poetry being in fact the art of wedding truth with pleasure; and it is epic poetry which sets itself to impart the most important truths by the most agreeable means. I must, then, conscientiously proportion the importance of my judgment to the eminent importance of *Paradise Lost*. Père Le Bossu is quite correct when he says that the moral counts first, the story illustrating it comes second. That is where Milton triumphs; with other poets, the moral is never anything but an incident or a consequence; with him the moral is the inspiring principle since his design was to set forth the ways of God to man, how the Christian faith conforms to reason and why we should obey the divine law. His subject is concerned with the world as a whole, not merely with the destruction of a city, the founding of a colony or the history of an empire. Compared with his, the characters of the most famous epics pale into insignificance. They are admirably drawn, the good and the wicked angels, man before and after the fall. Of the probable and the marvellous, there is little we can say; with Milton, the probable is the

[1]Louis Cazamian, *Histoire de la littérature anglaise,* Livre VIII, chap. I; *le Classicisme doctrinal: Johnson.*

marvellous and the marvellous the probable. So, too, there is little to remark about the machinery of the work since everything takes place as a result of the immediate intervention of heaven. Samuel Johnson adopts the points of view of the traditional critic and pronounces in accordance with what these tell him as to the structure of the work, the passions depicted, the diction, and he concludes this, the first part of his work, by giving the palm to Milton. Nevertheless it is the duty of an impartial critic to draw attention to omissions and imperfections, and so he proceeds to draw up the debit side of the account. The scheme of *Paradise Lost* involves this drawback: it does not show us either the deeds or the ways of men, so in none of the poet's greatest scenes, whether pleasing or terrible, are we conscious of any human interest. The theme demands the description of things which it is humanly impossible to describe. The allegory of Sin and Death is out of place: this clumsy device seems to him one of the poem's most marked defects. There is also some fault to be found with the mode of narration. Milton is unequal, as Addison pointed out: after all, he had to come down to earth sometimes. He imitated the Italians too slavishly and his desire to copy Ariosto led him to include a very inappropriate episode, the Paradise of Fools. He does not avoid punning or equivocal expressions. Such are the defects one might put in the balance against work of marvellous perfection. Anyone who thought the scales were even would be a person to be pitied.

That is a decidedly methodical way to go to work; it is a step forward, a step both peaceable and sure, along a road marked out once and for all. Samuel Johnson estimates every writer, living or dead, on similar lines. His gravity is pontifical; he keeps to the rules dictated by his reason, his guides are the Classics; his juridical system is based on the verdicts delivered by his predecessors on the critical bench. If he sometimes evinces a little less than his customary respect for authority, he tells us why. Again it is reason that counsels this or that divergence from the beaten track, reason freely exercised, less rigidly logical, but still a reason that leads him to mistrust the excesses of an undisciplined imagination, wild dreams and feverish ardours. His task, which implied obedience to a strict moral code, was to repel those enemy forces. However, he only knew them by their observable effects, he had never experienced them in himself, he had never felt himself disturbed by them.

When he came to address himself to Shakespeare, he found himself in contact with the very essence of the classical spirit, with that longing for universal and eternal truth which it was the aim of the classical spirit to attain. The life of a work depends on the duration of the esteem with which people regard it. What are the qualities that awaken this esteem? Shakespeare, beyond all others, knows how to portray the permanent, the deep-seated traits of human nature. He makes his dramas the perfect mirror of life. Some will have it that his Romans were not real Romans, nor his kings real kings. If that is so, it is not a defect but a merit, since it merely shows that he thought universals more important than accidentals. Another criticism calls for more serious consideration. Critics complained that Shakespeare mixed up comedy with tragedy. But was not this in order that he might portray life as it really is? He has his faults. He seems to have no clear moral purpose in view, his composition is careless, he does not seem to trouble himself how his plays are to end; his works are not unmarred sometimes by preciosities, sometimes by unseemly jests; his gentlefolk are not always distinguishable by their manners from his clowns. There is another shortcoming, but it is one for which Samuel Johnson cannot find it in his heart to condemn him: Shakespeare does not obey the law of the Three Unities. That rule was invented with the express purpose of bringing the drama into closer relation with actual life. Well, if Shakespeare has succeeded in depicting real life without it, what right has anyone to complain?

But now for some time past the English stage had been treating its patrons to a new presentation of the pathetic; and novels, too, had been eliciting floods of tears. And poetry appealed direct to the heart. It was all over, now, with those colourless, monotonous verses, those eclogues and idylls that unfolded their tale against a background of painted canvas; with tragedies written according to rule, with Young's *Busiris* and Fenton's *Marianne*; dead and gone, all of them, dying amid rounds of applause. In accordance with the inevitable ebb and flow of things, which makes us lose our taste for what we erstwhile loved, and yearn for something new, we know not what, a change was already coming over the theatre; already the revolt against the classical drama was beginning to take shape. But Samuel Johnson fought against it; he fought against it because he stood for principles that always to some extent hold good. There was about him, no one can deny, some of the grandeur that invests the stubborn defender of a beleaguered fortress, of the man who knows how to hold his position, and never gives in. And in particular, let us admit that he did all in his power to uphold the rights of eternal reason. Obstacles have their uses when they compel the assailants to look to their own weapons, to set their own armoury in order. That rôle was his. He affirmed, what can never be gainsaid, namely, that to write well we must have a clear and definite vocabulary, and a sound knowledge of grammar; that instead of being blindly subservient to the great models, we should bring ourselves clearly to understand in what their greatness consists; that we should bear in mind that confusion and incoherence are not necessarily the marks of talent, and that style, mind and spirit all need to be disciplined.

His country, vowed though it was to other gods, understood him. Men were grateful to him for building, stone by stone, year after year, from 1747 to 1755, the great edifice of the Dictionary, which bore witness to the probity, the lucidity, the stability of the language henceforth thereby assured; for having assigned to the English authors whose work had been examined by him, their due titles of nobility. Seated in the *Cheshire Cheese*, drinking his pint of beer, or his glass of port, he delivered himself of his oracles, which the faithful Boswell piously recorded. He said he had not lived in vain because, whatever the final verdict of mankind upon him might be, he had at least done his best to deserve well of it by endeavouring to refine the English language to the utmost, and had even added something to the elegance of its syntax and the harmony of its diction; and because he had, in the conduct of his life, set an example of uprightness and integrity. His contemporaries ratified this self-judgment; later generations did not belie it. Writing in the nineteenth century, Carlyle allotted to Samuel Johnson a place among the typically great Englishmen, and today we still number him, to use his own words, "among those writers who have lent fire to virtue and confidence to truth".

THE LITERATURE OF THE INTELLECT

The intellect now tasted a moment of pure delight. Nothing now to restrict its freedom—tradition, reverence, mystery, all gone! For a whole section of humanity the heart, as the seat of the feelings, had been put aside as an organ for which they had no use; as for the imagination, that was stark madness. But there remained the intellect, a gem of purest ray serene. What a joy it was to think, to use one's brains, and to think quickly! What an intellectual treat to think a thing out for oneself and then to explain it to others. At one time, there was supposed to be a sort of balance of powers, of which the intellect was but one. Then men turned to poetry, and the intellect fell behind. But between the two, there was reason, whose glittering coinage was flung about with reckless prodigality. Between Heaven above, which no one now made any attempt to pierce, and the depths of the unconscious, which no one was disposed to probe, men settled down in a plain and unmysterious country where they felt perfectly comfortable and at home, and which they proceeded to illumine in order to enhance its attractiveness.

The intellect was cultivated at Court, for by its means the royal mistresses maintained themselves in favour after their physical charms had faded. In town, too, it was much in vogue. Even your ordinary bourgeois thought much of it; even the man in the street. It entered into discussions about matters of taste, though taste still retained about it an indefinable "something" that was not a little puzzling. It wormed its way into the world of Art, and into the world of Literature, too, whereof it became a sort of tricksy Ariel.

Notwithstanding manifold differences, both individual and national, there was a certain family likeness among its various partisans. They were all very clear-cut in their ideas, all very confident, and all very keen-witted. The common ancestor of the whole brood was Fontenelle, who, though now a very old man, was still alive. One of the earliest of the younger family was Marivaux, who tried his hand at all manner of things, journalism, novel-writing picaresque or sentimental, to find at last his real vocation in the drama, the drama of ideas. He chose, as his particular theme, the narrow dividing-line between the first hesitant hint of dawning affection, and the frank avowal of the feelings; between love too shy to confess itself, love that was fain to deny itself, and love that was open and frankly avowed. The margin left him scanty room, but it sufficed. Between those narrow and restricting borders he executes all manner of mazy winds and turns, losing his thread, it would seem, for the mere pleasure of finding it again. Just as the student of Nature scans attentively the premonitory signs that portend a coming metamorphosis or change of state, so does he observe and note those subtle, elusive signs which seem at first to be drawing the characters away from their appointed destiny; whereas they are in truth but bringing them nearer to it. Strange comedies, his, surprises that fail to surprise us, since we see them coming from afar; our sole interest being in the manner of their coming. There are no incidents, no elaborate stage devices, scarcely any plot to speak of. His knights and ladies have not even got surnames of their own, and if his footmen and chamber-maids are better off in this respect, it is that they have borrowed theirs from the old-fashioned comedy. So, free and unhampered by any traditional conventions, he scores a striking success with this new departure of his, this plan to make affairs of the heart affairs of the head as well. His young ladies, his youthful suitors, his kind-hearted old fathers, his lacqueys and serving-wenches, are all people with brains. Even his boors, though they pretend to be dull-witted clowns, only do so in order to introduce a dash of variety into the otherwise completely highbrow atmosphere; and even when Harlequin is doing the farcical stuff his part requires, even when he is perpetrating some outrageous "bloomer", he manages, somehow, to tip us the wink that he is not such a fool after all, and hints that it costs him not a little even to look such an utter nincompoop. At last, when the whole business is cleared up, when it's no good pretending any longer, when everybody's real sentiments are laid bare, the curtain is rung down, the play is ended.

Goldoni, on the other hand, looks at it in a very different light. All the various stage tricks and devices he freely makes use of, old, new, good, bad and indifferent—he adopts them all. He trudges along with his wandering troupe. He could no more get on without them, than they without him. He had his work cut out and no mistake, turning out comedy after comedy. For a single carnival, he had to knock off sixteen. He can't put his pen down an instant. Some actress is waiting for her part; she simply must have it tomorrow, or maybe, this very day. He works like a slave, but he gets no richer. Any night he might be hissed off the stage. Well, if the thing is a flop, hard lines; but never mind, better luck next time. Things are quite different these days. Now it is all happy-go-lucky, slap-dash, hit or miss. No time for preparation; everything has to be done on the spur of the moment. No hankering after the *Comédie italienne* comfortably housed in some Paris playhouse; no *Théâtre français* for him, but just the old wagon of Thespis, lumbering along from town to town, and, at last, to finish up with, exile and a poverty-stricken old age. Nevertheless, he was one of those who could tell a hawk from a handsaw. The fates and the spirit of the age had combined to endow him with the quick, shrewd glance which, while not going right down to those deep places of the heart where rage may sometimes flare up in the very midst of laughter, observes, and takes in, at any rate what it sees on the surface. And that, too, is one aspect of humanity, if only a superficial one. He saunters along the Piazzetta, has a chat with an elderly senator, strolls into a café, or goes to pay a call. No matter what it is, he always manages to catch the typical trait, the characteristic look, the particular kink, or whatever he wants to get. Then, off he goes to put the subject of his snapshot into a comedy, sets him just where he ought to be and, by perfectly simple means, gives him just the degree of significance that becomes him. The result is never a failure, and is sometimes a masterpiece.

Ramon de la Cruz is a sort of Spanish cousin of his. He has the same insight, and the same simple technique, but a more biting satire. On broad canvases he is not very first-rate, but on smaller ones he excels. He studies the ways of the humbler classes in Madrid, how they behave themselves in the street, in the markets, on the Marché du Rostro, on holidays and on ordinary days; then he portrays them, and says, as he does so, "I write and the box-office dictates".

As for Wieland, may we not call him the *virtuoso* of the understanding? He is really too clever. He never sticks at anything.

He is so quick to recognize the defects, as well as the merits, of whatever the thing may be, that he loses faith in it. He gets something or other out of every great writer, but never takes a firm grip of anything. He comes under a host of different influences, but somehow one feels that whatever his enthusiasm at the moment may be, it is tinged with a longing for something else which he might have taken up and did not. He is more inquisitive about ideas than really absorbed in them. As soon as he has found out what they are about, his interest wanes, and he lets them drop. Even his irony is mere banter, and not to be taken seriously. If he got really angry it would imply that he had misconceived the object of his irony, and that would have been an unpardonable fault, worthy of a fool. If his novels seem interminable, that is because he ambles along without any particular object in view, putting off getting to his destination as long as he can, so as to enjoy as much as possible any delights that may crop up by the way. If his poetry is no more than an agreeable sort of prose, the reason is that he looked on his poetry-writing as nothing more than an amiable pastime. Greece is not his spiritual home, not even the Greece of the Anthology. No, he is much more at his ease with that European community blazoned on whose standard was the word "Intellect". It was not for nothing that he hymned the Graces; they gave ear to his petitioning, and responded to it, perhaps all too liberally.[1]

Wit—that was the fine flower of the age. It was a subtle essence that was captured and crystallized in apothegms, or disseminated in satires. It found its way into works of fiction; in fact it was in the very air you breathed. Of itself alone, even when nothing else went with it, it was enough to bring reputation and something like fame to its possessor. Take the Abbé Galiani, for instance, that little midget of a man who was secretary to the Neapolitan ambassador. He drops in at Mme d'Epinay's, it may be, or at the Baron d'Holbach's. They have been expecting him to turn up. He settles himself in an armchair, takes off his wig, which he finds a nuisance, and sticks it on his fist. Then off he starts; rattling on, fidgeting, gesticulating, twisting about like a thing on wires. The poet Dorat has just brought out an illustrated edition of his works. He would have gone under, comments Galiani, if it hadn't been for the *planches* (i.e. planks,

[1] *Musarion oder die Philosophie der Grazien,* 1768.

or plates). He tells the company he has just been reading M. de Silva on Tactics. The author says that the attacking forces would stand a better chance if their bayonets were longer and their rifles shorter; just like the Jesuits, who lengthened the Creed and abridged the Commandments. He says that the Opera ought to be moved to the Sèvres Gate, over against the Bull-ring. Loud noises should be kept well away from the town. He reports that Sophie Arnould, the singer, has about the finest asthma he ever heard. The Opera had been shifted from the Palais Royal to the Salle des Tuileries. People were protesting, because the hall was *sourde* (literally " deaf" but here "bad for sound"). "Lucky hall", said he. He said the Ambassador, his chief, was stupid and lazy. "A good job, too", he added. "What a menace he would be if he were stupid and energetic!" When he was called over the coals for some of his outrageous remarks, he said he was so used to being in people's bad books, he would feel like a fish out of water anywhere else. Saurin went out, said Diderot, and the Abbé Galiani came in, and with that engaging personage came gaiety, imagination, wit, folly, jesting—everything that helps us to forget the troubles of life for a while.

But the most famous example of the species is Voltaire. He is a marvel of cleverness, and if there's anything he does not understand, it is because he does not choose to understand it. So ready, so spontaneous is wit with him, that he seems to have endowed it with its rarest quality; he makes it seem natural. What this wit is, this wit with which he is so inexhaustibly supplied, he himself has told us:

What is called "wit" is sometimes a startling comparison, sometimes a delicate allusion, or it may be a play upon words; you use a word in one sense, knowing that your interlocutor will understand it in another. Or it is a sly way of bringing into juxtaposition ideas not usually considered in association; it may be some far-fetched metaphor; a search for something which the object under examination does not at first reveal, but which is there all the same. It is the art of finding a link between two unlikes, or a difference between two likes. It is the art of saying half of what you mean and leaving the rest to the imagination. And I would tell you a lot more about wit, if only I had more of it myself.

As for poetry, well, poetry, a feeling for poetry, was not the strong point about the literature of the period. Prose was what was wanted and a new style of prose at that. And that, a new style of prose, the age did in fact create. Breaking down the old-fashioned elaborate periods—it deemed them ponderous, even in hands that had wielded them with masterly skill—discarding simile, imagery, metaphor, as though it wanted to strip the idea of everything not of its very essence, eliminating from its vocabulary all vague, woolly or equivocal terms, it substituted a form immediately recognizable from its perfect simplicity, from its being always vital, direct and rapid, a form which precluded any misconception that might have been brought about as a result of ambiguity in the terms employed or from an over-elaborated, over-ornamental style. It went straight and speedily to the point, leaving out such intermediate stages as seemed superfluous, all over-cumbersome transitions, and those middle terms of which only the slow-witted have need. So thoroughly was it stripped and pared, so bare and naked a thing was it that when one admired it, it was not very easy to say what it was one was admiring. The only thing was to keep repeating, over and over again, how perfect it was. The docile servant of a clear-cut idea, a faithful messenger that never misinterpreted the sender, indeed you could hardly call it a messenger, so closely identified was it with the analytical spirit which, in this happy era of philosophy, was brought to bear on every possible subject. In France, prose was becoming limpidity itself; indeed, if truth be told, a little too limpid, for it was beginning to betray a lack of colour. In Germany, the labours which were to find their ultimate expression in Lessing's full-bodied and vigorous style, were approaching fulfilment. But in Italy, a war was in progress. There, the new school were all for framing their sentences on the Parisian model, and loaded their vocabulary with gallicisms. The purists called down the wrath of heaven on these impious ones. No doubt the impious ones went too far; but then, so did the purists. The result was that out of this interaction of opposing and contradictory forces, in Italy and throughout the whole of Europe, modern prose was brought to birth.

THE LITERATURE OF THE SOCIAL GRACES

The individual as such, that is to say whatever was unique and incommunicable about him, might be left for subsequent ages to consider. What predominantly interested this age was, not where he differed from, but where he resembled his brother man. Evidently, men told themselves, their likenesses they owed to Nature, their differences arose from habit and custom. The superiority of nature over custom is proved by this very priority in time. Thus, men applied themselves to investigating what united, rather than what separated, man from man; their object was to trace resemblances, not differences. They laid stress on the characteristics which led to the inclusion of the Egyptians and the Persians within our family of nations, not on the things that made for their exclusion. They pointed out what the Hottentot had in common with ourselves in his psychology, not on the things that belonged to him exclusively as a Hottentot. To draw closer the social bonds, that was one of the tasks assigned to literature. Speaking about Wieland, Amelia, Duchess of Weimar, said, "It is clear from his writings that the more he gets to know about the human heart in general, the less he gets to know about it in any given individual." The same might have been said of many another who tried to create, if not a single unanimous human heart, then at least a single, unanimous attitude of mind.

Never before had the word "correspond" been fraught with such profound significance. Letters, being nothing more nor less than conversation, talk, carried on in writing, retained all the vivacity of the spoken word. People who sat down to write a letter made believe they were continuing the conversation, and, if they were not actually in the salon where they would have liked to be, they at least imagined they were there. See, here is a letter being brought in. The company gather round, someone begins reading: "Your letter was charming, my dear Chevalier. Everyone to whom I read it thought so too. It brought you back to me as in your palmiest days." "I got d'Alembert to read your letter to Mme du Châtelet and Mme de Mirepoix. They made him read it again, two or three times over. They couldn't have enough of it, and, there's no doubt about it, it is a masterpiece."[1] They touched on all sorts of things, these letters, and their naturalness is something to admire. They never force the note; any straining after effect would have spoilt the whole thing. People would merely have smiled.

[1]Mme du Deffand to the Chevalier d'Aydie, 14th July, 1755.

They recount the little daily happenings, what's on at the Opera, the latest thing at the theatre, the comings and goings of various people; Mme de Pompadour is in a very bad way; it doesn't look as if she were going to recover. The King is terribly short of money, and it's not the first time. They discuss the latest publications, the *Apologie de l'abbé de Prades*, new instalments of the Encyclopaedia, Voltaire's pamphlets, Richardson's novels, *Pamela, Clarrissa, Grandison,* which they describe as high-life as a printer might see it, the sort of love-stories a Methodist preacher might have written. They touched on politics, they alluded to religion. With the rarest exceptions, the writer never talked about his own trials and tribulations, never made out that he was different from the rest of mankind, that he was a soul apart, never gave you to understand that he was the most hapless of mortals, born under an unlucky star, or how lonely he was among his fellow-men, how he dwelt, as it were, on an inaccessible island, condemned there to abide till the end of his days. On the contrary, a chameleon-like instinct prompted him to adapt himself to his correspondent, to take on his colour, his humour, to tell him all he could, without risking any rash revelations about himself.

From Paris, then, from London, Berlin, Milan, Rome, these letters went forth, and, voyaging thus from these centres to far-off places on the distant confines of Europe, they wove a vast network to and fro, along whose several threads thronged the ceaseless traffic of ideas. There were letters from Mme du Deffand, which bore into the very heart of Russia the wit and sparkle of her salon. There were letters from all manner of lesser female lights, Mme de Greffigny, Mme de Staal, and a host of minor Mme de Sévignés up and down the world. There were the letters of Fanny Burney, the letters of Lady Mary Wortley Montagu with all the news from Constantinople and the East. There was the Abbé Galiani, home in Naples now, and flashing message after message back to Paris. There was Horace Walpole, too. Frederick II's letters would have been unsurpassed for power and vivacity had it not been for Voltaire's. It may be said, without exaggeration, that in addition to his "works", every writer left behind him a quantity of correspondence equal and sometimes superior in value to his formal publications. The epistolary romance, the story told in letters, strikes us as artificial nowadays; it was natural enough to an age that looked on letter-writing, not as a burden, but as a daily diversion.

Encyclopaedia, Article *Hebdomadaire*, "of or appertaining to a week, or period of seven days, hence we have weekly gazettes, news-weeklies, publications appearing every seven days, such periodicals being the pabulum of the ignorant, the sort of thing that attracts people who want to be able to get a notion of ideas and discuss them, without taking the trouble to study them seriously. They are the bane and aversion of all conscientious students. No reputable writer ever got a worthy line out of them, no bad one was ever prevented by them from turning out bad work." Vain protests! How were you going to resist an invasion such as this, inspired as it was by this ever-growing desire to link up, to "get together"? The successors of Steele and Addison had made a fortune in their own country. Upwards of a hundred and fifty different periodicals were circulating among the British public in 1750, the year that Samuel Johnson brought out his *Rambler*. England was specially prolific in these edifying journals and they swarmed everywhere, even in countries that had only recently joined in the general movement, such as Hungary and Poland; nowhere, however, did they find the climate more favourable than in Germany. From 1713, when the series opened with *Der Vernünftige*, "The Man of Sense", and ending up with the year 1761, we may count no fewer than one hundred and eighty-two periodicals of a similar character. It was, as it were, an exchange of ideas, a sort of correspondence carried on betwixt publisher and reader, a bond of union between members of a given coterie who learn things together, read about the latest ideas together, and together find satisfaction in all those moral commonplaces about despising wealth, prizing virtue, and achieving happiness. And, as if all these various national periodicals were not enough, there were others, cosmopolitan ones, promulgating ideas which it was fast becoming not only a matter of ambition, but a moral duty to exchange.

Gradually the minor forms in the sphere of art took the place of the greater ones. Having failed with the Epic, they made the best they could of the madrigal. Brief lyrics about beauteous ladies and their gallants replaced poems of more ambitious length. The fashionable world, weary of comedies and tragedies, now fell back on proverbs, pithy sayings; grand opera became comic opera; the canzone was now the canzonetta. Similarly, in architecture, great châteaux, with their majestic wings, gave place to small and dainty dwellings. Just as in the world of art, little pictures took the place of imposing frescoes, just as, with furniture, the comfortable armchair ousted the throne-like stall, and just as, with life in general, the dainty replaced the grand, so in the world of literature, solemn, stately compositions had gone out of fashion. Philosophizing was still the vogue, but it was considered good form not to look too serious about it, and writers exchanged the fresco for the pastel, or the miniature. Even when the ferment was at its height, even in the days of the *Essay on Man* and the Encyclopaedia, the paradox existed. Or was it such a paradox after all? Was is not, rather, a strange association between seeming contraries of which we of today no longer possess the secret? You might have thought, about many and many a writer, that he was two men rolled into one, one stiff and solemn, the other all smiles, the most easy-going fellow imaginable; for example, you might have imagined there were two Gressets, one who composed the ode on *Ingratitude*:

> Quelle Furie au teint livide
> Souffle en ces lieux un noir venin?
> Sa main tient ce fer parricide
> Qui d'Agrippine ouvrit le sein;
> L'Insensible oubli, l'Insolence,
> Les sourdes haines, en silence,
> Entourent ce monstre éffronté,
> Et tour à tour leur main barbare
> Va remplir sa coupe au Tartare
> Des froides ondes du Léthé.[1]

and the Gresset who wrote *Ver-Vert* or the *Chartreuse*:

[1]What Fury with livid features breathes forth in these regions a dark poison? Her hand grasps the parricidal sword that pierced the breast of Agrippina; Oblivion that neither hears nor sees, Insolence and black Hatred in silence attend this brazen monster. From time to time they go in turn to fill in Tartarus its cup with the chill waters of Lethe.

Vainqueur du chagrin léthargique,
Par un heureux tour de penser,
Je sais me faire un jeu comique
Des peines que je vais tracer
Ainsi l'aimable poésie
Qui dans le reste de la vie
Porte assez peu d'utilité,
De l'objet le moins agréable
Vient adoucir l'austerité
Et nous sauve au moins par la fable
Des ennuis de la vérité.[1]

Nor were the men of genius slow to follow. There were two Montesquieus; one of them wrote a grave treatise about laws, the other made fun of them.

The world was full of paradoxes. Germany, carved up into pieces as she was, was beginning to grow conscious of herself. Why should she not have a literature of her own, as well as other countries? From the University of Halle, one of her ideological strongholds, there came forth three students, three friends, Johann Ludwig Wilhelm Gleim, Johann Peter Uz, and Johann Nikolaus Götz, who were the first to court the Lyric Muse. And whose lyre did they choose? Anacreon's. Anacreon was their master. They sang of Bacchus, his features all bedaubed with wine-lees, they sang of wine and feasting, of fair women and of love. Wilhelm was the living embodiment of the classico-rational spirit. And who was his model? Horace. Nothing pleased him more than to hear people speak of him as the German Horace. More surprising still was the case of Friedrich von Hagedorn. He pushed the classical spirit to the farthest possible limits. His all-absorbing aim was to purify the language and to chasten literary style. In his view the creative effort of the poet is not the soul endeavouring to reveal itself to the universe, or the soul's effort to capture the universe and make it her own; but the proper subordination of the parts to the whole. First he took up the French school, then the English, and he profited

[1]Vanquisher of listless Grief, I know how, by a happy turn of thought, to make light of the pains that will fall to my lot. This kindly poetry, which in ordinary life is of little practical use, makes the grimmest experience less austere, and by means of her fables saves us from the boredom of truth.

from this twofold lesson since he acquired a taste for the clear, the simple, the intelligible. But there was one thing he did not acquire and that was depth. Frivolity seemed to have nothing about it incompatible with his gravity, and of his liking for the frivolous he made no secret. Writing to Christian Ludwig Liscow on the 28th December, 1739, he says, "A smack of the sensual is the only thing lacking in your education. If you had that, you'd be perfection."

In Italy, there were a number of serious-minded, resolute people who, in alliance with the intellectuals, were trying to bring about a reform in the national economy and an improvement in rural conditions. But side by side with these graver activities, a whole army of smaller fry were busily turning out a lot of trumpery rhymes, little pretty-pretty things about nothing of note, a wedding, a birth, a christening, someone taking the veil, someone getting through an examination, recovering from an illness, somebody's birthday, such were some of the trifling occasions that led these poetasters to put pen to paper. The country was flooded with elegies, ballads, odes and sonnets. A fatal facility for turning out rhymes tempted these elegant loungers to pick up the pen and turn out their stuff by the yard. They found the same sort of diversion in composing quatrains or octets as the French did playing cup-and-ball. To M. le Marquis Pier Maria della Rosa, who, though Autumn has come, continues to live on in the country. To a pin that fastened the veil that hid Neaera's breast, and that Filinda purloined. To a sweet Nymph who wore a pink petticoat and a blue stomacher. On Crinatea's sweet canary. On presenting a darling little puppy to his mistress. Lofty themes, indeed. You might turn out a little ode in the morning and proffer it later on, as you might a pinch of snuff or a sugarplum. Verses were bandied like compliments or courteous salutations; it all being part of the ritual proceedings of a society whose members were just like actors and actresses, with their paint and their powder, their entrances and exits, their cues, their various rôles. There were the poets by profession who gained a precarious livelihood from their cultivation of the great; there were the amateurs who, for all the world, would never have given up the insignificant position they occupied in the procession that was trying to climb Parnassus. There were women poets, too, for the fact is that anybody and everybody had taken to rhyming. And they had their poems printed on superlative paper, on vellum, or even on rose-coloured silk. And they put them together into volumes, these masterpieces, things like *Lagrime in morte di un gatto*—"Tears on the death of a cat". These latter-day Anacreons and Horaces were just as plentiful in Italy as they were in Germany, only in Italy they did not take themselves quite so seriously. "What am I?" exclaimed Frugoni, a typical example of this butterfly breed, "Just a pedlar of rhymes, that is all; no poet." He was under no illusion. He knew well enough that when he died his verses would die with him and be heard of no more:

i versi miei
Tutti col mio morire
Sconoscuti morrano.

The thing was to make the most of this life. No sort of pleasure, were it never so insubstantial, was to be despised if it made life more agreeable. No strain of music however frail and fleeting but would help to swell the joyful diapason that was to soar upwards from the earth. Anacreon, as Gleim observed, bade avaunt to care and haunting fear. Horace, said Hagedorn, was a kindly philosopher, an Aristippus and no Diogenes, a friend to mankind; and Horace was a voluptuary, he stood for self-indulgence, for the cushioned life, as Voltaire frankly told him:

Je t'écris aujourd'hui, voluptueux Horace,
A toi qui respiras la mollesse et la grâce,
Qui, facile en tes vers et gai dans tes discours,
Chantas les doux loisirs, les vins et les amours.[1]

Thus the senses, puffed up with pride, clamoured for their share of recognition. Finally, it must be remembered that some of the outstanding ideas of the age, as defined by its leading men, had filtered through to the mob; the idea that pleasure ought to be grasped in any shape or form, the idea that pleasure was an essential ingredient of happiness. In those days,

[1]To thee I write today, O pleasure-loving Horace; to thee who breathest the air of gentle ease and grace, who, facile in thy verse and gay in thy discourse, didst sing of sweet repose, of wine, of love.

"Literature was one of life's adornments, one of the charms that help to create the happiness for which our nature yearns. Pleasure is the order of the day."[1]

But this literature of charm and culture might include erotic poetry, dubious stories, pornographic novels. Still, every now and again it achieved—and this is its crowning glory—a rare, an unprecedented grace; though not indeed a spontaneous, innocent grace, a thing unaware of itself, so to speak. Nevertheless, studied and self-conscious as it was, it was something so delicate, so fine that the secret of it escaped detection. A moment of winged music, a glimpse of some unfolding arabesque, a gleam of light mirrored on calm waters. It was as much the outcome of elaborate machinery as the apparatus required to produce stage-thunder. The opera, in fact, perfected as Metastasio had perfected it, was one vast machine. Take the most artificial form of composition it is possible to imagine, the *libretto*. Bear in mind that, as Baretti pointed out, it has, in the first place, to fulfil all the requirements of the composer; next to comply with whatever demands the vocalists may make on it, and, finally, to observe the strict convention which in some given act may require a solo, a duet, a recitative, or what not. Then it must conform to the limitations of a vocabulary to which any out-of-the-way word, any word too startlingly picturesque, or too harshly cacophonous would be anathema. There are other difficulties, and these are of Metastasio's own making. His libretto must needs conform to the pattern of tragic drama, and he invokes Aristotle as his authority. Such trifling departures from that pattern as he may have permitted himself were all made for a special purpose. All very hampering and restrictive; yet sometimes a touch of grace, of beauty will redeem the whole seemingly thankless composition; nay, at times it grows so beautiful, so entrancing that the heart is moved to tears. "So tender was the genius of Metastasio", says Stendhal, "that it made him avoid anything that might give pain, however slight, to the spectator. He refused to avail himself of anything calculated to rend the heart or harrow the feelings. No unhappy endings; never a hint of the sad realities of life; never a whisper of those chilling suspicions that eat like a canker into the tenderest affections. From the passions, he took just what was needed

[1]Gustave Lanson, *Voltaire,* 1910, Chap. V, *Le goût de Voltaire.*

to awaken the interest of the spectators, without jarring on their feelings. He exalted *la volupté*."

Take another method of approach: take a very minor instrument, the octosyllabic line, and a very arid-souled performer, Voltaire, a threadbare theme, the flight of time, oncoming age and Death which comes to claim its due. Yet the whole will be redeemed by an inimitable grace:

> Si vous voulez que j'aime encore,
> Rendez-moi l'âge des amours. . . .[1]

Like Wieland, the author of *Musarion, ou la Philosophie des Grâces* (1768): they, the folk of those days, had the Graces in their hearts and the love of Coypel before their eyes.[2]

THE LITERATURE OF FACT: HISTORY

We now come to one of the most difficult of their enterprises, the pursuit of fact in a fleeting past. The attempt had to be made in order that they might round off their conception of the world. As we survey them at their task, we shall behold in operation a process which some people have not hesitated to describe as a revolution in Western thought.[3]

Writers bent on reconstructing the past would have had no difficulty if they had had only outside enemies to contend with. These latter were numerous enough, but they were not very consistent: there were the showy, the rhetorical school for whom history was a succession of striking events, of deeds novel and strange, dramas of every kind, wars, rebellions, riots, trials and love-affairs. They penetrated into the private apartments of dead kings, recorded their deliberations, reported their speeches, delineated their features. These were historians of the dramatic school. Then there were the compilers, like Rollin, who confessed that in order to enrich and embellish his *Histoire ancienne*, he had freely borrowed from all and sundry, often without giving the name of the author he was laying under contribution, and that for the very good reason that, whenever it suited his purpose, he would take all sorts of liberties with

[1]If you would have me still to love, then give me back my youthful time again.
[2]Heinse referring to Wieland. Quoted by Victor Michel, *C. H. Wieland,* 1938.
[3]Friedrich Meinecke, *Die Entstehung des Historismus,* Berlin, 1936.

the passage he was quoting. Then there were those brazen people—or were they just simpletons?—who, without batting an eyelid, announced that they intended to write the complete history—civil, natural, political, religious—of all the countries of the world. Then, by way of contrast, there were others who were for serving up history in tabloid form: there was Père Buffier who talked a lot about his system of mnemonics. A single word, *Rabismaf*, would enable you to reel off all the kings of Aragon in their proper order, as well as their conquests, for, given the initials, the names come easily enough: Ramir, Alfonso, Barcelona 1138, Jacque, Sicily 1276, Martin, Alfonso V, Ferdinand V the Catholic. There were imitators of Père Buffier who, like him, wrote the history of France in rhyme:

> Pharamond, du début de l'empire romain,
> Fonda l'État des Francs vers l'an quatre-cent-vingt.
> Roi payen mais connu pour législateur sage,
> Il établit les lois, il en montra l'usage.
> Dans les Gaules jamais ce fondateur n'entra;
> De succéder aux rois les femmes il priva,
> Par la salique loi, qui fut toujours suivie. . . .[1]

Other pedagogues there were who composed schoolbooks in the form of question and answer; this sort of thing:

Question: Describe the character of Louis XI.

Answer: He was an astute politician and had his passions under complete control. He was brave, moderate in his pleasures, and outwardly devout, but he was suspicious, vindictive and an arch-dissembler. He was a powerful and despotic ruler and posterity has included him among the evil kings. . . .

Finally came glossaries of technical terms, chronological tables, which assigned doubtful dates to disputed events, without the slightest attempt to verify any of them. In short, of historians in the strict sense, there were none.

But it was within their own ranks, within themselves, that these innovators encountered their real foes. They knew perfectly

[1]Pharamond, at the beginning of the Roman Empire, founded the kingdom of the Franks about the year 420. He was a Pagan king but recognized as a sound legislator. He established the laws and showed how they were to be employed. This founder never made his way into the country of the Gauls; he deprived women of the right of succeeding kings by the Salic law, which was always observed.

well what a fund of patience they needed, yet they *would* scamp their work; they knew perfectly well that diligent research, profound study should be their sure foundation, but they did not care for study. A certain amount of reading, research, enquiry, that was well enough. But to go rummaging about among a lot of ancient archives, heaping up piles of old documents, forcing your way into repositories when the doors were not freely opened to you—all that sort of thing seemed to these gentlemen mere pedantic fussiness. They had a cordial hatred of Baldus, Scioppius, Lexicocrassus, Scriblerus and their like, tending to confound them with real men of learning. "The days of men like Vossius, Huet, Borchardt and Kircher are over and done with. All this learning, all this painful research is a weariness to the flesh. We find it much more to our taste to skim the surface of things, than to go lumbering about in the depths."[1] President de Brosses, finding himself at Modena with an hour to spare, went, he tells us, to the Library, where he saw Muratori, the illustrious scholar who brought out into the light of day the great outstanding landmarks of mediaeval Italy. "We found the old fellow, with his four white hairs on his bald pate, working away, regardless of the biting cold, fireless and hatless in that icy gallery, surrounded by a whole pile of antiques, and old Italian junk, for I cannot bring myself to dignify with the name of 'antique' everything connected with that deplorable age of darkness. I cannot conceive that, theological polemics excepted, there can be anything so unattractive as work of that kind."[2] President de Brosses is perfectly willing to see men like Du Cange and Muratori sacrificing themselves like Curtius and plunging into the chasm, but he is under no temptation to follow their example.

To acquire such a degree of self-devotion as that needs time; one has to get to it by degrees. But stripping and pruning the fact, ridding it of everything adventitious—that was an operation of some delicacy. There was a quality that was really extraneous to it but which had been so long and so closely associated with it that it seemed to be of the same substance, and that was the moral element. History must not be indifferent to the deeds of men, it must display vice defeated and virtue triumphant, the good

[1]Abbé Coyer, *Dissertations pour être lues*, 1755.

[2]Ch. de Brosses, *Lettres familières sur l'Italie.* No. 53, Visit to Modena.

rewarded and the wicked punished. That, our sires and our grandsires had repeated over and over again, and the generation following 1715 did not repudiate the heritage, they merely modified it. They stipulated that the morality thus introduced should be of the philosophic order; which simply meant that they substituted their own particular prejudice for that of their predecessors, so that they were no nearer getting to the bedrock residuum, though that was still their objective. Instead of imparting their lessons to the subjects of a country, they addressed them to those unhappy mortals who go by the name of "princes", men who were fated never to see men except behind a mask. They turned their attention, needless to say, to the Church; they were anti-clerical and anti-papal. Besides which there was that everlasting presence which tormented them, these new historians, and they were anti-Bossuetists from the bottom of their hearts. They made no effort to study the Middle Ages as a fact in history which they had to grasp, but as an error which they had to refute. When they came to deal with Mahometanism, they made it the text for a denunciation of the calumnies falsely levied against it by the Christians; as for the Crusades, they were an exhibition of stark madness. If they extolled the Renaissance, it was not because of its intrinsic merits, but because it had ushered in the Age of Reason. "History is philosophy teaching us by examples how we ought to conduct ourselves in all the situations of public and private life; consequently we should apply ourselves to it in a philosophic spirit."[1] So says Bolingbroke. But the most difficult thing to overcome was the habit of judging the past in the light of the present, and finding fault with the men of the past for being men of their own day. A certain Abbé once naïvely remarked: "Let us put ourselves back at the very dawn of the world's history; let us examine things as careful observers should." It never dawned on him that the earliest ages of the world were to be judged by eighteenth-century standards, seeing that those standards were valid for all time. Never suspecting that they were stultifying their own ideas, the rationalists "transformed questions of origin into questions of logic." The abstract was lying in wait for them just when it was the concrete which they were trying to attain. What they needed, to acquire the true historical sense, was a complete change in their conception

[1]Bolingbroke, *Letters on the Study and use of History,* 1752, No. III.

of truth, and in their intellectual approach. "Physical and mathematical proof should take precedence of moral proof, just as the latter should take precedence of historical proof."[1] That being their profound belief, was it to be expected that they would reverse this order of things against their own convictions and restore historical proof to its pride of place?

Of their practical aims, the primary one was this: History was to be something more than mere story-telling, it should be a science. *Divorcio de la Historia y de la Fabula.* Up to now, historians had only made of it a sort of tarnished mirror. They never dreamt of all the contradictions it could harbour, so long as it was not based on a foundation of solid fact; a spirit of error, a *lying spirit,* had pervaded it all through, and made it less worthy of credence than children's nursery-tales. To remedy this state of things, what had to be done was to institute the critical examination of evidence, whereupon all kinds of methods were proposed, all of them amounting to the same thing. "What we mean by history is a true and faithful narrative, a sincere and accurate account of events based on the testimony of eye-witnesses, on duly authenticated documents, or on the statements of trustworthy persons.

"An alleged historical fact may be regarded as duly authenticated when it is corroborated by a certain number of contemporary writers of satisfactory education and probity, provided always that their evidence is not rebutted by other persons of similar weight and standing." Thus speaks Lenglet du Fresnoy in his *Histoire justifiée contre les romans* (1735).

The ideal thing of course would be only to put down things you had seen with your own eyes, or of which you had had direct personal experience. So Frederick II went so far as to say. His idea was, no doubt, that the rulers of nations and the leaders of armies were the only people in a position to know, and therefore to report, the events for which they had been responsible. Failing direct, first-hand evidence, there was, of course, nothing for it but to rely on second-hand testimony; but this should always be regarded with suspicion, and not accepted without satisfactory guarantees of credibility. Hartley, and, after him, Priestley, suggested some sort of mathematical formula to gauge

[1]Diderot, *Introduction aux grands principes. Le prosélyte répondant par lui-même.* Œuvres, II, p. 81.

the degree of credibility to be attached to any given statement, this in unconscious deference to that geometrical spirit of theirs, which thus asserted its dominion over them. It was but continuing along the same lines when it suggested to them that they should take the probable as the sole criterion of truth. Anyhow they were not going to be taken in any more, if they could possibly help it. Who were the witnesses? What was their evidence worth? Were they intelligent people? Had they lived in a good sized town, in view of neighbours who could have corrected them if they had made a statement not strictly in accordance with the facts? Were they contemporaneous with the documents they quoted? Let us take care not to believe in any of those romantic stories recorded by obscure chroniclers away down in some ignorant and uncivilized province. Our business is to stick to facts, thoroughly well-authenticated facts, about which no sensible person could feel any doubt, things like the Battle of Pharsalia, or the capture of Constantinople by the Turks. So anxious were they for certitude that they would have gone the length of making a clean sweep of all ancient history. Levesque de Pouilly made a painful sensation when, in 1723, he read a paper before the Académie des Inscriptions casting doubt on the accuracy of the early history of Rome: "The dearth of any considerable historic remains, the ignorance or untrustworthiness of the chroniclers, compels us to say that we have no sure evidence to go upon concerning Romulus and the early kings, the defeat of the Gauls, or about any of those heroic deeds associated with the name of Regulus." Nevertheless, his view of the matter was soon to become general. The spirit of scepticism gained ground. What did we really know about primitive times? or about the Middle Ages? History proper should be held to start with the fifteenth century, not before. But at this stage a halt was called. There was another danger to be guarded against, and that was Pyrrhonism, universal doubt. We know nothing, properly speaking, except what is confirmed by incontestable evidence. What we have to do is to extend the area of such certitude as far as we can.

Secondly, we should recognize our limitations. The works that carried most weight today were not those that set themselves to pierce the infinities of space and time. There was, for example, the sound and monumental *Institutionum historiae ecclesiasticae libri quatuor* of Johann Lorenz von Mosheim, of which the first edition is dated 1720; there were monographs, too, *Histoire de Charles XII, Histoire du Siècle de Louis XIV* both by Voltaire; *History of the Reign of the Emperor Charles V*, by William Robertson. There were histories of races, of peoples, such as Montesquieu's *Histoire de la grandeur des Romains et de leur décadence,* followed, like the second rap of a postman's knock, by Gibbon's *Decline and Fall of the Roman Empire* (1776–1781). There were histories of nations, like David Hume's *History of Great Britain, History of England under the House of Tudor* (1754–1778), William Robertson's *History of Scotland* (1759). There was even a history of a region, a locality, the *Osnabrückische Geschichte* of Justus Möser (1768).

Thirdly, it was good-bye to the marvellous; and the marvellous, of course, included the supernatural. Never a Greek or a Roman but had given accounts of oracles, prodigies, prophecies and miracles. Many serious authors referred to them with the utmost gravity, and, in days gone by, the general run of people freely believed in them. They were none the less superstitions, all of them, and it was quite impossible to find any rational grounds for accepting them. They were invented to serve a purpose, then they were elaborated and embellished, and finally became a religious institution. Trumped-up nonsense, all of them, and to be rejected *en bloc*. The Bible itself came under the general ban.

"Now", said Burke in a letter to Gibbon, "the great map of humanity is unrolled." And that, indeed, was one of the things demanded. History was no longer to be devoted exclusively to descriptions of battles, to analysing the complicated wiles and ruses of diplomats, or to singing the praises of men who had been exalted to the status of heroes. Its main purpose should be the study of civilization. "Man is the subject of every history", says Bolingbroke. "If", said Duclos, "the history I write is not concerned with wars, nor politics, nor economics . . . people will be asking what kind of history I *do* propose to write. The answer is, the history of men and their manners and customs." And then Voltaire, "This is no mere account of military campaigns, but a study of men, their habits and customs." The statement thus reiterated is significant, the change it portends is of particular importance, and nowhere does it find more forcible expression than in the *Essai sur les Mœurs*. Deflected a little from its proper track by the obvious design to make it serve as a counterblast to Bossuet, and thus falling into the very faults which it presumed to condemn—too much haste, statements based on second- or third-hand evidence, mere compilation—it none the less remains one of the outstanding works of its time, one which future ages will treasure because it bears upon its pediment this device: "I aim at showing how human societies came into being, how life went on in the home, what arts were cultivated, rather than at telling over again the old tale of disasters and misfortune, the familiar warp and woof of history, those well-worn examples of human malice and depravity."

Well, did all this "enthusiasm for history"[1] enable them to bring their project to a successful end, the project, that is to say, of endowing history, once for all, with a firm and enduring character? Were they able to substitute for the stability and identity in which they had hitherto believed, the idea of evolution? Montesquieu, in his personal notes, records that he was greatly impressed by a theory of Vico's in which he speaks of *corsi e ricorsi*. In their earliest state, nations are barbarous, they make conquests and become amenable to law and order; they grow greater and at the same time more polished, this weakens them, they are conquered in their turn and relapse into barbarism. Virtually all the nations in the world revolve in this cycle. In his *Considérations sur les causes de la grandeur et de la décadence des Romains*, Montesquieu adheres to the idea of growth, maturity and decay. This idea of the passage from maturity to decay so impressed the generation as a whole that there was scarcely a single contemporary historian who did not adopt it. It is one of the most notable indications of the great man's influence. There is something pathetic about the way Voltaire, too, does his utmost to discover an upward evolutionary process in human things. Very gradual, it may be, very arduous and constantly beset with dangers and difficulties, and yet, every now and again, at some favoured moment in the course of civilization, it becomes discernible. Troubles, sufferings untold, the spirit of war, murder, rapine abroad in the world; nevertheless, amid all the havoc and destruction, there was manifest a love of order which secretly inspired mankind and preserved them from utter ruin. "It is

[1] Joh. Chr. Adelungs, *Pragmatische Staatsgeschichte Europens*. Gotha, 1762, p. 11.

one of Nature's never-failing sources of strength. To it we owe the code of nations; because of it the ministers of justice are held in respect in Tonkin, in the Island of Formosa, no less than in Rome." Voltaire breathes again, and takes heart of grace when he comes to one of those periods in history which are as dwellings in the homeless wilds, such as the age of Alexander, of Augustus, of Leo X, or of Louis XIV. He is grateful to those great men, for they keep him in good heart. For Lessing, the education of mankind is something that is still in process of becoming. The light of reason, even when it shines from without, is absorbed by the reason within which never suffers final extinction, but stubbornly pursues its onward course, and will pursue it till the day when heavenly truth and human truth shall unite together and shine as one. And now, after Lessing, the way is open for Herder.

Can they be said to have reached that concrete objectivity from which, at the outset, they were so far away? Not entirely. History, hitherto, has not amounted to a resurrection. Some have not been able to resist the temptation to dramatize their subject. Others have been too dry-as-dust. Others, again, carried away by their eloquence, have not always succeeded in re-creating the living simplicity of a real world. Things did not appear to them, so to speak, in flesh and blood. So much for the majority of them; but firmly based on the soil of his own little bit of native ground, realizing that if you dissect the chords of a symphony, the effect of the whole escapes you, knowing that brave deeds may cloak a grain of cowardice, and that altruism is not always so unselfish as it looks, Justus Möser it was who came nearest to the *Realgeschichte*. He had a sense—which increased as he progressed with his *Osnabrückische Geschichte*—of the complex nature of things. Still, he was and is the least European of all his philosophic contemporaries, seeing that his reputation, great as it was in Germany, did not extend beyond it, and that, compared with Montesquieu, Voltaire, Robertson and Gibbon, he remained comparatively unknown.

But did they renounce, as completely as they had proposed to do, the practice of explaining things in the light of general laws, and so running the risk of relapsing into the metaphysics which they had discarded? The answer is that they had not renounced it. It might be that the key to history was interest, self-love, or that idol, trade, as the Abbé Raynal maintained in his *Histoire philosophique et politique des établissements et du commerce des européens dans les deux Indes*; or perhaps some kind of Time-Spirit; or was it a combination of interests: "Men's minds are constantly influenced by three things; these are, their climate, their government and their religion. That is the only way to explain the enigma of this world."[1]

Or were we to take it, when we remembered how causes sometimes imperceptible were followed by the most stupendous results, that there was some mysterious Fate behind it all? They had resolved to concentrate on phenomena without seeking to discover their first causes; then, having made that resolution, it was to the discovery of first causes that they obstinately addressed themselves.

The result was that the history they wrote was not perfect; but when will the perfect history be written? Still, they did their work well. Theirs was a most difficult task, and they acquitted themselves with credit. Of erudition, research, they were inclined to fight shy, unless, that is to say, it could be made to yield some entertainment. Nevertheless, they did not underrate the importance of evidence, and they endeavoured to build on a basis of sound documentation. Pruning here, lopping there, they cleared the way for the future. Torn between two opposing forces, on the one side their own philosophy, which was to be empirical, respecting the fact and nothing but the fact, and, on the other, a natural tendency to the abstract, to the *a priori*, to the great systems to which, willy-nilly, reality must needs submit, they sacrificed sometimes, but not always, their private inclination to the historical method they had finally adopted. They left behind them masterpieces marked by that distinction which was characteristic of all the literature of the period.

[1]*Essai sur les Mœurs*. Chap. CXCVII.

IX

IDEAS AND MANNERS

THE ADVENTURER

IN those days no one could stop in one place. Here was Montesquieu, off on the search for political constitutions; Diderot, after holding out against the idea for a long time, at length made the journey to Russia. Then, one fine day, the youthful Goldsmith resolves to set out for the Continent, and set out he does, without a penny to his name, with no one to fall back on in case of need, and with no definite itinerary in view. However, off he goes, playing his flute at cottage doors in the hope of getting, maybe, a bowl of soup, or a shake-down in a barn. Holberg says goodbye to Denmark and takes the road, relying on his fine voice, as Goldsmith on his flute-playing, to get him along. On he goes, from country to country; learns French in Paris, and teaches it at Oxford. He was not a man to be balked by trifles. All these enquiring gentlemen, indeed, are as mobile as can be, and they are never satisfied, they've never seen enough. Exile brings them no repining. They don't mind knocking at strange doors, and the bread of the stranger leaves no bitterness in the mouth. Tossed by fate far beyond their native land, they profit by the occasion to improve their knowledge, and shape their minds anew. Voltaire has no bad time of it in London. He gets to know the language, the literature, and the mode of life, and all that is so much to the good. Nor does the Abbé Prévost fare so badly in Holland. Anyhow, that's where he sows his wild oats, and pretty plentifully withal. He fares even better in that happy island, which he quits reluctantly, with a hymn to her greatness on his lips. And Bolingbroke soon made himself at home as a noble lord of

France, with his mansion and his ornamental gardens. He gathers a following about him, and wields the intellectual sceptre. Winckelmann finds his spiritual home in Italy. Look at the host of persecuted philosophers that crowded about Frederick II in Berlin. No fugitives craving sanctuary, these; no more exiles; now we call them *cosmopolites*.

The word first appeared in the sixteenth century, but it had no run, and by the seventeenth it was virtually extinct. The eighteenth, however, saw its return to currency. Trévoux's dictionary, in 1721, has it under the form *cosmopolitain*. In those days, the word had two meanings; one, the pejorative, signifies a person of no fixed abode; the other, the complimentary, denotes a man who is at home wherever he may chance to be. It was the latter meaning that prevailed. In 1755, we have J. J. Rousseau talking about "Those great cosmopolitan minds that make light of the barriers designed to sunder nation from nation, and who, like the Sovereign Power that created them, embrace all mankind within the scope of their benevolence." The cosmopolitan, instead of being an object of scorn as once he was, because he had no country of his own, was now held in high esteem because he had so many.

It need not surprise us that the eternal spirit of adventure takes on the colour of the age. It was not now a matter of setting forth to win back the tomb of Christ, of driving the Turks from the Holy Places. Even expeditions to far-off lands beyond the seas were planned and organized on definite lines, commercial or exploratory. The heroic element had been relegated to literature. That was its final refuge and there it had to stay. Adventure was now a business, a calling, though a calling with a certain glamour about it. The adventurer, in silks and laces dight, complete with small-sword, was now a recognized social figure.

Sometimes he might come of a titled family, but usually he found it more convenient to forge his patent of nobility himself. Lorenzo da Ponte, forsaking his place of origin, which was the Ghetto, took the name of the bishop who had baptized him, and secured his entry into the seminary. The father of Casanova was an impecunious actor, his mother a cobbler's daughter. Giuseppe Balsamo, who was born in Sicily of humble parentage, and had been the scapegrace of the family, exchanged his plebeian surname for a very high-sounding patronymic; he called himself Cagliostro. And why not, pray? Aren't the letters of the alphabet common property?

The scene of the adventurer's exploits is not the green savannah, or the wide ocean, but some capital or other where your specious rascal can always manage to wriggle out of an awkward corner; unless, of course, he chose some little princeling's court where, life in the ordinary way being as dull as ditchwater, he would be welcomed with open arms as a heaven-sent cure for boredom. Forgetting all about his humble origin, quite unfettered by scruples, making out he was somebody very grand, he turns up one night from heaven knows where. In a few days he is off again leaving his friends to square up for him and pay the damage. He never stops long anywhere. All Europe is his hunting-ground. Egypt was not too far afield for that "crusader in reverse", the Marquis de Bonneval, who went to the East and became a pasha. Lorenzo da Ponte sailed for the New World and ended as a teacher of Italian in New York.

How in the world does the Adventurer contrive to get the wherewithal to cut such a dash? The fact is he hasn't a penny to his name. The carriage he drives in isn't his; his valet, if he has one, is his accomplice; his clothes aren't paid for; no one knows anything whatever about him. If they did they would soon show him the door. But he cuts a brilliant figure; he's got a certain veneer of culture; he talks airily of his knowledge of Latin and foreign languages; anyhow, he speaks French like a native, and that takes him anywhere. He's got a marvellous memory, and he skilfully belards his discourse with all manner of learned tags which he has picked up from time to time and retained for future use. Sometimes he is a poet and will turn out the *libretto* for an opera. He is fond of music, and an elegant dancer. Blessed with a ready wit, he is an excellent conversationalist and keeps the ball rolling with news, if he's got any; if he hasn't, he invents it. Add to all this an inexhaustible fund of daring and effrontery, and the power of a personality that fears neither God nor man.

The Adventurer profits by the vices of a disintegrating social order. No one knows now whom to respect or honour. Old standards have disappeared, authority is out of date. Better than those sour-faced moralists, have someone to make you laugh. Of course he must have his place at the card-table, and things warm up as soon as he is there. If he cheats, he won't be the only one. No one says anything about it unless he's caught red-handed slipping a card up his sleeve. But that's not likely; he's far too cute for that. He flings his money about like water, for your adventurer is no niggard; on the contrary, he will airily bestow a diamond here or a pearl necklace there, just as he thinks fit. With princely munificence, he tosses a purse bulging with money to the royal servants. As for the fair sex, he goes from triumph to triumph, from one belle to another, as is the fashion of the times. Even so, he is no more of a butterfly than that young officer friend of his who is so proud of his conquests, or that doddering old *roué* yonder, who has lost count of his. One eighteenth-century adventurer was taken to be a reincarnation of Don Juan, of Don Juan the lady-killer, of course. Another, the Chevalier d'Éon, kept people guessing all his life whether he was a man or a woman. Sometimes these gentry are honoured with a post in the secret service and used as agents in international politics. If you had lived in those days, you might quite possibly have run across a pseudo-religious adventurer, one Ramsay, who was in reality a freemason and Master of a Masonic Lodge. Then there were those mystery-men who gave out that they had studied at every university, seen service in every army, and hob-nobbed with all the great ones of the earth. Then again, there were those eerie people who seemed to belong to a tribe of ghosts, with their mysterious comings and goings, people who would swim into your ken like a meteor, and then as swiftly vanish again. They wielded supernatural powers, readily exploiting that residuum of superstition which reason is powerless to dispel, and which, as the century grows older, we shall see taking its revenge on reason. Sorcerers, soothsayers, occultists, hypnotists, prophets, magicians, they unearth treasure, foretell the future, mix magic potions to transform elderly dowagers into young girls of sixteen, heal the sick, and all but bring the dead to life again. One possesses the panacea for every ill; another has discovered the philosopher's stone; and yet another has conquered Time. "Dost remember, sirrah, the day on which Christ was crucified?" he asks his slave. "You forget, my lord, that I have been but fifteen hundred years in your lordship's service." Cagliostro, the Grand Copt, when his wife was Queen of Sheba, drank of a secret elixir he had found out, the elixir of immortality.

That did not prevent his dying in a prison cell, mad, or feigning madness. For he and his like failed to play out their comedy to a finish, and their end was dismal. Poverty overtakes them when they have squandered all their substance. Free as the air to begin with, it is in prison that they end their days. Fêted and made much of today, tomorrow sees them deserted by all their friends. They have no remorse to call them back to the paths of righteousness, only a futile and a vain regret. Some of them the irony of fate compels to drag out a dreary old age, full of complaints and grumbles. Of these, the punishment is late, but it is cruel.

However, society tightens up its control, for it discerns a corrupting influence in these men, which it likes not. Nevertheless society had furnished them with favourable conditions for their growth, or they would never have prospered as they did. They merely made a *reductio ad absurdum* and sometimes worse than that, of some of the ideas of the day. The Glittering Age; well, these adventurers were the spangles that made it glitter. It was the age of sharp practice. They did not hold up coaches and put the occupants to ransom; they did not commit robbery under arms. They just used their brains, their wits, their insight into character, not without a spice of contempt for the poor dupes who let themselves be taken in. What a gold mine for the needy, said the Chevalier des Grieux, is the folly of the wealthy and great! They liked to put a touch of the picturesque into their life-stories, these gentlemen.[1]

Writers make great capital out of this type of humanity. In fiction, the cloak-and-dagger hero tends more and more to give place to the adventurer. As for the theatre, see Goldoni on the look out for subjects! One day, he selects the wondrous marvels of *Madre Natura*, Mother Nature, for his theme; another, it is *Il filosofo inglese*, a disciple of Locke and Newton; then, in 1751, he presents *L'aventuriere onorato*, The Honourable Adventurer. But he—the adventurer—cuts a very colourless figure in print, compared with what he is in real life. Of the days that were vouchsafed him on earth he made a real masterpiece, using them

[1] We have availed ourselves in these pages of the essay on Casanova by Stefan Zweig in *Trois poètes de leur vie*, French translation, 1937.

for the ends he had at heart, fondly carving them into a flattering statue of himself. Literary memorials are of many kinds. There is the *Esprit des Lois* for one, there is the *Essai sur les Mœurs* for another, and, again, also bearing the unequivocal hall-mark of the eighteenth century, there are the *Memoirs of Casanova.*

WOMAN

Le Temple de Gnide; Le Voyage à Paphos, and, in particular Algarotti's *Il Congresso di Citera* (1745). Love has disappeared from the world and withdrawn to her own island. There she has convened a meeting of her council to consider the merits of a controversy that has recently arisen. The nations are at issue in regard to the right way to make love. Accordingly, they each select an ambassadress to represent them at the Court of Love. France's envoy is Mme de Jasy; England's, Lady Gravely; Italy is represented by Beatrice. Voluptas was appointed general secretary. It was to be clearly understood by all that there was one thing that was not under discussion, one thing that was above all controversy, and that was that Pleasure comes before everything, and is implanted by Nature in every human heart. Lady Gravely pulls a very wry face; the gentlemen in her country disdain the ladies, while the ladies, for their part, look on the gentlemen as bores. Mme de Jasy is all for brief, butterfly affairs. Away with those violent, overwhelming passions! Far better a passing fancy, seasoned with a dash of elegance and wit: *piacere senza pena.* Beatrice belauds ideal love. Not one stands up for the right cause. Voluptas sums up the pleadings and then makes known the will of the God of Love. It is not given to man to choose the object of his affections. He is drawn to her by an irresistible fate. His sole business, then, is to give her pleasure. What he has to do is to praise her up to the skies, and to remark on the shortcomings of her rivals—Chloe's shrill voice, Lesbia's ugly teeth, and so on. She must on no account be thwarted; if you would be her master, pretend you are her slave. Use every trick and device to win her favour, write choicely worded letters, get her maid on your side, take her about to garden parties and so on. Above all, choose the psychological moment to plead your suit. Never, for example, declare yourself on the very day she has seen her rival in a new frock of the very latest fashion.

Yes, that was the notion; people believed, or made out they did, that you could have pleasure without pain, *piacere senza pena*. Pleasure was nothing you had to be ashamed of; nothing you had to conceal, or feel uncomfortable about, nothing to repent of. The thing is really a feather in your cap, and it's easy enough to get it. If it had anything incongruous about it, it was the open way it was flaunted about: easy-going morals; the senses protested against the rigour with which they had always been repressed in days gone by. Now, when all the old disturbing hypotheses were, as far as possible, put aside, things like predestination and original sin; when it was satisfactorily established that whatever was natural was good, that pleasure was natural, and that the greatest of all pleasures was sensual pleasure, not, indeed, all women, but all who were in the fashion, conformed to the new Art of Love. Little brainless darlings, all paint, powder, and beauty-spots, with their silks, their satins, their brocades, their frills and furbelows, their trinkets, tripped daintily to the forefront. They swam in luxury, money floated round them in swirls and eddies. Dances, dinners, supper-parties were just items in one long, unending festival. Their wants must be humoured at all costs, provided they were but whims and nothing more. Passionate love? Mere madness! Plighted troth? Marriage vows? That sort of thing was quite out of date. Usbek had it that there was no country in the world where there were fewer jealous husbands than France. Not that they trusted their wives, oh, dear no! But they were so proud of their ill-fortune, that the only thing for it was to profit by it. Prince Angola is pursuing his education: his friend Almair assures him that the only remedy for boredom is change. The prince soon comes to look on pretty ladies as if they were goods up for sale, or transferable commodities. Expediency brought us together, convention kept us so, and I don't imagine it will hurt us much to dissolve the partnership.[1] Oegle was taken ill at the theatre. She did something so dreadful that there is nothing for her but to retire into seclusion, or to take the veil. The fact of the matter is this, her husband came to speak to her in her box, when she so far forgot herself as to look lovingly at him, and smilingly to

[1]Angola, *Histoire indienne*. A Agra, avec privilège du Grand Mogol, 1749.

press his hand.[1] You see? "Love tender and unfailing is something you only find in old-fashioned romances."[2]

Truth to tell, mistresses had become a sort of regular institution. Kings had mistresses. Louis XV had several, Madame de Pompadour being the best known. Men of high social position had them. "Why", Barbier the advocate used to declare, "fifteen out of twenty of the noble lords about the Court are living with women they aren't married to." After that, how can you blame the King? Even philosophers have their mistresses, every man-jack of them: Voltaire, d'Alembert, Diderot, Helvetius, the Baron d'Holbach. The Marquis d'Argens, who played *les Faublas* before its time, had more mistresses than he could count. As Mlle Quinault remarked, chastity was an artificial habit and quite contrary to nature, the invention, no doubt, of some half-starved, misshapen little dwarf, for no one at all presentable would ever think of concealing his identity.

No doubt Parisian society was more advanced than elsewhere, "advanced" in every sense of the word. Nevertheless, from what we read in memoirs and letters about other places, they too were not so far behind. No one will maintain that morals in Berlin and Potsdam were all they should have been. The princes of the various German courts had mistresses, although they may not always have wanted them. Still one has to do as others do. As for England, there was more coarseness there, more drunkenness, more corruption, open corruption, too, seeing that it had become a means of government. Bolingbroke began to fear lest the vices he practised, and of which he set the example, would end by unsettling the Constitution. But the difference was merely a matter of greater or less refinement. The story runs that when Queen Caroline was dying, she urged George II to marry again. "No", the weeping monarch replied, "I shall have mistresses." "Well, that need not stand in the way," said the dying woman. Italy sang the same tune, praising the dispassionate lover, the lover with no illusions:

> Fu gia caro un solo amante,
> Or quel tempo non e piu.

[1] *Les usages, par M. Tr. D. V., citoyen de Bordeaux.* Genève, 1762.

[2] *Mad. de Puisieux ou la nécessité d'être inconstant,* A Cologne; et se vend à Paris, 1762.

—"Time was when a woman was content with one lover, and no more. Those days are over." Or again, "Don't you see that women look on their lovers as playing-cards. They use them for a time, and when they've served their turn, toss them aside and ask for fresh ones." People travelling abroad note how the *cicisbeo* has wormed himself into the family circle. He installs himself alongside the husband, sometimes in the husband's place; he assists the lady at her toilet, he has his regular place in her withdrawing-room, goes visiting with her, accompanies her to the theatre. He pours out her chocolate, holds her powder-box and her fan, sits beside her in her carriage, and gives orders to the servants. Besides this *cavaliere servante*, there may be others, deputies, stop-gaps. The moralists may thunder, the poets may mock, the general public may cry "shame", or jeer, the *cicisbeo* holds his ground.

However, it must be added, in the interests of strict truth, that almost immediately afterwards, one might almost say simultaneously, another sort of change took place in the feminine world, very different from the liberty that degenerated into licence, or the coquetry that amounted to solicitation. Among the characteristics of the time, many and various as they were, there were some very different from those to which we have alluded. There were women who played an active part in the intellectual life of the day, not only participating in it, but sometimes leading it. They played their part in the intellectual world on equal terms with writers and scholars. There was less pedantry with them than with the men, and, so far as intelligence went, and of intelligence they undoubtedly had no lack, they displayed it more naturally. Often enough they came away from their convent school very indifferently stocked with knowledge; but they made up for that deficiency later on, prosecuting their studies with enthusiasm. Such was Mme du Châtelet, whom Voltaire chose for his Egeria. The pair withdrew from the world, and living in what people called that frightfully out-of-the-way place, Cirey, enlarged to the very utmost their sphere of study, and even then did not find it wide enough. They read Latin and Greek together, English and Italian. She asked a German scholar, Samuel König, to help her with her mathematics, and to continue the lessons she had had from Maupertuis and Clairaut. Meanwhile, Voltaire was devoting himself to physics, and interesting himself in an enquiry which the Académie des Sciences was conducting into the nature of fire. She also busied herself in this investigation, not merely as his collaborator, but as his rival. Then she took up philosophy. Voltaire recommended her to read Locke; she urged him to read Leibniz, and she had her way. A strange couple they were, spending their evenings with binomials and trinomials for their only company. There, then, we have a picture which shows us one aspect of the period, just as a different picture, the picture of a pair of lovers dreaming and shedding tears in the moonlight, will soon be showing us another—romanticism.

No less true to the life is yet another picture showing us a salon, Lady Montagu's in London, maybe, Caterina Doffin Tron's in Venice, Mme N . . .'s at Stockholm, but, conspicuous among all the salons of Europe, a French one, and of all those French salons which followed one another with the unbroken regularity of a dynasty until the days of the Revolution, and celebrated beyond all others, was the salon of Mme du Deffand in the Faubourg Saint-Germain; no palatial and solemn apartment, but a pleasant, comfortable room, with hangings of gold watered-silk, and curtains of the same material tied back with flame-coloured ribbon. Through a doorway you could see another room, with blue hangings, what-nots, and a wealth of elegant china. There, in a semi-circular armchair, which she called her tub—it is drawn up close to the fire, for the day is chilly—sits the woman who queens it over the intellectuals of Europe, gathered there at her invitation. Her wit, her vivacity, her wide and varied culture, her psychological insight, the world-wide character of her salon as a sort of intellectual refinery, the charm of good talk, where conversation was at once a diversion and a fine art—the fame of all these things extended to the farthest limits of the educated world. When she discovered that her *lectrice*, Julie de Lespinasse, had started a rival salon beneath her very roof, where the *élite* of her guests forgathered before going into her, the shock she felt did not arise from female jealousy alone, from resentment at ingratitude, from bitterness at the betrayal; no; what she had been robbed of was nothing more nor less than her *raison d'être*. Henceforth, it was not she, but another, who would be matching mind with mind, and pitting thinker against thinker, not she, but another who would be wielding the baton and conducting the great intellectual symphony.

"Every age in the history of Man, every succeeding generation, appears to have been dominated by some definite characteristic, some inner law, lofty, unique, imperious, moral in its nature, directing the course of events, and seeming, when regarded from a distance, to be the source from which history proceeds. A first glance at the eighteenth century discovers this general, constant essential characteristic, this supreme law of a society which is at once its crown, its physiognomy and its secret; the spirit of the time, the hub of the world, the centre from which everything radiates, the summit whence everything descends, the image on which all things are modelled is—woman."[1]

THE MAN OF LETTERS

The man of letters we shall have to put on a very exalted plane. It would be rank blasphemy now, in this eighteenth century, to say he was no more good to his country than a skittle-player. That would never do. According to the Abbé Raynal, he is now regarded as "a citizen of importance". He gets his living by his pen today. That's where the difference comes in. A book is a money-getter, now. You don't give your book to the bookseller, you sell it to him. There's a proper business arrangement now between author and bookseller; very profitable indeed for the bookseller but by no means a bad look-out for the author. In 1697, Dryden's translation of Virgil brought him in a matter of fourteen hundred pounds. Addison got most of his income from the public. Pope was quite comfortably off; his translations of the *Iliad* and *Odyssey* alone earned him some nine thousand pounds. As for his house at Twickenham, his garden and his ornamental grotto, he owed them all to his pen. Goldsmith did not exactly live like a lord, but he realized as time went on that he was in better case than he had been, and he expressed his gratitude to those kind and generous friends, his readers. Every educated member of society in buying the work of a man of letters helps to reward him. The old joke about authors, calling them a lot of hungry hangers-on, may have been a good enough one in its time, it would be a pretty bad one now.

[1]Edmond et Jules de Goncourt, *La femme au XVIIIe siècle,* 1862, Chap. IX.

Now, an author can decline an invitation to dinner without being afraid of offending a patron, or of finding an empty larder when he returns home. He may not be able to brag about his riches, but at any rate he has enough to live on. Lesage, we are told, was the first Frenchman to make a living out of his novels and his plays. Marivaux, ruined by Law's "System", managed to retrieve the position by his literary labours. Voltaire was a man of letters and very much the noble lord. True, he was also a financier.

Matters in Germany moved more slowly, but there, too, the theatre, translation work, and that now general resource, the press, had enabled writing men to cast off the yoke. Nikolai, the publisher, was a centre of attraction for all the leading men of the Aufklärung. In Italy, this was the question: "Writers of *Il Caffè*, answer me this, how is it men of letters were respected of old, but are respected now no longer?"[1] The question was beside the mark; literary men had no cause to grumble. The taste for reading had greatly increased, and they had profited accordingly. Scipione Maffei, Ludovico Antonio Muratori, Francesco Algarotti had all been duly rewarded. The Court of Vienna lavished money and distinctions on Metastasio. In short, anyone who knows anything about the place of literature in Europe in those days, will agree that never before was so much honour bestowed on men who had contributed to the general enlightenment, and to the diffusion of profitable knowledge.

The change was not without its effect on the content and, indeed, on the form, of the literary output. When a man wrote for pleasure, or with an eye to fame, he could take his time; there was no need to hurry. When, however, you had to get the thing done in order to pay the baker, or the landlord, you had to turn out as much as you could, and do it quickly. As soon as you had got one thing off your hands, you had to begin thinking about another. The periodicals were gluttons for copy. No time now to let a work compose itself, as one might say, by letting it mature slowly and surely. Further than that, the writer's contact with his readers is closer now, he shares their lives more intimately, and, above all, he feels freer; the whole point is there. Hard is the lot of the writer who has no longer a Mæcenas to fall back on. See; everybody's got a holiday today. The Crown Prince is

[1] Il Caffè, *Degli onori resi ai Letterati.* Semestre secondo, 1765.

about to enter the city, crowds are thronging the streets to see the procession go by. Only that cobbler there sits shut up in his shop. A journalist enters and expresses surprise. "Ah, well", says the cobbler, "I've got shoes to mend and deliver; no shutting up shop for me. I've got my living to earn, haven't I?" So it is with the journalist, and so it is with the writing man in general who tends to become more and more a publicist. He is compelled to go on working when everybody else is taking the day off.[1] Well, his lot may be harder, but he accepts it because it seems to him to have something higher, more dignified, about it. It may have its drawbacks, but it's got its fine side, too. Taking it all round, he likes his job under the new conditions. Johnson laughed at Gray because he—Gray—said he only wrote poetry when he felt in the mood. As for Johnson himself, he polished off his daily quota with great regularity, only too happy to think that literature was now a profession, and that patronage was a thing of the past.

"Authorship is a profession now, just like the army, the magistracy, the Church, or finance."[2] That sentence formed the text of a good deal of discussion. The history of the man of letters down the ages is briefly summed up. An attempt is made to define him. It is not so easy. A moral status is given him. Again and again, we are reminded that the republic of letters once consisted of mere *dilettanti*, who treated of matters of no significance so far as the general good was concerned; whereas, nowadays, its members were performing a public service.

So, no more truckling to the great. As for the philosophers, this was how they looked at the matter: Great men were the writer's friends because they paid the piper; they were his enemies because they called the tune he was to play. Literary men were not at all anxious to bring about a complete rupture. They accepted favours in cash or in kind, but what they would not put up with was being treated like paid servants. They thought it well to keep on good terms with the wealthy and great because it afforded them an opportunity of studying the tricks and manoeuvres of an important section of society; but there must be no suggestion of the master-and-servant relationship. Was not the author as good as any of the people who had so

[1]Marivaux, *Le Spectateur français*, 1722–1723, feuille 5.

[2]*Almanach des auteurs*, 1755.

long domineered over him? Nay, was he not in some ways their better? Was it not he, the author, who bestowed—the argument was well worn, but not, it seems, worn-out—the laurels that keep men's memory green? Was he not the mouthpiece of that new power in the world which we call Science? Was he not the monarch of the mind? Let the terms of the old alliance be revised, and let him, the author, take these "great men" for what, more often than not, they really were: men steeped in ignorance and injustice, without even the sorry distinction of knowing what they were unjust about. That is the only way to make him conscious of his real worth.

A cross-grained, quarrelsome tribe, no doubt; conceited, vainglorious, very fond of flattery; a race divided against itself, whose children rend and tear one another instead of making friends; a mongrel breed, displaying some of the noblest, and some of the basest qualities of the human character. Nevertheless, an unparalleled honour was promised it, could it but rid itself of its defects. Theirs was the task of refining the public taste, of explaining and interpreting ideas, and even of directing public action.

One day, Quesnay the physiocrat was calling on Mme de Pompadour, whose doctor he was, when he heard an important personage give out that the only way to settle these religious quarrels was to put an end to them by force: "The halberd was the thing to keep the country in order." Quesnay asked who was to wield the halberd, and as there was some hesitation about the reply, he supplied the answer himself: "Public opinion", he said. "Therefore it is on public opinion that we should act." Now it is the writers who mould public opinion. That is precisely what their business is, to bring daily pressure to bear on it. That is why their influence is so great, and that is what those wicked *grands seigneurs* are beginning to find out, and to be as much afraid of them as thieves are of the street lamp. However strong you may think you are, it is very bad policy to get on the wrong side of people whose words are read from one end of Europe to the other. With a stroke or two of the pen they may deal you a blow from which you may never recover. So princes, instead of treating them with disdain, would be well advised to turn to them for counsel. Men of letters saw themselves wielding, over the minds of generations to come, a far greater influence than monarchs ever wielded over the people of their day.

THE BOURGEOIS

It is a generally accepted fact that the eighteenth century witnessed the emergence of a new and powerful class, the *bourgeoisie*, the middle-class. We do not propose to examine this phenomenon from the economist's standpoint, giving figures, tracing the transfer of wealth, the rise and fall in prices, the variations in balances. What we do propose to consider is its effect on the history of ideas. The first thing that forces itself on our attention is that a brilliant and luxurious aristocracy was still holding its ground as the most important section of the population. Titles, honours, privileges, none of these things are its members willing to forgo. But while they pour out their wealth in order to keep up their rank, that rank itself is diminished by a process of revaluation, to which all are called upon to submit. The intellectuals contest the pretensions of the aristocracy. Sometimes, the aristocrats take no notice of their activities, and continue to ignore them. Sometimes they concur and go and join forces with the philosophers, a certain section of the party having always been ready to compass its own undoing. But quite apart from these people, the aristocrats as a body never really knew how to defend themselves. They either made no reply at all, or else an irrelevant one, to ideological adversaries who never relaxed their efforts to secure their downfall. These were not content any more to put forward the familiar argument of the moralist, the contention, namely, that noble blood is not so good as a noble heart, and that an honest locksmith is more to be respected than a dissolute nobleman. The new argument was no platitude and was the more effective in that it was directly connected with the latest conception of the State and Society, being steadily and uncompromisingly opposed to the notion of a permanently privileged class; the State is entitled to reward only such merits as are presently existing; Society only recognizes as worthy of recompense those who contribute directly to its welfare. If the distinctions so conferred were to be continued from father to son, that would constitute an infringement of the rule of justice, which alone should govern the relations between citizen and citizen. He alone is to be deemed noble who deserves well of his country and of mankind, not he whose ancestors long ago were deemed worthy of recompense by a group or collectivity which itself had no rational *locus standi*. Power belongs to all, it is only by delegation that it may be conferred on certain chosen representatives, whose authority is but temporary and always subject to revocation.

That spelt the end of hereditary distinctions. We foster a good breed of sporting dogs, and rear the puppies, so long as the strain keeps up; otherwise, we drown them. "Old title-deeds, ancient documents preserved in mediaeval castles, are they to confer on their inheritors a claim to the most exalted posts in Church or State, in the Courts of Justice, or the Army, irrespective of whether the said inheritors possess the talents necessary for the proper accomplishment of such duties? Because certain warlike aristocrats helped, at the peril of their lives, to conquer a kingdom or lay waste its provinces, is that any reason why their descendants, centuries later, should deem they had a right to oppress their vassals?"[1] The place of the feudal system in history ceased to be duly recognized and understood once it came to be regarded as nothing more nor less than "organized brigandage." And when, both in fact and theory, Europe deliberately set to work to obliterate the few remaining traces of feudalism, the rôle of the nobility was over.

We see, on the opposite side of the picture, a class not hitherto looked upon as qualified to fill the vacuum thus created, because they were supposed to be not sufficiently educated. For a number of reasons, conservative-minded people thought the lower classes were very well where they were. If they were raised any higher, perhaps their own position would be none too secure. The liberals looked on the proletariate as a tool, an instrument. There must be some people to do the work, even if they did have to suffer. The philosophers were inclined to hesitate. Doubtless there were crowds of paupers to be seen in the streets of London, and in some of the rural districts of France and Italy; true, there were peasant risings in Austria, Bohemia and Hungary, and for all this suffering the would-be reformer of the world and its ways could not but feel compassion. It was, they admitted, a great question how far the lower orders were to be treated as an inferior species. The spell-binders never really went into this delicate question, and fearful of making a mistake in their calculations, they filled the heads of their victims with all

[1]D'Holbach, *Éthocratie,* 1776, Chap. X.

the fairy tales they could think of. But, after all, do the spell-binders only use trickery? A man is susceptible of progress in proportion to his education; there are many who are not educated, many who can only be educated very gradually, or perhaps are not, and never will be, worth educating. Benevolence may well extend to the third category, the craftsmen, but not to the fourth, not to those callings which merely call for brawn, and the daily round of manual labour. When we speak of respectable people, people worth taking an interest in, we mean people whom it is possible to train and educate; but the riff-raff will never be anything but the riff-raff.

Here some protests are heard from those who propound and preach the gospel of Happiness: you say Happiness should be shared by all; are the working classes happy? You know perfectly well that they are not. The poor devil that has to till the soil, the mercenary when he has done his service—what have they to look forward to but grinding toil, want, and sickness? The labourer has to obey the orders of his idle, greedy boss, who has inherited the power to make him work for nothing. You treat the poor as if they had no brains, no good in them; nothing but their brute instincts. In your eyes, they are nothing but beasts of the field. They look human, but that is a mere illusion. But these are solitary protests, heard only here and there. It was to be one of Robespierre's grievances against the *Encyclopédistes* that they stopped short of the "rights of the people."[1]

[1]Abbé Coyer, *Dissertations pour être lues . . . La seconde, sur la nature du peuple,* La Haye, 1755. Abbé Raynal, *Histoire philosophique et politique des établissements et du commerce des européens,* 1770. Livre XVII, chap. XXXI.

Robespierre: Discours du 18 Floréal, an. II. In the *Gazette Nationale ou Moniteur universel,* 19 Floréal, an. II, 8 mai, 1794. "The most important and distinguished party was the one that went by the name of the *Encyclopédistes.* It included several worthy men, but a much greater number of ambitious and pretentious charlatans. Not a few of its leading men became important figures in the Government. Not to know something of its influence and its policy would argue a very imperfect notion of the prelude to our Revolution. As far as politics were concerned this party always drew the line at the Rights of the People; as regards the question of morals they were far in advance of the blind prejudices of religious people. Its leaders sometimes held forth against despotism, and they were fed by despots; sometimes they wrote attacks on kings, sometimes dedications in their honour. They penned speeches for courtiers and madrigals for courtesans. This party most zealously propagated those materialistic ideas which proved too much for the great and the witty. To the party in question we are in large measure indebted for that kind of practical philosophy which, reducing selfishness to a system, looks on human society as the battle-ground of cunning, which measures right and wrong by the yard-stick of success, which regards probity as a matter of taste or decorum, and the world as the heritage of the astute egoist.

On the one hand there were the powerful and great, who were to be cast down from their seat; on the other, there were the humble and meek, concerning whose promotion some doubts still lingered; and, between the two, a class who had not waited for the eighteenth century before beginning the upward climb. They were now to find their vindication in some of the ideas of the age. Some, at any rate, of the ideas subjacent to the fact are clearly manifest. The *bourgeoisie* did not become entirely itself till these ideas reached their full and unequivocal expression; that we should abandon the transcendental for the real, give up theorizing about the world, and make our own whatever it could give us. Joubert, pondering on the generation immediately preceding his own, put the matter in unforgettable words: "God has withdrawn within himself and hidden within the bosom of his own being; withdrawn even as the sun, when it hides behind a cloud. The sun of the spirit is visible to them no more. . . . With nothing now to wake them to ecstasy, nothing to excite their lofty contemplation, able no more to gaze upon God, they busy themselves with the world."[1] Then, again, there was the idea of liberty, and how potent that was we have already seen. Then there was the idea that a citizen's worth was to be gauged by the amount of property he owned. Whether his wealth was derived from trade, from the land, or from industry, the idea was the same: every man who has a stake in the country, has an interest in the country's welfare; and whatever the rank which circumstances assign him, it is always and necessarily as a property-owner, always on the strength of his possessions, that he speaks and is listened to; always from his property that he derives the right to be represented. So says the Encyclopaedia.

Thus the majority of those who were of a philosophical turn of mind were of the middle class, and new forms of literature were addressed to a middle-class public. So literature makes some quick approaches to a class whose frontiers are not clearly defined, but whose distinguishing mark was the possession of wealth: *Le paysan parvenu, La paysanne parvenue, La nouvelle paysanne parvenue, Le soldat parvenu*. And then the theatre; more heartily than it laughed at *le Bourgeois Gentilhomme*, it praised

[1]*Les cahiers de Joseph Joubert,* text edited from the original manuscripts by André Beaunier, 1938, Vol. I, p. 102.

The London Merchant. This latter, a worthy but sententious individual, has a business man's code of honour superimposed upon the ordinary one. Lillo makes him assert that, as to be called a merchant does not necessarily derogate from one's rank as a gentleman, so a gentleman is not necessarily excluded from the dignity which invests the merchant. And the *drame larmoyant,* while opening the door to sentimentalism, marks a definite stage in social evolution. The bourgeois, having won his livelihood, now wins his title-deeds. The advent, however, of the great industrial era was not yet reflected in literature. That was reserved for the nineteenth century.

THE FREEMASONS

A strange paradox: Here are people who won't have any more to do with a Church of any kind, attending some sort of mysterious chapel of their own. Here are people who have turned their backs on rites and symbols, inventing rites and symbols of their own devising; an initiatory ceremonial, columns painted on canvas representing the temple of Solomon, the flaming star, the set-square, the spirit-level; people who have done away with mysteries and rent asunder every veil, who proclaim that all matters of foreign policy should be debated in the open, here are these same people pledging themselves to secrecy by the most solemn of oaths: "I promise and make oath before the Great Architect of the Universe and this Most Honourable Company never to divulge the secrets of the masons or of masonry, never to be the cause, direct or indirect, of the said secrets' being revealed, engraven or printed in any language or written characters whatsoever. And all this I promise on pain of having my throat cut, my tongue torn out and my heart rent asunder, and buried in the depths of the sea, or burned and reduced to ashes and then scattered to the winds, so that my memory may be completely obliterated from the minds of men and masons." Rationalists would be found searching the records of remote antiquity for traces of a mysticism which, with some of them, would one day take the place of reason. Thus did the opponents of sects found a sect of their own.

But apart from these outward manifestations, the prevailing spirit of the times is unquestionably discernible in these men.

They conform to the new conception of existence, the conception which will have nothing to do with the self-denial, the melancholy, the hopelessness which find their corollary in the hope of a better world beyond the grave:

> Sur un chemin couvert de mille fleurs
> Le Franc-Maçon parcourt la vie
> En cherchant le plaisir, en fuyant les douleurs.
> De la morale d'Épicure
> Il suit toujours les douces lois. . . .[1]

That is why, in their initial gatherings, they instituted love-feasts, banquets, the loving-cup, the singing of Bacchanalian songs. They fling away the Crown of Thorns, and bind their brows with roses.

They would have liked to revolutionize society, but they were not strong enough. What they needed was a brotherhood, an international brotherhood. They would unite and be as one great band of brothers. The devotion of the members, one to another, should be one of their laws. If a member visits a particular town or city, he will receive help and hospitality from his brother members there. If he is in any sort of distress, that distress will be relieved; if he is in some difficulty or other, he will be duly extricated. All he has to do is to give the sign; he will be recognized. *Les Vrais amis, la Bonne Amitié, la Parfaite Amitié*, names such as these were often given to their lodges. If local differences become apparent, if the various countries tend severally to lend their own national colour to these separate entities of the general confederation, we shall find the leaders doing their utmost to restore unity, for in unity lay their strength.

No one was more eager than they for that political freedom which was one of the aspirations of the age:

> Le cri de la nature, ami, c'est Liberté!
> Ce droit si cher à l'homme est ici respecté.
> Égaux sans anarchie et libre sans licence,
> Obéir à nos lois fait notre indépendance.[2]

[1]Along a path bestrewn with flowers, the Freemason fares through life, looking for pleasure and shunning pain. The gentle laws of Epicurus are the gospel that he follows.

[2]The cry of nature, friend, is Liberty! this right so dear to man is here respected. Equality without anarchy, liberty without licence, in obedience to our laws lies our freedom.

War to tyrants and despots; away with privilege; down with every authority other than the one they recognize. "This level which we carry with us teaches us to to measure men that we may respect their human qualities and not be overawed by worldly honours." "The Freemason is a free man, the friend alike of rich and poor, provided they be worthy."

For a long time, your Freemason was a deist. He would be neither a "godless libertine" nor a "stupid atheist". This may explain how it was that some of the clergy were mixed up with it until quite late on in its development. Nevertheless, it was definitely anti-Christian. It professed to adhere to "that broad religion on which all men are agreed". That meant "Natural Religion". And so, when the atheists approached; when the philosophers, realizing that Freemasonry was fighting their battle and that it was the most valuable of allies—when either of them, deists, or atheists—sought admission to its ranks, they were received with open arms.

This similarity of aims and intentions, this doctrine of mutual help and support, brought about the swift and widespread extension of the movement. On the 24th June, 1717, the members of the four lodges who were accustomed to hold their meetings in the taverns known as *The Goose and Grid, The Crown, The Apple Tree, The Roman and the Grapes*, met in combined session to found the Grand Lodge, London. In 1723, Anderson provided the Society with a set of statutes. Thereafter, Freemasonry became one of the most conspicuous centres of activity in the age of enlightenment. It increased with remarkable rapidity on the Continent, spreading to one after another of all the countries of Europe. If one were to chart the stages in its progressive conquest, we should see how the great commercial centres, seaports, capital cities, all fell before it. The precise route might be determined sometimes by some chance contagion, but as often as not it followed the age-old track of trade-routes, migrations, and invasions. Members who went travelling from place to place, merchants, diplomats, sailors, soldiers, founded lodges on their lines of route, or wherever they might settle. The same may be said even of prisoners of war when they were transferred from camp to camp; it is true even of peripatetic actors, of strolling players. The English name was retained for a time, free masons, or *fri-maçons* as the French sometimes wrote it. The first lodge in Rome was founded in the year 1735 as a result of the efforts of certain members of the Jacobite party who were living in exile there. It contained in its statutes a provision that a knowledge of English should be regarded as an essential condition of membership. Later on, the various nations translated the word into their several languages. The governments of the several countries proscribed the association, the Church condemned it. The Florentine lodge, founded by the English in 1733, was denounced to the Holy Office, and closed down. The fiercest aspersions were cast upon the poet Crudeli, one of its members. Freemasonry in any shape or form was proscribed to the whole Christian world by a Bull issued by Pope Clement XII in 1738. In 1751, Benedict XIV repeated the condemnation. But Freemasonry defied both governments and the Church. Lodges multiplied, and into them flocked notabilities, prosperous citizens, members of the learned professions. As far back as 1738, Chambers' Dictionary included the word and added this comment: The Freemasons are a body well worthy of consideration by reason both of their numbers and character. The movement has gained in importance by the accession of certain members of the nobility; the Marquis Joseph François de Bellegarde, gentleman of the bedchamber to Charles Emmanuel III, founded the first lodge at Chambéry, the Lodge of which Joseph de Maistre was later to become a member; and which was the parent lodge for the Savoy and Piedmont. Raimondo di Sangro, prince of San Severo, became Grand Master of the Naples lodge. The Duc d'Antin, the Comte de Clermont and the Duc de Chartres were Grand Masters in France. Of still more exalted rank, François de Lorraine, who was to espouse Maria Theresa of Austria, Empress of Germany, became a mason in the Low Countries. Frederick II joined the order in 1738, while he was still Crown Prince; in 1744, we behold him Grand Master of the Three Globes lodge, Berlin. Queen Maria Carolina of Naples was a freemason. At first, women were excluded from membership. Candidates, to be eligible, had to be "persons of good reputation, dependable, of good family, ripe in age and judgment". Slaves, women, immoral persons, men of scandalous behaviour were rigidly excluded. To evil livers the door remained shut, but women were later received in special lodges.

The 7th April, 1778, witnesses the apotheosis of this influential body. That was the day on which Voltaire became a member of the Lodge of the Nine Sisters, founded in Paris in 1776, of which first Helvetius and afterwards Lalande were the moving spirits. Dispensed from the ceremonies of initiation, escorted into the hall by a commission of nine delegates, who had gone to meet him, he came in leaning on the arm of Benjamin Franklin. To the questions on morals and philosophy put to him by the Worshipful Master, he made reply amid loud applause from the assembled company. The black curtain was drawn back revealing the Orient brilliantly illuminated. The proselyte took the oath and was granted his apprenticeship. He was girt with the apron of Helvetius. Such was the entry into the Society of the Freemasons of the man who had worked with them so long that the members of his lodge were amazed that he had not joined them years before.

THE PHILOSOPHER

He had no connexion with Doctor Atqui and Doctor Ergo, those gluttons for syllogisms and enthymemes, revelling in their *barbara* and their *baralipton*; nothing in common with the Schoolmen, who, like advocates pleading a hopeless cause, used all their art to embroil the simplest of issues by pompous declamation and subtle sophistry; or with those scarecrow figures swathed in black gowns with wide sleeves, a tall bonnet on their head, who haunted the schools in order to instruct the young how to convert the hypothetical into the factual, and *vice-versa*. Men like those belonged to the dark ages. Let the dark ages keep them and bury them deep. Don't let them come and cast their sinister shadow over us today. Nor had our philosopher anything in common with the metaphysicians, or any such speculative dreamers, or with those shallow-minded egoists who claimed a name too good for them by half, saying that they took with equanimity—that is to say lying down—whatever life might offer. The word had to stand because it meant love of wisdom, but in order that there might be no mistake about its true significance, some sort of distinctive epithet was tacked on to it; such as " the new philosopher", "the practical philosopher".

The past had given us, one after the other, the Saint, the Knight, the Courtier, the Gentleman; now we are offered yet another pattern man, the Philosopher.

There is no lack of definitions. We will content ourselves with the most explicit, the one given in the Encyclopaedia. It is not enough to talk of philosophy as indicating a retired and sequestered mode of life, some outward show of wisdom combined with a certain amount of reading; that is not enough. Nor does the renunciation of all prejudice in regard to revealed religion meet the case. That would be taking the consequence for the cause. The cause lies deeper. "The Philosopher is a human machine, just as any other man is, but he is a machine so constituted that he reflects on his own movements. . . . He is a clock which sometimes, so to speak, does the winding-up itself." The spirit of observation, of enquiry is, then, the essential thing; no opinion but must be submitted to this initial test. The critical spirit, in which most of our fellow creatures are lacking, acting as they do without being aware of the causes that prompt them, whirled away by their passions they know not whither—the critical spirit belongs to the reason, which latter is to the philosopher what, according to St. Augustine, grace is to the Christian.

Wander forth far and wide, even as do the bees . . . then return to our nook and distil your honey. Only from observation of the facts are true principles to be arrived at; on facts is based a science at once certain and limited; certain in its results, limited in its scope. Certitude is ours when we feel that we have received from whatever we have been examining the sort of clear and precise impression that our judgment requires. We come to a halt when the nature of the thing contemplated, or the imperfection of our faculties, warns us that we can go no farther. At the certitude, the philosopher rejoices; at the barrier, he does not chafe. He can speak with certainty of nothing save that of which he has a mental grasp, he must needs hold his peace when he comes to the reality of substances. So much the worse, and yet so much the better. He takes himself for what he is, not for what it may seem to the imagination he might be. While refraining from making any definite pronouncement on a matter beyond his ken, he nevertheless inclines to the view that he is composed, not of two different elements, matter and mind, but of one single element, namely matter endowed with the power of thought. The air, of its own accord, is capable of producing sound; fire, of its own accord, excites the sensation of heat; the eyes, of themselves, see; the ears, of themselves, hear; similarly, then, the substance of the brain is susceptible of thought; it thinks.

Realizing how the fancy and over-hasty conclusions may lead one astray; convinced that truth is only to be arrived at by the method by it prescribed, the philosophic mind is wholly concerned with observation, and the accurate relating of everything to its true principles.

But if it was to remain a mere matter of complacent meditation, chewing the cud of satisfaction at having corrected an age-old error of the understanding, it would be working *in vacuo*. Our philosopher does not look upon himself as an exile in this world; he does not in the least regard himself as being on enemy territory. Like a wise economist he wants to enjoy the good things which Nature offers. His aim is to find pleasure with others and to find it, it is necessary to make it; thus he endeavours to be agreeable to those with whom chance, or his own deliberate choice, has brought him into association, and so doing he finds that which is agreeable to himself. He is an *honnête homme*, a gentleman, who makes it his endeavour to give pleasure to others and to be of service to them. He spends his time partly in a solitude that enables him to possess his soul in peace, partly in commerce with his fellows, which enables him to live. He is full of the milk of human kindness, and we may say of him that the social order is the only divinity he recognizes on earth.

Whereas the devotee is animated either by religious zeal or by self-interest, the philosopher is actuated by a sense of order and by the dictates of reason. The motives which govern his behaviour are all the stronger for being both disinterested and natural. The idea of the rude, unpolished man is as remote from the idea of the philosopher as would be the idea of dullness of intellect.

He has the ambition, and quite properly so, of extending his dominion. If he were called upon to direct the course of things on earth, earth would be the better for it. When the Emperor Antoninus declared that nations would be happy when kings were philosophers, or philosophers kings, he was perfectly right. The superstitious man ill performs the loftier functions, because he looks on himself as being an exile here on earth, because his kingdom is not of this world. The wise man, on the other hand, when raised to the lofty sphere of authority, will have but one object in his mind, and that is the public good.

He is no more prone to blush for his passions than he is to despise material good. He readily avails himself of whatever contributes to the amenities of life. Over and above the bare necessities, he likes to have a margin as it were, the little something extra that will enable him to live like a gentleman, the little more that spells the difference between contentment and constraint; the little more which gives to life its grace and charm. Of course we shall esteem him none the less if he remains a poor man, but we shall exclude him from our society unless he manages to rid himself of the burden of want. Straitened circumstances which mar our own well-being, rob us also of all delicate enjoyments, and exclude us from the society of civilized people. In short, the philosopher is a person of good repute, who does everything in the light of reason, a man who combines with a thoughtful and well-balanced mind, rectitude of moral conduct and the qualities which go to the making of a good member of society. That is how he saw himself.

VICTORY IN SIGHT

Between 1720 and 1750 there was a period of hesitation in which the word seems not as yet to have attained its full significance. After that, it became definitely crystallized, and it was adopted by an aggressive faction which blazoned it on their banners. When Rousseau, so far as he was concerned, decided to have nothing to do with it, he repudiated a doctrine. If any additional characteristic enriched it later on, it was a touch of pride. After 1760, Europe seemed to be conquered, the battle won.

That is what the philosophers themselves kept on telling us. They went about saying that they had rounded the difficult corner; that the promised land was in sight; that the general fermentation had not been barren of results, and that those results were fruitful; that the days of barbarism were over and done with; that the age was now enlightened; that reason had been purged of all its dross. Whatever envious tongues may say, ours is the age of reason, of thinking men and women. It promises us a better future, for sooner or later, as the light steals on, it strikes the eyes even of those who deem it in their best interests to destroy it. It is undeniable that monarchs are more tolerant than they have ever been. A generation is now arising which will hold fanaticism in abhorrence. The highest places will one day be filled by philosophers; our reign is at hand. It remains for us to hasten on the advent of that happy day. So they went on and on, in the same strain. The prize, it seemed, was assured; the fulfilment of their hopes, the happiness of mankind, was at hand.

England, the home of free thought, they looked on as definitely theirs. In France, the majority of the strategic positions, the salons, the Academy, were in their hands. Even in that solid bastion, the Sorbonne, there were some ominous cracks. More than that, the world of fashion was definitely plumping for the philosophers. "The wealthiest districts of Switzerland", Geneva, which had nearly thrown over Calvin, and Lausanne "were giving great satisfaction." So, too, with the seven United Provinces. The Latin countries seemed to be lagging behind a little. Rome was holding out, and Rome was coming in for some pretty harsh words; but after a time Milan and Naples appeared as bright spots in the general darkness; neither Tuscany nor Parma displayed reluctance and there were plenty of Italians who reported that among them, too, Philosphy was gaining ground daily. Spain was beginning to free herself from the prejudices which, despite her natural resources, had kept her so long in swaddling clouts. Still, looking at the situation as a whole, it was on the Northern countries that the eye rested with the most gratifying satisfaction:

C'est du Nord aujourd'hui que nous vient la lumière . . .

It is from the North that the light comes to us today. For Scandinavia had gone over to the school of Reason. Ten years later, Poland was completely free of the yoke; Frederick II and Catherine of Russia were taking the lead in the philosophic campaign; sooner or later the last remaining fanatics of the South

PART THREE

DISAGGREGATION

BOOK I

I

"BECOMING"

NOW another matter for observation will be engaging our attention; we shall see how, within those symmetrical designs which we have just been examining, there were hidden certain inconsistencies, certain contradictory elements, which ultimately rendered them nugatory, at least in part. We shall in fact be witnesses of one of those transitions which make the history of ideas one ceaseless transformation scene; we shall see a doctrine brought to nought, not by any hostile intervention from without, but by the operation of some inherent defect within. We shall see how flaws remained undetected within a system that was seemingly so faultless; we shall see how a victory, prematurely proclaimed, turned out to be no victory at all, and how, yet once again, a mighty effort to bring happiness to mankind was doomed to end in failure.

Were they absolutely sure, those building experts, that their plans were without a flaw? And those philosophers, were they so perfectly confident that that philosophy of theirs had led them at last to the eternal verities? Were they, to begin with, so convinced that they had confined the spirit within a formula so perfect that it would remain there a prisoner in perpetuity? If they were, there was a cobbler's son in Königsberg who did not share their certitude. Before they had time to put the coping stone on their system, he stepped in, and demolished it. Emmanuel Kant began to re-examine the theories propounded by Locke, Berkeley and Hume. Metaphysics was, and could be, nothing but the science of the limits of human reason. He agreed with it thus far, but he thought that where it went wrong, where it fell short, was in neglecting to define the specific quality, the essential attributes of the powers contained within those limits. That meant that the whole task still remained to be done, despite all their efforts. He began by getting together as much human knowledge as he was able. He made acquaintance with the natural sciences, with geometry, mechanics, astronomy, and finally reduced the whole matter to one single problem, a problem that people thought had been solved, but which had not: What is knowledge? At length, ready for the fray, he published, in 1781, his *Critique of Pure Reason*. Henceforth, the mind was no longer a *camera obscura* whose sole function it was to receive impressions from without; it was a prism which refracted the sense-data from the universe outside it, which only became ours by virtue of such transformation. Our senses perceived in accordance with *a priori* forms, or conditions. The understanding performed its office of linking together, combining, in accordance with *a priori* categories; knowledge depended on an *a priori* element which organized it. No longer, now, were we the slaves of Natural Law. In morality, as well as in psychology, it was our minds that made the law. This was revolutionary, and it looked like upsetting every previous philosophy, it looked as if the sage Locke, the admirable Locke, the one really great thinker since Plato, would be put in the shade. What were the causes? What could have paved the way for such a drastic change? How did the break up of the empirical system begin—a doctrine which, for a space, had deemed it held the whole of Europe in its power? Where were the cracks? What faults did Time reveal? Was there not something wrong at the very start? Was it not that Nature, so perpetually invoked, had never been properly defined? Was not the word susceptible of a hundred different interpretations?

As for the heart, the seat of the emotions, that, of course, was quite out of the picture; everyone was agreed on that. It was beating precious slowly those days; in fact the tiresome intruder had almost been put to silence. And yet . . .

1731. *Histoire du Chevalier des Grieux et de Manon Lescaut*, by the Abbé Prévost.

An unfrocked monk, who sought refuge, first in Holland, then in England, where he found himself at loggerheads with the law and narrowly escaped hanging, had the gift of endowing his characters with feelings so deep and tender, of imparting to his phrases a music so sweet and plaintive, that people could not restrain their tears as they read his story. Des Grieux's arguments melted away like snow before the warmth of Manon's smile.

1740. *Pamela, or Virtue Rewarded.*
A London printer, who at one time thought of launching out into authorship with a series of letters supposed to deal with all the varied circumstances of life, put into the hands of a young peasant-girl a pen that never grew weary: Pamela tells the story of the long persecution she underwent at the hands of a certain young lord who tried his very best to overcome her virtue. All England was in tears. Soon after came Clarissa, whose sufferings outdid the tribulations of the sorely persecuted Pamela.

1761. *La Nouvelle Héloïse.*
"O Julie, how fatal to be dowered by heaven with a sensitive heart!" An adventurer, a barbarian from Switzerland, a musician's apprentice who had not troubled to learn the rules before he took up writing; a living paradox who ran counter to every recognized idea, who declared that the Arts and Letters had done a disservice to mankind, who protested against the inequalities of the social order, who exalted and lent dignity to love. No more should love be a tame and domesticated thing. It should be wild and forceful and nothing should withstand its immeasurable expansion. It should disrupt and bring to nought the edifice man's intellect had raised, it would rejoice and make merry amid the ruins.

1774. *Die Leiden des jungen Werthers.*
"I withdraw within myself, and there I find a whole world! albeit a world of forebodings and shadowy fragments, rather than of clear-cut images." When he created Werther, the youthful Goethe had a new human type in mind. In Werther's case love would be but one more addition to the intolerable burden of one whom society irritated and life embittered, one whose dearest wish was to mingle, beyond the grave, with the spirit of the Universe.

1784. *Studies of Nature.*
Bernardin de Saint-Pierre, an egoist, an embittered, peevish spirit, yet outwardly so gentle, so full of feeling, was astute enough to put on to some imaginary island the love he had never

met with in any civilized land. "I wholly reject this alleged source of knowledge, this 'reason', as we call it." Imagine that, when books proclaiming the supremacy of the reason were coming out in a continuous stream; imagine such language, such exuberance, such violence of expression in the very midst of the sentimental drought! Here, yet again, we may discern the effect of that hidden process which comes to tamper with something we thought was securely our own. What psychological compulsion, what subtle and at first almost imperceptible influences were at work, what disruptions, nay what complicities, what compromises, what errors of judgment could have led the Philosopher to set free the Anti-philosopher? What could have led him deliberately to let loose the Man of Feeling?

"From Locke to Frederick II, from Newton to Joseph II, from d'Alembert and Voltaire to Christian Wolff and Justus Möser, ideas must have described an almost infinite curve to have brought men so diverse as these within a single span. All the same, it is as a single group that we have to consider them. All of them were pressing on in one and the same direction; all of them were more or less antagonistic to the past, to what was old, to the day before yesterday; all were bent on discovering and adopting whatever might help to increase the happiness of man and add to the amenities of life."[1] That was true enough; these men did form one single group; you might almost call it a brotherhood. They were inspired by a common purpose; they believed themselves to be marching to the same tune, and towards the same goal. Already, the promised land was in sight, even now they were about to set foot on it. But when was there a group that did not dissolve in the long run? The stronger the personalities composing it, the less likely are they to get along together. Each of them will want to find a truer truth, a better truth than his neighbour's, which he will decline to accept. In this case, the relation of man to the Deity, on which everything depended and which was supposed to have been settled once for all, was continually being taken up and examined anew, and with ever-varying results. And so, the very unity of the Aufklärung was at stake.

[1]Gyula Szekfu, *Les lumières,* In *l'Histoire hongroise,* par Valentin Homan et Gyula Szekfu, tome V, livre VI. *XVIIIe siècle, Troisième Partie.*

In 1802, the church doors will be flung wide, the bells will be pealing out across the skies as though they had never ceased to call us; a poet, a poet in prose, will call on all the enchantments of the imagination, on all the promptings of the heart to help him in writing his *Génie du Christianisme*. Chateaubriand, turning his back on "enlightenment", will display the treasures of the shadows. "Nothing there is that is fair, or sweet, or great in life but it is veiled in mystery. The most wonderful sensations are those that move us a little vaguely; modesty, chaste love, virtuous affection—all have their secrets. It might be said that responsive hearts need no words to convey their meaning, that they are as doors ajar. And innocence, which is but saint-like ignorance, is not that, too, the most ineffable of mysteries? A child is happy because he knows nothing; old age is dismal because it knows all. Fortunate it is for the old that, when the mysteries of life are over, the mysteries of death begin." Thus there rose up again the very thing which the philosophers had been so anxious to destroy. But would this revulsion of sentiment, beckoning men back along the road to faith, have had the power it did, if deism had been the sort of thing to satisfy the human conscience? Or if it had had the force of a doctrine perfectly consistent with itself? Or if it had exhibited perfect unity, and had not been divided against itself? Or if it had not permitted individuals and nations to exercise a freedom of choice, which, in the end, amounted to spiritual anarchy? Or, finally, if that universal value which it claimed to possess had resulted in the constitution of a wider catholicity instead of in a wholesale dismemberment, which was in fact its end?

What we have now to examine is, first, the antinomies which were inherent in the idea of Nature, the watchword of the age. Secondly, the philosophical origins of the man of feeling. Thirdly, the variants, the different shades of meaning, connoted by the word "deism". For these, as we look back on it all, were the several agents which brought about the disintegration of the philosophy of knowledge.

II

NATURE AND REASON

YES; Nature and Reason were united by an indissoluble tie. That much was certain. Nothing was clearer, nothing was more firmly established, or more often inculcated by the sages. Nature was rational, Reason was natural. A perfect arrangement. Psychological fancies that had no basis in Nature were like certain forests of the North which, having no roots in the soil, were carried away by a gust of wind. But ideas which Nature implanted in the mind and were in strict accordance with her laws, these were unshakable. Yes, perhaps. Yet, how did it come about that there was still a certain feeling of embarrassment in the air, and that, just when the formula equating Nature with Reason seemed to have established Knowledge on an immovable foundation?

Nature was too rich in its composition, too complex in its attributes, too potent in its effects to be imprisoned in a formula, and the formula gave way under the strain. Despite all their efforts to elucidate it by analysis, to get possession of it through science, to reduce it to some easily intelligible concept, those same wise and learned men who should have been basking in the warmth of certitude, still went on giving the word all manner of different and sometimes directly contradictory interpretations. Conscious of all this, they began to behold in Nature the reappearance of that Mystery which they were bent on banishing from the world. Hence their embarrassment and their irritation. At one moment, they declared that Nature was a mother whose thoughts were wholly centred on supplying the needs of her children; the moment after, that she had a profound disdain for the individual, her sole care being for the species; and, finally, that she cared for nothing and nobody, and went her own inexorable way. They said that she was as secret as a conjuror, who only displayed the result of his operations; they also said that she was so readily communicative, so manifest, so open that he who ran might read. They declared that she had purposes of her own, that she was full of attentiveness, scruples, subtleties, delicacies; and also that she was completely indifferent, or else positively hostile. Putting these contradictory interpretations end to end, one after another, you arrived at one long string of contradictions, you were faced with a catalogue you could only turn over with a sensation of irony, a gesture of despair.

Often it was only a matter of figures of speech, of rhetorical commonplaces, or metaphorical flourishes. However, they put up with them as something to go upon, or, maybe, as a cogent argument, or even a final answer. The more they kept saying that they were following Nature, that they were obeying Nature, the better they were pleased, and the less they agreed. Nothing was more disturbing to the Western conscience, an historian of ideas[1] has justly remarked, then this continual recourse to a shibboleth whose antinomies varied in character with the period, and with the individuals who swore by it. The Philosophers of the age of enlightenment, so far from dispelling the confusion, did but add to it. Nature and beneficence; natural politics; natural morality—all very dubious alliances, these, and not the least dubious was the statement which prepared the way for all the rest—the statement which equated Nature with Reason.

Did our idea of logic always square with Nature's? Voltaire, the Grand Inquisitor in the matter of questionable ideas, summoned this one among others to appear before his judgment seat. If we have to put fifty pounds of energy into our arms to lift a single pound; if the heart has to make a quite incommensurate effort to expel a drop of blood; if a carp lays millions of eggs in order to reproduce one or two of its species; if an oak-tree has to shed countless acorns to produce one sapling, and does not always succeed even then, such outrageous expenditure, such reckless profusion, is surely anything but reasonable. Similarly, Nature has poisoned the intercourse of the sexes over three-quarters of the earth's surface with a dreadful

[1]*Prolegomena to the History of Primitivism,* by A. O. Lovejoy, in the *Contribution to the History of Primitivism, Primitivism and related ideas in Antiquity,* by A. O. Lovejoy and G. Boas. Baltimore, 1935.

disease which affects mankind alone, a disease not the result of debauchery and excess, but one which arose among an island people living lives of primeval innocence. Who will say, after that, that Nature, incomprehensible Nature, despises not her own handiwork and confounds not her own designs? The philosopher—and the philosopher was Voltaire himself—asked her, nay, implored her to reply: "What art thou, Nature? I live in thee; for fifty years I have been seeking thee, and still I have not found thee!" But Nature made answer, saying, the Egyptians, that ancient race, had already made her the same reproach. They called her Isis, and had put a veil over her head that none had lifted.

The Philosopher

My dearest mother, come tell me I pray thee wherefore thou dost exist, wherefore anything existeth?

Nature

I make answer unto thee, even as I have made answer for many a century to those who have questioned me concerning first principles. That answer is "I know nought about them."[1]

The majority of the choir went on singing a hymn with the old familiar verses, Nature never deviates from the truth; Nature and Truth are everywhere the same, and Reason shows forth their identity; Nature never says one thing and Wisdom another. Follow in the firm steps of Nature and you will never go astray. The majority of the choir continued to sing a magnificat to Nature, for that she had had the foresight to create substitute plants in regions where wheat, rye and barley were not. Aye, in certain parts of Norway and Germany which were particularly barren, Nature had shown men the way to make bread out of a certain kind of earth which would keep good for forty years: admirable precaution on the part of Nature thus to compensate for the barrenness of those unfortunate lands. The majority of the choir kept harping on the old familiar sayings; Nature no longer abhorred a vacuum, that had gone out of fashion; but it always had to abhor something, and now it abhorred the opposite; Nature never worked in

[1]Voltaire, *Nature, Dialogue entre le Philosophe et la Nature.* In *Questions sur l'Encyclopédie,* 1771.

vain; Nature always went the shortest way to work. It sounded like a litany.

But some of the voices sang a different tune. We will follow Nature, they said, as soon as you have shown us exactly what it is; and that you will not do. You keep on harping on the same word, using it with the greatest freedom, though you have no real idea of what it means. You flourish it with great impressiveness in the forefront of your writings, yet it never seems to enter your heads that you yourselves are making use of the very same sort of metaphysical jargon as you condemn. Let us give a wide berth to the sort of people who, under pretext of explaining Nature, give us for truth unintelligible theories born of their own imaginations. . . . These disaffected gentlemen averred that whenever they got back to the realities of things, they felt as if their heads were going round as they contemplated the scene of disorder in order, and noted the caprices of Nature, at once lavish and miserly. They felt overwhelmed by such a multiplicity of contradictory phenomena, and all of them natural!

Possibly the Nature-worshippers might have extricated themselves from their dilemma had not empiricism itself involved them in their greatest difficulty.

Seeing that the empiricists laid it down as a principle that it was fundamentally impossible for us to get to know anything about substances, and that consequently it is absurd to make a definite assertion of any kind concerning them, what right has anyone to ascribe properties to those same substances? To be logical, the empiricists should have stuck to that ignorance of theirs, so often and so freely proclaimed. They only got out of it by the most inexcusable act of faith. Moreover, since their knowledge was confined to the sensations they perceived in their minds, they had no right to assume that, outside their minds, something called Nature, or what you will, had any existence at all.

And now behold, here was a great thinker at hand to give form to the argument. It was in 1713 that Berkeley brought out his *Dialogues between Hylas and Philonous*; they had crossed the Channel in translation, but not until a considerable interval had elapsed. They seemed somewhat disconcerting. At dawn, in the light of the rising sun, Philonous, the friend of Mind, was pacing deep in thought. He encountered Hylas, the friend of Matter, and the two fell into a discussion. Was Philonous really serious when he affirmed that there was no such thing as material substance? The thing was possible, no doubt. Yes, and an irrefutable certainty, according to Philonous, who, with incomparable dialectical skill, proceeded to prove his statement. We cannot conclude from our perceptions that external objects exist, for our perceptions are the only things of which we can speak with certainty. Anything very hot burns us and causes pain: are we to say that that pain is in the body whose contact has burned us? We know that sugar is sweet and wormwood bitter; are we to take it that the bitterness is in the wormwood, and the sweetness in the sugar? These sensations are in ourselves; they change when we are ill. The same is true of scents and sounds. Can we say of the wave of air which strikes the drum of our ear that it is sharp or flat? The same with colours. We know well enough that substances have not the colours we assign to them, as yellow, when we have the jaundice.

Hylas would have none of this, and cudgelled his brain for arguments to reduce his interlocutor to silence. It was no good. To be is to perceive, and to be perceived; nothing more. Habit, custom, or our own unreasonable fancies lead us to look for some sort of substratum, some substance underlying sense-data and wholly within ourselves. Better make haste and confess our error. We have recognized, once for all, that we have no idea, positive or relative, of what matter really is. We are as ignorant of what it is in itself as we are of its accidental relationships. That being so, let us keep within the limits which we ourselves have established. Or as Hylas, now at last convinced, expressed it: let us keep, if we must, the expression to which we have been so long accustomed, and talk about matter; but when it comes to defining what it really is, well there is no such thing, if we mean some substance destitute of thought, and existing outside the mind; but there *is* such a thing, if we mean by the word something sensible, whose existence consists in its being perceived.

Berkeley, the idealist, pursued, with gentle persistency, the demonstration of his theories. He went to the New World and there endeavoured to establish a seminary in which young

Englishmen and young Americans should rub shoulders for the good of the Christian religion. Returning to Europe he was appointed Bishop of Cloyne in Ireland, his native country; but he still went on with his philosophic task. In 1740, in a work which he entitled *Siris*, or reflexions on the subject of tar-water, etc., he reached the topmost peaks, whence he gazed with ravished eyes on the beauty of the Mind-Universe. He made known the virtues of tar-water, whose marvellous powers he had learned in far-off lands among the savages, a cure for every ill, impurities of the blood and intestinal ulcer, consumption and erysipelas, wasting diseases and hysteria, the gravel and dropsy, gangrene and scurvy, smallpox, gout and fever; equally efficacious whether with children or the aged, men and women, seafarers or stay-at-homes. From tar he went on to the volatile salts contained therein, from volatile salts to the air, from the air to the ether, to the Wisdom which distributes it, the pure and invisible fire, for it is impossible to take a single step forward in the explanation of phenomena unless we admit the presence and immediate action of an immaterial agent who interconnects, moves and disposes all things according to the laws, and in fulfilment of the purposes, which seem good in his sight. Mechanical philosophers study only the rules and the operation of the process, not the cause thereof; for nothing mechanical is or could be a cause. Only a mind, strictly speaking, can be a cause. Berkeley did not reject the Newtonian theory of attraction; he enlarged upon it. When it is alleged that all the movements and all the changes that take place in the world are caused by attraction; that the elasticity of the air, the movement of water, the descent of heavy bodies and the ascent of light ones are to be ascribed to the same law; when, from the imperceptible attraction of minute particles within the smallest possible distances, are deduced cohesion, dissolution, coagulation, animal secretion, fermentation and every kind of chemical action; when it is added that, without such principles, there would be no movement in the world, and that if they ceased to operate all movement would cease—when all this has been said, all we really know, all we have really arrived at is that bodies move in accordance with a certain order and that they do not impart motion to themselves. . . .

Berkeley was a thorn in the philosophers' flesh; though not

so much on account of his apologetic. He had a great contempt for the "small fry" of the free-thinking class. It was his wish and aim that his doctrine should result directly in a fresh proof of the existence of God: things apprehensible by the senses having no existence save in the mind, it was necessary to admit the reality of a Mind which was none other than God. Of that line of argument his unbelieving readers made short work; it seemed to them to be a mere corollary; all the same they felt that this Berkeley was a great stumbling-block. How were they to refute a man with whom their only quarrel was that he drove home their own argument to its logical conclusion? It was easy enough to laugh at him and to say, for example, that ten thousand men slain by ten thousand cannon shot were, in reality, but ten thousand conceptions of the mind; that when a man puts his wife with child, it is merely one idea lodged within another idea, from which a third idea is born. It was still easier to fly into a rage: what preposterous nonsense will men think of next? What monstrous rubbish to deny the existence of the external world! And then it had to be admitted that neither ridicule nor indignation met the case. On the front page of the French translation of the Dialogues of Hylas and Philonous was an engraving of a child who, seeing his face in a mirror, was trying to take hold of it; the child was laughing at his mistake. But the words underneath indicated that it was wrong of him to laugh. *Quid rides? Fabula de te narratur.*

How patiently, for three-quarters of a century, was the search carried on for some convincing evidence that would show, beyond dispute, whether sensation was purely subjective, or whether it corresponded to some reality external to us. Imagine a blind man suddenly getting his sight back; would he have any real idea of distance? An experiment on these lines had first occurred to the learned M. Molineux, who wrote Locke a letter in which he put forward the suggestion as follows: Take the case of a man blind from birth who has reached a mature age. He has been taught to distinguish by touch between a cube and a globe, both made of the same metal and both as near as may be of the same bulk, so that he is able to tell which is the cube and which the globe. Now suppose that, the cube and the globe both being placed on a table, the blind man suddenly begins to see; the question is whether, by merely looking at them, without taking them in his hands, he would be able to distinguish between them and to say which was the cube and which the globe. Molineux said he would not; and Locke, too, said he would not; Berkeley declared that he would not: a person blind from birth who began to see would at first, by merely looking, have no idea whatever of distance. The sun and the stars would seem to him to be in his eye, or rather in his mind.

This of course was all pure hypothesis and no one could say how a real flesh-and-blood blind man would comport himself in such circumstances, when lo! experimental surgery came to the aid of philosophy. A surgeon named Cheselden had found out how to operate for cataract. In 1728, he described how he had carried out the operation in question on a lad of thirteen or fourteen. He had cleared one eye, to start with; the result was that the patient could not take in distances; he thought the various things he saw were touching his eyes, just as the things he handled touched his skin. It was two months before he could convince himself that pictures represented solid bodies. Seeing his father's likeness on a watch-case, he marvelled that a man's face could be contained in so small a space. He thought that there was nothing beyond the range of what he saw. The other eye was operated on a year later, and with this second eye he saw things much bigger than with the first, and some sort of adjustment had been necessary. Similar experiments carried out on a number of different subjects had given like results. It takes a long time for the mind to acquire a sense of distance.

The question concerning people born blind who obtained their sight was occupying some of the leading minds of the day; it was a test which they had neither the right nor the desire to evade. Diderot thought a propitious opportunity was within his reach: Réaumur had taken under his wing a certain Prussian oculist named Hilmer, who also operated for cataract; Diderot had got leave to be present when the work was going on. He was grievously disappointed, because he thought the whole thing was a fraud; but behold, the operation was over, and the man could see. All the philosophic considerations had to be started over again. It would be necessary, however, to refute Berkeley in order to expose the defect of "a system which, to the disgrace of the human intellect and of philosophy, was at once the most difficult to combat, and the most absurd of all". The best thing was to call in the aid of a specialist in the matter of the human mind, one whose knowledge of the subject might enable him to put his finger on the precise point on which Philonous had gone astray.[1] This was how it came about that Condillac was invited to come to the aid of Nature in her hour of need.

He addressed himself to his task; he refuted Berkeley, or at all events he did his best.[2] Everything we know comes to us through our senses; that much is certain; our sensations are but modes of being; that is no less so. Well then, how can we affirm that anything exists external to ourselves? All we perceive are states of our mind, variously modified. We should, then, be, and have to remain, where we were, if our sensations were limited to those of smell, hearing, taste and sight; we should take it that we were smell, sound, taste, colour. The sense of touch would do nothing to dispel our ignorance regarding things external to us if we remained motionless. We should never perceive anything but the sensations which the air surrounding us would make us feel. We should feel hot or cold, we should be conscious of pain or pleasure, and all these things would still be modes of being in which we should perceive neither the circumambient atmosphere, nor any other body; we should be conscious only of ourselves. But then, we move; when we put our hand on the things about us, we experience a sensation of a special kind, we feel a resistance. This is where Berkeley's theory breaks down: this resistance can only be offered to us by objects external to ourselves; therefore the external world *does* exist.

Whether or not the sense of touch possesses the specific quality which Condillac ascribed to it, was a debatable point. What was certain, however, what ran counter to Diderot's requirements, what aggravated the difficulty instead of dispelling it, was that the deeper Condillac delved into the matter, the more obviously he departed from Isis and Physis and concentrated his attention on the soul, the more he was allowing his incipient empiricism to lead him towards a spiritual interpretation of things. He was

[1]Diderot, *Lettre sur les aveugles, à l'usage de ceux qui voient*, 1749.

[2]Condillac, *Traité des Sensations*, 1754. Based on the *Précis de la seconde partie.*

a disciple of Locke and he acknowledged his debt, never realizing that it was heavy enough to crush him. In many ways he had corrected his master, particularly in regard to the ambiguity exhibited by the latter, who considered ideas sometimes as images of inapprehensible realities, sometimes as the inward adjustment of our sensations, truth being no more than the correspondence of their relations. The French philosopher had chosen the second alternative and clung to it more and more persistently. The amazing spectacle of the mind's interior was enough to keep him occupied; he had no interest in what went on outside it. Sensation, a mental fact; the multiplicity of sensations which do not require to be arranged in a hierarchical order, but to be organized; their organization by virtue of signs which lend them a general character; knowledge of these signs which are furnished by language; the logic of the mind, the algebra of the mind: such according to him, was the real science. The refutation of Berkeley had been after all a mere incident in his career. He abandoned Berkeley, but the path he chose as particularly his own led him farther and farther from the philosophers who had solicited his aid.

And now, to play his part in the explanation of Nature, there came on the scene, not an adversary like Berkeley, not a doubtful friend like Condillac, but a real friend, a brother, whose rôle was to demolish the family mansion from the inside. And his name was David Hume.

A philosopher of the enlightened school was he; and he was so in a variety of different fashions. To begin with a decision which he took: it must have been an act of great courage for him to quit his native Scotland at the age of twenty-four, to give up the law and trade, and to go and settle down in France so that he might work in freedom at the cultivation of his mind. From 1735 to 1737 he remained at La Flèche working on his *Treatise of Human Nature*, the first two volumes of which were published in 1739, and the third in 1740. He was a philosopher in his universal curiosity and in his desire to find a solution to the problems which, he observed, were everlastingly being debated round about him. No one proclaimed himself more attentive to the facts and to the facts alone, or more remote from the dreams of the metaphysicians. He hoped, and there were many others who hoped the same, that he would at length succeed in disengaging from the general mass the unique, the central fact, which should be the key to the whole universe, and make him, David Hume, the Newton of the Intellect. His tone was in tune with the times; there was nothing of the pedant about him; he did not quote from the Classics, and he was sparing in his use of technical terms; and if, despite all this, there *was* a suspicion of the pedant about him, he wore his pedantry with an air. He was sociable, a good mixer, and he did not hold aloof from public affairs; as a matter of fact, he had a decided aptitude for directing them. He had a whole host of antipathies, he was anti-enthusiasm, anti-sentiment, anti-superstition, anti-miracles, anti any sort of faith whatever. His style of argument, of writing, was the soul of clarity. He was fond of juggling with ideas; he seemed to be able to make them do just what he liked; but this amusement was rather terrifying. His earlier literary ventures had not come up to his expectations, but he stuck to his guns and finally achieved fame. In 1763, when he came back to Paris, this time as secretary to the British Ambassador, he was received with something approaching transport. Invited everywhere, welcomed, fêted, a familiar figure in the salons, a great diner-out, David Hume was the Philosopher Triumphant. And it was this same philosopher who was the undoing of Philosophy.

And now behold him explaining to the deists that they had succumbed to the temptation of anthropomorphism just like the veriest religious simpletons alive. He started by making liberal concessions to them: they were perfectly right in upholding the need for natural religion as a bulwark against wholesale scepticism, that being incompatible with action. The fundamental error of pyrrhonism is this: it assumes that man is permanently in a state of mind in which, as a matter of fact, he only is at certain times; the most sceptical of men must make up his mind sometimes, or he would die. Here then is something that points the way to a *Credo*. But how had these deists pictured their Supreme Being. They recognized that they had no experience of the divine attributes, that the essence of that Being—his mode of existence, his qualities—were completely hidden from them; they ought to have stopped there, but, instead, they conceived of God's intelligence as modelled on their own. Contemplating the world, and the parts of which it was composed, they perceived that this world was none other than a vast machine divided into an infinite number of smaller machines, which latter were themselves capable of incalculable subdivision. These divers machines seemed to be adjusted severally one to another with a perfection that captured the imagination of anyone who had looked into them. The curious adaptation of means to ends, discernible throughout the whole of Nature, seemed to reproduce, though on a vastly wider scale, the outcome of human ingenuity, of the destiny, the ideas, the intelligence, the wisdom of man. Inasmuch, therefore, as the effects were similar, the deists had been led to infer by analogy that the causes also were similar; and that the author of Nature was in some degree like a human being, though the faculties he possessed were infinitely more powerful, as befitted the greatness of his work. By this *a posteriori* argument, and by it alone, the partisans of Natural Religion had upheld their cause, never realizing how weak and irrational it was.

In the same serene and placid manner, stating the facts, calmly explaining—things were thus and not otherwise, and that was all there was to be said about it—Hume found fault with our method of reasoning. We hold the idea of causation to be essential; the relationship between cause and effect is the corner-stone of our science and our philosophy. But this relationship was in no way justified by the facts. Look for a moment into our own mind; it contains present impressions, and remembered impressions, which latter we call ideas. All we can do is to associate these impressions and these ideas; and, in so doing, we assume between them the existence of logical relations of which we have no assurance whatever. Without any justification, we transform into a law of causation what never was, never is, and never can be anything but a succession in time. What is called cause is an object so followed by another object that the presence of the first makes us think of the second; we are not entitled to affirm any necessary connexion between the two. The following propositions are both equally possible: the sun will rise tomorrow; the sun will not rise tomorrow. We have got into the way of uniting the two terms, without any assurance that the union is justified. The metaphysician knows nothing more obscure than the notions of power, force, energy and connexion. "The world in which we live is a great theatre in which all the machinery is hidden; we do not see the motive power, the cause of events is concealed from us; threatened unceasingly with countless misfortunes, we have not the foresight to avoid them or the power to drive them away; we are continually hovering betwixt life and death, disease and health, plenty and famine. Secret causes outpour on the human race both good and evil; they operate often when we least expect them, and their mode of operation is a mystery."

Hence there is science no longer, but only the uncertain recurrence of particular cases. There is no more philosophy, only arbitrary interpretations of the unknowable. Nature is no more; there is nothing but the Great Unknown. There are no laws of Nature, but merely appearances which we interpret erroneously. No more reason, only a chaos of sensations. No definite conclusions, but only certain impressions that seem to us more vivid than others and which we consequently prefer. No more of "I", or "Me", just a glittering swarm of inexplicable presences. Let us speak no more of a universe regulated by a wisdom, whereof the reflexion becomes our wisdom; speak we only of a swarm of phenomena.

The celebrated Mr. Hume was a sceptic pure and unadulterated. Entering into the game, playing it with due regard for the rules, he ended with defeat final and complete. Howbeit, he was not grieved, not even disappointed. It was his partners who suffered most. His reasoning—if the word had now any meaning—seemed ingenuous; hardly a trace of malice was discernible in his seemingly innocent air. Little by little he lured his hearers on towards the precipice and little did they realize what pleasure it gave him gently to conduct them thither. In actual practice he stopped short of causing a revolution; he had no wish to be crushed beneath the last remaining columns of the temple. He advocated a certain moderation in wisdom, and he himself set the example. Was it prudence on his part? He knew how risky it was to go poking about in drains which spread infection round about them; how dangerous to disturb the plague in the underground places in which it is confined; he declared that truths which might harm society, if such there were, should give place to beneficent and salutary errors; other-wise, men persecute you; and, if they cannot refute you, conspire to bury you in eternal oblivion. Contemptuousness perhaps; or did his scepticism really fail him at the end, telling him that the illusions on which men feed are after all not of such great importance that one must always refuse to share them?

Contradictors, dissentients, underminers—let them do their worst! They were powerless, it seemed, against the unshakable conviction that truths brought out by reason are possessed of a transcendental value. Evidence enjoyed this privilege: it had no need to ask leave of the Ancients or the Moderns to display itself. It induced in everyone an inward conviction amounting to the highest order of certitude. It was a compelling force. Whoso beheld it was powerless to say it nay. Just as it is not ours to say that day is night, so are we powerless to escape the evidence of fact. With regard to what is evident, our liberty is at an end; we can but yield to it, and yield it our full consent. Now this idea, so completely incompatible with empiricism, yet withal so familiar to empirics, whence came it, if not from Descartes?

We have stated that Locke was the moving spirit of the age, and we do not modify our opinion; we said that his influence was felt in every branch of intellectual activity, and that we firmly repeat. We are aware that in a number of cases Descartes is pictured as a slave bound to the chariot of the conqueror, and a number of writings proclaim the discomfiture of the vanquished. The law that governs human affairs ordains that the old shall give place to the new, and now, his turn having come, Descartes has had to take his leave. He overthrew the great ones among the schoolmen, and is now himself overthrown: he has had his day; now let him fade away, treated as he himself treated the scholastics. He wrote the romance of the soul, not its history. He knew not the origin nor the generation of ideas. With his "whirlpools", he made nonsense of nature. They mock at him, these same writers, and call him René the visionary; they vilify him, and say that he was false to his own convictions. When he was making preparations for constructing a system, he was for basing it on the doctrine of the void; hearing from a friend that that hypothesis was not in fashion at Court, he changed his plan and instead of the void, chose its opposite. There were testimonies all agreeing that Descartes had been eclipsed, in physics by Newton, in philosophy by Locke. If we are to accept the dates given by contemporary authorities, it would be about 1730 that what were called his chimaeras were abandoned.

But other testimonies, no less authentic, reveal that his influence was much more active than first impressions would lead one to suppose; moreover, we are all well aware that no one flogs a dead horse. The eighteenth century was both Lockian and Cartesian, and if that sounds like a paradox, that is not our fault, we have but to put it on record. Do not let us be content with saying that Locke survived through Malebranche, who still wielded considerable influence, particularly on French thinkers, for Malebranche, while deriving from Descartes and faithfully adhering to some of his earlier ideas, found his ultimate goal, be it remembered, in Berkeley's idealism, nay, more than that, in Spinoza, of whom we shall have something to say hereafter. No; Descartes is here, Descartes himself, and in his own right, and many are his manifestations.

In the foreground of the picture, to defend his shade, stand the Old Guard. Fontenelle, still bearing arms, is there; so is the Abbé Terrasson, the man who said that anyone who did not think like Descartes, not in mathematics alone, but in literature, was not worthy of the age; and Mairan, too, who preached Cartesianism to the Académie des Sciences until his dying day. Next came the forces of the spiritual and the material; their reasons were different, but they both had their source in his teaching. The former were ever grateful to him for demonstrating the existence of God and the immateriality of the soul, and for putting free-thought to rout by his alliance with reason. A certain Abbé Genest put his doctrine in verse, happy to take shelter behind this bulwark of the Faith:

> Je marche à la faveur d'une heureuse clarté,
> Les mystères de la Nature
> Vont sortir devant moi de leur obscurité.
> Un homme parmi nous s'offre pour me conduire;
> Dès que par sa Méthode on commence à s'instruire,
> Un chemin plus connu mène à la vérité. . . .[1]

[1] I go forward by favour of an auspicious light, the mysteries of Nature will emerge before my gaze from their obscurity. There is a man among us who offers to be my guide. As soon as we begin to learn by the light of his Method, a better known road leads to the truth. . . .

"Descartes came on the scene! Armed with all the forces of genius, he dared, single-handed, to fight for the cause of Philosophy and Reason against a universe in thrall to the Peripatetics. Vast, sublime, profound was his mind, but, it may be, over-daring; yet to Descartes will belong the eternal glory of having led the thinking world along the way to the truth, even if he did not always have the glory of reaching it himself. To this auspicious genius it is that philosophy owes her rehabilitation and her immense progress". Thus speaks a Jesuit, Father Phara; another Jesuit, Father Paulian, came out with a work in three volumes which he called *Traité de paix entre Descartes et Newton*. For the Jesuits, having banished the Cartesian philosophy from their scheme of studies, and long striven against it—yet not so fiercely but that some obstinate partisan might crop up among them here and there—had at length taken him to their bosom. Apart from Malebranche and Descartes, declared Père André, there was no salvation in philosophy. Descartes' mission, Père Antoine Guénard used to say, was to announce to men that to be a Philosopher it sufficed not merely to believe; one must also think. However, the anti-religionists recalled, for their part, that Descartes had boasted that he would build a world, provided he was furnished with the material and the movement. So La Mettrie took up his defence against those objectionable little philosophers, apers of Locke, against M. Goudin who had let his tongue run away with him in his animadversions, against M. Deslandes who never really understood him; the fact was that, recognized in his true light, he was an astute materialist who had never been free to develop his own ideas; he had only spoken of the soul because he had to, at a time when his merits were better calculated to retard his fortunes than to advance them. He was the originator of all those endless discussions about the souls of animals; from the animal-machine to the man-machine was no far cry. What it amounts to is that Descartes, never having hung up a sign-board outside his Clarity Inn, anybody and everybody might lodge his opinions there.

Recent references to him, whether they bore on such major works as the *Esprit des Lois,* or the *Encyclopédie*; or whether their purpose was to trace the trend of thought throughout the different countries of Europe, all show how persistent was the influence of the "Great philosopher of France", of "*Renato, genio grande e creatore*", "*sublime e benemerito genio*"; they show, too, how great was the effort to sacrifice neither the empiricism of Locke, nor the rationalism of Descartes. In 1765, when it seemed clear that the former had come out the winner, they awarded the latter a consolation prize that looked uncommonly like an apotheosis. The Académie française had offered a prize for the best panegyric on Descartes; a specialist in the line, one Antoine Léonard Thomas, was adjudged the winner. The reading of the discourse "aroused prodigious enthusiasm". In fine, rhetorical phrases, Thomas reminded his audience that a hundred years before, the ashes of Descartes had been brought home from Stockholm to Paris and that then no one had been allowed to pronounce a funeral oration in the philosopher's honour; but now the time to make amends had come. Doubtless a number of his ideas had since been discarded; not so his mind, his soul; that kept marching on and had its faithful followers. Descartes had brought about a revolution whose effects would last for ever. Betwixt Aristotle and Descartes there yawned a gulf of two thousand years; and he concluded by saying that the author of the *Discours de la Méthode* was a living presence everywhere, in London, Berlin, Leipzig, Florence, and as far afield as St. Petersburg. In 1771, His Majesty the King of Sweden visited Paris, where he was received by the Academy and regaled with a Dialogue between Descartes and Christina of Sweden in the Elysian Fields.

In the Elysian Fields his shade was entitled to rejoice. If it was freely admitted that he had erred on certain points, it was equally plain that the very weapons employed to oppose him were weapons that he himself had forged, and that to him were owed those dawning gleams that had ushered in the Age of Light. He had taught the doctrine of methodical doubt, he had inculcated the importance of orderly thought, of analysis; reliance on the fact, and the transcendental value of reason; all deductions made, the debt that we owed him was still immense. The philosophers forgot just one thing and that was that the transcendental value of the reason was based by him on the attributes of God. They had so often declared, these philosophers, that they found the attributes of God quite inconceivable that the Cartesian backing, logically speaking, should have meant nothing to them. Ingenuous creatures, they denied the principle, and retained the consequences.

Perhaps we may find, in the fact we have been bringing out, a means of terminating a controversy which is still going on. We know the systematic vigour with which Taine persisted in seeing in eighteenth-century philosophy nothing but pure abstraction, and this in spite of its being pointed out to him that the thinkers of those days cherished nothing more dearly than the rule of beginning with the most scrupulously attentive investigation of the facts, coming back again and again to the facts and of bringing about at last a practical reconstruction of society. Might it not justly be said that ideas in those days were paradoxically both rationalistic and empirical at one and the same time? They were empirical in stating that there was nothing *a priori* in the mind; and rationalistic in that they believed in the *a priori* character of the Reason; empirical when they professed that Nature was no more than the record of our impressions, our sense-data; rationalistic, when they affirmed that Nature was Reason.

Leibniz, too, and Spinoza, claimed a place for themselves. Leibniz was rejected on the same grounds as, and sometimes even more trenchantly than, Descartes; they talked about extravagances, about the dreams of a doctrinaire, about the vague meanderings of a charlatan, and offered other similarly polite remarks.

But on the practical plane, things happened very differently. One of these days, it may be, someone will undertake an exhaustive study of this great subject. In the meanwhile, perhaps we may be permitted to suggest some of the lines such an enquiry might take. To begin with it would call attention to the fact that the respective positions of Descartes and Leibniz are widely different in point of time. Whereas the former represents a movement already long established in the world, on which the movement initiated by Locke was superimposed, without crushing it out of existence, the latter's starting point dates from a time when the eighteenth century was already well under way. While, therefore, the one was concerned with the exploitation of wealth long in hand, the other was confronted with treasure but recently discovered. Leibniz died in 1716;

his *Theodicée* appeared in 1710, three-quarters of a century after the *Discours de la Méthode*, and twenty years after the *Essay concerning the Human Understanding*; the *Monadologie* saw the light for the first time in the *Acta Eruditorum* of Leipzig in 1721. Towards extracting the many articles of Leibniz from the learned publications in which they lay embedded, and introducing the substance of his philosophy to a wider circle than that of his immediate disciples, much work was undertaken late on in the century by various publishers, popularizers and editors, among them, Gottsched, Élie de Jaucourt, König, Dutens, Raspe and others. This does not imply that his influence was any the less profound, but merely that it had not been immediately appreciated; that it had to be explored, and that it had sometimes been underestimated by reason of the difficulty of disengaging it from among the many doctrines which had reached, or already outlived, their maturity.

The study we envisage would note the fact that, while Europe aimed at being a community, each nation was for preserving its own particular predilections, so that France remained, in spite of herself, more deeply committed to Descartes, while England favoured Locke, and Germany Leibniz. The more widely the last-named country communicated her ideas, the more widely her Leibnizian predilections began to operate. Leibniz was not merely the inspirer of German lyricism—Gottsched's ode is dedicated to him—he was the very soul of Germany.

Next, our commentator would note a sentiment of some complexity; a consciousness of the presence of a genius of such exceptional powers that one was overtaken by a feeling of something akin to remorse for failing fully to understand him and so to do full justice to his great qualities. Père Castel was astonished to discover that a man who had done little but set forth his fleeting ideas, plans and promises in journals no less transient than they, and who had written a *Theodicée* which, after all, had nothing so very sublime about it, was, nevertheless, worthy of such deep attention; d'Alembert, remote from him as he was, could not but offer him the admiration to which the loftiness of his views in every sphere, the prodigious extent of his knowledge, and above all the philosophic spirit with which he had illumined it, so richly entitled him. Diderot came humbly to the stool of repentance. It had been alleged, possibly with some justification, that he had not rendered to the philosopher the homage he deserved. Well, then, he made up for the omission, and blithely: he was far too tenacious of the honour of the human species ever to have thought of depreciating its illustrious representatives; besides that, their works, handed down to posterity, would testify to later ages in their favour; they would lose no inch of their stature; but those who had neglected them would look uncommonly small. There were scarcely more than four or five people whose genius had done honour to humanity, Hérault de Séchelles reports him as saying, "Newton, Bacon, Leibniz, Montesquieu and myself." As regards Newton, he discovered a great principle, but he spent his whole life working out sums to prove it; in the matter of style, there is nothing much to be got from him. Buffon ascribed greater importance to Leibniz than to Bacon himself. He declared that Leibniz carried all before him at the point of his genius.

It would be further pointed out that if traces of him appear unexpectedly in unlikely places, among the most divergent of writers, in the old Muratori, for example, and the youthful Turgot, the reason is that people often adopted his views on particular matters without deeming themselves obliged to subscribe to the whole of the system of which they formed a part. Here it would be appropriate to make mention of the assistance demanded of him against the negations of Bayle, and the way in which it was contrived to bring out the conciliatory qualities of his philosophy; of his place in the evolution of history; of the part played by him in the diffusion of optimism, a subject, incidentally, with which we ourselves propose to deal in our next chapter. Then there is the frequency with which his famous principles are appealed to: Reason sufficing; the Economy of Forces; the Indiscernible, and, perhaps most important of all, the Principle of Continuity which lent substance to the belief in the existence of an endless scale of living creatures. In a certain sense, Leibniz, a mathematician and a physicist, though by no means a naturalist, was yet the inspirer of natural history. Says Charles Bonnet: "M. Trembley's discovery has greatly widened our knowledge of the organic system. It has thrown a valuable light on that marvellous gradation which some philosophers had perceived in the works of Nature.

Leibniz said that Nature did not work *per saltum*; and it is most remarkable that the metaphysics of that great man led him to suspect the existence of some such living thing as the polypus. It is not often that the metaphysician is so happy in his explanations of Nature."[1]

And so, after all these different approaches to him, themselves a proof of his omnipresence, we should be brought to the consideration of his essential rôle. Leibniz symbolized the counter-offensive of metaphysics. His part it was to remind us that when every conceivable malediction had been heaped upon it, it was to metaphysics we had to go if we would learn aught of the mystery of Being, and lay bare the ultimate secret. We are not thinking only of those who, without being conscious of any notable inconvenience, adopted both Descartes and Locke, and then the Leibnizian solution into the bargain. We are speaking of some very decided partisans of the enlightened school who at a particular juncture looked like falling into heresy because it was in vain that they went on explaining matter in terms of matter, motion in terms of motion. Very singular is the case of Mme du Châtelet, who, having begun on a work of pure physics, admits a dose of metaphysics and finishes up a Leibnizian. Still more curious is the case of Maupertuis whose *Essai sur la formation des êtres organisés* (1754) starts with materialism and then invokes the aid of Leibniz and his spiritualism. Maupertuis begins by saying that so many previous attempts to explain Nature having met with no success, he himself is going to try his hand. The secret is that Nature consists of elements, that is to say, particles of matter so minute as not to admit of being split up any further; these elements or particles combine together to form bodies. What remains to be explained is how these atoms are organized. The gross particles postulated by Epicurus, and subsequently by Lucretius, offered no solution of the problem. Even the laws of matter, such as attraction, would throw but an imperfect light on the phenomena of life. So, therefore, it was necessary to imagine "some principle of intelligence, something akin to what we term desire, or aversion, or memory. . . ." Let there be no mistake about it; what we have here is the monad. This puts La Mettrie into a towering

[1]Charles Bonnet, *Considérations sur les corps organisés,* Part I, Chap. XII. Consult his *Vue du Leibnizianisme,* Œuvres, Ed. of 1783, tome VII.

rage: these Leibnizians with their monads have done more to spiritualize matter than to materialize the soul; everybody knows about these precious monads since the brilliant conquest the Leibnizians made when they won over Mme du Châtelet. This gang adds to its numbers every day, and we shall soon have to get another Descartes to come along and purge metaphysics of those vague obscurities with which the mind too often regales itself.

And now Spinoza. Here we encounter once again the same gestures of disgust, the same shouts of opprobrium, the same repulsion, with which the story of his life had been received, and which had followed on a first acquaintance with the *Tractatus theologico-politicus* and with the *Ethic*. The same familiar insults were hurled at this unbelieving dog, this criminal, this filthy cur. The same scorn was poured out on that theory of infinite substance which could but excite contempt and abhorrence, on the system which, subtracting the infinite from the infinite, arrived at nothing, the most absurd which had ever been thought of since philosophers had thought at all. And there was the same anxiety to avoid the slightest suspicion of being tainted with Spinozaism, as if it had been some shameful disease.

It was not only Christians, Catholic and Protestant, who dreaded the pest; the majority of the philosophers, taking their cue from Bayle, turned their backs on Spinoza. Neither Bolingbroke nor Wolff was for risking the leap into topsy-turvy land. As for Condillac, he said that Spinoza simply did not know what he was talking about; his definitions were vague, and his axioms inaccurate; his proportions were the creation of his fancy and had nothing in them calculated to lead to a knowledge of things. That said, he stopped short: "I should have been just as foolish to attack the phantoms it engendered as were those knights-errant who charged at spectres and enchanters." And how should a man like the Baron d'Holbach have done any better? "There is every reason to believe that, had it not been for the persecution and ill-treatment inflicted on him by the chief of the synagogue, Spinoza might quite possibly have never thought of his system." People were willing to admit, at a pinch, that he was not the kind of hypocrite who would skilfully conceal the impiety of his dogmas beneath a cloak of moral austerity, and a display of sham righteousness; they admitted that his life was stainless. But his philosophy incurred a reproach from which nothing could absolve him: it was not clear, and by the same token, it was not sound. It was, in fact, unintelligible, and that was a very good thing. Had it been understandable it would have made converts; but being a puzzle, it was left on the shelf.

At the same time, there were termites at work. Clandestine manuscripts were going about; they did not enable you to get hold of him from end to end, but they gave you the gist of him: we know now that a number of these manuscripts under various titles served as vehicles for his ideas. So-called refutations, under cover of making mince-meat of him, were really a means of making him known. *Réfutation des erreurs de Benoît de Spinoza, par M. de Fénelon . . . , par le P. Lami, bénédictin, et par M. le comte de Boulainvilliers,* Bruxelles, 1731. M. le Comte de Boulainvilliers, pretending to controvert Spinoza, in reality interpreted him. Then there were reckless fellows, rebels, who found him much to their taste; and little bands of independents, or shall we call them active cells. Every now and again, a great scandal: some defiant individual, ostracized by society because he had boasted of being the genuine disciple of the accursed one, had stuck to his guns.

Then, somewhere about the middle of the century, a change came about. Instead of a general scrimmage which had this about it, that neither those who attacked him, nor any of his scanty band of defenders could form any very exact idea of the power of his teaching, there was now apparent a sort of uneasy curiosity, a feeling that prompted a closer acquaintance with his work, so that one might get to know what was really at the bottom of it. And Biblical exegetists, whom no difficulties discouraged, and who were used to squeezing the last drop of juice out of the texts they were studying, reached the *Ethic* by way of the *Tractatus,* and both these books became the subject of their meditations. They no longer looked on Spinoza as an atheist; they recognized him for what he really was, that is to say, a pantheist. In an atmosphere that was becoming increasingly revolutionary, he becomes the centre of a renewed ferment, and the ferment works.

Yes, it works; it finds its way into the ideas and theories of the Aufklärer, exegetists, publicists, philosophers; it became an integral part of that explanation of the Universe which, one day, Lessing, the greatest of them all, was destined to unfold. Rarely in the history of ideas has a comparable resurrection been recorded.

Nature is not to be equated with reason. So say today our thinkers and our learned men; and, among them an illustrious biologist, Charles Nicolle. "Nature is neither beautiful nor kind. She knows nothing about the logical and the illogical; nothing about reason. Nature is." Of all the failings of Reason, the most widely met with is that of ascribing its own attribute of ratiocination, its own reasoning faculty to the phenomena it is examining. "Having outgrown the employment of a superficial observation and an extravagant imagination, it became the rule to bring this reason of ours to bear on every mortal thing; and quite unwarrantably, for what we did was to invest things with laws which were merely those of our own mind. "The fittingness of the bond is a creation of our own mind, arising from the necessity it is under of representing facts under a rational guise. The human mind distorts phenomena by subjecting them to the rule of logic." "As primeval man used to invest the objects and creatures about him with a spirit as uncouth as his own, so have the philosophers introduced into this latest heap of outworn images of the divine that part of themselves which they considered the most ethereal, which they held to be purely spiritual, the image of their reason."[1]

In the very heart of the *philosophie des lumières*, there exists an essential disharmony, for has not this same philosophy melted together into a single doctrine, empiricism, Cartesianism, Leibnizianism, and finally Spinozaism? We are not merely amusing ourselves by drawing upon our imagination for a philosophy laden with these incoherences and calling it the philosophy of the age. It is the philosophers themselves who boasted of being eclectics; we are only recording their avowal of the fact. "My friend", writes Voltaire, "I have always been an eclectic; I have taken from all the different schools whatever struck me as having the most likelihood about it". Then the Encyclopaedia: Turn up *Eclecticism*; what do we find? "The eclectic is a

[1]Charles Nicolle, *La Nature. Conception et morale biologiques*, 1934.

philosopher who, treading underfoot prejudice, tradition, antiquity, universal consent, in a word, everything that enslaves the minds of the great majority, dares to think for himself, to go back to the clearest general principles, to examine and discuss, and never to admit anything save on the testimony of his reason and experience, and then, after an analysis, carried out without bias or partiality, of all the philosophies, to extract from them a philosophy for his private use, one that shall be peculiarly and personally his own . . ."

That is why Europe, to put some order into the theory of knowledge, had need of Kant.

III

NATURE AND GOODNESS: OPTIMISM

NATURE is kind. That is what the philosophers thought to begin with. It is also what they ceased to think after maturer reflexion.

Why is there so much suffering on this earth? Why so much injustice, and why so many crimes? If there is a God, and if he is all-wise and all-good, why has he tolerated, why has he incited evil? Ever since the days of Job, perhaps of Adam, this same question has been cried aloud to Heaven.

A determination to treat the question, not from the religious point of view but as a matter of pure philosophy took shape as far back as 1702. If in those days William King's treatise *De Origine Mali* scored some success and excited a good deal of sensation it was because he gave point and weight to ideas that so far had been vague and scattered. In short, he refused to bring Christianity into the matter at all, albeit he was one of its staunch defenders. In a Latin that still savoured of the Schoolmen, weightily and powerfully, this Anglican bishop, appealing to his readers' intelligence and not to their faith, proved that God would not have been either all-powerful or all-good, if he had not tolerated evil, for evil is but a privation, a lack, and these, privation and lacking, are an essential condition of the existence of created beings. When, of his goodness, God decided to create, he could not create perfection, but only imperfection, which is at any rate superior to nullity.

However, Bayle when reading an analysis of King's book by Bernard, raised a whole heap of questions. Could it be said that God created the world for his own glory? Can we really say that evil had to be? Are there not two forces contending for the mastery of the world, the force of Good and the force of Evil? But is even that a tenable hypothesis? What explanation ought we to adopt in such a dilemma? The origin of evil is hidden in obscurity; and more difficult to trace than the sources of the Nile: "it is outside the range of human reason".

Pursuing his reflections and starting a new discussion with the M. Bernard just mentioned, he soon came up against another aspect of the same problem. This Nature that is being dinned into our ears so much, this Nature which we are told is so wise and good, it would be well to look into it a little more closely. Let them tell us, on the one hand, "what exactly is a thing that emanates from Nature"; and, on the other, "if to know whether a thing is good, it is enough to know that we are taught it by Nature". We are told that children ought to honour their parents, because it is in Nature. "Now there is hardly any word which is used more vaguely than the word nature; people are constantly using it in all sorts of contexts, now in one sense, now in another, and hardly ever keeping to one precise and definite meaning". How is one to distinguish what is innate from what is acquired, in the case of the young?

But—and this is the important point—it does not follow that what comes from Nature, is necessarily good and just. We see in human nature a number of things that are anything but good, yet there can be no doubt that Nature is wholly responsible for them. If we would attain to wisdom, nothing is more necessary than that we should avoid what Nature prompts us to do under the headings of revenge, pride and inchastity. Have not laws, both human and divine, been necessary to put a curb on Nature? Had it not been for them, how would it have fared with the human race? The state of nature is a state of morbidity.[1]

How, indeed, should we trample on our inmost being and deny what is plain evidence? How can we minimize the horrors of war and bloodshed, make the sick believe that their sufferings are lighter than they imagine, and persuade grief-stricken mothers that they should not mourn for their children lying dead in the cradle. So now comes Shaftesbury to exchange Christian severity for rational peace of mind.

We have already seen how he mitigated the tragic element in life; how he brought the divine down to a human level; we

[1] *Réponse aux questions d'un provincial,* I, chap. LXXIV *et sqq.*, Chap. XCV *et sqq.*

know his words, "Nature has no malice". We have seen the effort he made within the space of a few years, from 1707 to 1711, to change the moral outlook; henceforth, all was freedom, familiarity, ease and comfort—happiness on an earth calmed and consoled by the beauty of the rainbow.

Nevertheless, something more than the work of a dilettante was required, however powerful his influence, and now Leibniz came to lend a hand. Of all the various parts of his doctrine, one in particular had a conspicuous effect on minds hungry for comfort and that was the one which he had built up as a breakwater against the scepticism of Pierre Bayle, and against his Manichaeism as well. It was to be found in his miscellaneous writings, articles, letters, discussions, rejoinders and more especially in his *Essais de Théodicée sur la bonté de Dieu, la liberté de l'homme, et l'origine du mal* (1710). To start with, he had reduced the rank of natural catastrophes and pain and suffering; he had made use of an old-fashioned term and called them physical evils, and already they seemed less grievous. As to metaphysical ill, what we call an evil from our own particular point of view, is not such in the general order of things. A line may have all sorts of turns and twists, backwards and forwards, up and down, and other variations, so many of them that there seems to be neither rhyme nor reason in it, particularly when we are looking only at a part of the line; and yet it may possibly admit of an interpretation in which a geometrician would discover the meaning and the propriety of all these seeming irregularities. The same considerations apply to what look to us like glaring defects in the Universe. Our sight is too imperfect to permit of our taking in the vast, complex whole. If this or that particular detail seems to us to be amiss, it is because we cannot see and understand the plan of things in its entirety.

Lastly there is moral evil. Something must be done to account for, to explain, our faults, our vices; our poltroonery, our crimes; that terrible complacency, and, worse still, that morbid temptation of ours for wrong-doing, and that strange perversion which somehow crept in and corrupted our most seemingly pure intentions; the hidden work of the taint-worm within us. To explain this problem of evil, Leibniz outlined an imposing picture. He conjured up an idea of all the countless worlds as God might have passed them in review before selecting one worthy to be called forth from nothingness. He pictured God making choice of the one which was least marred by imperfection. In the interspace, which our reason shows to be necessary as constituting the difference between creature and creator, evil takes up its abode, as one of the necessary constituents of the whole.

Supreme wisdom, united with a goodness no less infinite than itself, could not but choose the best. For, inasmuch as a lesser evil is a kind of good, so a lesser good is a kind of evil, if it stands in the way of a greater good; and there would have been some fault to find in God's action if he had neglected to choose the better alternative.

Our world then is the least evil of all possible worlds; or, to express it in positive terms, it is the best of all possible worlds. In the temple of Memphis stood a lofty pyramid of globes piled on the top of one another. When asked by a traveller what this pyramid, what these globes signified, the priest-guardian of the temple replied that they represented all possible kinds of worlds and that the best one was at the top. The traveller, eager to see this most perfect of worlds, mounted to the very top of the pyramid and there the first thing that met his gaze was Tarquin about to ravish Lucretia. We are astounded; but wait; let us penetrate more deeply into the profound significance of this symbol. If Tarquin had not raped Lucretia, there would have been no Roman Republic; Roman civilization would never have assumed the form it did, or spread over all the known world; it would not have provided a framework for Christianity when it came into being. Thus this crime was destined to have its place in a world essentially imperfect; but it was also destined to play its part in bringing about a greater good. This rational assignment of a function to evil was welcomed and fondly embraced, like a long expected friend. Jean Christian Wolff expressed it in a formula and passed it on to the German universities; while in France, people were told "This world of ours is the best of all possible worlds; in it we have the maximum of variety combined with the maximum of order. All the arguments people may advance after contemplating the evils that prevail in the world disappear in the light of this Principle".[1]

[1]Mme du Châtelet, *Institutions de Physique,* 1740.

Evil was less extensive, less profound; evil was understandable; at this point, a parallel but not altogether similar argument, obtained contemporary approval and pulled in the same direction. The great ascending scale of living things in the universe, occupying each its own proper rung, implies a certain lawful permanence and a logical value in that which *is*. Philosophy was getting poetical in Pope's *Essay on Man*; and it was becoming emotional. O Fool that seest not that of all possible worlds the Infinite Wisdom hath chosen the best; that thou hast thine own place in that great chain of beings which reaches up from nothingness to God! Thou askest wherefore God did not make thee greater than thou art: ask rather wherefore he did not make thee smaller still. Thou knowest how limited are thy faculties, that thou canst perceive but a tiny part of the immensity of things, yet wouldst thou judge of eternal Justice. Faculties more delicate, wert thou to obtain them, might add perchance to thy unhappiness. Hold thy peace; accept thy lot; in the faultless plan which arranges all things as Nature would have them, any change would destroy the general harmony and lead to chaos. He reminds the reader of the humility which befits his condition; he suggests a creed; he would fain engrave on the very depths of his heart, the statutes of his own belief:

> All Nature is but Art, unknown to thee;
> All Chance, direction, which thou canst not see;
> All discord, harmony not understood;
> All partial evil, universal Good;
> And, spite of Pride, in erring Reason's spite,
> One truth is clear; whatever is is right.

We demand to be happy, and quite rightly so; but be it understood that this happiness must be social and not individual; of such a nature, in short, that any suffering we might feel, might well be the tiny measure of poison purposely included in the physician's prescription. And now, let us build up this happy state to which this race of ours aspires; the acquisition and maintenance of health, peace of mind and the practice of virtue. True, the wicked flourish; true, the good are cut off before their time: it is none the less true that in the general plan of things, all that is, is well. The poet repeats that formula so often that he gives it the power of an incantation, as though he thought there were no other means of compelling our assent. *Whatever is, is right.* It looks simple enough, but what a world of complexity lies beneath. Pope did not accept the whole of Leibniz; he did not hold with him entirely. "All is as little evil as possible"—"All is well": there is some difference between the two, as anyone can see. However, for the time being, such differences were swallowed up in the main stream.

Almost at the same time—the year was 1734—there came from literary Germany another poem about the origin of evil. Albrecht von Haller was not only a doctor of medicine, an anatomist, a botanist, and a physiologist; he also cultivated the poetic Muse; and he meant to show those English that they were not the only ones capable of writing philosophic verse. His poem, a didactical lyric, was entitled *Die Alpen.* He aimed at showing that mountains were not the terrible things people took them for, but imposing and beautiful, and his work won him a considerable reputation. He did not stop there, and through him Switzerland, coming in after the many other countries already involved, was to find herself participating in the great discussion. Hence his cantata in three parts, *Ueber den Ursprung des Uebels.*

From some silent, solitary mountain-top you let your gaze linger on the wide expanse of country that lies outstretched beneath your feet, and there all seems peace and happiness. You get the notion that the world was created in order that those who lived in its might be happy; all nature is inspired by a spirit of universal good. But if you give heed to the voice within, if you reflect awhile, if you pause to consider what life really is, how false and illusory that happiness will seem to be! Children of sorrow, we are condemned to toil, even as we fare along the road to death:

Elende Sterbliche! zur Pein erschaffen Wesen!

To those who have eyes to see, all takes on another hue; they now see nothing but Evil, even in the sovran shrine of Good; and the hymn of joy becomes a plaint of passionate entreaty, where man and his whole destiny are involved: O God of goodness, God of justice, wherefore didst thou choose a world where agony and sin for ever reign? Because, obeying what his own wisdom told him, this God could but choose that world which was as little as possible removed from perfection; because he chose the one most worthy of being brought from the realm of the might-be into the world that is,

> Der Welten wurdigste gewann die Wurklichkeit

The same unvaried theme begins yet again: God, in conformity with the principles of logic, created a long chain of beings descending by a series of degrees from himself to the lowest depths of the abyss; we are a part of an immense whole whereof we cannot grasp the pattern or the harmony. Just beneath himself, he has placed the angels; a little lower down are men; part angel, part beast. To men, he has given a physical conscience and a moral conscience; to men, he has given two ruling motives, love of themselves and love of their neighbour, which, together, induce them to seek happiness. Though everything was organized for good, evil came into existence because God left his creatures free to do as they liked, hence the fall of the angels striving too ambitiously after perfection; hence the sin of Adam and his fall; hence our feeble resistance and our failings. Happy indeed are they who, by the fulfilment of their duty, still keep their place within the plan divine!

We have now come to one of those rare moments in history when all seems peace and harmony, just before the various components renounce their obligations, and resume their freedom of action by a resort to arms. The philosophers had been doing their best to find a plausible explanation of a painful enigma and thought that they had found one. The pietists approved. The moralists were grateful to them for strengthening the foundations of virtue. The poets, forgoing all that was dark and sombre save for the purposes of contrast, were lavish of their rose and azure; the dismal tones that Matthew Prior had put into the mouth of Solomon to express the wretchedness of man,

> Born to lament, to labour, and to die,

gave place to hymns of gratitude. Conservatives, well-found folk, Tories by temperament, by conviction, by tradition came to lend their aid:[1] the world and its ways are not so bad after all; some poor there are bound to be, people to do the rough work, domestics and so on; if there weren't, the whole social scheme would be upset; gentlemen would have no one to serve them, and the fruits of idleness would be licence, poverty and violence. This general accord, which for a time united individuals and nations alike, so far lacked a label; but now, here it is, *optimism*. The word made its first appearance in the *Mémoires de Trévoux* for February, 1737; the *Dictionnaire de Trévoux* admitted it in 1752, and the *Dictionnaire de l'Académie française* ten years later. But by then, the Berlin Academy had already adopted it in connexion with one of those competitions which played so conspicuous a part in the intellectual life of the time. In 1753, it had set the following subject for the year 1755: "Candidates are required to examine the philosophic system of Pope as set forth in the proposition: All is right. It will be necessary (1) to determine the precise meaning of this proposition in the light of its author's premises, (2) to compare it with the system of optimism, or choosing what is best, so as to bring out clearly where they agree and where they differ; (3) to adduce reasons which, in the candidate's view, would justify the retention or rejection of the system in question." It is clear that the Berlin Academy intended everyone to have his due, that Leibniz should have what belonged to Leibniz, and Pope what belonged to Pope. The prize was awarded to Adolf Friedrich Rheinard, whose paper was duly translated and published in German.[2]—Now 1755 was the year of the Lisbon earthquake.

That year Nature produced more than an epidemic or a typhoon to emphasize, by way of exception, her customary benevolence; she caused the earth to shake and gape wide. Lisbon, that charming and picturesque city, whose inhabitants are so uniformly kind and gentle; and prosperous withal, being the third busiest port in Europe after Amsterdam and London; and a Christian city to boot, filled with churches and convents, with masses and other religious offices and processions always going on—

[1]Soame Jenyns, Esq., *A Free Inquiry into the Nature and Origin of Evil*, 1757.

[2]Herrn Adolf Friedrich Rheinard, *Vergleichung des Lehrgebaüdes des Herrn Pope von der Vollkommenheit der Welt, mit dem System des Herrn von Leibniz, nebst einer Untersuchung der Lehre der besten Welt*, Leipzig, 1757. *Abhandlung von der Lehre der besten Welt, aus dem franzosischen*, Wism, 1757.

Lisbon had been laid in ruins. On the first of November, All Saints' Day, an earthquake had demolished houses, public buildings and the city walls; a tidal wave had followed; and then some of the population had done what they could to complete the disaster by pillage and looting.

The news of this catastrophe filled the scientists with the gravest concern and they addressed themselves with renewed ardour to their researches into the mysterious cause of earthquakes; Père Feijoo, for example, in neighbouring Spain, said that electric fluid was the explanation.[1] This event had considerably disturbed those philosophers who had been so active in doing away with evil, physical evil included, and were now brought face to face with a reality which they had somehow overlooked in their speculations. There was one in particular, one whom we come across at every turn, who found himself in a notable quandary, and that was Voltaire.

Voltaire, at first, had had a great respect for Leibniz. That was when he knew him only by repute. He examined him more closely when Mme du Châtelet caused him a certain amount of intellectual jealousy by becoming unaccountably enamoured of this German metaphysician's ideas: why couldn't she have been content with Locke and the great Newton? For that reason, he did not feel drawn to him. However, if there was anything in his theories that struck him as acceptable, it was this providential optimism. He argued that there must be more good than evil in this world, since so few people wanted to quit it. No one had any business to go complaining about it in the name of humanity in general, or to abjure the Sovereign of the universe, merely because some of his subjects were in a bad way. Leibniz, then, he found a considerable resource. His monads of course were the purest moonshine; but not so his optimism; that was based on sound reasoning.

But doubts came over him; he felt a need to bolster up his faith in this idea; he was like Babouc in the *Monde comme il va* (1746), who couldn't make up his mind. There was a good deal to find fault with in Paris-Persepolis; and Ituriel, one of the *genii* who preside over empires, wonders whether it would not be best to destroy the sinful city altogether. Babouc, sent to carry out investigations on the spot, is doubtful; he keeps on

[1] *Nuevo Systhema sobre la causa physica de los terremotos*, 1756.

weighing the pros and cons. At last he decides what to do: "He had a little statue made by the best craftsman in the town; it was composed of every metal, all kinds of earth, of stones both precious and worthless. Then he took it to Ituriel." "Are you minded", he said, "to break this pretty statue, because it is not all gold and diamonds?" Ituriel took the hint. He decided to give up thinking about improving things in Persepolis, and just let the world go on its own old way. "After all", he said, "if things are not as good as they might be, they are at any rate bearable."

Voltaire's stories always give you something to ponder about. There is *Zadig* (1747–1748) for example. All the fairy-tales of the East do not avail to banish his cares. Zadig is wise, he is good, and he is just, but he is not happy. He is rich; he has health and good looks, a sagacious understanding, an upright heart and loyal; everything, in fact, to ensure his happiness. But neither woman, nor a life of solitude, nor learning, nor power brings him the felicity he longs for. Envy, jealousy, stupidity, cruelty all are arrayed against him and bring him from disaster to disaster, to his complete undoing. What is life then but a cruel farce, without any rhyme or reason about it, and so astoundingly constituted that the most trifling causes produce the most terrifying effects? So Zadig, revolving these things in his breast, comes to see men "as they really are, a lot of insects devouring one another on a drop of mud". But at this point the white-bearded hermit, the companion of his travels, intervenes; the hermit who talks most sensibly and behaves quite inexplicably, stealing a bowl of gold enriched with emeralds and precious stones from a rich man who had given them a royal welcome; bestowing this same golden bowl on a miser who had refused them everything; setting fire to the house of a generous host, murdering the young nephew of a charitable and virtuous widow who had given them asylum. No wonder Zadig was amazed. Then the hermit transfigured himself, and assuming the form of the angel Jesrad, gave the explanation of it all, an explanation which every succeeding episode had made more urgent. Those crimes, incomprehensible to our understanding, are by no means so in the light of the universal order; on the contrary they would bring forth fruit and increase the sum total of good. The spendthrift will be more careful of his belongings; the miser more thoughtful for his guests; a vast treasure lay hidden beneath the burnt-out house; the young nephew would have murdered his aunt. So these seeming crimes had their parts to play in the best possible of worlds. . . . Zadig, however, was not entirely satisfied with this explanation: "But supposing all had been good and there had been no evil at all?" "Then", said Jesrad, "this world would have been a different one altogether, and the inter-relation of events would have belonged to a different order of wisdom; and that order, being perfect, could be none other than the eternal abode of the Supreme Being, whom nought that is evil can approach. . . ." "But . . .," Zadig began. Before the word was out of his mouth, the angel was winging his way towards the tenth sphere. Zadig, falling on his knees, glorified Providence, and bowed his head. Thus we see that in 1748, Voltaire was still disposed to submit; but . . .

When he heard about the Lisbon disaster, the problem of evil, which had been not so much solved as shelved, not so much settled as softened and toned down, came up again in tragic shape, and his ideas, already wavering, received a rude shock; he was sorely troubled. His *Poème sur le désastre de Lisbonne*, for all its faults, was none the less pathetic. Look at all those fires and all that ruin; hark to those groans, those shrieks; remember that the blow has fallen on the innocent and the just: can we still say, dare we say, amid our sobs, that all is good? To whisper that the heirs of the slaughtered ones would be the better off, that the masons would gain by the money they would get for rebuilding the houses, that the animals would grow fat on the corpses buried beneath the ruins would be sheer blasphemy. Pope is no doubt worthy of esteem and admiration, but there was no agreeing to his dictum; there was no getting away from the sad and ancient truth, there is evil in the world. The saying "All is good", taken in its literal sense, and excluding any expectation of a future life, is but to mock at the sorrows of our existence. In his letters, where he expresses himself more freely, Voltaire denounces the absolute formula of Pope, but the day was to come when he would no longer abide even by the more qualified one of Leibniz: "You must surely feel that Pope's 'All is well' is but a jest, and not a jest to be played off on the unhappy. I tell you that out of every hundred men, there are at least ninety who deserve commiseration. 'All is well', therefore, clearly does not fit the human race" (20th June, 1756).

Candide, ou l'optimisme. Traduit de l'allemand de M. le Docteur Ralph, avec les additions qu'on a trouvées dans la poche du docteur lorsqu'il mourut à Minden, l'an de grâce 1759. "'Tis Job in modern dress", said Frederick II; "*Candide*", said Cardinal de Bernis, "has made the Optimistic school look ridiculous."

Nimble, agile; and there's *matter* in it; observations, as accurate as profound, amaze you with the truth of their psychology, put forth with so careless and rapid an air, that they don't seem to take themselves seriously. Never was there such skill in hinting at a thing, without going into details, calling up ideas, and going straight on, like a man with too much wealth that sheds his riches as he goes along, without taking the trouble to look behind him; a host of arrows, of light shafts that go ringing through the air; the cut and thrust of a pitiless intelligence, of a ruthless irony; all the old stock-in-trade, voyages, utopias, adventures in the Old World and the New, shipwrecks, *autos-da-fé*, Eldorados, furbished up and given fresh life by a sparkling imagination; a sensation of feverish pace due to the suppression of all superfluous transitions; a troop of gesticulating puppets, a *danse macabre* of comical marionettes—such is *Candide*. And underneath all this glitter, sadness profound. We are compelled to laugh at all these devices designed to excite our mirth; yet what is the issue of it all, all these drolleries? Despair! We are dazzled, and then, behold the Dark River again wherein all our hopes and all our illusions are engulfed.

Alas, poor Candide! And still more miserable Cunegonde! And the ludicrous Pangloss, struggling against wind and tide, going about and shouting that all is well, that everything is to be explained by reason sufficing, and by harmony pre-established: neither diseases, nor deaths by drowning, nor fires, nor iniquities, nor crimes avail to dishearten him. Beaten, hanged, drawn and quartered, a miserable slave toiling at the oar in Turkish galleys, he still adheres to his first opinion: "For", he says, "I am a philosopher, and it ill becomes me to unsay my words; Leibniz never could be in the wrong." The spectacle which the earth presents is one of horror: nothing but wars, butchery, tyrannies, robbery and rape; as it is now, so it was in the past, and so it will be in the future, for the hawks have always devoured the pigeons when they could get them, and devour them they always will. But all is for the best in the best possible of worlds.

This caricature was too much for Optimism. "What is this optimism?" asked Cacambo. "Alas", said Candide, "it is a mania for maintaining that all is good when all is bad." "But there is some good somewhere", said Candide. "Maybe", said Martin, "but I've never come across it." And then, this question: "If this be the best of all possible worlds, what are the others like?" At length, when Voltaire gets tired of pulling the strings that work his characters, and then in a trice brings them to hand as promptly as he had dispersed them, the troupe find themselves once more united, on a farm. Candide is looking very woebegone; the fair Cunegonde looks as if she had been burnt black, with her scraggy neck, crow's feet about her eyes, arms all red and chapped; Pangloss, who looks like a tramp, is covered with pimples; his eyes have no life in them, his nose is all eaten away, his mouth is lop-sided, teeth turned black, and he's got a frightful cough, which makes him spit out a tooth every time a fit comes on. That is what life has done for them! However, at long last, they come upon the great secret, the secret that is going to let them live out the remainder of their wretched lives in peace; what they have to do is to cultivate their garden. That is no perfunctory *dénouement*; it involves an idea of due and necessary resignation, it means a call to work, work which fends off our three great evils, boredom, vice, and want. And this garden is in itself a symbol of our limitations. But is it possible for us to cultivate our garden without being interfered with by our neighbours, caressed or cuffed by the wind, lashed by rain; never casting a glance beyond the fence, never gazing at the horizon, never lifting our eyes to the stars? The remedy corresponds well enough with a certain aspect of empirical philosophy; but after all it is only an expedient, a makeshift, a confession of defeat, a sort of curling up, as it were, so that evil, albeit triumphant, may get less of a hold upon us, just a way of making the best of an unintelligible world which reason, all-sufficing reason, is powerless to explain.

After *Candide*, there was no more to be said; the case was finished, and the case was lost. Not that optimism suddenly disappeared completely; a doctrine lives on for a long time, even when wounded, even when its soul has fled.

Still, most people when they mentioned the word, did so with a smile of irony, when, that is to say, they did not speak of it with anger or rancour. Mme d'Épinay's secretary, in a letter dated the 11th November, 1771, was explaining that the Marquise was indisposed, and took the liberty of adding something on his own account: "People say, 'All is well'; a fine saying, and all the finer in that at the present moment I can't see anything, not a single thing, to justify it. All is well; and I say, anyhow, *that* is not well!" Mme d'Épinay herself, apropos of M. de Mora's spitting blood, was telling the Abbé Galiani that he was one of those who were fated to die young, "and that tells you how untrue it is to say 'All is well' "(6th June, 1772). Whereupon the jest-loving Abbé began talking about the "best of all impossible worlds".

Alliances began to crumble. Christian apologists warned their followers of the determinism which they discerned in the "All is well" idea. The materialists took another line: Nature knows nothing about categories of good and evil. Whatever is, has got to be; God did not create any margin where imperfection has its place, because there is no God and no creation. The eternal laws require the preservation of the various species, and the suffering of individuals does not concern them. Those who exalted the feelings, the passionate school, who were making ready to come on after the philosophers, only asked to be allowed to sing their sorrows and to nurse their pain. The sceptics began to fall back on their first position:

> D'où vient le mal? Eh, plus je l'examine,
> Et moins je vois quelle est son origine.[1]

And then people went on suffering their ills, and that was all there was to be said. The man who had seen his mistress die, who had lived happily, if not always tranquilly, with her,

[1]Whence cometh ill? The more I enquire into the matter, the more obscure appears its origin. *Vers sur l'inexistence de Dieu, composés par Frédéric II quelques années avant sa mort* (*Œuvres*, Ed. de 1848, tome XIV).

bewailed his loneliness: "When, tired out with work or with people, as I quickly am, I find myself alone and isolated in this best possible of worlds, I feel terrified and icy cold. I feel like a man with a long stretch of desert in front of him and the precipice of death at the end of it, and no hope of coming across a single soul who would grieve if he saw him fall into it, or give him another thought after he had disappeared."[1]

As the century wore on, it left its old loves behind it. New, far-reaching ambitions would have none of the compromise that optimism seemed to them to stand for. Kant was developing along very significant lines. He believed, to begin with, that all was for the best in the best possible of worlds. Earthquakes had not shaken him. They just seemed to him a logical consequence of the conditions of our life on earth; an evil that might be fraught with good, for, at any rate, the inhabitants of Toeplitz, where many more medicinal springs had appeared, would have good reason to chant a *Te Deum*, while the people of Lisbon were intoning dirges for the dead. Again, in 1759, in his *Essai de quelques considérations sur l'optimisme*, he came to the support of Leibniz with a very carefully wrought argument. But he was to change his views, and later on he disavowed the works belonging to this period of his life and asked that they should be wholly disregarded; he finally declared that all the philosophic experiments in Theodicée had proved failures.[2]

It was not he, however, who was to mark, as he did in the theory of knowledge, the great divergence. When Jean Jacques was reading the poem on the Lisbon disaster, his belief in the natural goodness of man had been rudely shaken, and he took up his pen to write at length to the author. A letter dated the 18th August, 1756, reveals the mental perturbation which Voltaire's change of opinion had caused him: "Man, have patience, Pope and Leibniz used to tell me; your ills are a necessary effect of your own nature and of the constitution of

[1]D'Alembert to Frederick II, 27th Feb., 1777.

[2]1756: *Von der Ursachen der Erdschütterung bei Gelegenheit des Unglücks, welches die Westliche Länder von Europa gegen das Ende des vorigen Jahres betroffen hat.—Geschichte und Naturbeschreibung der merkwürdigsten Vorfälle des Erdbebens, welches an dem Ende des 1775sten Jahres einen grossen Theil der Erde erschüttert hat.—Fortgesetze Betrachtung der seit einigen Zeit wahrgenommenen Erdserschütterungen.*

1759: *Versuch einiger Betrachtungen über den Optimismus.*

1791: *Ueber das Mislingen aller philosophischen Versuche in der Theodicee.*

1793: *Die Religion innerhalb der Grenzen der blossen Vernunft.*

this universe. The eternal and beneficent Being who governs it would fain have preserved you from them: of all the possible economies, he chose the one which combined the minimum of evil with the maximum of good, or, to put the thing more crudely if we must, if he has not done better, it is because he was not able to do better." Now what does your poem say? "Suffer for ever, hapless one. If it was a God who created you, doubtless he is all-powerful and could prevent all your ills: never then nourish the hope that they will end, for none can tell for what reason you exist, if it be not to suffer and to die." But he did not for that reason exalt Dr. Pangloss. Rather he shifted the bearings of the problem. If Nature had remained good, man had grown evil. For this wickedness of man, a wickedness he had acquired, he had a remedy to propose, and that was the *Contrat social*. That is why Europe, having reconsidered the matter, had come to the conclusion that all was not well, and therefore was for refashioning a world that was not the best of all possible worlds; that is why Europe had need of Jean Jacques Rousseau.

IV

NATURAL POLITICS AND ENLIGHTENED DESPOTISM

THERE were some difficulties about Natural Politics. . . . A wise old Troglodyte, on being offered the supreme power, burst into a flood of tears. Up to then, he and his brother Troglodytes had lived in a state of blissful equality; power was a yoke men wanted to impose on virtue.

Cyrus took twenty-four years fitting himself for the royal power. He went and dwelt among the Medes, whose luxurious and effeminate mode of life might well have corrupted him, but did not; then he betook himself to the shores of the Persian Gulf, and there Zoroaster in person instructed him in the wisdom of the Magi. Thence he went, successively, to Egypt, land of wisdom, where the memory of Hermes Trismegistus was revived for him; to Sparta, where Leonidas gave him an insight into military discipline; to Athens, where Solon explained to him the laws of the Athenian constitution; to Crete to learn about the laws of Minos and to converse with Pythagoras, who unfolded to him the Orphic doctrine regarding the Golden Age; to Cyprus, where his stay was of the briefest, for he shunned the Temple of Paphos; to Tyre, that most flourishing commercial city. Thus he became a philosopher, and reigned with ease over a contented people, and conquered the East, not so much by force of arms as by the prestige of his virtues.

Then, in Egypt, we have Sethos; in Aquitaine, the Comte Ménandre de Rivéra. Handsome, wise, cultivated, and a model of good sense, Comte Ménandre de Rivéra was summoned to the Court, whither he went with much reluctance, for he knew that the young prince, though not really bad at heart, had been corrupted by flatterers, and had given over the government of the kingdom to a scheming sycophant; the State was tottering; the workman groaned under his heavy burden; the farm-hand, quitting his plough, rushed away to the town, where he learnt a lot of useless things and exchanged his innocence for profitable knavery. The Comte de Rivéra arrived in the nick of time; he defeated the Lycatians in battle, but stopped the fighting the moment his victory was assured; the King was sick and ailing, but he worked his cure, recommending him plenty of physical exercise, plenty of open air, and a frugal diet; he soothed his passions, reawakened his sense of duty; a peace-loving soldier, baffling plotters, unmasking traitors, weaving through the warp of all his days the thread of love and friendship, he lived happily for the rest of his life.

Altogether too innocent, these stories;[1] too innocent these maxims: Any policy that was not inspired by pure goodness would destroy itself; the more freedom a nation had, the greater its cultivation, and the greater its cultivation the stronger it became. Four or five sound laws were enough to put virtue on a firm basis. So with aspirations; they, too, were over-simplified: for example: Why could not a few philosophers get together and legislate, and so put an end to evil and injustice once for all?

It had to be recognized, however, that kings did not so much mind being kings; nor, in the republics, were the stadtholders, or the doges, so anxious to lay down office. It was the same all through; ministers, secretaries of State, supervisors, managing clerks; they were all alike, and anyone who held any sort of office, no matter how insignificant, far from rejecting with tears an ill-omened post of authority, clung to it with all his might, as has always been the way with our species. Perhaps, after all, there is no other right than that of might, and the world is the home of the strong; perhaps what the natural law comes to is that the big things eat up the little. There was no guarantee that political freedom, even if it came about, would turn out to be the universal panacea. It might be rash to centre all our hopes on that, without bearing in mind the other

[1]Montesquieu, *Lettres Persanes,* No. XIV, 1721. Ramsay, *La Nouvelle Cyropédie ou Les voyages de Cyrus,* 1727. Abbé Terrasson, *Séthos,* 1731. Johann Michael von Loen, *Der redliche Mann am Hofe, oder die Begebenheiten des Grafen von Rivera,* 1740. The theory of the "philosopher-captain" is set forth in *Il Capitano filosofo,* by Paolo Mattia Doria, 1739.

kinds of servitude that remained undealt with. Social reform ought to go hand in hand with political reform, otherwise the anomaly would certainly breed trouble one of these days. Some people went so far as to say that the old-fashioned slavery went on just the same, but that it was called by a less forbidding name. Navvies, day-labourers in town and country, were just slaves. All they had gained by the change of name was to be haunted by the constant fear of starvation. It was said they were free; the truth was that, if they cared for nobody, nobody cared for them. The day was not far off when Robespierre would be blaming the Encyclopaedists for forgetting all about the most down-trodden and the most deserving class of all.

You could not stop a war, once it was started, by throwing yourself between the contending armies, with a dove in one hand, and an olive-branch in the other. The soldiers would not fling away their rifles, or the officers break their swords, merely because someone made them an eloquent speech. In any case, if they did sign a treaty, the rulers would merely tear it up. In 1742, the year before he died, the Abbé de Saint Pierre sent the King of Prussia yet another work on the way to re-establish peace in Europe, and to put it on a firm and lasting basis. And that was in the middle of the war of the Spanish Succession. In 1766, some philanthropically minded person had founded a prize of six hundred *livres* for the best speech in favour of peace. But behold, not one orator but three; not one prize, but three; to be awarded, not by one body, but by three, the Académie française, the Société typographique at Berne, and some Dutch literary society. The French were quickest off the mark; they were the first to pronounce their verdict and it was M. de la Harpe that the Academy judged the winner. But despite these floods of eloquence, it was always peace tomorrow, never peace today.

A few theories, a few dissertations, and a few pious hopes did not tend to improve things very rapidly. The slightest progress in the right direction took time. People thought they were going to do wonders, and then, all of a sudden, the feeling came over them that they were putting up a vain fight against some vast and inscrutable power. Sometimes Grimm would pause a little in the middle of those fine theories which he insinuated into his literary criticisms, and at such moments his musings took a sombre tone. Brutus, Cassius, Cicero, Cato, great men these; but all their noble utterances availed not to stay the decadence of Rome. We are proud of our age, we boast that it is finer than any that preceded it, and we are wrong. We are wrong to suppose that philosophy's tranquil rule can follow peacefully upon long and stormy periods of unreason and folly, and bring lasting repose, serenity and happiness to the human race; a pleasing error, but an error all the same, and it had to be acknowledged. "Whatever may be the advantages we attribute to this age of ours, it is evident that they benefit only the chosen few, and that the mass of the people have no share in them. Whatever modifications the national spirit may undergo, and there is no limit to them, man at bottom always remains the same, and, so wretched is his plight, that the more he seems to need truth and happiness for his very existence, the more inexorably is he dragged down—and it has been so in every age —to misery and lies." Grimm wonders how it is that history had not long ago disabused his friends the philosophers and himself of the deceitful allurements of an ideal perfection that must remain for ever unattainable. To restore his equanimity, he went and saw his friend Diderot, the modern Socrates, as he called him. Diderot enlarged with great eloquence on the power of virtue, the supremacy of reason, and the progress of the philosophic way of looking at things. As he was holding forth, a footman entered the room and gasped out in trembling tones: "The King is dead!" It was the day Damiens made his murderous attempt.

You might have thought you were looking at a minuet: the Princes bow to the Philosophers, the Philosophers return the bow. As if the mighty ones had forgotten how they had persecuted, and were still persecuting, writers who were trying to undermine their authority; and as if the writers had forgotten about the furious rhetoric they had hurled, and were still hurling, against the tyrants! They declared that for ages past all that kings had done was to strive to put chains about their people, and they bowed low to those same kings! Despotism was getting to mean something new. All that had to be done was to tack on an adjective and call it "enlightened" despotism.

Certainly, the phenomenon was not a little complex; you

could, if you tried, find some points of contact between this enlightened despotism and the philosophy of light, which would go some way towards explaining the misapprehension. The enlightened despots were warring against privilege, and that, to begin with, was a common line of action. They contemplated a vast egalitarian reform, they were for destroying all traces, and there were still too many, of the old feudal system. Ardently progressive, they adopted any economic measure that might be calculated to advance the prosperity of their respective peoples. The philosophers were useful because they gave lustre to their reign. And then, most important of all, the centralized administration which they set going, created order in place of disorder; order the mirrored image of universal reason; they were rationalizing government. Reason, no sooner invoked, promptly supported their policy: Euclid, too, was a despot. One might go so far as to say that it belonged to the mind that was the strongest, the intelligence that was the most clear-sighted, and to the understanding that was the most unerring, to be a ruler; so that inherited power was sanctioned in their case by natural law. More than that; if utility was the sole measure of right behaviour, why should not a great nation subjugate one in which the standard of life was lower? Why should it be taxed with wrongdoing, if the result of its conquests was a further substantial addition to the sum-total of human happiness?

But whatever might seem to be the possibilities of agreement, they did but mask a basic, an irreconcilable antagonism: on the one side, the totalitarian State directing and controlling all the activities of its members; on the other side, the liberal or constitutional State. If those who argued in favour of the liberal form of government made common cause with the representatives of despotism, they were betraying their own political philosophy. You either had to bend nature to your will, or else let her have a free hand; either the maximum of interference, or the minimum. Either the spontaneous virtue of the eternal laws, or the will of one man dominating everything, the law included.

A form of government was coming to the fore in Europe which took no stock of constitutions, the balance of power, and the uneasy suspicion that some one power might outstrip all the others. The die had been cast in 1740, when Frederick II succeeded the Roi-Sergent. Farewell to anti-Machiavellianism!

What he had to do now was to get to know his business; curb his impulsiveness; overcome his horror of the battlefield, his fear; find out people's weak spots the better to profit by them; get command of his physique and, when his mind said "march", make his body obey; make the most of his unrivalled intelligence; become the cleverest of the clever, the strongest of the strong; foreign policy, war, civil administration, finance, industry and even education—all these he must take in hand. Everything, down to the smallest detail, must depend upon one sole central will. He must transform his present meagre inheritance into one of the first, and if possible, *the* first, power in Europe. That was his task. He was not merely the servant of the State; he *was* the State. Never, throughout that century, was there a more arresting personality, and the age contemplated him with admiration. Between the poet, the musician, the dilettante of Rheinsberg and Old Fritz with his dirty clothes, his limbs deformed by gout, his nose all stained with snuff, how many different beings were united in one? The general who on the night of battle recites Racine, and imagines himself one of Racine's heroes. The traveller summoning to his carriage-door burgomasters and justices; who questions the peasants about their plough-lands, about their cows, and the supply of salt. The ironist, the high-and-mighty one, the "quiz", the jester, the skin-flint who counted every farthing, and the man of genius. The tireless official who has his subordinates up before him in his office and wants almost as much out of them as he takes out of himself. Then there is the philosopher of Sans-Souci, and the artful diplomatist who checkmates Austria, France, and England, though his procedure may be a little questionable, though he may hit below the belt. And besides these, a host of other incarnations, all of them, by divers routes, making for one and the same goal: the greatness of Prussia.

Over against him, face to face, behold his adversary, Maria Theresa; and when her time comes to pass on into the chapel of the Capuchins, to take her place in the vault of the Hapsburgs, behold her son, Joseph II! A despot doing his best to play the kindly father of his people, looking on his imperial office as a sacred mission, trying, and trying in vain, to make everybody happy. Unification, centralization, rationalization, these were the aims that he pursued, hurrying from Vienna to Budapest, to

Prague, to Brussels, to see everything for himself, give an eye to everything, and suffer nothing to remain as it was, never doubting the fundamental wisdom of his decrees, decrees which had merely to be promulgated in order to become immediately effective; turning everything upside down, in his zeal for improvement. There was something touching about this zeal of his, this passion for the public good. Headstrong, irritable, impetuous; sick with fatigue and exhaustion, working himself to death, heart-broken to see that men refused to be angels or to recognize as a beneficent archangel this Emperor of theirs who wore the twin aureole of Enlightenment and Right Divine. Yet he had done his utmost to bring everything, the Church included, under state-control. In 1763, while he was still getting his hand in, so to speak, there appeared a book which created a wide sensation: *Justini Febronii J.C. de statu Ecclesiae et legitima potestate Romani Pontificis liber singularis.* Under the name Febronius was concealed, with a care and a success that few incognitos have achieved, the name of the author, who was none other than Hontheim, Bishop-suffragan of Treves. The thesis he put forward was well calculated to produce a shock throughout the length and breadth of Christendom. It amounted to saying that the Papal rule had been but one long usurpation; that the time had arrived to replace it by an oligarchy of bishops, a body itself deriving its authority by delation from the democracy of the priests and the faithful. The Pope was to be left in possession of his executive functions, but the legislative power was to reside with him no longer; the power to define doctrines binding on the Church Universal was to belong exclusively to the General Councils. To bring about this reform, it would be necessary for the Pope himself to play his part, as well as the prelacy, the theologians and the monarch. The latter was to sustain the preponderating rôle. He was sovereign Lord over his subjects, and he would protect them against all papal and ecclesiastical encroachment. . . . All this was a compound of Jansenism and natural law, reinforced by all the arguments against Rome that had ever been made to do duty. To those monarchs whose policy it was that religion should not be a power apart, but a department subject to their royal jurisdiction, the occasion was far too tempting a one to be neglected; but Febronius's best disciple was Joseph II.

Catherine II suffered nature to have her way, in so far as her private life was concerned, and her favourites knew well enough how imperious were nature's demands upon her. But it was to the service of the Russian State, to the welfare and advancement of Russia that she devoted her sovereign intellectual gifts, her political sagacity, and all the power of her will. She allowed herself no rest till two object had been attained: in the foreign sphere, the destruction of Poland, the weakening of Turkey and the dismemberment of Sweden; in the domestic sphere, the establishment of her authority in place of the anarchy in which her immediate predecessors had left the Empire; Catherine the Great would resume the task of Peter the Great. A woman of genius, the Comte de Ségur called her. "Proud, tender-hearted and victorious", like Louis XIV, said the Prince de Ligne.

There were other monarchs who were included in the category of enlightened despots, Gustavus III of Sweden, Christian VII of Denmark, Stanislas Augustus of Poland, and even Charles III of Spain; and when sovereigns ran short, there were the ministers who supported them; there was Charles III's Count d'Aranda; Pombal was Joseph I's right-hand man; there was Dutillot at Parma, Tanucci at Naples. All were striking, powerful personalities, very different from those lily-faced sons of Telemachus whom the philosophers depicted as representing the ideal of kingship. To this imperious breed, to these realists who acknowledged no reason but reasons of State, to these spiritual sons of Machiavelli, the apostles of the English constitution addressed their smiles of approval. Not perhaps quite so freely in the case of Joseph II; but without any reservation whatever in that of Pombal, since he had expelled the Jesuits; for that is what it always came back to. "Down with the Church!" was always the rallying cry. They also fully approved of d'Aranda, Dutillot, and Tanucci; and when they came to Catherine II, their encomiums knew no bounds, and they indulged in more flowers of rhetoric than the most abject of sycophants. She was the Semiramis of the North; Algarotti discovered Paradise itself amid the snows of Russia; Carlo Gastone della Torre di Rezzonico dedicated his *Ragionamento sulla filosofia del secolo XVIII* (1778) to Her Imperial Majesty; a pact signed and sealed between Philosophy and the State. She had announced her intention of bestowing a Code on her subjects, and to this end she summoned to a conference in Moscow, deputies from all her provinces, and told them that the country was not made for the sovereign, but the sovereign for the country. She had ideas for reforming the whole legal system, for bringing educational methods up to date. She invited artists to adorn her palaces and her capital; she wanted to have an *Encyclopédiste* as her grandson's tutor, and, in default of d'Alembert, she engaged a Swiss republican; she kept up a friendly correspondence with Mme Geoffrin. When Robertson published his *History of Charles V*, she sent him a gold snuff-box and gave him to understand that his book went with her on all her travels; either that, or Montesquieu's *Esprit des Lois*; and she had Marmontel's *Bélisaire* translated into Russian. As for Diderot, her protégé, her client, who said the only journey he ever wanted to make was to St. Petersburg, you ought to have heard him giving vent to his enthusiasm! If she had a fault, it was that she was too kind; there was not a trace of the despot in her character, in her purposes, or in her deeds. You felt you were a slave in the countries that called themselves free, but over there, in *her* country, you breathed the very air of freedom. But the man the philosophers loved most of all was the representative of the Leviathan State, Frederick II. He, they said, was greater than the greatest of the Roman emperors. He had bestowed happiness on his people, provided Europe with the pattern of the model ruler, and paved the way for the happiness of generations to come. And so on, and so on. Because he was himself a philosopher and had taken the trouble to study the systems that purported to reveal the meaning of life; because he had a very real love of letters and was, in a sense, a man of letters himself; because he gave asylum in his Academy to all who suffered persecution in the cause of freedom of thought; because he was a deist, and, in his inmost heart, something more than that, in short an atheist; and because he was a genius—for all these reasons, "the philosophers and men of letters in every land have long looked upon you, Sire, as their leader and their model".[1]

We all know how these princes and their successors behaved later on, when the French Revolution translated these philosophers' ideas into action; we all know about the Holy Alliance.

[1]D'Alembert to Frederick II, 7th March, 1763.

V

NATURE AND FREEDOM: LAWS ARE NECESSARY RELATIONS DERIVING FROM THE NATURE OF THINGS

NATURAL morality had its difficulties. Was it so certain that Nature, in the long run, always sanctioned what was good and punished what was evil, as the case might be? Was the abstemious man never ill, and was it the voluptuary's fate always to become so? Was the evil-doer always punished by remorse? And the thief, was it a fact that as soon as he came to his senses and realized he had done wrong, he hurried off to give back what he had stolen? In short, was not true morality a protest against the blindness and indifference of nature in the raw?

Again, was it so sure that the interest of the individual always coincided with the interest of the community? That what was good for an individual bee was always good for the hive as a whole? Here was this Mandeville, as he called himself, who in his *Fable* maintained precisely the contrary. The lesson of that tale was a long way from being forgotten. No need to go delving into books; wasn't it obvious, if you looked at life in its everyday aspect, that the ruin of one merchant meant more customers for another? One man's loss is another man's gain, and "It's an ill wind that blows nobody any good", runs the popular adage. If we go down to the very bedrock of things, we see that morality and interest, even social as distinct from individual interest, are things of a different nature. In fact, disinterestedness is a necessary ingredient of morality in the strict sense of that word. Do good unto him from whom thou expectest nothing, aye, even if he wisheth thee harm; and not, Do good unto him from whom thou expectest a benefit in return.

Now, was Epicurus a master to be followed? How far were we going in our pursuit of this rehabilitated Pleasure? Those old-fashioned austerities, was there not, after all, some reason at the back of them? Was it without motive, from bile, or misanthropy that some crazy being had imposed them on the human conscience? Nowadays writers were treating morality as if it were like the new style of architecture, which aimed at convenience rather than at grandeur. No one nowadays thought of denying himself, of putting the brake on; nothing was less fashionable. The result was a rapid slackening of discipline. That had to be recognized. "To some extent the regard for glory and true worth is slowly losing ground among us. Philosophy has gained ground, and the old ideas about heroism, and bravery, and chivalry, have faded away. Indifference about the life to come, which leads to softness and self-indulgence in this one, renders us careless and incapable of anything that demands an effort." So much for the French; now for the English: Love of freedom, zeal for the honour and prosperity of the country, desire for fame are changed into a general indifference, into base submission and a frenzied desire for wealth.[1] And now for the voice of the age as a whole: "As in what I say to you I am not affected by any sort of ill-humour, and as I look upon things in general with more or less indifference, I am not going to tell you that there never was an age more corrupt than this one; possibly, indeed, we ought to ascribe to folly a good deal of what has been debited to corruption; nevertheless, I do think that there never was an age more indecent than this one."[2]

Moral laws, codes of morality—that was a branch of science that presented no difficulty, or should not have done, now that morals, like politics, had been linked up with anthropology. Yet nothing was done, no move was made, owing to the fact that those who had undertaken the work had become aware of its extreme difficulty. Morality based on religious dogma had been rejected as being too rigid, and as deriving from an authority external to man. Dogmatic morality having been put aside, and, it being understood that natural morality was to take its place, the old eternal question arose once more: What was

[1] Bolingbroke, *Letters on the Spirit of Patriotism,* 1749, Letter II.

[2] Duclos, *Mémoires sur les mœurs de ce siècle,* 1751.

it, what did it lead to, this Nature which everyone interpreted according to his own ideas? Now, there was not one morality, but several; as many, indeed, as there were would-be interpreters of the misty and elusive oracle. An indication of the confusion into which men's consciences were thrown is to be found in the multitude of attempted solutions that followed so hard one upon another. As the latest treatise invariably began by correcting, or demolishing the arguments of its predecessors, so was the work of the latest comer fated to be demolished in its turn. There was an immense expenditure of ingenuity and honest endeavour, and the only product of it all was just so much lumber. What men hoped for was some great convincing movement that would enlist the support of all, and give the impression that the truth was in it, and so set all minds at rest. Far from that being the case, there was nothing for them to contemplate but the unedifying spectacle of schools and individuals wrangling interminably among themselves. What principles should be rejected seemed clear enough; what principles should be adopted was not so clear.

Let us now consider just a few of the many treatises each of which gave a definite solution and, in each case, a different one. In 1726, Francis Hutcheson, professor of moral science and natural philosophy at Glasgow, brought out his *Inquiry into our Ideas of Beauty and Virtue*. The starting-point was unchanged; as usual, it was agreed that the only important truths were those that contributed to human happiness. But the difficulty began when the choice of means came to be considered. It was no use having recourse to the reason, reason was not strong enough, and all who had gone to it for a system of morality, the Stoics for example, had met with no success. Nor did mere sensation offer any better hopes, since it did not lie with us whether it was pleasant, or the reverse: it was passive. But there was a sense, a sense at which Shaftesbury had already hinted, a sense of a special and peculiar quality, a sixth sense, an inner sense expressly designed to enable us to discriminate in the matter of moral conduct and of beauty. "The author of nature has led us to virtue by means much surer than any the moralists have been pleased to imagine, I mean by an instinct almost as powerful as that which urges us to ensure the preservation of our being."

1736. Louis Jean Lévesque de Pouilly, *Réflexions sur les sentiments agréables, et sur le plaisir attaché à la vertu.*

Our instinct and our feelings are more potent agents than our reason in bringing us into the paths of virtue, though they may not belong to the intellectual order. The subject was one of which it was only possible to treat hypothetically, since in this matter Nature had covered her countenance with a veil; nevertheless, we have grounds for thinking that an object of an agreeable nature causes certain fibres of the brain to vibrate without in any way weakening or exhausting them; whereas anything painful hurts those fibres; while things that are merely tedious and boring leave them inert. Thus, the perception of the beautiful and the good is dependent merely on the movements of matter.

1741. *Essays, Moral and Political,* by David Hume.

Hutcheson was right enough when he proved the inanity of a moral system based on reason. The faculty which enables us to distinguish the true from the false is not the same as that which enables us to distinguish good from evil. Morality, instead of being founded on unalterable relations recognizable by the mind as being as universally true as a proposition in Euclid, depends on the mental likes and dislikes of each particular person. But Hutcheson failed to press home his own principles. How is one to recognize the moral rectitude of the feelings of any given individual? By a certain degree of consent, or of opposition, observable in other people. "We shall describe as virtuous any action that is accompanied by the unanimous approbation of men, and we shall call vicious any action which incurs blame and censure." If David Hume had wanted to ridicule Hutcheson, he could not have done better. But he was not joking; he followed his own line of argument and finished up by dissolving morality, even as he had disintegrated reason.

1759. Adam Smith, *Theory of Moral Sentiments.*

Some explanation of morals must be found, and up to now the key has been lacking. Hutcheson was wrong, and Hume, though he glimpsed the truth, failed to take hold of it. Morality is not a matter that depends on the approbation, or disapprobation of our fellow men, but on a certain emotion that we feel, and which finds, or does not find, a like emotion in the hearts of others. We shall refer to it by the name of sympathy, in the etymological meaning of the word.

This brief list is impressive. As we have seen, a theory of morals began to take shape in accordance with the logical notions of the philosophers, the enlightened school, and it already bore within itself a twofold element; there was the rational element—let us be virtuous, because virtue is the reflexion of the order of the universe; then, there is the empirical element, let us be virtuous, because our sensations tell us to seek what is good and to eschew evil; because our first law is the conservation of our being, and because our being cannot be conserved without recourse to the society of which it is a member, and which will pay it interest on the capital entrusted to it. But at the same time, other philosophers, starting with the same premises, were arriving at conclusions that were fundamentally different, referring to something called instinct, whose nature and meaning they varied to suit themselves whenever it pleased them. But the prospect as a whole was incomparably more complex; England and Scotland had not completed their endeavour to construct an independent system of their own, when Germany began on another. Intermingled with works of high distinction which were coming to be regarded as guides, which were read and studied and reprinted and talked about and criticized, we must take note of a host of other heresies. We must remember that in a composite work which aimed at promulgating doctrine, such as the *Encyclopédie*, these various moral systems rubbed shoulders without seeming to have any suspicion that they were severally incompatible; that theories do not cease to proliferate just when we give up studying them. There was Jeremy Bentham, and James Oswald, and Thomas Reid; and we shall understand the profound significance of that naïve reflexion of Adam Smith's, who said that all the systems that had been brought out prior to his own, being founded on natural principles, were sound in some degree; but as the view of nature from which those principles were derived was partial and incomplete, they were also in some degree unsound.

Just as Nature was not rational, not kindly, not adapted to

any one polity more than to another, so also was she not virtuous; and the opponents of natural morality did not fail to point out to its supporters that they started with an error at the very outset: to say that virtue was natural to man was to state something that the whole of mankind knew to be false. What was true, on the other hand, was that to strive to curb the lawlessness of Nature was not folly, not cruelty, but wisdom and love; and that it was the duty of every thinking being to combat the unruly promptings of blind Nature.

The truth was that when you came to consult Nature on any specific matter, she answered both "yea" and "nay". Was it lawful to commit suicide? Yes, because Nature permitted it. If anyone found that existence had become so hateful to him as to be tolerable no longer, and if he consequently did away with himself, he was but obeying a power which, having imposed this suffering upon him, had furnished him with the means of putting an end to it. The idea of a pact in such circumstances is inadmissible. As soon as the pact becomes burdensome, the question of observing it does not arise. Nature envisages mutual advantages between the contracting parties; when those advantages cease to operate, the contract lapses. Again, was suicide lawful? No, for Nature's business was with the maintenance of the species, and the individual who destroys himself contravenes Nature's law. Nature aims at the conservation of whatsoever she has created; it is not for the creature to decide when his rôle in the great ensemble has ended. The quarrel went on and on; one of those quarrels of which the age has furnished us with so many examples, that age which, whenever a debate was opened, felt itself stirred to the depths of its intellectual being. This time the occasion was furnished by Johann Robeck's *De Morte voluntaria Philosophorum et Bonorum Virorum* (1736) which maintained that such men as Brutus and Cato could not be accused of cowardice, or of folly, and least of all of committing a crime. Socrates, he held, had died a voluntary, much rather than a compulsory, death. Robeck was right; Robeck was wrong.

The pathos that surrounds the name of Vauvenargues is brought vividly home to us by the series of mournful pictures which portray his life; there is the child whom no one loves;

the youth whom no one understands; the young army lieutenant living a life of boredom in little obscure garrisons; the fighting man who looks to war to bring him the chance of displaying a valour that has lain fallow for so long; then the same man broken and infirm, all his dreams dispelled; the sick man with his chronic cough, his failing eyesight, his face disfigured by smallpox, finding his way to Paris, there to finish out his thirty-two years of life in a second-rate hotel, in a dingy street. Pathos, too, in his lofty spirit, his courage, and in the restraint with which he voices his unending plaint: when he takes his walk in the Luxembourg gardens and beholds the poor wretches about him borne down by their hard lot; old folks trying to hide their poverty as though it were something to be ashamed of; young people dazzled by the glitter of vain ambition; and others that hazard all kinds of futile plans to escape from the obscurity of their drab existence: his mind is disturbed and ill at ease, he feels a sense of kinship with these unhappy folk, but the cry that rises to his lips is a cry, not of rebellion, but of compassion. There is pathos in his longing to be remembered by posterity: he casts his bottle on the waves, in it a few thoughts, a few reflexions, a few essays, and he wonders, not too hopefully, whether they will preserve his name from foundering in the waters of eternal oblivion. Pathos, no less, in the way he sets to work, adopting a form which he thinks the least personal, the most unfailingly objective, and which, nevertheless, is full of avowals and regrets, each fragment being but an instalment of one perpetual confession. Finally, there is pathos in the way in which the spirit of the times strove to put its mark upon him, trying to impose on him its leading thinkers, its favourite reading, its philosophic systems, which, nevertheless, failed to gain entrance to the hidden recesses of a mind able to live in itself while it lived in the world, a mind so constituted as to reject everything that was foreign to its essence, and to retain only that which was congenial to it, only that which it loved and longed for.

His form, his style, was plain and unadorned, yet for all that, it sometimes vibrates with emotion, and then we catch glimpses of the growth of a system of morality which ends as something peculiarly his own. He is under no illusion about Nature: "Whether we are speaking of kings, or peoples, or mere individuals, it is always the strong that domineer over the weak. And the same thing holds good among animals, in the material world, and with the elements, etc., so that the whole universe is based on a system of brute force, and the order which we blame with some *prima facie* justification, is Nature's most general, most absolute, most invariable and oldest law." Nor did he deceive himself in regard to happiness; life, from one point of view, is an evil. Inequality of birth, and the almost insurmountable injustice involved in the unequal distribution of wealth, which is bestowed or withheld apparently at random—all this makes life a cruel experience for those not favoured by fortune. However, we must play our part; the present slips between our fingers and is gone; our thoughts and ideas are born to die, we are powerless to retain them; our sole resource lies in unwearying action and meeting the perpetual flux of things with perpetual renovation. Therefore, what we do should be directed towards achieving permanence; all our actions should be associated with the preservative and not with the destructive forces of the universe; we should strive to attain to virtue, the counter-agent of corruption, decay and annihilation; to virtue, the conqueror of evil; for if virtue were vanquished in its never-ending conflict with vice, the sole antidote to vice would disappear, and vice would bring to pass the complete annihilation of our species. There is virtue, there is vice; both exist: to plump for vice would be to plump for death. One may be the dupe of vice; one cannot be the dupe of virtue. The man that renders the greatest service to the world is he who gives the loftiest example of virtue, virtue that creates and restores; such a man we call a hero. The hero does not linger in the background; no victim he of that faint-heartedness that leads mankind in general towards their own undoing. If his actions are extravagant, as they sometimes may be, they are always in the grand manner. The fairest recompense is his, the prize which is envied even by those who pretend to disdain it; his guerdon is fame. He is charitable, compassionate, on occasion even homely and familiar; yet, though he never loses contact with the general run of men whose failings he shares and understands, he has the gift of taking his stand above them and acting as their guide. The pure metal that is in us he separates from its surrounding dross, he it exalts and makes it shine. He is the star that directs the mariner voyaging over the darkling waters of the trackless sea.

It was a challenge to all who had disparaged the hero in days gone by, and to all who should continue to do so; the protest of a lofty spirit who would have nought to do with insidious compromise. It was a reminder of that everlasting truth; morality must ever take the upward way, be the path never so difficult, the goal never so far above us.

Free-will or fatalism? Everything hung on the answer to that question. "I know of no system of morality, whether civil or Christian, that does not jealously adhere to the dogma of free-will."[1]

One might have been listening to two antiphonal choirs, singing alternately, one answering the other, but the second of the two gaining in volume, and boldness of attack.

We are free, sang the first choir, a somewhat heterogeneous body, free, for God has left us to choose for ourselves between two roads, whereof the one leads to salvation, the other to perdition. We are free. The Supreme Being would never have made mere puppets of us, himself pulling the strings. We are free; were we not so, there could not possibly be any sort of government; warnings, instructions, orders, penalties, rewards, would serve no useful purpose; you might just as well preach to an oak in an endeavour to persuade it to become an orange-tree. Inasmuch as we know from experience that it is possible to correct men, we may take it they are not automata. We are free; doubtless our thoughts are determined by our sensations, but our actions are not; therefore freedom is definable as the power to act, or not to act, as our thoughts may prescribe. If we were not free, everything would go on precisely as if we were. Let us then take it that free we are. What we have there, is clearly a truth of the intuitive order, of which the proof, the sole proof, is analogous to that employed to demonstrate the existence of bodies. Independent beings could not have a keener consciousness of their independence than we have of ours. Suppose we were subject to a higher and ineluctable power, things would go on precisely as they do

[1] Abbé Terrasson, *La Philosophie applicable à tous les objets de l'esprit et de la raison*, 1754, p. 96.

now; we should not give up putting robbers into prison, or hanging murderers on the gallows. But to try and penetrate deeper into a matter like this, means plunging into a sea of uncertainties.[1]

No; we are not free. The mind is passive and has no influence on the elements that impinge upon it from without, nor on any combination thereof. Action being the result of a mental operation governed by certain conditions, is itself similarly conditioned. Therefore man is governed by necessity. We are not free, we are dependent on a blind, material force which gives life to all creatures and acts without knowing that it acts. The world is one vast machine and we are the least significant of its works; we are in no way privileged beings; we cannot call our souls our own at any moment in our lives; what we do and intend to do is always the sequel of what we have been. The rule of Fate is Nature's fixed and changeless order: you deny that miracles are possible; how then should you admit that there is such a thing as freedom? The group who gave expression to these ideas started with Anthony Collins, who, in 1717, had published a compendium on determinism which was still consulted, *A Philosophical Inquiry concerning Human Liberty*, and went on to include the Baron d'Holbach, whose *Système de la Nature* appeared in 1770. He tinged his negations with a shade of proud satisfaction: we are governed by necessities far more numerous and far more complex than those to which the animal world is subject, and therein lies our superiority over them; let us rejoice that this is so. This awe-inspiring Destiny which brings all things beneath its sway, let us look at it with a steady eye; do not let us be like those folk of feeble understanding who imagine they possess a freedom which they are incapable even of defining. Let us submit to our chain with a good grace, since submit we must, and when our time comes, let us join without repining the mighty host of the departed. There is a sort of pleasurable excitement in tracking, one after another, through the infinite network of cause and effect, the way in which some wholly insignificant incident, a word or a gesture, will grow and grow till it culminates at last in some gigantic catastrophe, or revolution. When we take stock of the ludicrous disproportion that sometimes exists between cause and effect,

[1] D'Alembert, *Éléments de philosophie,* VII, Morale.

when we hear that the assassination of that good king Henri IV was all brought about by a false step made one day by a certain Brahmin on the banks of the Ganges, we may be pardoned if we indulge in a little irony on the subject of fatalism.[1]

"This question of freedom is the great stumbling-block in philosophy."[2] Let us betake ourselves straightway to the man who, beyond all others, was conscious of finding it in his path, and could not get it out of his way, the man whose pride it was to have discovered the spirit of the laws, the essence of the law eternal: did eternal law imply determinism, or did it leave scope for the exercise of our will?

One could hardly call Montesquieu a dramatic character; lyrical indeed he sometimes was, as though in spite of himself; but dramatic, never. We may say of him that he had the feeling of being in a dilemma from which he never escaped.

Laws are the necessary relations which derive from the nature of things

Necessary: the expression is a serious one. Between a given climate and a given individual there exists an ineluctable connexion; the individual will be what the particular degree of latitude, the geological formation and superficial character of the earth, its soil and its products, the sky and the wind, compel him to be; a Chinaman is what the Chinese climate makes him. Chinese, Africans, Americans are what they are, and you cannot alter them, nor any other inhabitant of this world; nor the moon, nor the sun, nor the milky way.

That necessity is not the only one; it is but one among countless others which weigh upon us. Consider: suicides are common in England; that is an established fact. Why is this?

[1]Voltaire, *Dialogue d'un Brachmane et d'un Jésuite.* The Brahmin: I am, such as you behold me, one of the chief causes of the lamentable death of your good King Henri IV, which as you see makes me sorely to grieve. This is how Destiny arranged the matter: Putting forward my left foot, I was the unfortunate cause of my friend Eriban, a Persian merchant, falling in the water and being drowned. He had a very pretty wife who married an Armenian trader by whom she had a daughter who married a Greek. The daughter of the said Greek went to live in France where she married the father of Ravaillac. If none of these things had happened, the fortunes of the Houses of France and Austria would as you see, have taken a different turn. The European set-up would have been different, the wars between Germany and Turkey would have had different results. That would have affected Persia and Persia would have affected the Indies. You see how the whole thing was brought about by my left foot, which was linked up with all the events in the Universe, past, present and to come.

[2]Euler, *Lettres à une Princesse d'Allemagne,* Letter 83, 13th December, 1760.

The mania arises from a defect in the flow of the nervous fluid. In the absence of this nervous current the motive power of the machine is lacking, and the machine itself declines to work. It is not that the spirit is conscious of any pain, it is that it finds existence difficult; so the Englishman puts an end to himself. The peoples of the North are energetic, the peoples of the South are indolent; all a matter of nerve tissues. These vary under conditions of heat or cold. "A cold atmosphere contracts the extremity of our bodily tissues; that makes them react more vigorously, and helps to send the blood well back into the heart. By diminishing the length of the tissues, it increases their power. Warm air, on the other hand, relaxes the extremities of the tissues, and thereby diminishes their strength and resilience." For this reason the Eastern races will always be effeminate, self-indulgent, and fit subjects for despotic rule; it is why the Northern races are always vigorous and active.

If we were tempted to show astonishment at this intrusion of fibres into the *Esprit des Lois*, we should greatly upset Montesquieu, for he attached great importance to them. It is all very well to say that sensation is at the bottom of all our activities, but the question is, how is sensation translated into action? By means of the fibres. The fibre apprehends the sensation and records it; the more tenuous and supple the fibre, the more promptly it informs the mind of what is taking place, and the more readily it reminds it of previous sensations. The mind is like a spider in the middle of its web; slender filaments bringing notice to it of the sensations which are disturbing them, of the presence of foreign bodies which set them in motion. In order to be quite sure of his ground, the learned member of the Bordeaux Academy undertook some experiments; we may imagine him, a picturesque figure bending over a microscope to examine a sheep's tongue with the minutest scrutiny. "I have examined the outer tissue of a sheep's tongue at the part where, to the naked eye, it looks as if it were covered with little mounds; looking at them through the microscope, I observed that these mounds or hillocks were covered with a number of tiny hairs or a kind of down. Between the mounds, there were pyramids which, at the tips, looked like tiny paint-brushes. It would appear very likely that these pyramids are the chief organs of taste. I then froze half the tongue, when it became apparent to the naked eye that the mounds had shrunk considerably, indeed a few rows of them had disappeared entirely within their sheaths. I then put the tissue under the microscope and saw no further trace of any pyramids. As the tongue was gradually warmed up, I could see with my unaided vision that the mounds seemed to be rising again, and when I looked through the microscope, the tiny tufts began to reappear." No matter whether it was sheeps' tongues or Siberians, it was clear that frost acted on the extremities of their fibres and affected the constitution of the being as a whole. Thus sorely, at one stage of his career, was Montesquieu tempted to explain the *Esprit des Lois* in terms of matter.

It was, however, a temptation he expressly put aside, if not always in the detail of his treatment, where traces of it are frequently to be met with, at all events when he came to make declarations of principle:

People who have declared that blind fate has brought about all the effects we see in the world, have committed themselves to a great absurdity; for what could be more absurd than that blind fate should produce intelligent beings?

Blind fate, well no, we agree. But here comes in another risk, and one a good deal more subtle. It is contained in a formula closely associated with the one quoted, and corrective of it:

There is a primitive reason, and laws are the connexions which exist between it and the various beings, and between these beings in their mutual relationships. It follows that creation, which appears to be an arbitrary act, implies laws as invariable as the fatalism of the atheists.

It was an idea equally dear to Montesquieu. He had brought it out in his *Lettres Persanes*, and it was the very backbone of his *Considérations*. This rationalized fatalism of his began to look uncommonly like Spinoza's.

That is precisely what the upholders of orthodoxy had observed the moment his great work appeared, and they had taxed him in so many words with reviving the ideas of the *Ethic*. Finding himself obliged to publish a *Défense* against his various critics, Montesquieu could not avoid explaining his position on this point also. He was not a "Spinozist." His reply, on this matter, was short and sharp. How could such a charge be levelled against him, seeing the pains he had been at to distinguish clearly between the material and the spiritual worlds; seeing, too, how he had stated that God's relationships with the world were those of its Creator and Preserver? A God who is both Creator and Preserver is directly opposed to pantheism; "Spare me then this calumny; a Spinozist I never was, and never shall be."

The fact of the matter is that a strong personality like his could not endure a system which makes no distinction between one's *ego* and universal substance, regarding it merely as a mode of that substance. His own private memoranda, his *Cahiers*, show him preparing his arguments on this matter. What! here is a great genius making use of all manner of mathematical arguments, which are alleged to be very powerful and are in fact very obscure, to drag my soul down to the level of my body, and to convince me that I shall die like an insect! He robs me of everything I deemed to be peculiarly my own! I should be more completely lost in infinite space than a drop of water in the ocean. This same philosopher would also like to do me the favour of robbing me of my inward freedom. He deprives my actions of all motive, and relieves me from any concern about morality. He does me the honour of wishing that I may be a crimeless criminal about whom no one will have the right to make any complaint. I am under many obligations to this philosopher. . . .

Such is his line of argument, such are the terms of his passionate revolt against Spinoza. Far be it from us to doubt the word of so great a man; nor shall we heed what his contemporaries thought about him; and we are ready to put aside the impression that the doctrine he condemns is to be found, if not in its full perfection, at all events in fragmentary traces, in the *Esprit des Lois*; all the same we shall have to admit the presence of another doctrine, the doctrine of the Stoics, for whom the world was Reason and Necessity. From any connexion between the Stoics and himself Montesquieu also defended himself, but this time half-heartedly, unconvincingly, and with seeming reluctance; something after the manner of one who, having to disown some very dear friends, still retains some lingering affection for them. He had so often praised their lofty moral code, so often belauded their most illustrious representatives, and expressed his admiration of the Roman Emperors who had followed in their steps; he had so openly avowed that, if he had not been born within the Christian fold, he would have been among their disciples; and in the course of his own intellectual training he had been on such familiar terms with them—he had even annexed a formula of theirs which he had come across in Cicero, "law is the reason of Great Jupiter"—that it was now no easy matter to sever the connexion. For them, as for him, the universe was the effect of a rational cause, a unique cause containing within itself the concatenation of all subsidiary causes; for them, as for him, everything was the necessary consequence of cause and effect.

What a stupendous *tour de force* he had to execute in order to find a loophole for human freedom of will! How agonized is that opening passage in which he does his utmost to account for the exceptions he has to admit in the operation of an otherwise invariable law!

It is of course essential that the intellectual world, the world of the mind, should be as well regulated as the physical world. The intellectual world, the world of the mind, is a long way from being as well regulated as the physical world; for, though the former has laws which by their nature are invariable, it does not obey them as constantly as the physical world obeys its own. The reason is that individual intelligences are by nature limited, and consequently liable to error; furthermore, it is their nature to act of their own accord. Therefore, they do not consistently observe their primary laws, and even those which they make for themselves, they do not always obey.

Another idea, Stoic like the first one, the idea, namely, that the ideal moral law should be modelled on the pattern of the physical; individual intelligences are restricted by their very nature and consequently liable to error; an idea that might accord with Leibniz: if human nature were perfect it would merge in the divine. It is their nature to act of their own accord; that is the whole point at issue. There is the same factitious juxtaposition of ideas as he proceeds to enlarge on his theme, and all it amounts to is that he has erected at the entrance to the *Esprit des Lois* an arch that is majestic indeed, but most laboriously and artificially constructed.

Man, being a physical being, is, like other bodies, governed by invariable laws. As a thinking being, he is constantly violating the laws laid down by God, and varies those which he has made himself. He must needs be his own guide; but his faculties are limited; he is subject to ignorance and error, as are all finite intelligences; such feeble acquisitions as he makes, even these he loses again; being a creature of the senses, he is liable to all kind of passions. Such a being might at any time forget his creator; God has called him back to Himself by the laws of religion. Such a being might at any time become forgetful of himself; the philosophers have warned him of that by means of the moral law. Though made to live in society, he might forget his fellow men; the lawgivers have brought him back to the path of duty by means of civil and political laws.

That is not all. For to finish up with, man might improve upon the reason of great Jove himself, and make laws that should surpass the primitive ones. Just as in the days of the Stoics human nature had striven to produce of itself an admirable school of thought resembling those plants brought forth by the earth in places that have never seen the sun; so, in Montesquieu's day, men would not leave things as they found them, and human nature set itself to make a fresh endeavour. It would mitigate, and perhaps abolish the oppression which the centuries had perpetuated; it would teach respect for the rights of the individual, it would surround him with guarantees of such a nature as to be held inviolable. Subjects and rulers should alike practise moderation; practical wisdom should be added to the effort of the pure intellect in the attempt to do away with error. Worrying his head no more about those fatalistic ideas that would make us all consequences instead of causes, Montesquieu marked out a place for himself in the crusade for liberty. If he could so contrive that everybody should have new motives for loving his duty, his ruler, his country and her laws; for increasing his sense of well-being in whatever country, under whatever form of government and whatever his position; that those who were in command should grow in the knowledge of what it behoved them to ordain, and that those who obeyed should find a new pleasure in obedience—then Montesquieu would die the happiest of mortals. He would die the happiest of mortals, but leaving to others the task of reconciling inevitability with progress.

BOOK II

I

SENTIMENT: UNEASINESS: POTENCIA SENSITIVA EN EL OMBRE

THE Man of Feeling; the Man of Reason; two human types succeeding one another; one arriving, the other departing. . . . But supposing things did not happen on quite so simple a plan. What if there had been a certain secret understanding between the two? What if Philosophy had assisted Sentiment to express itself and had actually contributed to its victory?

That certain very matter-of-fact writers did not exclude sentiment, or even sentimentalism, from their works; that the tragedians made full use of passion, and occasionally of affection, in their dramas; that Sheridan, for example, could be emotional and keenly critical by turns; that Goldsmith painted the Vicar of Wakefield and his family in a manner midway between smiles and tears—all this we know, but do not intend to insist upon, for it would simply amount to saying that psychologies are complex things, and that the writers of the day sometimes remembered it; and all this would be too obvious to need recording. Nor shall we dwell on the fact that, if sentiment resolutely turned its back on philosophy, philosophy very timidly extended the hand of peace and reconciliation to sentiment. The philosopher indulged in flights of eloquence; it was his way of being lyrical; he was not above putting a little *tremolo* into his voice. The philosopher's indignation was mingled with tears, and, sworn enemy though he was of enthusiasm, he gave some spectacular exhibitions of it. He did not often ask himself what this strange "I", this *ego* of ours, really was, this *ego* whose elements were in a state of perpetual dissolution, but which nevertheless maintained its unity; for ever changing, and for ever the same. Sometimes, however, he *did* enquire, and the answer he gave was that this mysterious "I" was not, perhaps, a fact cognizable by the understanding, but a power of which we were made conscious through the feelings. The philosopher believed that truth possessed an intuitive quality. But these points of contact are few and far between, and it is not they that we shall consider. What we are looking for is some influence more weighty and more general.

The concrete sciences were a great eye-opener. If you wanted to collect plants you had to go out into the fields and forests, and climb some of the lower slopes of mountain ranges. A movement had been started which brought people to make careful observation of the different forms of life, of exciting interest in them to begin with, and then admiration. When he was twenty-five years old, Linnaeus decided he would study the flora of Lapland on the spot, and on the 12th May, 1732, he left Upsala by the North Gate, breathing in with delight the springtime air. "The sky was bright and genial; a gentle breeze from the West lent a refreshing coolness to the air; a dark patch of cloud was rising in the West. The buds of the birch trees were beginning to burst into leaf; the foliage on most trees was fairly advanced, only the elm and the ash still remained bare. The lark was singing high up in the air; after a mile or so, we came to the entrance to a forest; there the lark left us, but on the crest of the pine, the blackbird poured forth his song of love." The young scientist who could thus taste the delights of the Swedish springtime, shy and chilly as it was as yet, was to become something more than the foremost botanist of the age; a great portrayer of the open-air life, he left behind him a name ever to be held in honour by the lovers of Nature. Similarly Buffon, though a studio artist he, was to achieve a fame no less illustrious. It was in 1740 that he began to unfold a store of pictures more arresting than any that the popular eye had yet beheld; pictures which the professional illustrators lost no time in stereotyping.

Science lent another aspect to the surface of the world, and to the depths beneath it. It had been once a little place enough, kitchen-garden and orchard, with a desert here and there by way of contrast; at the most, a garden such as those they have in England. But Science, with its work of exploration, showed how immense it really was; revealing in it such a wealth of strange *fauna* and *flora* as it almost pained one to contemplate; the world was full of life, full to overflowing. Time was when it was thought of as a thing almost of yesterday; with just a few thousands of years behind it; a very paltry score. But now Science endowed it with a stupendous past, telling of primeval chaos, of the action of mighty waters, of oceans diminishing in depth, of the first mountain-tops appearing above the watery surface; of effects wrought by fire, of erupting volcanoes, of fiery furnaces, of cavernous depths suddenly gaping wide, of subsidences, of shocks that brought whole continents into being, or made them disappear. Unconscionable pangs of childbirth indeed! Science enriched the picture with "the countless multitude of worlds contained within the confines of the mighty universe". She enriched it in every conceivable and inconceivable manner, presenting it as a sort of writhing, agonized polyp, conjuring up deformed and monstrous creatures lacking some essential organ, and so doomed from their birth to inevitable extinction, calling up visions more awe-inspiring than those of the Apocalypse, upsurges of force bringing vast systems into being, causing collapse and destruction, no less great; rivers, torrents of atoms discharged by the tireless energy of matter, without beginning and without end. The world had been looked on as something fixed and stable. Not so; this same Science required that we should accustom ourselves to regarding it as something undergoing a ceaseless process of evolution. Nature was stable no more. "Though it may appear, at first sight, that its great works go on without change or variation; though even in the frailest and most transitory of its productions it may seem to be perpetually and consistently the same, since new copies of the same original types are brought constantly before our eyes, yet if we look a little closer, we shall see that its course is not so absolutely uniform; we shall notice that it is subject to unmistakable variations, and undergoes successive modifications, readily assuming fresh combinations, fresh mutations, both of form and matter. Nature has passed through a number of different stages; the earth's surface has assumed a succession of different aspects; even climates have varied, and everything in the physical universe, no less than in the moral, is involved in a process of continuous and progressive movement."[1]

We may here note the origin of one of those themes that were to become such favourites with the romantic poets. Project into ethereal space those manifestations of the forces of nature

[1]Buffon, *Les Époques de la nature*, 1774.

and we shall have the visions of Lamartine; imagine the great ladder of living beings extending from the lowliest of creatures up to God himself, mark the course of the various evolutions and metempsychoses and we shall likewise have the visions which haunt the meditations of Victor Hugo.

The attitude of revolt which was taken up at the beginning of their poetical careers by Ugo Foscolo, Wordsworth and Coleridge, which was assumed intermittently by Keats, and consistently displayed by Byron, had several origins, but one of them was the trend of ideas in the eighteenth century.

Libertà va cercando, ch'è si cara is the epigraph to the novel *Ultime lettere di Jacopo Ortis*; he goes forth looking for liberty, for liberty that is so dear. That same liberty, not only Jacopo Ortis, but his predecessors, his contemporaries, and his successors as well, prized dearly. Rationalism declined to take account of any but universal values in the human being; but by dissociating him from authority, from tradition, indeed from any regulating influence external to himself, it had let him loose with a vengeance. Now, independent at last of any promptings save such as came from within himself, he was master of his own actions. For all that he did he was answerable only to himself. That initial, basic liberty implied all the rest. There is more logic than might at first appear in this pronouncement of the Abbé Raynal's: " 'If you lay a hand on me, I shall kill myself', said Clarissa to Lovelace; but I should warn anyone who attempted to interfere with my liberty, and say, 'If you come any nearer I shall put a knife into you'; and I should be talking much better sense than Clarissa."[1] Freedom for the individual, freedom of thought, freedom for the passions, freedom for the writer to say what he will. We are completely misguided when we insist on going, for our authority, for our pattern, to our grandsires. Let us stand on our own feet and show ourselves for what we really are. It is no paradox to say that, if there was a romanticism which had its roots in the distant past, which in religion was theocratic, in politics conservative, and which in consequence would have nothing to do with the new-fangled ideas of the modern school, there was also a liberal romanticism, liberal, even anarchical; there was Shelley, for example; and Stendhal.

[1] *Histoire phil. et politique des établissements et du commerce des Européens dans les deux Indes*, 1770, Livre XI.

Bearing all this in mind, let us now pass on to another question; let us take part in the quest of the psychologists as they attempt to discover, sparing neither time nor labour, some faculty of the non-rational order which enables us, not only to recognize beauty, but to create it.

What is beauty? Another problem, and a problem all the more difficult to resolve because psychologists, logicians, metaphysicians, all bent on finding the answer, were joined by a host of painters, sculptors, engravers and even caricaturists, all anxious to put in their word, as they had a perfect right to do, but all making confusion worse confounded. Put the question to any mixed company; ask them what this beauty is that has such power to charm; what is its nature, what is the basic idea of the thing; ask them whether it is relative or absolute; ask them whether what they consider beautiful in France would be considered equally so in China. Ask them whether there is a standard or canon of beauty on which all the derivative beauties which we behold here below are modelled. Then what a pell-mell of ideas ensues, what a babel of voices, and what a host of doubts are cast upon matters of which, of all things in the world, we felt most certain. And then, when you try to pin any of them down, when you ask them to explain themselves, to say what they really mean, most of them will be unable to tell you.[1]

Of course there was one way out of the dilemma, or, rather a way of not getting into it at all. All that was necessary was to stand firmly by the classical doctrine. Beauty was a reflexion of the true. After that, there was nothing more to be said. The definition, valid for all times and for all places, was as unique as Nature itself. The way to capture the true was to imitate Nature; or to imitate the masters who had done so, and done so to perfection. Even if one gave oneself a little latitude, if, for the strict truth, one substituted what looked like the truth, Beauty, being thus dependent on some inward reasoning process, still retained a rationalistic character. After all, as Crousaz observed, variety within general unity, regularity, order, proportion—these things are not mere will-o'-the-wisps.[2]

But that is precisely what the heretics would not agree to.

[1]Le P. André, *Traité sur le Beau,* 1741. *Premier Discours.*

[2]Crousaz, *Traité du Beau,* 1715.

For heretics there were, and the orthodox, like the Abbé Le Batteux, were exceedingly angry with them. And as the main question was split up into a host of subsidiary ones, insinuations against the classical doctrine infiltrated into a number of replies on matters of detail, each of which helped to undermine confidence in the original position. Taste it was that decided what was beautiful and what was not; but then what *was* taste? It was difficult to go on maintaining that it was never anything but a purely intellectual process. What is that "Je ne sais quoi", that "indefinable something", which always insists on cropping up when we find ourselves at a loss for an argument or an explanation, which has something of mystery about it, and whose very name is a torment to the understanding? The sublime, which seems to elude all attempts to define it, what is it? And genius, what is that? Then, in a neighbouring whirlpool of questions, what, exactly is poetry? How do we distinguish between the real thing and the spurious? From other countries there come a flood of poetic forms, so called, that do not square with ours; so too, in remote ages we catch glimpses of forms equally at variance with our own. But they all claim to be called poetry. Then, what about painting? and sculpture? and architecture? The old definitions are out of date.

Thus any number of rebellious protests were heard against the state of mind which Antonio Conti, scholar, man of letters and citizen of the world recorded as reigning in high places on Parnassus: "They have introduced into the realm of *Belles Lettres* the spirit and the method of M. Descartes, and they judge of poetry and eloquence without any regard to their effect on the senses." The senses demanded official recognition; and two countries which, though under the influence of a pseudo-classical revival, could not but feel a certain predilection for them, namely, England and Italy, were glad to put it on record that they were still present with them. While the English theorizers, schismatics by nature, were busy with their heterodox explanations, a poet, one Mark Akenside, began singing *The Pleasures of Imagination.* The year was 1744. As poetry, pretty second-rate I daresay; didactic, priding itself on imitating Virgil and Horace, and highly delighted at recapturing the cadences of Pope—second-rate, maybe, but all the same putting a universe of Beauty for a universe of Reason, and isolating the singular nature of the pleasure which

Beauty awakens in us, analysing the charm that lays its spell upon our responsive hearts, and chanting the advent of a new divinity:

> Thou, smiling queen of every tuneful breast,
> Indulgent Fancy . . . ![1]

The Italian doctrinaires, great as was their attachment to all-sovereign Reason, did not want her to be such a tyrant as to suffer none to exist beside her. On the contrary, they put in a claim for other faculties, imaginative and sensuous, and gave examples of their influence. Possibly their published writings and their letters kindled the revolt which Bodmer and Breitinger carried on in Switzerland against the sterilities of Gottsched.

It was very necessary that Beauty should pass from the objective to the subjective; from the absolute to the relative, and that, instead of depending on some ontological conception, it should depend rather on a modality of our being, since that was what empiricism demanded. What do we mean when we talk about "the Beautiful"? What is Beauty? Sublimated passion, answered the Abbé Dubos. It is essential that we should experience the passions, but they often cause us to suffer. It is the function of Art to make us feel the passions without the pain which they bring in their train. "Painters and poets excite these passions in us artificially, by putting before us imitations of those things which are of a nature to excite our passions in reality." In a room in which we are intended to enjoy ourselves a picture portraying the terrible sacrifice of Jephtha's daughter proves more enthralling than another picture illustrating some happy theme. The sight of the knife, of the victim, of the stream of blood fills us with horror. But while the portrayal of this tragic deed loses nothing of its appeal to the emotions, it suppresses the pain which the act, had it been real, would have inflicted upon us. This answer to the question was destined to travel a long way in the minds of men, to be discussed and argued about, rejected here, accepted there. If men were perfectly healthy and cheerful, Pietro Verri was later on to declare, there would be no such thing as the Fine-Arts. They it was that took our minds off our hidden troubles. Whether these unrecognized pains came from the action of something impinging on our physical organism, or whether they proceeded from moral

[1] *The Pleasures of Imagination,* Book I, lines 9–10.

sensations beyond our cognizance, they secretly tormented us; and though they eluded our attempts to trace them, they were with us all the same. But some beautiful music, a beautiful picture or a fine play will beguile us of this pain. The crowning triumph of an artist's skill was to stir up painful sensations within us solely in order to put an end to them.

What is Beauty? Let us be logical, answered Francis Hutcheson, the same that had so vehemently denounced rational morality. Let us begin at the beginning, let us start with sensations. Some sensations differ in kind from any others; and cannot be affiliated with any of them. They touch a particular chord within us, they awaken a special feeling, the feeling for beauty. This inward faculty procures us a pleasure of a peculiar kind, quite different from that which we derive from a knowledge of the principles, the proportions, the causes of things, or the use to which they may be put. Reason may furnish a supplementary pleasure by showing us some practical advantage, or by affording us the sort of satisfaction that comes from knowledge, but reason is not its essence. To conclude; if we were lacking in this inward feeling, we might say, when speaking of buildings, or gardens, or clothes or an equipage of any sort, that they were becoming, useful, convenient and so on, but we should never say they were beautiful.[1]

So a fresh start was made. It often meant a step backwards. The stone would slip from their hands, and back it would roll again to the bottom. But again it was heaved up, with the same fierce energy as we have so often seen already. In 1735, the science which people were seeking to establish, was given a name; Alexander Gottlieb Baumgarten, a disciple of Wolff's and a brother of the exegetist, referred to it as the science of aesthetics. That was in the thesis he wrote for his doctorate under the title, *Meditationes philosophicae de nonnullis ad poema pertinentibus*. However, the word lay buried in the text till Baumgarten retrieved it and used it as the title of a fuller work on the same subject, *Aesthetica*, the first volume of which was published in the year 1750. The work was not a masterpiece, and in some respects a good deal less spirited than many of its predecessors. The important, the really significant, thing about it was the title, indicating, as it did, a plan to construct a new system of values, a

[1]*Inquiry into the original of our ideas of beauty and virtue*, 1725.

new code of laws, a *Theoria liberalium artium*, and as indicating that this mode of apprehending things through the senses, though still esteemed by Baumgarten inferior to knowledge gained through the intellect, was now receiving its charter, and vindicating its rights.

A signal effort—that is what it amounted to—to withdraw from the intellect, from the reasoning faculty, its claim to be sole judge where the beautiful was concerned; a vigorous attempt to have this prerogative transferred to another department of the mind. Then came the discovery announced to the Spanish public by the padre Feijoo even as the look-out man cries "Land ho!" when his vessel approaches some unfamiliar shore, *Descubrimiento de una nueva Faculdad o Potencia sensitiva en el ombre.*

Behold, first, the son of a humble shoemaker earning his bread by acting as guide to a blind man; now, a lad who, in spite of everything, contrives to get a little schooling and reproaches his teachers with being no friends of the Muses, since Greek is as scarce a thing with them as fine gold; now, the young man who, hearing that the library of the learned Fabricius was to be put up for sale at Hamburg, takes the road thither, prepared if need be to go hungry on the way, so that he may attend the auction and buy some Greek book; next, the schoolmaster, teaching little grubby urchins how to read, and forgetting his troubles in his devotion to Homer; next, the librarian, consumed by one absorbing passion, which is to perfect his knowledge of antiquity, and who reads through the *Iliad* and the *Odyssey* thrice in a single winter; the Lutheran who turns Catholic because he sees a chance of getting a job of some sort in Rome; the Brandenburger who thinks that he only begins to live on the day he sets foot on Latin soil—*Italiam, Italiam!* This man, Johann Joachim Winckelmann, is swept onwards to classical antiquity as though by the wind of Destiny. It is not only this vocation of the man that is surprising, but also the way in which he is borne along to the contemplation of Greek beauty in its ideal perfection. He spurns everything that partakes of the *baroque*, and even the sort of cheap-jack Hellenism that seemed to please his contemporaries well enough; and fixing his gaze on the noble statues of the age of Pericles, he cries: Behold true Beauty! Know it by its simplicity. Even as the depths of the sea are calm however furiously the storms may rage upon its surface, so are the faces of these statues, calm amid all the welter of surrounding passions, the marble index of spirits ever serene and undisturbed. Nothing mars their peaceful harmony.

The discovery of the remains of Herculanum had, of course, a great effect on people, but it affected them gradually, not all at once. The picture of a bygone world was not revealed in a single flash. Bronzes and statues were brought to light one by one. The work of excavation took a long time. On the other hand, the *Gedanken über die Nachahmung der griechischen Werke in der Malerei und Bildhauer Kunst* (1755) and the *Geschichte der Kunst des Alterthums* (1764) illuminated the scene as with a sudden wave of floodlight. Not only did Greece appear in all her naked purity; but the whole attitude towards art underwent a fundamental change. Art was now seen to be a sharer in that evolutionary process to which all created things are subject; that is to say, it was born, it passed on to maturity, and thence to decay and death, just like a man or a plant. Fully to comprehend it, one must observe it in its successive stages; its early manifestations cannot but charm us with their touching simplicity; and the fruits of its autumn time, these too we needs must love, but with a love tinged with sadness, the sadness we cannot but feel at the passing of all things beautiful. And between those faltering beginnings and those melancholy farewells, let us love with full and grateful hearts such master-works as have captured for us on earth the image, the incarnation, of perfection. No more was art the inexplicable product of some recipe cunningly applied; now, you could see it germinate, bloom, and fade away; it was a phenomenon of actual life.

It is curious to reflect that, long before Sentiment broke loose and tore away with such speed as to upset the equilibrium of our faculties, to cast off the restraints of rationalism, and to transform life into a lyrical chant; long before the appearance on the stage of those passionate heroes we have called to mind, as far back as 1690, as the *Essay concerning Human Understanding*, the Man of Desire had secured his Declaration of Rights. Locke had shown that the mind was passive, and this initial statement of his was fraught with a load of consequences, not fully developed. But he had also shown that the mind was active, too, since it worked on the *sense-data* conveyed to it. Now, the essential principle of this activity was *uneasiness*; desire:

The uneasiness a man finds in himself upon the absence of anything whose present enjoyment carries the idea of delight with it, is what we call desire; *which is greater or less, as that uneasiness is more or less vehement. Where, by the by, it may perhaps be of some use to remark, that the chief, if not only spur to human industry and action is* uneasiness.

Locke's successor and emendator, Condillac, laid great stress on the psychology of desire:

To desire is the most urgent of all our needs; and so, no sooner has one desire been satisfied, than we begin to long for something else. Frequently, we indulge several desires at once, or if we cannot, we reserve for a later and more convenient period those which present circumstances forbid us to entertain. Thus our passions return to us again and again, one after another, and wax more and more numerous, and we live on only that we may desire, and only in so far as we desire.

Then he goes on to deal with the psychology of tedium, of boredom, *ennui*. The marble statue which came to life as soon as it obtained the power of feeling recalls the pleasant situations in which she had found herself; from that time forward, indifference seemed to her unbearable; the discomfort she felt was what we call *ennui*. *Ennui* is a thing that lasts and waxes in intensity; it becomes as grievous to bear as actual pain. The mind clutches at any and everything calculated to dispel it. Fear of *ennui* it is that makes the majority of men busy in mind and body. This fear impels them to look about for anything that will stir the emotions, even if it stirs them to excess and brings them suffering. *Ennui* sends the working-classes to the gallows, and rich people to the theatre; it sends old women to their prayers and dismal acts of penitence; it turns courtiers into plotters and conspirators. "But it is particularly in those societies in which the *grandes passions* are strictly curbed, either by a rigid moral code, or by legal enactments that *ennui* plays its leading rôle; in such conditions it may be described as the universal incitement." Sensible, stolid folk are inferior to passionate; without passion, one cannot be a poet. "Feeling is the soul of poetry." Whence come these words? From what enthusiastic romanticist? They are writ in the book entitled *De l'Esprit*, and its author is Helvetius.

What it comes to is that in Nature you can find anything; even Romanticism.

II

THE FEELINGS: THE PRIMITIVE AND THE CIVILIZED

THERE are times when civilized man feels a sense of weariness, weariness of self. He would give a lot to be able to cast off the burden he carries on his shoulders, but did not put there, the accumulated result, the refinements, the complications, of thousands of years of human endeavour, a burden which he finds beyond endurance. What is he but the fruit, the ultimate product of an age-old artificiality? Life runs smoothly enough, but somehow, the stream seems contaminated, and that very smoothness displeases him; he calls it pampering, molly-coddling. What he craves for is the simple life. He would not mind roughing it, if he had to; a plain supper and a bed on the hard ground. Oh, for a stream of living waters to wash him clean!

To this sort of feeling, which, like so many others, goes and comes in alternating waves, the eighteenth century man was no stranger. In his elegant drawing-room, with its pictures by Lancret or Gainsborough, its furniture by Boule or Chippendale, he has sat and longed for a breath of the large air. Comfortably ensconced in his stall at the play, he has loudly applauded the quips and sallies of *Arlequin Sauvage*. The means of escape have never been plentiful; there were very few of them in those days. The excesses, the wild extravagances, the follies which a later age hoped would lead to the ineffable, the undreamt of, had not as yet been thought of. He had to make shift with the exotic and the marvellous. He laughed at sorcerers and necromancers, yet he beheld the future in a glass of water, and invited the departed to come and hold converse with him.

Then he would dream he was retracing his steps along the path of time. He dwelt among the Spartans. Ceasing to regard Homer as the great poet who had only lacked a little *savoir-faire* to achieve perfection, he looked with envy on the manners and customs of the ancient Greeks, those kings who knew the number of their cows, their goats and their sheep, who prepared their own meals; that Queen Arete who wove the material for her husband's garments; that royal princess Nausicaa who washed the linen of her household in a neighbouring stream. And farther back still in the abysm of time, he came face to face with the Noble Savage, and loved him.

The Noble Savage came straight from the hands of Nature; he was still to be met with, just as he was at the beginning of the world, in certain regions difficult of access where, alas! people were forever trying to get him to adopt the ridiculous customs of the European. Now here was a traveller painting him in livelier colours, in clearer outline, with a more emphatic brush, as though he wanted to make a gift of him to the new age. This traveller, the Baron de La Hontan, had ended his career of adventure in 1715. He was a born rebel, and when he had seen some service with the King's army in Canada, he eventually abandoned the white people to go and dwell among the redskins. Never did anyone paint so dazzling a portrait, never had his friends the Savages been portrayed in livelier hues. They were handsome, active, strong and tireless; and happy, because they had loyally adhered to the habits and religion derived from Nature. They recognized neither *meum* nor *tuum*, knew nought of money, that root of all evil, and cared not for arts or sciences. Then, by way of contrast, La Hontan drew a picture of civilized man, burlesquing his absurd blue coat, his red stockings, his black hat with its white tuft, and his green ribbons; mocking his fine airs, his polite greetings, his bowings and scrapings, his ceremonious obeisances, and his bombastic speech, his physique vitiated by drugs and sauces, and, worst of all, his mind poisoned by superstition. Foolish Frenchmen, who thought they were reviling a foe when they called him a savage! The Man of Nature was the personification of virtue, truth and happiness. It was not enough to praise the people of China or Siam; they had already fallen from their high estate, with their judges, their priests, and their mandarins. There was only one thing to do: say good-bye to the Old World and become a Huron!

Other symbolic characters there were who came along in the wake of La Hontan's mouthpiece, the anarchical Adario. The first dark-skinned hero—black as ebony, he was, with teeth like white enamel—Oroonoko, was brought to England by the novelist Mrs. Aphra Behn. He afterwards figured on the stage. Oroonoko, whose misfortunes were great, and attributable for the most part to the treachery of white men, was nothing like so unfortunate as the unhappy Yariko, the female savage. A young English trader, Inkle by name, fair-haired and fresh-complexioned, well-bred, with polished manners, set sail from London to do business in the West Indies. They landed on an island on their way across, and all his companions were massacred by the natives. He, however, had been saved by the fair Yariko, who concealed him in a cave, dressed his wounds, brought him food, and took him to her bosom; all for dear love of him. After a time, an English vessel appeared on the horizon and drew near. Inkle went on board and, moved to compassion by the young woman's devotion, took her with him. But the time came when he realized all the time and money he had wasted on his adventure, and, though she was with child by him, Inkle sold Yariko to a slave-dealer. Novels, tragedies, dramas, operas, poems, epistles, elegies, fables, songs, paintings, drawings, engravings—all spread abroad and popularized this touching story. A diptych was offered to the view; in one panel, was the traitor, the scoundrel, the villain; in the other, the noble, generous but ill-fated soul. And the former was the European, the latter, the child of Nature!

The notion of some deviation of which humanity had been guilty, and for which it was undergoing punishment, a punishment which became more grievous as men drew farther and farther from the course that had been destined for them; insistence on the value of simplicity, spontaneousness, as compared with the artificial and the premeditated; the determination to seek the ideal pattern of humanity in the earliest ages, or in places into which contamination had not yet entered; the hope of discovering happiness by going backwards; a feeling of rebelliousness, of discontent with things as they were; maladjustments, regrets, longings and, what was an almost physical sensation, a mighty hunger for fresh air; pictures which disprized the real, and invested some bygone age with a dreamlike beauty—such were some of the elements which went to the making of that complex thing called primitivism.

But, at the same time, pictures, feelings, purposes, ideas were completing the formation of a complex of a diametrically opposite character.

Man's earliest state was that of a brute beast. Anyone who set out to discover what things were like in the earliest times, instead of seeing noble beings, creatures of light, might equally well picture to himself beings hardly distinguishable from the lower animals, without speech, without altars, and without tombs, wandering in the great forest that was then the earth; barbarous hordes who disputed their prey with wild animals.

Those specimens of humanity who have remained in a state of nature, far from possessing the beauty with which some people would invest them, are nothing less than repulsive. There are no savages more closely resembling the real thing than the Hottentots; the Iroquois were drawing-room darlings in comparison. Now Hottentots have flat noses, they are covered all over with a coating of black grease; their hair reeks with the stench of rancid oil. Tquassow speaks in terms of glowing admiration of the charms of the fair Knomquaïha: "He was struck with the shining hue of her complexion, as brilliant as the jet-black down which covers the black pigs of Hessaqua; he was transported with delight as he contemplated the splayed cartilage of her nose, and his eyes lingered with enchantment on the flabby beauty of her breasts which hung down to the level of her navel." Knomquaïha adds another cunning touch to her attractions: "Her face, which shone like carefully polished ebony, was agreeably diversified by patches of red earth, and presented the appearance of night's sable veils all besprent with stars. She sprinkled her limbs with ashes and perfumed them with charred civet. Round her arms and legs were intertwined the shining intestines of a heifer. From her neck was suspended a pouch made of the stomach of a kid. The wings of an ostrich shadowed the fleshy protuberances of her posterior, and in front she wore an apron made from the hirsute ears of a lion."[1] A pretty picture, that, to put up against the idealized portrait of the Noble Savage! What is more, the scientists pointed out that there was not, nor ever had been, any such thing as the Noble Savage; that history and exploration clearly proved the existence of many different kinds of savages, the majority of them still fierce and, when opportunity offered, anthropophagous. Faced with these facts, the *ferini*, that is, those who maintained that primitive humanity was on a level with brute-beasts, carried the day against the *anti-ferini*, and scored a point.

Artifice was not at all in favour, but Art was looked upon as sacred. Artifice smothered Nature; but it was necessary that Nature should be corrected, brought into order, by Art. So profound was that conviction in those days that it animated all manifestations of beauty, whether literary or plastic. It was developed in innumerable treatises, it governed the rules of composition, and an attempt was made to unite both concepts in one, as thus: all our notions, whatsoever they were, were natural; art was natural. People were quite ready to accept the view that Nature, in the real sense, was Nature transformed by Art; by Art, Nature was broadened, corrected and polished; thistles and brambles were cleared away, the rose and the vine flourished in their place; Nature, properly so called, was not the barren mountain, but rather the tilled field. Sometimes Nature herself was looked on as the artist, for she worked on a plan that she herself had fixed, she quietly prepared the germs of her productions, made a rough sketch of every living thing, patiently labouring to bring them to perfection, within a certain limit of time. Her first attempts were failures; nothing daunted, she tried again, only to bring them at last to that wonderful pertection which moves us to admiration.

Who could say whether the ideal so restlessly longed for was a heritage from the past, or whether it was nothing of the kind, but a hope for the future? Was the line of our destiny a descending or an ascending one? Should we look behind us for that golden age, which, try as we would, we could never recapture, or should we look to find it at the end of the road on which we were faring? Here the idea of progress came in. Its influence on contemporary thought has been rightly pointed

[1]Lessing, *Laocoon,* 1766, Par. XXV.

out; we have been reminded how Turgot first solemnly proclaimed it before a learned assembly at the Sorbonne on the 11th December, 1750. Nature, they were told, is perpetually dying and coming to life again, whereas "the human race, viewed from its earliest beginning, presents itself to the eyes of the philosopher as a vast whole which, like every individual being, has its time of childhood and of progress. . . . Manners become gentler; the mind becomes more enlightened; nations, hitherto living in isolation, draw nearer to one another; trade and political relations link up the various quarters of the globe; and the whole body of mankind, through vicissitudes of calm and tempest, of fair days and foul, continues its onward march, albeit with tardy steps, towards an ever nearing perfection." Now let us discover, if we can, the sources of those springs which went to swell this mighty current.

The quarrel of the Ancients and the Moderns had been a challenge to the Greek and Latin classics to justify the prerogatives they enjoyed; it went farther, and dissected the motives which were at the bottom of the revolt. The basic fact is clear enough: Leibniz had enunciated the idea of continuity, and that in itself might well be one of the components of a process which needed time for its fulfilment. Science, at all events, was growing; that was something nobody could deny; any schoolboy knew more about geometry than Pythagoras ever did. The latest branch of knowledge, Natural History, in all its various branches, had not only enlarged our field of enquiry, but had furnished us with a method which set no limit to our progress. And at the same time it had given us a firm hold on our power. Nor was our material progress any less incontestable. We had available a host of conveniences which our ancestors never even dreamt of; the mechanical arts were at once increasing the supplies and lowering the cost of all these things. Of more recent date was political progress. Governments were beginning to find out where their true principles lay; before another century had past, internal equilibrium and universal arbitration would definitely guarantee the security of their citizens. Then, more recent still, there was social progress, with a theory that was at all events taking shape, as thus: the consciousness of the need we had one of another would render us increasingly humane; happiness, though it might not be equally shared by all, would extend to an ever-increasing number of individuals; well-being would become more generally diffused; the division of labour would render toil less onerous.

There was something about the atmosphere which, as they breathed it, caused the adversaries to soften. The recollection of the original sin, of Adam's expulsion from the Garden of Eden, and the curse that hung over his unhappy posterity, grew less poignant; a God of Mercy began to get the better of the God of Justice; a certain number of Christians favoured the idea of a progress that would never reach any precise limit, but would continue indefinitely till it approximated to the joys of Paradise. Divine perfection could not but vouchsafe to mortals on this earth unending progress towards perfection. Divine science knew well enough that what comes first in the order of nature is less perfect than what comes later. Divine wisdom, having created, and put at our disposal, the means for bettering our lot, could hardly forbid us to make use of them; as a matter of fact, Divine Truth had always favoured a process of development in religion; polytheism had been followed by monotheism; monotheism by Judaism; Judaism by Christianity. The selection of the people to whom the deposit of truth was to be entrusted had been carefully pre-ordained; the true faith had been revealed little by little, and the revelation was not yet complete; the Church had been compelled to advance step by step. So with the individual soul; it passed from darkness through successive stages of ever-growing light. For that reason, it would have been wrong to suppose that we were living in a retrograde age; why not—it would be far better—share in the general movement? The confident belief that the present age was more enlightened than those which had preceded it was a thing to make us quicken our pace. It was England that promulgated these ideas. Lay folk and pastors who took this line felt sure that their arguments would help to confound the ungodly, and particularly the man Tindal, who had given out that it was absurd to suppose that God had waited for Tiberius to come to the throne, in order to manifest himself to man. There were not two truths, said Tindal and his followers; and either Christianity was true, in which case it was contained in, merged with, eternal truth, or it was false. There are not two truths, their adversaries replied, but there is a gradually unfolding truth. Nothing ever operates *per saltum*. This is true of Christianity; it is true of revelation. Progress is the law of the spiritual world.[1]

Irradiating all the various manifestations of intellectual activity, empirical reasoning was actively at work. Reason was not innate. It somehow formed, fortified, and completed itself. Lessing made a decisive contribution to the idea of progress when he postulated in the history of the species the same evolutionary process that operates in the individual, interpreting reason as a kind of gradual becoming.

All these considerations put together carried conviction. "We are infinitely more worthy than our ancestors. Men are better behaved than they ever were, more polished, more enlightened, more humane. Our forefathers of Francis I's day lived like barbarians, and behaved like savages. Nowadays, everything has changed for the better. In my opinion, the Abbé de Saint Pierre is perfectly right in what he says about the human race progressing little by little towards universal reason." In these words, which are those of a European observer, one Jean François de Boissy, a Swiss who had travelled in France and Germany, and had lived for a time in Holland, we recognize a note of confident assurance. All that remained now to be done was to go on from the progress already attained and confirmed to consider what it promised for the future, from discontinuity to continuity, from believing in progress to theorizing about it. That was a task which, later on, Condorcet was to undertake: *Esquisse d'un tableau historique des progrès de l'esprit humain* (1794).

Before now, we have had to make out certificates of baptism for newborn words, and now, here is another. Civilization in French was originally a legal term; it denoted the process by which a case was transferred from the criminal to the civil court. Without wholly losing its juridical sense, it was now used for the first time to indicate the difference which separates a savage community from a state governed by law, and this in a book by "the late M. Boulanger", entitled *l'Antiquité dévoilée par ses usages* (1766): "When the people of a savage race come to take on civilization, we must never set a term to the process by giving them fixed and irrevocable laws; they must be taught to regard

[1]Ronald S. Crane, *Anglican Apologetics and the Idea of Progress. Modern Philology*, 1934.

the legislation imposed upon them as a stage in a continuous process." As the book of the late M. Boulanger was published by the Baron d'Holbach, we are in some doubt to which of the two we should assign its paternity. Be that as it may, in the ensuing years the word took on the meaning which we give it today. It took its place at the head of a hierarchy of words; at the very bottom came the savage state, then barbarism, then civility, politeness, then "a wise control", and finally, civilization —"the triumph and the efflorescence of reason, not only in the constitutional, political and administrative spheres, but in the moral, religious and intellectual spheres as well".[1]

If, instead of worrying our heads about the abstract meaning and exact definition of the word, we prefer a lively, witty and satirical picture of the thing itself, something that would serve to illustrate the penury of the primitive age and the triumph of civilization, we can have one at a much earlier date. It is to be found in Voltaire's *Le Mondain* (1736) and his *La Défense du Mondain* (1737). Our fathers were poor; is there any merit in being poor? They lived frugal lives; no virtue in that; they didn't know any better. Cincinnatus returned to his plough because he had nothing better to do. Don't talk to us about Ithaca and Salentum, let Fénelon sound their praises as he will. Nothing in the world would induce us to live in either of them. The so-called Golden Age wasn't golden at all; it was iron. The beatitude of the first couple in that primeval garden, ere yet they had eaten of the fruit of the tree of the knowledge of good and evil, was the purest illusion:

> Mon cher Adam, mon gourmand, mon bon père,
> Que faisais-tu dans les jardins d'Eden?
> Travaillais-tu pour ce sot genre humain?
> Caressais-tu Madame Ève, ma mère?
> Avouez-moi que vous aviez tous deux
> Les ongles longs, un peu noirs et crasseux,
> La chevelure un peu mal ordonnée,
> Le teint bruni, la peau bise et tannée,
> Sans propreté l'amour le plus heureux
> N'est plus l'amour, c'est un besoin honteux.

[1] Lucien Febvre, *Civilisation, Évolution d'un mot et d'un groupe d'idées,* 1930.

Bientôt lassés de leur belle aventure,
Dessous un chêne ils soupent galamment
Avec de l'eau, du millet et des glands;
Le repas fait, ils dorment sur la dure;
Voilà l'état de la pure nature.[1]

In these days pleasure is offered to us in countless dainty and delightful forms; we enjoy the products that come to us from every quarter of the globe. The fine arts vie with one another to enchant the eye; we have attractive houses to live in; we take our walks in beautiful gardens; we have carriages, perfumed baths, tables tastefully set out, appetising dishes, champagne, pleasant little supper-parties. Let us confess, what it would be hypocrisy to deny, let everyone boldly cry:

The Earthly Paradise is here, where I am.

People hesitated as to which road to take, especially when they came to consider the inherent nature of the two alternatives. Arts and Letters—were they a blessing, or a bane? It was true that this product of prosperity had a corrupting effect on morals, and that moral corruption brought empires to ruin; it was none the less true that refinement and good taste lent a charm to life, and that man, devoid of the delights of grace and beauty, would be the most miserable of animals. If you started talking about luxury and its effects, you were lost. Any Tom, Dick or Harry might take up his pen and elaborate an apology, or an indictment; verbiage without end, "an unlimited source of twaddle". Luxury was a danger in itself; luxury was only dangerous in ill-governed States. There were two brands of luxury, one culpable, the other salutary. Or two other kinds, one aristocratic and the other popular. Aye, and yet two more, luxury in the early stages, which was harmless, and the luxury which led people on to acquire adornments which they had not the money to pay for;

[1]My dear Adam, my greedy one, my father dear, what were you doing in Eden's garden? Were you working for that stupid human race? Were you caressing Madame Eve, my mother? Come now, confess, you both had long, black and rather filthy nails, your hair a little unkempt, your complexion swarthy, your skin weatherbeaten and tanned. Love without cleanliness, however happy, is not love at all but a disgusting appetite. Soon weary of their brave adventure they sup in gallant style beneath an oak on raw grain, acorns and water. The meal finished, they lie down to sleep on the hard ground. Such was the state of pure nature.

and that was, of course, to be condemned. Others came to the conclusion that it was a waste of time to argue about the matter at all. There the thing was, whether you liked it or not, and you had to put up with it. Helvetius declared himself in favour of primitive habits and customs, for equality of conditions for all, and for luxury. Baron d'Holbach was opposed to luxury, but all for civilization. The outcome of a widespread enquiry about primitivism recently carried out in the lower grades of English eighteenth-century literature—popular novels, cheap tracts, second-rate poems, etc., revealed a wide diffusion of the fashionable philosophy, but showed that its various conflicting tendencies were very dimly apprehended. It was not a little surprising to find, side by side and rubbing shoulders in the most brotherly manner in the self-same book, the idea that the world was degenerating, and the idea that it was doing precisely the opposite.[1] The hero, or the heroine, would be going blithely along, without any consciousness of inconsistency, towards a Nature all happy, but departed, and a Nature no less happy, but still to come.

However, it was in no such hazy regions, but in the full light of day, and in full panoply, that Physis and Anti-Physis confronted each other; and precisely when Physis was carrying all Europe before it in the matter of the feelings, Anti-Physis was establishing its supremacy over it in the sphere of action.

About half-way through the century, a great change did in fact take place in the domain of political economy. The trading system was beginning to give place to the school which held that the land and its cultivation was the source of all wealth. Mercantilism had taken fully three centuries to run its course; it had firmly established itself, had received government support, had found a great minister, Colbert, to put it systematically into practice; and finally, the theorists seized on it and dressed it up in formulas. National wealth could only be derived from the skilful political manipulation of the precious metals; consequently the winning of those metals should be left in the hands of the State. The State would encourage exports and reduce

[1] *A Documentary History of Primitivism and related Ideas*. Vol. I: *Primitivism and related Ideas in Antiquity*, by Arthur O. Lovejoy, George Boas, Baltimore, 1935. *Primitivism and related Ideas in English Popular Literature of the Eighteenth Century*, by Lois Withney. Baltimore, 1934.

imports, so as to secure a favourable trade balance. Seeing that everybody could not be a winner at one and the same time, it would take all necessary steps to assure victory in its rivalry with its neighbours, and to establish its hegemony over all of them. And so it was; the merchant team, Melon, Dutot, Véron de Forbonnais, with their Essays and Reflexions on commerce, gave place to another team, Gournay, Quesnay, Mirabeau, Turgot, Lemercier de la Rivière, and this one, learned, eloquent and inspired with the enthusiasm usual in converts, took the field with a new plan of action and a new philosophy. Physis was their rallying cry. Long enough had people held the belief that gold and silver constituted wealth; the land, and only the land, was a producer. Industry was sterile because it was precarious, because it might be transferred abroad, and because it was perpetually under the menace of some change or other. Even when all was going well with it, its activities were second-hand, never doing anything but manipulate what it had got from the land. Sterile, too, was the income derived from capital, always a burdensome and iniquitous levy. But the land—that was a different matter. The land was productive, it created wealth, and it did so regularly every year; the power which produced and multiplied the soil's fertility was agriculture. The world's prosperity was all derived from the land; that was the fundamental principle on which all our activities should be based: politics, morals, education, everything.

The mercantile school bore mainly the trade-mark of England; the agricultural, the trade-mark of France: thus the latter was an ideology. All the various ideas which we have shown as going the round—liberalism which allows laws to act of themselves with the minimum of interference; enlightened despotism, which, being enlightened, always told on the side of reason; the sacrosanct character of property; the interest of each is the interest of all—these things kept cropping up again and again in the homilies of their several apostles; all these ideas, and this one in particular, namely, that the whole world might easily be put to rights thanks to a few principles that had at last been recognized; it was the easiest thing in the world not to meddle with the good which was in process of coming about of itself; measures sufficient for ensuring the well-being of the vastest empire might be contained in fifty pages, or, at the most, in sixty. Here again it seemed that Nature was fated to come into the picture; and so in fact she did. She came on in the guise of the kindly and provident mother who, by the succession of the seasons, tells us when it is time to sow, and when to gather in the harvest; who causes the rain to descend upon the pastures, and the sun to shine upon the orchards, who never wearies in bringing forth good things in abundance, provided only man plays his part. The Physiocrat is he who feels himself one with the essential laws of the natural order; Physiocracy is Nature's code.

It was with delight that the *Journal économique*, the party organ, recorded the adhesion of the neighbouring countries. An Academy of Agriculture was set on foot in Florence; the Swedish nation evoked general admiration for its lofty wisdom in founding an Academy whose chief concern was to study the nature and the peculiar properties of the country, and to exploit them to the best advantage; throughout the length and breadth of Germany an eager attempt was being made to imitate England in her economic rôle; Holland realized that an important place in the republic should be given to the owners of land. Naturally, therefore, public interest in Europe was particularly aroused when Louis XV decided to put the workability of this new agricultural policy to the test of practical experiment. If it was to work satisfactorily, it was necessary that corn should fetch a good price; and in order that corn should fetch a good price, it was necessary to give free play to the law of supply and demand; a fair field and no favour. A declaration dated May, 1763, which was followed by a further notice in July of the following year, enacted that corn should circulate freely within the kingdom, and gave permission for its export abroad. Then unforeseen difficulties arose; there were miscalculations; and a crop failure, affecting several provinces, necessitated some reactionary measures: the Abbé Terray, who was appointed Comptroller-General in 1769, though he did not entirely revert to protection, greatly curtailed the scope of the measures recently adopted. He fell from power in 1774, and great hopes were aroused when it became known that Turgot had been appointed in his place. Turgot was a friend of Gournay's, and had served his apprenticeship to public life as governor of Limoges; he was a philosopher, and had the public weal at heart. He gave out in his statement of policy that, while he was in office, there would be no going bankrupt, no increase in taxation, no loans. Turgot was welcomed with enthusiasm. But that did not last long. He soon became a target for attack; his popularity declined; he was the man who robbed the people of their food. He was dismissed from office on the 12th May, 1776, and Physiocracy, although he had never wholly identified himself with it, shared in his downfall. This is not wholly to be ascribed to circumstances peculiar to France; 1776 was the year that witnessed the publication of Adam Smith's *An Inquiry into the Nature and Causes of the Wealth of Nations*. Adam Smith started from Nature, as did everyone else. Once more, man had only to act in accordance with the Code of Nature. But this time, the Code spoke a different language. Work was now the great thing, the ultimate source of wealth. Already you could hear the looms humming; the nucleus was the family no longer, but the workshop; already, the economic centre of gravity had shifted; the industrial era was at hand, and with it, fresh progress, and fresh ills, for all mankind.

III

DIDEROT

"WHEN we essay to delineate Rousseau by contrasting him with the philosophers of his time, there is one of them who provides us with something of a problem, and that is Diderot, Diderot the Nature-worshipper, the sensation-monger, the well-spring of enthusiasm. Roughly speaking, we should say that he was a sort of understudy to Rousseau, playing his part, and often indistinguishable from him."[1] However, the fact is that if we attempt a rigid classification and put things as it were into separate water-tight compartments, Reason in this one, Sentiment in that, and so on, Diderot is undoubtedly something of a puzzle. Nevertheless, to anyone setting out to trace the course of intellectual and spiritual evolution, Diderot is useful, indeed he is indispensable, for he typifies the precarious and temporary coalition of two forces which were soon to part company, and pursue their separate ways.

What an excellent companion he was! What a picturesque figure, swathed in the ample folds of his grey plush frock-coat, its pockets crammed with books; or in that ancient dressing-gown which still lives on for posterity in his description of it! So frank, so free, without a trace of pose or affectation. You never felt that you were not wanted, still less like someone trying to pump him against his will. Pump him! You just had to sit back in your chair and listen; listen as he unburdened himself of all that was in his mind, the whole day long. On one occasion Garat went to see him and could not manage to get a word in edgeways. Diderot started by laying down what the legislature ought to do, what laws they ought to pass, then he ran through five or six plots that he thought would make good plays, then he said what he thought about Tacitus and translations, acted a scene from Terence, sang a song he had made up impromptu at some

[1]Gustave Lanson, *Histoire de la littérature française*. *Jean-Jacques Rousseau*; Début.

supper-party or other and finally, having recited a comedy, told the youthful Garat that he was an admirable conversationalist and bade him a cordial farewell. Bubbling over with energy, his head was full of all sorts of ideas, plans, projects, dreams. Writing one day to Mme d'Épinay, Rousseau, who knew his Diderot, said, "I am undone if he arranges to come and see me. He'll plan to come over and over again, yet not once shall I see him. He's the kind of man you have to go and dig out by force if you want to make him do what he wants to do." On another occasion he says, "For my part, what I think about it is that the ante-meridian Diderot will always be wanting to go and see you, and that the post-meridian Diderot will never see you. You know how rheumatism gets hold of him sometimes; and when he's not soaring on his two great wings as high as the sun, he's to be found doubled-up on the ground, unable to budge an inch." Diderot of the morning, Diderot of the night; Diderot up in the skies, Diderot on all fours—yes, that is Diderot, that is the man right enough. And what a generous fellow he was, too! How prodigal with his belongings, his money, his time, his energies and even his writings. He was one of those rare men of letters who are not so desperately attached to their writings. He did not mind putting them on one side, leaving them in manuscript, letting his friends have them, or abandoning them to their fate, like apples fallen from a tree which had hundreds more to send after them. A little unpolished, a little plebeian, he would sample at a supper party bottle after bottle of champagne red or sparkling, of Canary sack, to say nothing of several kinds of liqueur, and after dinner he was not above letting go a button or two for comfort. And he was headstrong and no mistake, forever butting in and meddling with things that did not concern him. He was hail fellow well met with everyone and very free with his friendly embraces and slaps on the back; a little overpowering, but never mean, or petty or hypocritical, never envious, and even his faults had something half-attractive about them. So teeming was his brain, so prodigal was he of information and ideas, that, though you might come across profounder geniuses, you would never meet a richer one.

His riches were various and sharply contrasted, yet they got on peaceably enough together; he gave them house room without feeling the least uneasy because of their diversity. And why should he have felt uneasy? He was but too glad to behold this spate of incongruities flowing in upon him, only, in due time, to flow forth from him again.

Here is an epigraph, "My parents left behind them a son called 'Denis the Philosopher'; I am that son."

He is Denis the Philosopher. He is one of the brethren; he knows them all, for he has grouped them all around him, and with some of them he is on intimate terms, Grimm, Helvetius, d'Alembert, Condillac, the Baron d'Holbach; he admires Montesquieu, to whom he has solemnly rendered homage. He does not care much for Voltaire, their characters are too unlike, but Voltaire esteems him, because he considers him one of the leading members of the philosophic confraternity. For this reason he wanted to get him into the Academy. If the Atlas who bore the Encyclopaedia on his shoulders were to make one of the Forty, that body would be considerably strengthened. In Diderot's view, there could be no limit to what the philosopher might aspire to; the magistrate dispenses justice; the philosopher teachers him to distinguish justice from injustice. The soldier fights for his country; the philosopher makes him understand what his country really is. The priest calls on the people to pay honour to the gods; the philosopher explains to the priest what the gods are. The sovereign rules over all; the philosopher instructs him as to the origin and limitations of his power. If he had the management of things, he would adorn the brows of the philosopher with the civic crown, *ob servatos cives*.

He was responsible for the metaphor, to which we have already alluded, about knowledge being destined to dispel the tracts of darkness that still obscured the surface of the earth. To him, too, we owe that picture of Experiment in the guise of a giant, bringing down the pillars of the Temple of Error. He followed every successive step in the evolution of science, proceeding from geometry to mathematical physics, and from mathematical physics to natural history; he took a passionate interest in anatomy and physiology; he studied fibres and tissues, nerves, bones and the various organs; he had seen flesh palpitate and the blood circulate, he had taken away from the metaphysician the right to talk authoritatively about man, and conferred it on the doctor.

Examining his ideas about morality is more or less like retracing the dogmas and the tentative theories of the philosophers: the taste for examining moral problems; moral science; rational morality; morality which connects the interests of the individual with the interests of the race. On the other hand, there was the disappointment at the failure to arrive at any definite moral code; the feeling that morality is a relative matter; the uncomfortable suspicion that the morality which was suitable to the scholar, the intellectual, was not equally adapted to the multitude; and, above all, that growing determinism which denied that there was, or could be, any such thing as morality at all. Jacques the Fatalist's master would have been only too pleased to regard himself as a free agent; but the arguments that Jacques the Fatalist threw into the scales tipped the balance towards the negative; we are what the general order of things and our own particular organization compel us to be. We are powerless to alter the laws which condition our lives; therefore, if freedom is a word devoid of meaning, as philosophically speaking it is, nothing that we do is deserving either of praise or blame, there is no such thing as vice or virtue, and nothing which calls for reward or punishment.

And that is the same Diderot who raised his voice in denunciation of tyrants; who declared that man possessed an indisputable right to political freedom; that the members of the State voluntarily dispossessed themselves of a portion of their liberty in order to entrust it to a power which exercised its authority solely by delegation; a power safeguarding security and property; the same Diderot who, in the matter of the training of the young, was all for taking education out of the hands of the regular clergy and making it a government responsibility, at once obligatory and non-clerical; a system in which Latin should give place to modern languages; in which teachers should pay careful attention to the stages in the development of the child's understanding, beginning with what was quite simple, and proceeding by degrees to the more complex; the kind of education which should aim at producing men of science, agriculturists, economists, in a word the sort of men who would be capable of rendering useful service to the State; a system of education in which the useful arts, its special care, should occupy the place of honour. It was that same Diderot, eager to know everything, who, like everyone else, had sought to discover the basic principle of the fine arts. He had read Plato and St. Augustine, Shaftesbury and Hutcheson, the Abbé Le Batteux and Père André, Wolff and Hagedorn, everyone in fact that was readable and a good few that were not. After learning so many conflicting ideas, he found himself in some perplexity. Finally he decided to define Beauty in the following terms. "I apply the term beautiful in respect of the external world to whatever contains within itself something that awakens in my understanding the idea of relationship, of association; and, in respect of myself, anything which awakens that idea"; association being "an operation of the understanding which considers either a being or a quality in so far as it implies the existence of another being or another quality." "Regard Beauty as a matter concerning the perception of relations, and you will have the history of its progress from the birth of the world down to the present day."

That Diderot did not make anti-clericalism the dominant business of his life; all the same, he was one of Christ's most violent accusers in the great trial. To begin with he professed Deism, but he soon got beyond that. If you don't believe in the gods, why banish them to the intermundane spaces? Better deny them outright. And that is what he did. He turned atheist. He believed, as did Naigeon, who followed him as a dog follows its master, that all would be peace and happiness on earth if only the idea of God could be obliterated. Towards God he was filled with wrath, bitterness and rage; witness his story about the misanthropist who hid himself in a cave and meditated long and deeply as to how he should take vengeance on the human race. At length he came out of his cave shouting loudly, God! God! "His voice resounded from pole to pole, and behold, men fell to quarrelling, hating and cutting one another's throats. And they've been doing the same thing ever since that abominable name was pronounced, and they will go on doing it till the process of the ages is accomplished." Materialist as he was, he believed in the atoms of Epicurus and Lucretius, assigning to them, however, the sort of dim sensibility and intelligence with which Maupertuis had invested them; and he treated himself to the pleasure of looking on at the birth and destruction of worlds.

If we were to stop short at this aspect of his character, he would somehow contrive to protest, even from the depths of the realm of shadows. When Van Loo painted his portrait, he was not pleased with it. Van Loo had only brought out one physiognomy, one kind of expression, whereas, said Diderot, "I had a hundred different ones a day, according to the mood that was on me. I was serene, sad, dreamy, tender, violent, passionate, eager. The outward signs of my many and varying states of mind chased one another so rapidly across my face that the painter's eye caught a different one from moment to moment, and never got me aright." So, too, with his mind; he was Pantophilus, the universal lover. What he liked best for himself was the impromptu effusion, and, next to that, dialogue, where one voice affirms and the other denies; Himself and The Other. Not to put too fine a point on it, let us say that there was always something of Himself in the Other and something of the Other in Himself. It was always a case of the Neveu de Rameau and his Interlocutor. Not that he was hesitant, or undecided, or like that personage Manzoni was later on to describe, the man who was always against everything, whatever it was. In point of fact he took up a very definite stand, but so all-embracing was his intellectual outlook that he always kept a soft spot in his heart for things his reason had told him to abandon. It was well said that into the plain solid truth which so many of his contemporaries looked upon as fixed and stable he imported the mobility of life and so made truth something that was mobile too. His mind, acting on the various data that came before it, deprived them of their stability so that he was like some magical Master of the Ceremonies making his company continually assume whatever forms he might for the moment desire. That is the key to all the various Diderots that inhabited a single body. But now let us turn from the man who by means of the Encyclopaedia heralded in the age of enlightenment and contemplate him who by the influence he undoubtedly exerted over the pioneers of the *Sturm und Drang*, proved to be himself one of the pioneers of romanticism in Europe.

Here is another epigraph: "If Nature ever made a sensitive soul, that soul, and you know it, is mine."

And first of all the soul imaginative. A ceaseless outpouring of rough sketches, themes, expansions, alluring digressions, a host of works in one. A full-blooded, vital force that looked on reality as a poorish thing compared with what that force itself could produce. Comfortably installed in a corner of his habitation, the imaginative man piled up dream upon dream. No need for him to travel in order to make discoveries; why come down from the garret to the cellar, and mount up again from the cellar to the garret, when you can dream so well sitting in the same armchair? If it so happens that he does accept an invitation to the country, he goes with a romantic outfit in which some subtle *nuances* are already packed. From his window at Le Grandval he descries the little wood which weather-fends the dwelling against the northern blast, the little brook that flows by brambles and reeds, by mossy banks and pebbly beaches, and the view strikes him as "picturesque and wild". Of a night he loves to lie in his bed and listen to the billowing wind, to the rain lashing the eaves, to the storm that makes the branches loud, and to the ceaseless undertone that sounds like a never-ending diapason through it all. Save for Langres and Bourbonne, that was about the limit of his wanderings, until, as an old man and despite his vows, he went to Russia. All the same he contributed, and that mightily, to bringing the beauties of Nature into the stock of human acquisitions. Take pictures: he will describe so vividly the landscapes he has seen at the Salons, rocks, precipices, ruins, sunsets, moonlight, and, in particular, shipwrecks, that the privileged few who read him are in the end quite carried away by his magic. Who was it that gave these pieces of advice to the artist? "Don't leave your studio, unless it be to consult Nature. Live with her in the open fields. Go and gaze at the sunrise and the sunset, see the sky as it adorns itself with coloured clouds. Go and walk in the meadows among the flocks and herds. See the blades of grass all glistening with drops of dew."[1] It was Diderot. Who was it told poetry the way it should go, saying, "Poetry requires something of the vast, the uncouth, the untamed"?[2] That, too, was Diderot. His heart is in a ferment. He is thrilled he knows not why; nor wherefore he is sad, nor wherefore he rejoices. His whole being is stirred, and tears betray the intensity

[1] *Salon de* 1765. Lauterbourg.

[2] *De la poésie dramatique,* XVIII, *Des Mœurs.*

of his emotion. Diderot gives his daughter in marriage, and then sheds tears of grief at losing her; he sees that she is happy, and behold he weeps for love of her; his thoughts turn to the death of his parents and he weeps tears of hopeless grief. Diderot will fly into such a rage that he will tear his hair, and strike his head against the wall—"The worst of it is I can never put myself into such a rage as to quiet my entrails even for a few days on end." Diderot never continues in the peaceful state that comes of a contented mind; his temperature is always above normal; he burns with feverish sensibility.

So far from being ashamed of itself, that sensibility glories in its transports—if there is someone that does not share them, that "someone" is greatly to be pitied. It keeps bursting out into "O my friend!" "O my Sophie!" for the living; for the dead, "O Seneca!" It scolds, it hustles, it frets. It strikes attitudes, it piles on the pathetic, it surveys itself in the glass, and listens to itself approvingly. It is quite individual, unique; and it is fatal. It overdoes the dramatic, and becomes—just melodrama.

Such faculties as those, given free play, differentiate him from his friends; he is as different from d'Alembert, for example, as fire is from ice. They inspire him, atheist though he be, with words of praise for the Catholic religion. Who, he asks, witnessing the Good Friday devotions, or looking on at a Corpus Christi procession, seeing the majesty of it, listening to the chanting of the priests and the responses of the crowd, impressed by the sombre magnificence and solemnity which always accompany religious ceremonial, who could help protesting at those "absurd rigorists" who remain unmoved? Thus it happened that the enemy of Christianity associated himself, for the nonce, with those apologists who seek to show that religion is true because it is touching. A materialist, he firmly believed in the supremacy of the mind, the spirit; a determinist, he would not admit, when he dwelt on his love for Sophie Volland, that it had any origin other than his own personal and independent choice; he was furious when Naigeon ascribed it to the influence of a passing comet, and he chafed angrily against a philosophy which his heart could not but force him to deny. He was a tyrant-hater, but he had a tremendous enthusiasm for Catherine of Russia. Professing a moral code based on self-interest, the code he practised was wholly one of sentiment; he made much of a maxim already regrettably illustrated by the Abbé Prévost, the motto that said everything is permitted to a man provided he has a kind heart. A professed aesthete, he made Beauty something to be accounted for by the reason; yet in spite of all his pet theories about government, utility, morality, philosophy, the ideal and many another besides, he finished up as the champion of sincerity as opposed to artifice, upholding the "inward spirit" of the artist against the bondage of convention, and proclaiming the emotional value of the arts. "Be moved", he said when others said, "Be sensible". At the same time, he extolled the emotional value of the stage. O unfeeling onlooker, why did you come to the theatre, if not to weep? And he revelled in tears; he wept as he read about the woes of Pamela and Clarissa, and, across the sundering distance, he embraced Richardson, all bathed in tears.

Everything yields to analysis; or would do if our psychological life were not animated by tiny dim perceptions so minute that they elude the analyst. Everything we do should be guided by method; if, that is to say, method were not a cold and clumsy process, infinitely inferior to the spirit of invention which lives and moves and stirs in a manner all its own; compared with genius, method was like the call of the cuckoo compared with the song of the nightingale. And how delightful to go and launch out on a boundless sea of hypotheses, of majestic systems which, may be, were not sound, but were at all events seductive. With that sensibility of his, he endowed the infinitely small, the indivisible particles of matter; he sent it heavenward as far as to the stars. By means of it he counted on setting death itself at defiance. The marble tomb which had inurned the bodies of two lovers, would crumble into dust and mingle with the soil around it; the soil would feed the cells of the plants, and the plants the cells of living beings, and two of these might one day remember and recognize each other again. His philosophic speculations took a lyrical tone:

The first vows exchanged by two beings of flesh and blood were made at the foot of a rock which was crumbling into dust. To bear witness to their constancy, they called aloud to a heaven whose aspect was ceaselessly changing; all was evanescent, all was changing, within them and around them, and they deemed that their hearts were immune from vicissitude.[1]

[1] *Jacques le Fataliste,* Œuvres, tome VI, p. 117.

The only thing which that poetic effusion lacks is metre, and with that Alfred de Musset supplies it in his *Souvenir*:

> Oui, les premiers baisers, oui les premiers serments
> Que deux êtres mortels échangèrent sur terre,
> Ce fut au pied d'un arbre effeuillé par les vents,
> Et sur un roc en poussière.
> Ils prirent à témoin de leur joie éphémère
> Un ciel toujours voilé qui change à tout moment,
> Et des astres sans nom que leur propre lumière
> Dévore incessamment. . . .[1]

If we were trying to collect together the various meanings we have seen gathering round the word Nature, we should find a good many, if not all, in Diderot.

For him, according to the moment, the day, the mood, the caprice, the train of thought, the theory, the system, whatever happened to be uppermost at the particular time, Nature was the aggregate of all the phenomena external to ourselves; and our understanding is the little square upon which the image of it comes to be depicted. It is all that is created; men ought to erect a mighty temple to Nature, in which specimens of all the animals and all the plants in existence should be shown. Nature is benevolent and full of kindnesses; sometimes she is pleased to plant a sensitive soul and a tender heart in a man of the humblest station. Nature is an artist; she made the sky blue, and of her green she wove the earth's Spring mantle; in our art we imitate the cunning with which she has dissembled the scheme of her effects. Nature knows her business; she never produces anything that has not some part to play, no evil without its remedy, and in particular no form of government in which some limits are not set to the sufferings of the people. Nature is artful; of set purpose she made love and hate terrible, because her aim is the reproduction and conservation of the species; the force of the human passions is always proportioned to that end. Nature busies herself with the minutest details;

[1]Yes the first time two mortals exchanged kisses and vows on earth was at the foot of a tree despoiled of its leaves by the winds and on a rock crumbling into dust.
They called to bear witness to their transient joy a heaven for ever veiled and changing every moment and nameless stars which their own light was ceaselessly devouring.

she prepares the cellular tissue, she fabricates membranes, aided in that, it is true, by sickness and chance. Nature is just and punishes offences against society; you live a life of debauchery, you will have the dropsy.

Nature is indifferent; provided the race goes on, she is satisfied; she cares nothing for good or evil. And Nature is capricious; the race is made up of individuals, but of individuals she recks nothing. Nature works by fits and starts; sometimes she will remain for an age in a sort of torpor, as though exhausted; sometimes she bestirs herself to make great men. Nature is capable of strange blunders and does not always give good counsel in time of danger. Nature is treacherous; beware of always yielding to her lure. She is cruel, and exterminates those whose organism accords ill with the laws of the universe. She is the unrelenting foe of man and pursues him from the day of his birth. Man, if he would survive, must fight against her in company with other men, his brothers. She is immoral; she is always trying to benefit herself at the expense of others. She is incoherent; and she is blind. She does not *will* anything; she simply *is*. And is that strictly true? A multiplicity and concatenation of various contingencies, she has no intrinsic *raison d'être*. Can our senses take cognizance of her? Some of the causes of sensible phenomena are outside the range of our senses. . . .

However, among all these different meanings, and we do not claim to have exhausted the list, there is one that seems to preponderate in his mind—Nature is the hidden instinct which inspires the individual, and gives him his great and privileged position. Were it not for this instinct, there would be no strong characters, no original types, no geniuses. Without it we should just be borne along, with everything else that is, on the great ever-flowing stream. For we go our way, never getting any clear idea of the place we occupy, or the limits of time assigned to us; we flit past like so many May-flies; the world is a composite whole perpetually tending to its own destruction, a swift succession of beings that follow closely one upon another, press hard on one another's heels, and disappear; but for all that, the individual obtains, by the intensity of his powers, what time denies him. Save for this instinct we should be, each one of us, but a slave in a drove of slaves. It is open to the individual to create a compromise between the spontaneous and the studied, between the untutored and the corrupt; he may quite well decide to build himself a dwelling mid-way between the cot and the castle; but just as he begins to think about contenting himself with this compromise, he gives a shout and scuttles away:

> L'enfant de la nature abhorre l'esclavage;
> Implacable ennemi de toute autorité,
> Il s'indigne du joug; la contrainte l'outrage;
> Liberté, c'est son Voeu; son cri, c'est Liberté.
> Au mépris des liens de la société,
> Il réclame en secret son antique apanage.
> Des mœurs ou grimaces d'usage
> Ont beau servir de voile à sa férocité;
> Une hypocrite urbanité,
> Les souplesses d'un tigre enchainé dans sa cage,
> Ne trompent point l'oeil du sage;
> Et dans les murs de la cité,
> Il reconnaît l'homme sauvage
> S'agitant dans les fers dont il est garrotté.[1]

Thus does the eleutheromaniac, the fanatic of freedom, behold himself beneath the guise of the citizen. He is thrilled as he reads the account that Bougainville gives of his sojourn in the happy isle where his vessels came to anchor; he feels a stirring in that residue of the wild, the untamed, that lingers far down in the depths of his soul. He would fain be as that Tahitian who delights in all the joys of primitive existence. But he realizes that that is impossible, and so he finds himself in conflict, not only with society, but with himself, the combat which rends the romantic's heart asunder. "Would you like to hear an epitome of almost all our troubles? Well, this is it. There once existed a natural man, child of nature. Into this natural man was introduced an artificial man; and there started within

[1]The child of Nature abhors slavery; implacable foe of all authority, he rages at the yoke, constraint infuriates him. Liberty is his longing, Liberty his cry. Scorning the bonds of society he secretly lays claim to his ancient appanage. The manners and make customary make-believe faces are powerless to hide his ferocity; a sham urbanity, the graceful movements of a tiger shut up in its cage do not deceive the wise man's eye; and in the city walls he recognizes the man of the wilds chafing at the fetters by which he is bound. *Les Eleuthéromanes*, 1772.

the cave a civil war which went on for life. Sometimes the natural man gets the better, sometimes he is floored by the moral and artificial man; in either case the unhappy monster is pulled about, pinioned, tortured, broken on the wheel. Forever moaning, forever woebegone, whether because some hollow expectation of glory transports and intoxicates him, or because some false idea of shame hampers him, and casts him down."[1]

When Rousseau came to visit Diderot, while he was a prisoner in the castle of Vincennes, he told him about the subject set for competition by the Dijon Academy, *Has progress in the sciences and the arts contributed to the corruption or to the purification of morals?* Did Diderot, inventive man, advise him to run counter to received opinion and thus start him on the career which was in due time to lead him to upset the whole psychology of Europe? Of course we shall never know exactly what took place that day, but some such intervention on his part is within the range of possibility. From that moment it was all over with me, said Jean Jacques. From that moment a new attitude towards life came into being.

[1] *Supplément au voyage de Bougainville, ou Dialogue entre A et B.* Written in 1772. *Œuvres,* tome II, p. 246.

BOOK III

I

THE VARIOUS DEISMS: BOLINGBROKE AND POPE

SO the philosophers of the enlightened school did not resolve the problems which arose from their recourse to Nature, and forces opposed to the goddess of Reason were let loose beneath their eyes, in their very midst, and, occasionally, at their invitation. We now come to what was probably the most serious of the divergences which brought about the disintegration of their doctrine, concerning as it does the relations between human and divine. Religion, *a* religion, there was still to be, and Atheism was the enemy. But can you have a religion without dogma? A religion without a Church? If religion is something that binds, can there be such a thing as a religion which does not bind? "An important question to settle is whether this part of the army constitutes a corps. For here there are no churches, no altars, no sacrifices, no guides. There is no common standard to follow, no general regulations to obey; the host is split up into more or less numerous bands, each of them jealous of its independence."[1] The fact of the matter is, that instead of the unity it was hoped to attain, what really resulted was dispersal, isolation, and hopeless divergences regarding that simple affirmation, I believe in God: Well, but in what sort of a God *do* you believe? When one comes to look closely into the matter, it is clear that there was not one deism, but several, all different, all mutually opposed, and even at daggers drawn with one another. Pope's deism is not Voltaire's, and Voltaire's was worlds away from Lessing's. That being so, it was obviously all over with unity of belief.

Here is a portrait. A libertine in his young days, a cynic; never troubling to conceal his vices, merely remarking that he hoped they would be made up for by his virtues; a

[1]Diderot, *La Promenade du sceptique*, 1747.

great lady-killer and a lover of the sex, retaining a fondness for them even after he had settled down, giving himself the airs of a celebrated coquette; an English peer, fully aware of what his rank required of him, namely sumptuous living, lavish expenditure, much liberality, mansions, gardens, invitations, receptions, friends and a large acquaintance; an affability which did not exclude a touch of *hauteur*, just enough to keep people in their place; a politician of some weight, since he had been a long time in office, and, when he fell from it, finding himself perhaps in a still more advantageous position as leader of the Opposition. He was well acquainted with the art of keeping a party together, and he knew with accuracy the price of a conscience, and this perhaps, as well as a natural inclination, accounted for the hardly perceptible disdain he entertained for humanity in general, who usually resembled the specimens he had commanded, or purchased; a cultivated mind, particularly on the surface; an intelligence as swift as it was brilliant; a memory that enabled him to make apt use of what he had read, and he had read a lot. An excellent public speaker, a wonderful talker, too, it would seem; we wish we could have heard him, for his books are a trifle disappointing; even in his lifetime, people were greatly carried away at a first reading, but somewhat less so at the second. As for his writings, he did not so much publish them as let them fall from him, and his output consisted of letters, essays, brochures, rather than of books complete in themselves. A citizen of the world, he had turned two prolonged periods of exile to account by making France his second home, and he was as much at ease in French as he was in his mother-tongue. He was a philosopher, but one who regarded his rule of life as better adapted to the privileged few than to the general run, and he himself did not always practise what he preached. He let his ideas have full rein, remembering, however, that as a Tory and the soul of the Conservative Party, there were some things that he ought to conserve. Such was Henry St. John, now, by the grace of Queen Anne, Viscount Bolingbroke.

And here is another character, a poet. As a child, the only companions he had known were the poets, English, French, Italian, Latin and Greek; in his 'teens he was always writing verse, nothing but verse, and a little later on, when he was a young man, his poems passed from hand to hand, rousing murmurs of admiration. A prodigy this, and nothing less, and when he was no more than three-and-twenty he had won the foremost place among the writers of his day. The gods had not endowed him with a great profundity of ideas, nor with a strikingly creative imagination; what they *had* given him was a fine sense of rhythm and harmony. He was of a morbidly sensitive nature, uneasy, anxious, and, if the wind blew a little, he took it for a storm, and a storm directed against himself. Caresses even, he would take for scratches. If someone paid him a compliment, he would fancy there was mischief at the back of it. His life, which was uneventful and, to outward view, entirely happy, was a perpetual torment. Continually taking offence, he gave offence in return, and he was not backward in doing so, often going out of his way to hurt people's feelings; then he would say how unjustly he was treated. His parents were Papists and he, a poor sickly-looking, misshapen creature, was a Papist himself, and he had not been to any of the recognized schools. Not the eulogies that were showered on him, nor success, nor riches availed to efface the memory of his shy and lonely childhood. Patronized and made much of by the great, though he was but the son of a draper, he vented his bitterness on other men of letters. He said they were a lot of criminals whose jealousy poisoned every success he gained. He did his utmost to wound them to the quick, that being what he imagined they wanted to do to him. He called enemies, those who *were* his enemies, those who might have been, or who might have one day become his enemies, and those who never said anything about him at all. Ah! they said nothing. That meant they were persecuting him by their silence!

M. de Silhouette, one of his French translators, speaks of "M. Pope, the greatest poet in England, and one of the finest geniuses that have ever been".

Early in his career he had got to know Bolingbroke; the acquaintance was renewed and strengthened when the latter, on returning from France, took up his residence at Dawley in Middlesex. Twickenham, where Pope lived, was not far off, and they had been on neighbourly terms. The poet lacked but one thing; he had never taken up philosophy; this was a singular and almost unpardonable omission. Anyone who did not philosophize in verse was not doing his duty. Bolingbroke got him to realize this, and became his instructor, responding to his almost desperate appeal:

> Come then, my friend! my Genius! Come along!
> O master of the poet, and the song!

His lordship and the writer take their walks in the great park intersected by trim alley-ways. Bolingbroke, stouter than he was in his young days, his features, later on to be ravaged by cancer, showing traces of dissipation and hard work; Pope, a shivering, frail and ailing figure, listens submissively to his lesson. And this is the lesson: Let your Muse continue her incomparable songs, but let her no longer be content with diverting and amusing men; let her instruct and reform them. A task more worthy of her must now be undertaken. Many books have I consulted; the schoolmen, children of the dark ages, birds of the night; St. Thomas, that presumptuous one, that mad-brained metaphysician; Leibniz, one of the vainest and most chimerical of minds that were ever included in the ranks of thinking men; and many another of every sort and kind; Plato, whose mistake it was to shadow forth on the walls of the cavern the phantoms of ideas; Socrates, another visionary; the Stoics, who were too hard; the Epicureans, who were too soft. Still, I never encountered the truth.

So, I descended within the depths of my own being, and there I found waiting for me a surer guide than any of those will-o'-the-wisps I had hitherto so thoughtlessly followed. I divested myself of all derivative notions, which it is a waste of time to consider, and went down to plain bed-rock principles; I gave ear to my reason. Is it not better to put our reason once for all in the place of men who have proved their inability to judge for us? Let us judge for ourselves. . . . Real knowledge is no inexplicable effect of some supernatural revelation; science, too, if it is to be real, must come from below, not from above; it must be human, not divine. At this point Bolingbroke enunciates a conclusive statement: Truth of existence is truth of knowledge. The fact, and nothing but the fact; that alone commands knowledge, and leads us onward to truth.

Let us be quite clear about this reason, which inward

observation shows us to be there. So feeble and limited is it that it does not permit us to explore the transcendental. Let us constantly proclaim this weakness and limitation, when we become aware of them, for all our errors, all our misfortunes arise from our fancying we can reach things beyond our capacity. If our species were to last on for thousands of generations, and if, during all that time, men went on with their enquiries, they would still be unable to penetrate the secret of things; the substance, the essence would still be unattainable, and first causes still beyond our ken. Nay, if the whole human race were doomed to come to an end, man would disappear from the face of the globe knowing not the why nor the wherefore of the world, of life, of the bodily form he had indued. Reason, as an instrument of intellectual activity, is our very good friend; when it attempts to reach out and grasp the supernatural, it is the very fountainhead of error. Reason is adapted to deal with whatever is accessible to it, whatever is within its scope, but with nothing else.

It follows that if our knowledge is real knowledge, it must be superficial. It cannot tell us what God is, but it can tell us that God exists. It, in fact, discerns a natural law whose workings are manifested both outside our minds and within them. Another dictum of his, no less decisive, no less pregnant was this: Nature and truth are the same everywhere, and reason shows them everywhere alike. Reason proves to us that there is an order in the facts, and this order is the guarantee of truth; it is also the guarantee of God's existence. We cannot conceive an orderly creation apart from a mind that willed such an order. This consideration should answer the needs of our moral being. It leads us, that is to say, to render to God the respect, the gratitude which we owe to him; in conformity alike with our inward promptings and with our own interests, it encourages us to treat others as we should wish others to treat us.

This conviction Bolingbroke had retained from his early days; but during his exile he had matured it somewhat. Though not formally a believer, he had declined the sort of atheism which a learned Frenchman, Lévesque de Pouilly, invited him to embrace. He had brought himself to decide on a middle-of-the-road philosophy, and that philosophy it was that Pope was now to propagate.

The first Epistle of the *Essay on Man* appeared in February, 1733; the second and third followed in the course of the same year. They came out anonymously, for Pope was not sure of success. The fourth Epistle, which did bear his name, came out in January, 1734.

It was a declaration of faith, and a startling one. For the first time in its career, deism became poetry; it emerged from the study of the philosopher, and betook itself to the multitude; and it was adorned with beauty. The *Essay on Man* was so pure in language and diction that England acknowledged it a masterpiece. Other countries welcomed it as well, and set about translating it. The process had begun, and there was no stopping it. When the first renderings had appeared, one in verse and one in prose, along came an imitation, a paraphrase; then another interpreter would appear to try his hand at the same adventure. In 1762 a volume came out with the poem translated into several languages, and this volume was many times reprinted, a piece of rare good fortune. The popularity of the *Essay on Man* lasted well on to the end of the century, and beyond that.

It was the declaration of faith of the new religion; public opinion was under no misapprehension about that. As early as 1737, a Lausanne pastor, who was in no small repute in his own country and outside it, Jean Pierre de Crousaz, devoted a whole work to refuting it. The year after he followed this up with another attack, this time levelled against one of the French translators of the book, the Abbé du Resnel; Pope—this was his line—was at fault in sharing the optimism of Leibniz; Pope had endorsed the doctrine of fatalism; Pope—though he may not have been completely aware of it—had ranged himself with the ungodly. The impetuous Warburton, who, to start with, had rather manhandled his compatriot, no sooner saw him attacked than he burst out into fire and fury, defended him with might and main, and fiercely refuted the refutations of de Crousaz.

Poor Louis Racine, heir to a name too great for him, was extraordinarily well-intentioned; the only thing he lacked was genius. He, a Christian to the backbone, saw how unbelief was growing, and tried to stem the tide. He went for his inspiration to Bossuet and Pascal; he expounded the doctrine of grace in verse; in verse he defended the Faith. In a poem entitled *La Religion*, which appeared in 1742, he picked out a few of the prime movers, denounced the *Essay on Man*, and went so far as to honour Pope by devoting two Epistles to him. Not, as he explained to J. B. Rousseau, who wrote him approvingly from Holland, that he had the good fortune to be able to read Pope, England's most celebrated poet, in the original; he did not claim to be attacking his real sentiments, about which he was not certain, but he *was* attacking the sentiments which had become current since his *Essay*, whether properly understood or not, had been before the public. Louis Racine's verses were not first-rate; that did not prevent them from being well received. They ran into more than one edition and were even translated. The Chevalier de Ramsay, one of Fénelon's converts, took up the cudgels on behalf of "the English Homer". Pope's aim, according to him, was to show that, starting with a degraded Nature, everything is proportioned, in weight, measure and harmony to the state of a fallen being, who suffers, who deserves to suffer, and cannot be restored. The Abbé J. B. Gaultier, a Jansenist, was against Pope, whom he dubbed a disciple of Spinoza; Père Tournemine was in favour of the *Essay*, the only people to be hurt by it being those corrupt minds that turn everything to poison. In short, there was a lively set-to, and it went on for a long time.

Pope suffered, as well he might. Bewildered by all the noise going on about him, he thanked Warburton very warmly for defending him, begged Ramsay to do what he could, and wrote to Louis Racine to explain matters. His principles, he assured him, were diametrically opposed to Spinoza's, and even to Leibniz; indeed he regarded them as being quite in conformity with what M. Pascal and the Archbishop of Cambrai would have held about the matter. He went farther; to give a conspicuous proof of the soundness of his ideas, he published a hymn which he entitled, *The Universal Prayer* (1738). The mischief-makers would see quite plainly that he was faithful to the spirit of the Gospel.

But his attempt to smoothe things over met with scant success. The God he invoked, though he was the Father of all things and had existed before the Creation, was none the less He whom saints, savages and sages all worshipped indiscriminately;

Father of all! in every age
In every clime adored,
By Saints, by Savage, and by Sage
Jehova, Jove, or Lord!

The result was that he only added fuel to the fire. They called his hymn the deist's Prayer.

A declaration of faith it was, and a prayer. Virtually all Bolingbroke's ideas were to be found in it; but how different it was as a whole, if only in its tone! And how faltering, how perplexed was the line of thought! The *Essay on Man* still moves us, in spite of changes in taste. It moves us because we become aware of a tremulous sensibility, as of a spirit, which the dictates of reason do not wholly avail to satisfy. No sooner does it profess itself convinced, than it must needs be convinced anew. Pope is engaged with an interlocutor whom he feels he must win over at any price, an interlocutor whom he questions sharply, whom he scolds and grumbles at, and with whom at times he gets thoroughly angry, so stubborn and obstinate he seems to be. This adversary never utters a word, yet we feel his presence all the time; this adversary is none other than the poet himself, none other than that part of his conscience which holds back, or keeps out of the way. There is something moving about these contradictions, about that untimely way of giving in, of throwing up his hand and so disturbing a security, a certainty, constantly proclaimed, but never finally grasped. His formulas, often repeated, are absolute in their clarity; in a few lines, sometimes in a single line, they contain axioms which could not have been expressed with greater force and harmony. There is not perhaps in the whole world any poetry of the didactic order which imprints itself more readily on the memory. Man must accept his lot; man should be contented, man occupies his due place in the universe; man must admit the existence of an intelligence infinitely superior to his own, an intelligence which knows thoroughly what it knows, and does thoroughly what it does; man must believe in the existence of a Supreme Being, who could not have planned the world otherwise than for the general good; each one of these articles of his teaching finds its expression in a decisive maxim. This firmness of touch in the outward form of the thing contrasts strangely with all those vacillations, hesitations, doubts, appeals and rejections.

Deism as poetry; deism still in the nebulous state. It had been Pope's intention "to steer a middle course between the extremes of seemingly opposite doctrines, and, borrowing from them all, to devise a system of morality which should be temperate without being inconsistent, and brief without being incomplete". And what he had succeeded in producing was a medley of inconsistencies. The reader discerned in him, and rightly, Paganism, Pantheism, Fatalism and a persistent strain of Catholicism; for he spoke of a state of nature, a perfectly happy state, which had become corrupted, thus opening the door to belief in the doctrine of original sin. "The realization of anarchy," Thomas de Quincey was to call it; and Taine, "An amalgam of warring philosophies", while Louis Cazamian says "His most powerful philosophical dissertation, the *Essay on Man*, is made up of a quantity of commonplaces, warmed up afresh and tricked out with up-to-date ideas.

A deism with alloys; a deism in which a number of psychological data still survived, though they were the very things it was desired to put beyond the pale; an attempt to achieve a rational demonstration; and an acceptance of the element of mystery.

II

DEISMS: VOLTAIRE

IF he had never existed, would the character of the century have been the same?

He bestowed on deism his ineffaceable imprint. He it was who fashioned it anew; or, if another metaphor be preferred, it was he who filtered the brew. When his work was done, it was a pure crystalline liquor that remained. To see how true that is, let us read over again the book that was one of the manuals of English deism. *The Religion of Nature Delineated*, by William Wollaston, which was published in 1722. The book earned a fortune in the original and in translation. Compared with the Voltairean concentration, it reads like so much windy verbiage. Instead of Wollaston's lengthy dissertations, here we have a few rapid demonstrations, a few adroit expositions, all so clear that a child might grasp them; here we have imperious, authoritative pronouncements that come upon one with the force of law.

He it was who insisted on argument from final causes; it was through him that man was grateful to the Supreme Being, who, not content with assigning him his just place, had also bestowed on him the gift of pleasure:

> Mortels, venez à lui, mais par reconnaissance;
> La nature, attentive à remplir nos désirs,
> Vous appelle à ce Dieu par la voix des plaisirs.
> Nul encor n'a chanté sa bonté tout entière;
> Par le seul mouvement il conduit la matière:
> Mais c'est par le plaisir qu'il conduit les humains.[1]

[1]Mortals, come to him, but come in gratitude; Nature, punctual in fulfilling our desires, calls you to this God with the voice of pleasures. No one yet hath sung of all his goodness. Matter he leads by mere mechanical means, but men and women by the power of pleasure. *Cinquième Discours sur l'Homme*, 1739.

He it was who indicated in precise terms where we were to stop: believe in God, yes; but refuse to talk about his nature, refuse to speak about how he goes to work. A cricket finding himself in the presence of an imperial palace recognizes that the edifice is the work of some being more powerful than a cricket, but he is not such a fool as to dogmatize about the said being.[1] Let us imitate the wisdom of the cricket.

> Soit qu'un être inconnu, par lui seul existant
> Ait tiré depuis peu l'univers du néant;
> Soit qu'il ait arrangé la matière éternelle,
> Qu'elle nage en son sein, ou qu'il règne loin d'elle;
> Que l'âme, ce flambeau si souvent ténébreux,
> Ou soit un de nos sens, ou subsiste sans eux,
> Vous êtes sous la main de cet Être invisible. . . .[2]

So we are not to speculate about the soul; what do I know of it? Or about the Beyond: what do I know of it? Whenever we try to affirm a thing, we come up against the same impossibility, recognized as a preliminary fact. It was he who drew up the Creed of the doctrine. A single page suffices for it; see *Dictionnaire Philosophique*, under *Théiste*:

> *The theist is a man firmly persuaded of the existence of a Supreme Being as good as he is powerful, who made all beings extended, vegetative, sentient, thinking; who perpetuates their species, punishes their crimes without cruelty, and rewards their virtuous deeds with kindness.*
>
> *The theist does not know how God punishes, how he shows favour, how he pardons; for he is not so foolhardy as to flatter himself that he knows how God does things; yet he knows that God does act, and that he is just. The difficulties connected with the idea of Providence do not shake his faith, because they are only great difficulties, and are not in the nature of proofs; he is subject to this Providence, although he only perceives some of its effects and*

[1] Voltaire, *Catéchisme chinois*. In *Dictionnaire philosophique,* 1764.

[2] Whether a being unknown, and self-existent drew a little while since the universe out of chaos, whether he arranged eternal matter, whether it floats in his bosom, or whether he reigns remote from it, whether the soul, that torch so often dim be one of our senses or whether it subsists apart from them, you are under the hand of that Invisible Being.

external manifestations; and judging of the things he does not see by the things that he does, he deems that this Providence extends to all places and to all ages.

United on this principle with the rest of the Universe, he embraces none of the sects, all of which contradict one another. His religion is the oldest and the most widespread, for the simple worship of a God preceded all the systems in the world. He speaks a language which all peoples understand, whereas they do not understand one another. He has brothers from Peking to Cayenne, and he counts all wise men as his brothers. He holds that religion consists neither in the opinions advanced by some unintelligible school of metaphysics, nor in vain show, but in worship and justice. Do what is right, that is his religion; submit to God, that is his doctrine. The Mahometan cries to him, "Take heed to thyself, if thou makest not the pilgrimage to Mecca!" "Woe betide thee," says some monk to him "if thou journey not to Our Lady of Loretto!" He laughs at Loretto and Mecca; but he succours the poor and protects the oppressed.

He it was who gave such a valuable lift to deism by supplying it with illustrations. Tell people that you will have nothing to do with anthropomorphism in any shape or form, and you will stand a poor chance of being understood by the majority of your readers. But you will excite their amusement if you write in this vein: "I really must tell you about something that happened to me a little while back. I had just had a little place put up at the bottom of the garden, and I heard a mole talking about it with a cockchafer. 'That's a fine building', said the mole, 'it must have taken a very powerful mole to turn out a bit of work like that.' 'Go on', said the cockchafer, 'you're fooling; it was a cockchafer, a regular genius of a cockchafer who put up that building, let me tell you.' After that, I made up my mind to give up arguing."[1] If you say that in your opinion deism possesses a universal authority, you will still be in the realm of abstractions; but you will be concrete and picturesque if you put it like this: "I turned up all the passages people quote in order to prove conclusively that everybody who had never lived in the Sorbonne district, as, for example, the Chinese, Indians, Scythians, Greeks, Romans, Germans, Africans, Americans, whites, blacks, redskins and yellowskins, woolly heads and hairy

[1] *Dictionnaire philosophique*, 1764, Article: *Dieu.*

heads, bristly chins and smooth chins—that all alike were damned beyond recall, as it was quite right they should be; and that it could only be some horrible and abominable mind which could ever imagine that God could possibly have shown pity to a single one of these good people."[1]

Above all, he stands out more conspicuously than any for having made truth a synonym of clarity. A philosopher indeed he was, in so far as his art was impregnated with ideas, in so far as he was continually asking himself,

> Ce que c'est que l'esprit, l'espace, la matière,
> L'éternité, le temps, le ressort, la lumière,
> Étranges questions. . . .[2]

A philosopher in that there was no philosophy, near or remote, ancient or modern, which did not excite his curiosity and seem worthy of consideration. But if we mean by philosophers those over-bold people who presume to regard their theories as a creation equal to the creation of the universe, who essay to give our prison windows an opening on the unknown and the stupendous, who offer to explain the mysterious to us in a nutshell, then Voltaire belongs not to the tribe. The man who most unequivocally rejected metaphysics again is Voltaire. He advanced a few steps in the direction of Spinoza, and then drew back: Baruch Spinoza, full well do I know that you have lived an exemplary life, let calumny say what it will; I know too that you were no atheist, in the rough and ready meaning ordinarily attached to the word; I know that you have essayed some dizzying flights; however, I am not going to follow you, and I disown you, because you are not clear. Leibniz, I know full well that you were a genius; I know that you sought to find harmony in all things, that you detected continuity everywhere, that you did not hesitate to grapple with evil itself, in order to explain it. But I don't like you, and I don't hesitate to tell you that you are a little ridiculous, that there is a touch of the charlatan about you, and that you don't really understand what you mean yourself. I say a fig for you, because you have talked

[1]*Seconde anecdote sur Bélisaire,* 1767.

[2]What is mind, space, matter, eternity, time, strength, light, strange questions. . . . *Deuxième discours sur l'homme,* 1739.

about dim perceptions, because those monads of yours are not clear. Wolff, you are voluminous, verbose and ponderous, and I decline to take you into consideration, even if the Crown Prince of Prussia does think something of you, for the fact is you are not clear. Now Locke *is* simple and clear, and that is why I side with him and his wisdom.

He went so far in this direction, that his ideas began to lack consistency; all he wanted was that every piece in his collection should be transparent, even if it did not fit in very well with the pieces next to it. Being a follower of Locke, he laid down that there was nothing innate in our minds; unless, of course, there were such things as innate dispositions; which put the whole thing back in the melting-pot again. He believed firmly in the value of a strict moral system; but the more deeply he pondered on things, the less sure he became about freedom. Morality and fatalism seemed to him two principles both equally clear; if they did not settle down comfortably together, so much the worse for them. The unknown God, in whom he placed his trust, would reward the good and punish the guilty; but he was doubtful about that other life where the good were to be rewarded and the wicked punished. The one and only thing that was true absolutely was the fact which analysis had shorn of everything extraneous, so as to leave it no other mark but clearness. "A chaos of clarities" is still one of the best definitions that have been given of the general body of his ideas, of his philosophy as a whole. Just as he began to feel ill at ease the moment he approached the regions of the undefined, the imperceptible, the unconscious, so also he knew nothing about evolutionary theories, the hidden progressions of time, the travail of "becoming". That which is intelligible is fixed; fixity of languages, fixity of species, fixity of Nature. Reason was fixed, it had never had any other form than that which his contemporaries and himself had given it, and it never would; the present lit up the past. If ever there were two incompatible modes of speech, they were Vico's and Voltaire's.

From deism he had taken away the aristocratic and quasi-sceptical air it owed to Bolingbroke, and the poetical air it owed to Pope, so as to make it a thing intimately connected with life and its activities. He was under no illusion about life, often contemplating it with a poignant sense of its imperfections.

Quid est felicitas? Foes contend fiercely against you; friends betray you; the women you love deceive you, or die. The history of the human race is frightful to contemplate. Putting together a few of the sentences employed by the author in his endeavour to depict it, we can construct the speech for the prosecution: mass-murders in the East, mass-murders in the New World; wars of every kind; and, among the worst of them, the wars of religion; "Is this history which I have just finished, the history of serpents and tigers? No, it is the history of mankind; tigers and serpents would never treat their fellows so." "Times there are when the whole earth is one great scene of slaughter, and those times occur too often." "The history of the great events that have taken place in this world is little else than a story of crime." "Such is the deplorable state of mankind that the most divine of remedies have been turned to poison." *Quid est justitia?* Criminals are rewarded and just men suffer; young people and little children die, and no one can say wherefore; the aged are sunk in misery. Causes and effects are so ill-proportioned, you might take it all for a piece of buffoonery. Vanity of vanities.

Quid est veritas? Ignorance everlasting. We see no farther than the tips of our noses; the rivers do not flow so swiftly to the sea as men are borne along to error. "Pilate said to Jesus, what is truth? And having said it, went forth. It is a pity for the human race that Pilate departed without waiting to hear the answer. We should then know what truth is."[1] *De las cosas mas seguras, la mas segura es dudar*: of all safe things, the safest is to doubt. But doubts are dismal things. The fact is that if Nature had not bestowed on man two excellent antidotes, a love of work and a cheerful heart, he would long ago have died of despair.

Seeing we can do nothing to alter the evils for which we are not responsible, at all events let us mitigate those which we inflict on ourselves, let us put on the armour of wisdom and moderation and make more deliberate use of the benefits which are offered us. There are the refinements of civilization; the freedom of the mind. And here—as few or none of his predecessors had done—he interposes directly in the conduct of life. He puts up a fight not only for his general principles, but

[1]*Questions sur l'Encyclopédie*, Article *Vérité*, 1772.

for their application in particular instances, in regard to which he proceeds to discuss their efficacy and value; he deems he will be leaving his task unfinished if he does not work to bring about increased production, a better administration and juster laws; if he does not rescue those unhappy ones who have been unjustly condemned, or rehabilitate their memory. A third antidote remains to him. He uses it; it is action.

He determined to stand up to Pascal;[1] and that, not merely by the way, as it were, like certain other people who did not miss the chance of referring to him disapprovingly as "one of those melancholy moralists who are perpetually reproaching us with our happiness";[2] not like that, but in a duel to the death. Voltaire would slay Pascal, and the deed should be his glory. He would defy him in the lists, and Europe should look on and award judgment. He would bring Pascal on to the field, he would hurl him to the ground, he would make an end of him. "Come, now Pascal, have at thee!" He knew that he was very great; well, so be it; with his sling he would lay low this Goliath.

He comes on, he skips, he bounds. No good trying to rein in a passion which, beginning with a show of respect, will soon be descending to downright insult. At first, he compels himself to use a gentle tone; he will merely take the liberty of amending one or two of the *Pensées*, for these, as is well known, were left in a somewhat imperfect state. By correcting them he will be doing a service, not only to their author, but to religion as well. But that attitude he is incapable of keeping up for long. Every argument he brings forward, sets him quivering and puts him in a rage. It is all over with that show of calm. Before long he begins contradicting, word for word. That is contrary to any kind of order, says Pascal. That is in accordance with every kind of order, answers Voltaire. Montaigne's foolish idea of portraying himself, said Pascal. Montaigne's charming idea of portraying himself, artlessly, as he did, says Voltaire. He is sharp with his adversary. How could a man like M. Pascal possibly fall into such a commonplace blunder as that? He attacks his style, and calls it gibberish. He then criticizes his

[1]*Lettres philosophiques*, 1734. Lettre XXV. *Remarques sur les pensées de M. Pascal.*
[2]Adam Smith, *The Theory of Moral Sentiments*, 1759, Part III.

ideas; such-and-such an idea is as absurd as it is metaphysical, another is puerile and a trifle unseemly, yet another is mere fanaticism. Man is neither a brute, nor an angel, and the trouble is that anyone who tries to play the angel shows up the brute, said Pascal. And anyone who tries to subdue the passions instead of regulating them is trying to play the angel; what he is really hinting at is that Pascal is playing the *bête*.

Gradually it becomes evident, almost pathetically so, that the difference between them will never be composed. On the one side these *Pensées* which carry with them the trace of the mental anguish, the terror in which they were conceived, these fragments which derive their profound significance from the fact of their being the whole story of a human experience, the dissolute life, the uneasy stirrings, the questing, the illness, the conversion, science and erudition coming to lend their aid to religion; the joy of the man who has at last found what he was seeking, and, full of trust, flings himself into the protecting arms of Christ, of the man who from now onwards holds the eternal truth within his grasp. Here is the proselyte who offers his brethren the solution which this sorrowful and triumphant experience has offered to a spirit now and eternally freed from doubt. A man who has lived once again through the agony of the Mount of Olives, who has climbed the hill of Calvary. Here we have a religious explanation of the world: the misery within us, death that calls to us, prisoners who come forth from their dungeon to die each in his turn; the original tare that vitiates our lives; our inability to cure, or even to mitigate, the perversion which lies at the roots of our being, and leaves us no resource but to turn away our heads and seek to forget it in diversion. Our greatness is a memory, and a longing.

The sole explanation which enables us to resolve this contradiction, to unveil this mystery, is the Christian religion, our happy state when we issued from the hands of God, the freedom of choice that was granted to us, our choice of sin, and redemption. It is the only religion which assures us of its truth, because it takes into account all parts and portions of the problem; because its truth is borne home to us both by reason and by intuition; and, finally, because its truth is confirmed by the prophecies and miracles. It is one great whole, whereof all the parts hold firmly together; a solution which restores a meaning to our destiny.

All visions of a "sublime misanthropist", says the adversary, the self-appointed adversary from the other side. The sentiment of sin is but one prejudice among many. Yes, we do suffer sometimes; but the rule does not operate so imperiously as not to admit of mitigation. A regard for ourselves has been imparted to us for the purpose of ensuring our self-preservation; some agreeable enjoyments are available to us; Paris and London, those rich and well-ordered cities, do they resemble a desert island, or a prison cell? Another enigma; man is in his rightful place in the order of creation; he is only unreasonable when he tries to quit it; he must accept his condition; no wise man would go and hang himself because he cannot tell how it feels to behold God face to face, or because he cannot unravel the mystery of the Trinity. A man might just as well think there was no hope for him because he had not got four feet and a pair of wings. No secret instinct, or dim reminder of our pristine greatness, prompts us to seek diversion; but much more probably an instinct, not at all secret, which urges us to seek out other men and to form a society with them. No need, therefore, to conjure up some decline, some downfall, unless we are to take it that the tribulations of a cab-horse prove that horses were at one time all big and fat and never felt the stroke of a whip; and that from the day, long ago, when one of them went and gorged too many oats, all its descendants were condemned to draw cabs. None of those bets which might lose us what we had got, under the pretext that what we really wanted was the absolute! What is this absolute? There's no such thing. There is only the relative. By a bet, only a few of the luckier ones would benefit; if God had come only for a chosen few, it were better not to trust in God at all. A very different sort of greatness from that of the God of the Christians, is the God that knows no anger, whom all the Universe adores, and to whom we gain access through the exercise of our reason. No room in a well-balanced mind for intuitions, raptures, ecstasies; it is ridiculous to say that the heart has reasons, which the reason knows not of; the thing is a contradiction in terms. Tradition; only that of a coarse and stupid people; no prophecies; miracles never! Fortified by these convictions, the only ones which an accurate estimate of our limited faculties and the realities of our existence permit us to entertain, we shall come to understand the true significance of our destiny.

Henceforth there was no mistaking the situation. Two distinct categories of mind; we had to decide to which we preferred to subscribe. Two interpretations of life; we had to choose between them. Since light we were to have, should we choose the natural light with Voltaire, or the supernatural with Pascal?

It looked as if he were dowered with eternal youth. At seventy, at eighty, and even when he was on the brink of the grave, he was still performing his gambols. "I am as supple as an eel and as lively as a lizard, and still working like a squirrel." His mind, too, was just as supple, just as lively; and the wheel kept on turning. To look at, he was "as thin as death and as ugly as sin"; but he had lost nothing of the "mobility of his fiery soul". "M. Pigalle", he writes, "must come and do a model of my face; but I ought to have a face; you could hardly guess where it ought to be. My eyes are sunk three inches in my head, my cheeks are like so much old parchment gummed on to bones that have nothing to hold on to; the few teeth I had left have departed." All the same he retained all his fighting force and his determination to take the lead. He gave orders to the philosophers, urged them to unite together, instructed them in tactics. "He was the Lord of Ferney, with all its appurtenances, rents, tithes, enfeoffments, acts of homage, fiefs, emphyteutics, all the rights and powers of a feudal overlord, including that of life and death. Of all this he was not a little proud, but not so proud as he was of feeling that he was one of the intellectual Princes of Europe. Never a letter did he write but it passed from hand to hand, never a page but it had its effect on the popular mind, never a book but it attained celebrity. He boasted that he had the ace of trumps in his hand, and was sure to win his match with time. Every traveller made a point of coming and paying his respects. Fathers of families brought their children to him, so that in after years they might be able to say that they had had the honour of beholding the great man. If anyone, say for example the Count von Falkenstein, whose name concealed no less a personage than the future Emperor Joseph II, passed through without stopping, he took offence as though at a personal affront. Was ever a man more certain of being immortal?

However, a sort of process of crystallization was going on in his mind. It has been appositely remarked that somewhere about 1760, he submitted himself to a sort of searching of the conscience, which brought about, not a change, but a hardening. He shut himself in upon himself. To the sentimental appeal which Richardson had voiced, he turned a deaf ear. The transformation in the English attitude of mind, which he himself had initiated thirty years before, no longer interested him. As for the Wesleyan movement, he took no notice of it. Shakespeare himself was now no longer a barbarian of genius; he was just a barbarian. Dante, whom he had considered as one composed of coarse material which, however, glittered here and there with gold and diamonds, was now but a sort of madman. As for his Italian contemporaries, the only ones worth considering were a few who had the good sense to think as he did, Bettinelli, for example; the rest were a pack of imbecile critics who were so wrong-headed as to criticize him, men like Baretti, who taxed him with his turn-coat ideas about Shakespeare. In the Italian movement, in the search for a way that should lead to the country's resurrection, he evinced no interest at all. Of the literary awakening in Germany, he had no suspicion.

At the same time, his opposition to Christianity grew stronger, more exacerbated; it was becoming an obsession. This spirit, so charming, so delicate, so sober, became violent and wholly extravagant when it was a matter of "crushing the infamous", as he used to express it. Whether it was that the final victory of his cause, which seemed to him close at hand, emboldened and excited him; whether he was angered by the resistance which was still being opposed to him; whether that resistance, within himself and against himself, had grown deeper, so that, having declared every night that the foe was irretrievably vanquished, he felt every morning that he had got to renew the conflict, and lay him low—whatever the reason, the feelings of hostility which had possessed him as a young man, he now whipped to a frenzy. The thing became a mania. From the factory at Ferney, more redoubtable to religious folk than those in Amsterdam, London, Paris or Berlin, there poured forth an unrelenting stream of pamphlets which displayed alike the genius of the artist and the zeal of the sectary. To his atheistic denials he gave expression not ten times, not a hundred, but in a thousand different shapes and forms, so that an obsession characteristic of the age in general, became for him nothing short of life itself; he would not, and he could not, shake it off. The Bible was devoid of beauty, devoid of grandeur; the Gospel had brought nothing but disaster to the world; the Church throughout and without exception was nothing but folly or corruption. Not a single confessor of the faith that was not a fanatic; the purest, the noblest were dragged in the mire; St. Francis himself was disendowed of his gentle aureole and became a poor, witless creature. A caricature-like simplification, a determination never to enter into the reasons of his opponent, to ignore, or to distort, unending repetition—such were some of his methods. When we come to read one or other of the sermons, the catechisms, the speeches, the dialogues or the tales he flung by the handful up and down the world, we are astounded at a manner that seems constantly to gain in ease, at a touch ever more piquantly picturesque, and a style that grows more and more natural; but when you have got through ten or twenty, the propaganda-machinery at the back of it all becomes apparent. He was the originator of that cheap mode of attack, wholly unworthy of him, which consists in telling people that they should not believe in Christianity, because the Bible tells us that the Devil took Christ up on to a high mountain and showed him all the kingdoms of the earth, whereas it is impossible to see all the kingdoms of the earth from the top of any mountain; or it may be because the Church requires the faithful to regard Friday as a day of abstinence. When he thought he would, he descended to the depths of the ignoble. Of this we could offer many examples, were it not for soiling our lips. In thus degrading himself, he was disloyal to the memory of his friend Bayle who, though no less hostile to tradition, to authority, and to religion, never abandoned the grand manner.

"What a number of different characters he invented for our instruction", says Mably. "Hardly ever presenting himself under his real name, he is now a theologian, now a philosopher, now a Chinaman, now an almoner of the King of Prussia, now an Indian, now an atheist, and now a deist, or heaven knows what. He writes for all sorts of minds, even for those who are more responsive to a jest or a pun than to an argument."[1] As a matter of fact, that was his favourite weapon, irony. He wielded it so effectively that no one has ever equalled him, and, perhaps, no one ever will. He used it, quite justifiably, to counter exaggerations, but he came in the end to employ it indiscriminately, against all manner of things, not only against idols, but against things whose disappearance debased and impoverished mankind, against generous enthusiasms and ardours of the spirit. He bequeathed this irony of his to a clumsy, coarse-grained race that acquired the habit of laughing at whatever they could not understand.

He took on a more than human aspect; he was—the word is Diderot's—the Antichrist. But to that extreme a part at any rate of Europe declined to follow him, beholding in him now nothing but "the genius of Hate."[2] The dissentients include not only those who were soon to appeal to the heart to provide them with the delights which the reason denied them; not only his enemies, and they were innumerable, but even some of his friends, who were beginning to draw away from him with feelings of alarm. Among the members of the enlightened school, one Genovesi reproached him with stirring up amongst men a violence which was very much at variance with an exhortation which, for his part, he was much given to repeating, and that was "Love ye one another." Then, a certain Alessandro Verri talked about those French philosophers who, if they could have had their way, would have set up an Inquisition to deal with people who did not think as they did. People like Nicolai, Mendelssohn, August Wilhelm Schlegel, and Johann August Eberhardt considered that, if he was not careful, he would ruin their cause. Voltaire was at last coming to inspire them with fear.

D'Alembert one day conceived the notion that it would be a good thing to set up, opposite the ancient abode surmounted by the Cross, where men were wont to seek refuge from the ills of life, a second building. It would be his task to point out the advantages of the idea; he would bring out the logical character of his plan, and explain how comfortably people might live in his

[1] *Du développement, des progrès et des bornes de la raison.* Œuvres, Vol. XV, p. 7.

[2] "Voltaire ist der Genie des Hasses", H. A. Korff, *Voltaire im literarischen Deutschland der* 18 *Jahrhunderts, Heidelberg,* 1918, Zweister Buch, pp. 235 *et sqq.*

two dwellings. Having done that he would leave them free to choose; a man could take up his abode in whichever house he preferred; there were to be no recriminations about the past, no rending each other asunder. Each would do what his conscience told him, while respecting the conscientious decisions of others. All this was very fine, no doubt; too fine, for it was far too remote from the ways of our species. French deism, by-passing Pope, and linking up with the school of Toland and Collins, was essentially aggressive. That the eighteenth century witnessed the birth of a race of men, thereafter perpetuated, whose sole spiritual nourishment was anti-clericalism, who made anti-clericalism the sole item on their programme, and who deemed that that would suffice to remodel governments, to perfect societies, and lead the way to happiness—for this, many men are responsible—and not all of them belong to the Encyclopaedist camp—but none of them to the same degree as Voltaire.

III

DEISMS: LESSING

GOTTLOB EPHRAÏM LESSING had a few traits in common with the thinkers of the English and French schools. Who ever longed for clearness, for light, more ardently than he? And he gained his object, not by treating his quest as a sport and trusting in some lucky chance to get him through, but by sheer hard work, by the exercise of patience and determination. As a critic, who ever played the part more faithfully than he? He felt as if he himself were personally challenged by the things he read, and he came down with his full weight on their authors, never making the slightest allowance for human frailty. Nothing was left of his adversaries when he had finished with them, because, for him, men merely stood for ideas, and to ideas that were unsound he gave no quarter. I am not, he was accustomed to say, one of those privileged beings who create beauty spontaneously, straight away. I am no magician, no enchanter; I am a critic, and through criticism it is that I find my way to art. So many reckless statements were flying about the world, that to restore the balance of things, he was always ready to ally himself with the critical opposition. Any generally received view or opinion straightway made a rebel of him; he only had to start reading books in favour of religion, which were so numerous as to constitute three-quarters of the whole German book-output, to become all on fire to know what the remaining quarter had to say. Every time an adverse verdict was delivered, he lodged an appeal. Like his English and French confrères, he had read, and studied, and busied himself with research beyond all belief. When he was a schoolboy, one of his masters said he was like a young horse that needed a double ration of oats; he had gone on eating double, aye and quadruple, rations ever since. Being the hungry fellow he was, he thought that any sort of printed thing was worth reading, even if it was only for the fun of running some absurdity to earth; but he liked best to read the things he was not obliged to know about, the things that other people did not know about, things that were off the beaten track, on the by-path, so to speak. The result was that, later on, the enormous quantity of unpublished and out of the way material he had accumulated, provided him with an immense arsenal on which he freely drew in all his controversies.

And like his confrères, he was quite indefatigable; in the first place, from necessity, because, as far as he could, he supported himself by his pen; in the second place, from inclination, and we see him dramatist, aesthete, theologian, philosopher, journalist, leaving behind him a host of fragments, essays, material for works begun or projected, but never finished. Neither books nor manuscripts took on all their savour for him until, having left them awhile to go and sniff in a little of the air of life, he came back to them once more. That battling and storm-tossed life, life which, if it was to be well-lived, should be fraught with unnumbered experiences, including high adventure and incursions into Bohemia, that life, how dearly he cherished it! It was on no plain, hum-drum pattern that he cut his coat out of the modest piece of cloth allotted to each of us. It was the ministry that awaited him. He had been sent to Leipzig University to read with a view to taking orders. However, his pious family had been terribly shocked to hear that he was more often to be seen in the wings of Mme Neuberg's theatre than in the lecture-room, that he was translating plays, and even writing some himself. Our student, Gottlob Ephraïm, had made up his mind to throw off his shyness, his awkwardness; no more of the impecunious theological student for him; he made up his mind that he would go out into the world and get used to mixing with people, and, to start with, he would learn fencing and dancing. Books, he said—and this was one of his settled convictions—books may make a good scholar; but, of themselves, they will never make a man. That cold, frigid book-learning, leaves no imprint on the mind but that of dead letters.

This preliminary crisis was to be followed by several more. A sudden impulse takes hold of him. He must get out of this place; so without so much as a good-bye, he packs up his traps, leaving behind him, however, a few unpaid accounts. He will be going now any moment. He has already gone. He has settled himself in at Leipzig and is beginning to make a name, when off he dashes to Berlin; then, from Berlin, back again to Leipzig, whence he starts on a journey across Europe, a journey interrupted, at the first stage, by the war. This man, with his military bearing, quite at home amongst soldiers, and secretary to the Prussian Government attached to General Tauenzin commanding the fortress of Breslau, this man is Lessing, yes, the same Lessing. Of an evening, he sits down to cards and plays a very careful hand. If anyone remarked on the serious way he took the game, he would say, what's the good of playing at all, if your heart isn't in it? All that, however, did not interfere with his reading, his studies, his meditations, or prevent him from keeping an observant eye on the queer characters around him, some of whom he brought into his best play, *Mina von Barnhelm*. Then another fade-out: no more truck with government and army; behold him now a member of the council of the Hamburg theatre! All this chopping and changing about was not mere caprice. In fact, these changes were the patent of his freedom. Weak people allow themselves to get into a groove, and suffer themselves, with resignation, and sometimes with joy, to become slaves of their business, their habits and their environment; whereas the stronger sort, as soon as they feel themselves in danger of becoming fixtures, make an effort and break free. Off with the chains, fling wide the doors, shake off the dust of our feet on the things we have loved, and then each time we do so, let us be ourselves once more. Money! Don't let us bother about money! And every venture leaves Lessing worse off financially than he was before, because money meant nothing to him, because he spent it freely, nay, actually flung it away. But every fresh venture left him richer in humanity.

There were certain inward qualities with which he was not endowed, such as an inventive imagination, suppleness of mind, a sensitiveness to the finer shades; he was hard, and he could be decidedly distant; there was, too, a suspicion of schoolmasterish pedantry about him. He had chosen his bit of ground, and he kept to his own furrow, without looking very closely at the meadows or the mountains, the trees or the flowers. He admired his friend Ewald Christian von Kleist, who found repose and delight in the contemplation of Nature. For his own part, when he wanted a little amusement, he would go and talk literature or philosophy in the tavern with a few of his own kidney. This is not to say that he was insensitive; his shafts of irony, his fits of anger, his outbursts of fury show that clearly enough; but he was certainly not sentimental. Klopstock got on his nerves, and so did the other etherialists; and he had a very lukewarm sympathy with the passions of the youthful Werther. Love occupied but few of his thoughts. Did that man ever really love anybody, who declared that he had never written a woman a letter which could not be shown to a third party? Were all his confidences of the intellectual order? Did he ever even dream? Love, however, he did, though without confidences, and without dreams. He married, pretty late on in years, a companion whom he had selected as being the best possible among a species always difficult to understand. The child that Eva König bore him died when but a few days old, and, dying, took his mother with him. Heartbroken, Lessing gave utterance to a moving plaint; he had not been extravagant, he had only asked for that modest share of happiness which is vouchsafed to other men; but that share had been denied him. What he lamented above all was the dawn of a new intelligence of unknown possibilities and then its swift extinction. He would bear his cross, and to lighten the burden, he would betake himself to work once more. A dose of laudanum, shall we say? A dose of laudanum made up of theological and literary occupations that would help him to get through the days, one after another, always the same, tomorrow like today. Yes; he would become again what he had been before, an intellect on the march.

A friend of his, called Mylius, was the publisher of a journal which went by the name of *Der Freigeist*. The name would have suited Lessing. He belonged to the family of unfettered spirits.

But Lessing, if he bore the mark of his times, was not indistinguishably merged in the general herd; he was the officer in command. At some of the ideas and aims of the day we can see him shrugging his shoulders with an air of contempt. Locke, a thinker who has said the last word on philosophy? Pope, a metaphysician? Those two he leaves in the land of Gulliver, and turns to some other companions of a different calibre—Spinoza, Leibniz. On Wolff he comes down with all his irony. "Generally speaking there is no lack of systematic works in Germany. Take a few accepted definitions, deduce from them in the most admirable manner whatever suits our case, that is an art in which we may defy all the countries in the world to rival us." A certain infusion of the practical element is necessary, that we agree; when the paralytic receives the electrical discharges that are for his benefit, he does not ask whether it was Nollet or Franklin who had the rights of the matter, or whether neither of them had. But don't go and let him think that to explain a thing all you have to do is to take note of it. Your task, you say, is to win over the many; well and good, if your talents lie that way. All the same, people who act on those who are going to act on the crowd are a superior species. A dazzling show of diamonds, real or sham, is one thing; a sound demonstration which carries conviction to thoughtful men is quite another. Will a man who has spent all his time on the lighter kind of literature, or in playing the flute, feel quite satisfied with himself when he approaches the term of his existence? Will he, in his own mind, be the sort of man to pass through the gates of the tomb with undiminished head? A plain demonstration has no need to be tricked out with lace and finery. People either like it, or they don't like it. Ill betide those who don't. They are soiled past curing. All they do is vain. Useless to try and rub things clean, if the sponge is dirty.

He was all impatience to see what Winckelmann's book would have to say; he looked to it to bring him the enlightenment he hoped for on the classical conception of Beauty, and he was quite disposed to admire it. But admiration, with him, was never so fervent as to take the edge off his critical faculty. Now, Winckelmann's work was not only a history of Art; he added to it a theory of Beauty: yet another one. He alleged that the basic principles of Art, in spite of all that had been written on the matter, had never been gone into as deeply as the subject deserved. Beauty, he said, was still one of Nature's mysteries, but he was going to give the full and final explanation of it. Thus he brought into the matter the Divine Essence, of which these works of beauty are the human expression. "Supreme beauty resides in God. The idea of human beauty grows nearer perfection in proportion as it conforms to, and harmonizes with, the Supreme Being, with that Being whom the idea of unity and indivisibility enables us to distinguish from matter. This notion of Beauty is as of a substance withdrawn from matter by the action of fire, as a spirit seeking to create for itself an image of the first reasoning creature formed by the Divine Intelligence."

Whereupon, Lessing girds on his armour once more and enters the lists; it delighted him to measure swords with a champion he respected. Anyhow, there could be no holding back. A fallacy must not be allowed a free run. It could never be admitted that Greek art was the archetype of Beauty, no matter in what particular form it existed; impossible to allow its principles to be applied to all the arts, particularly to poetry. No doubt Laocoon and his sons, in the coils of a monstrous serpent, retained in their expression, their gestures, their attitude in general, a look of majesty; it did not properly befit the sculptor to reproduce pain which, by its distorting effect upon the features, would have been a thing of ugliness. But the Philoctetes of Sophocles does not shrink from giving vent to his pain with groans; and Homer's heroes weep, and moan, and fly into fits of anger. It follows that there must be a difference in the two arts. And the difference is this. The painter and the sculptor are both concerned with perpetuating a single moment of time, the conditions of their art leaves them no choice in the matter; as this moment is invested by them with perpetuity, it follows that nothing of a kind which we look on as transitory should be imparted to it. The poet, on the other hand, does not concentrate his attention on single moment; it is open to him to take an event at its beginning, to trace its development and finally to bring it to its end. Poetry, therefore, cannot properly be treated like the plastic arts. Nor is the difference simply one of changing times and tastes; it is not to be explained by the fact that the Ancients loved only a calm beauty, being so much in love with calmness that, when Iphigenia is being sacrificed, Timantes throws a mantle over Agamemnon's face, which he could not have depicted agonized, distorted, hideous; whereas the Moderns have broader tastes. It is not that. No, the difference is a specific one.[1]

Lessing repeated his argument in a variety of forms, all leading

[1] *Laokoon: oder über die Grenzen der Malerei und Poesie,* 1766.

to the same conclusion: my theory retains all its cogency; succession in time is the domain of the poet; that of the painter and sculptor is space. It took all that to sever the ancient alliance, *Ut pictura poesis*; to overthrow the currently accepted notions on a host of aesthetical subjects required all the vigour, all the combativeness, all the tenacity of this same doughty fighter. And he, with undiminished zest, went on casting down the idols. Poetry, being more adaptable, less rigid, than the other arts, might quite well depict ugliness, using it as a sort of ingredient: in the case of the ludicrous, ugliness impotent; in the case of the tragic, ugliness cruel. Poetry, being richer than the other arts, had no need of mythological symbolism, the Scales of Justice, Strength leaning against her Pillar, the Curb of Moderation, not being so destitute of expressiveness as all that. Poetry was not reduced to the pass of returning again and again to universally familiar types, like Venus, Mars or Jupiter. Invention, properly speaking, had little importance for the artist; a well-worn theme was an assistance to him rather than a drawback. For the poet, however, inventiveness, originality, was more important than execution. On his way, as he went along, Lessing restored Shakespeare to his throne, invalidated rules, denounced dogmatism, vindicated spontaneity, demanded that the living should be allowed not to resemble the dead, even the illustrious dead. But his great, his all-important work was the emancipation of poetry. It was not of the essence of poetry to be didactic, any more than it was to be minutely descriptive. Haller, in his poem *Die Alpen* crammed in such a wealth of description that nothing remained for the reader's imagination to work upon; Ariosto, instead of spreading out his portrait of Alcine over several stanzas, ought to have put in a few touches and left us free to make a dream-picture of our own. There was in poetry what it said; but there was another and more potent element, what it did *not* say, but what it suggested. True poetry belonged to the ineffable. In these terms he was always ready and eager to proclaim its power. But nothing came so near his heart as the solution of the religious problem. Everything depended on that.

In him there still lived on the soul of his father, the pastor, and of those many other pastors, his ancestors; believers, apostles, who had never contented themselves with a merely perfunctory performance of their duties; their creed was the sole food of their spiritual life, these defenders of the faith, these children of God. Of such a heritage one does not dispossess oneself at will. Even on the day when a man formally discards his orthodox religion, it still remains with him and still he looks on it with affection. Religion is a serious thing; only the small-minded make it a jesting matter; that, Lessing maintained and never ceased to maintain. Religion is not to be trifled with, to be joked about, it is a form of Truth and Truth never sneers. Doubtless, he thought it a duty to clear away the corruptions which had crept into it, and so he came to add his voice to the chorus that denounced superstition; so he came to put in his word against the Crusades, saying that they were the crowning achievement of Papal policy and had given rise to the most horrible persecutions of which fanaticism had ever been guilty; so he declared that he was living at a time when the voice of sane reason was too clearly heard for any madman who needlessly, and regardless of his civil duties, threw himself light-heartedly into the jaws of death, and boasted that this made him one of the noble army of martyrs; and so it was that he painted in very black colours ignorant monks and knavish bishops. But knights of the Crusades, untimely martyrs, bad priests, did not in his eyes embody the essence, the everlasting power of religion.

A deist after his own fashion, he demanded that he should be distinguished from others so calling themselves, who knew nothing about the deeper philosophy, who were not to be classed as reasoning Christians but as purveyors of unreason. At the start of his career, the fates had brought him into contact with Voltaire for whom he conceived a violent aversion. Voltaire, when in Berlin, had engaged as his secretary a professor of French named Richier whom he had asked to look out for a German capable of acting as his translator. Whereupon, Richier suggested a friend of his, young Gottlob Ephraïm Lessing, who was very clever and very poor. At first things went along pretty well; but Richier was incautious enough to lend Lessing the manuscript of *Le Siècle de Louis XIV*. Voltaire wanted it back. Lessing, however, had left Berlin, taking the document with him. When his friend asked him to return it, he replied, in a letter half-respectful, half-bantering, that it had never entered his head to keep the work, but that he had not quite finished it, adding that he could not resist the temptation of reading to the very end the work of so perfect a writer. Still less, had it been in his mind to translate it, for he was aware that the work was already in hand; worthily to translate M. de Voltaire one would have to give oneself to the devil. Furthermore, he had the impression that much cry was being made about little wool, and was sure that Richier would soon be forgiven. Then Voltaire himself wrote to Lessing in flattering terms, for he did not want him to disappear with the manuscript, but also threateningly, telling him that he was not going to make light of the affair, and that M. Lessing's career would receive rather a nasty jolt if he, Voltaire, had to take legal steps to get his property returned to him. Lessing, feeling very indignant, wrote back a letter in Latin. The letter in question is no longer extant, but Lessing afterwards said that Voltaire would have had no call to stick it up in his window. The manuscript was given back and the quarrel blew over, not, however, without leaving in the mind of the youth the seeds of an enmity which grew and developed in the man.

This was the time when the German mind was beginning to grow conscious of possessing a specific character of its own, a character which had to be asserted, in the first place for its own sake, and, secondly, for the sake of the neighbouring peoples. It was felt, though as yet obscurely, and only among the leading spirits, that the assertion of this character, and of its dignity, implied a claim to a place in the sun, and would result in the public recognition of such a claim. A swarm of little States, separated, divided! Yes, but also a reaching-out, a striving towards, a common spirit, such that when the moment came, after prolonged preparation, it would be a matter of practical politics. There was a desire to manifest the existence of a national body of ideas, the first appeal of the fatherland.

The Aufklärer fully intended to play a part in the movement that was drawing Europe towards the philosophy of Enlightenment; but they did not intend to be swallowed up in it; on the contrary they reserved a particular rôle for themselves. According to what they said, the English were philosophers up to a point, and no farther; they were too high-and-mighty to read the Germans, too much in love with their own ease and comfort to delve down very deeply into ideas. The French were brilliant, careless, and superficial. English people philosophized with their sensations, the French with their wit; only the Germans with their reason.[1] The Germans, wrote the *Allgemeine Deutsche Bibliothek*, which catered not only for the Berliners and the Prussians, but for readers and contributors throughout all German-speaking lands—the Germans have the ability to fill a place that no other country could occupy. They are level-headed, and not the sort of people to be carried off their feet by any extravagant flight of fancy. Nature has endowed them with a taste for scholarship; they take their stand midway between misleading doubts which are but aberrations of the mind, and the uncurbed enthusiasms of an over-heated imagination. The reproach that is generally made to them is that their national character consists in their not having any at all.[2]

Of this intellectual Germany, Lessing was the leading citizen. But what he took himself to be was a citizen of the world, and he made no bones about advertizing it: he had not the slightest desire to be reputed a patriot; that was the last thing in the world he wanted. Love of country meant nothing to him, and he had no inclination to hanker after that heroic failing. In point of fact, he was German to the core; one of the creators of the new German spirit. Leipzig, Berlin, Hamburg—each of the towns in which he established himself, as though from mere blind wilfulness, had its part to play in the grand adventure, the shaping of a nation. Leipzig, the centre of the life intellectual, the capital of the book-world, of fashion, elegance, the drama, criticism; Berlin, animated by the genius of Frederick II; Hamburg, the international exchange. The governmental secretary attached to General Tauenzin, the man that drinks deep and plays high, finds himself playing a part in the decisive ordeal for Prussia and Germany, the Seven Years' War.

Teachers who were not content with repeating over and over again the doctrines of the great masters, and were for arousing the younger folk; pastors who ascribed the growth of incredulity

[1]Moses Mendelssohn to Lessing, 20th February, 1758.

[2]*Allgemeine Deutsche Bibliothek*, 1765, article I: *Ibid.*, 1768, vol. VI, compte-rendu de l'ouvrage *Von dem deutschen Nationalgeiste*, Francfurt-am-Mein, 1765; and *Noch etwas Zum deutschen Nationalgeiste*, Lindau am Bodensee, 1766.

to the fact that a great many of their confrères, imagining they were teaching the true God, only beheld his distorted shadow; scholars, exegetists, who imagined they were putting new life into the sacred tree; critics who inspired the educational reviews with their ideas—all alike complained of seeing Germany smothered beneath the burden of old-fashioned orthodoxy. And Lessing gave ear to their demand. To espouse the cause of the so-called heresiarchs unjustly condemned; to champion the cause of the Moravian Brotherhood against their persecutors; always, whenever occasion offered, to play the part of the Samaritan against the Pharisee—all this was his delight. But among these many combats, one stands out as conspicuously remarkable in that it whipped his attacks and the anger of his opponents, into a paroxysm of fury. He was then at Wolfenbuttel. For want of anything better, he had accepted the post of curator of the library of the Grand Duke of Brunswick. He was forty-two, and still in the prime of life; nevertheless, he felt weary and dispirited; this defeat in his struggle with fate, this very mediocre post, this "any port in a storm" sort of job, this acquiescing in servitude. . . . Yet this was the moment when he hurled at Lutheran orthodoxy his shattering attack.

Samuel Reimarus was a scholarly and peace-loving professor, who taught oriental languages at the *lycée* in his native city, Hamburg. Content to pursue the even tenor of his life, a good husband and father, he gave one the impression of a man whose way of life was crystal-clear. He had written some highly esteemed books defending natural religion and combating atheism, arguing in particular that the marvellous organization of insect life could be explained in no other way than as resulting from the wisdom of the Supreme Being. This worthy man regarded the approach of death with a steady eye. On the 19th February, 1768, he invited a few of his special friends to dine with him, so that he might take his leave of them. Three days later, he fell ill, and on the 1st March, 1768, he died.

Now his most secret ideas had remained hidden, but he had set them down in a manuscript superscribed with the words *Schutzschrift für die Vernünftigen Verehrer Gottes*, Apology for the rational worshippers of God; and this manuscript, of which his friends knew nothing, though a few of the more intimate of them suspected its existence, might have remained for ever unknown had not Lessing chanced to become acquainted with it and, in 1774, and again in 1777 and 1778, published passages from it, without giving the author's name, under the title, *Fragmente eines Ungenannten*, passages from an unknown writer.

Now, it is no Jean Meslier that we have here over again. Reimarus indulges in none of that individual's outbursts of anger and devastating rage; it is no personal quarrel between himself and his Lord that he must vent; he does not suffer himself to be inflamed by a fiery flood of rancour which, sweeping on, consumes everything in its path. On the contrary, he believed with the utmost sincerity that he was making his way towards God, clearing away the thorns and the briars, driving the hordes of the godless and the idolatrous before him, pointing out the source of vice and evil, and thoroughly convinced that he would have purified earth and the heavens, when he had destroyed the belief in revealed religion. He was amazingly sure of himself; he says repeatedly that he means to see things clearly, as they really are, *ich will die Sache klar machen*; and he has another saying which in his view clearly expresses the fundamental laws of reason, *Ein jedes Ding ist, was es ist; ein Ding kann nicht zugleich sein und nicht sein*; everything is what it is; a thing cannot at the same time both be and not be. Thus equipped, Reimarus addresses himself to an examination of the Old Testament, not hesitating to interrupt his critical labours at intervals to give utterance to passionate exclamations, interrogations, appeals; ah, how quickly do our minds fall into error! How is it possible that, for generation after generation, things so manifestly contradictory could have been looked upon as true! A religion which is good and wise in its essence cannot but have exponents both good and wise; look then at the characters of the Bible; look at David; they were neither good nor wise; they were vindictive, greedy, immoral; therefore, a religion founded on the Jewish tradition cannot be good and wise, cannot be true. There is in all the world no story that claims to come more directly from God; and never one in which the depositories of the divine commands were less worthy to receive them; that means it is a Jewish story, not a divine one, that we are concerned with. A religion which claims to furnish men with a code of moral conduct should give its rules in a precise form, intelligible to everyone, clear cut in their expression, and in their content. Now, the Bible contains no such teaching; it does not even consider the soul as immortal; for that reason, its precepts cannot proceed from a divine revelation.

Reimarus applies the same mode of treatment to the Gospels: The New Testament, which should contain one single truth, but which, drawn up by four persons, varies as regards times and places, the particular words used, and the nature of the acts performed, is contradictory and therefore cannot be matter for belief. Protestantism then comes under examination: the doctrine of Justification by Faith—is that in conformity with reason? Or belief in Original Sin? Protestantism, like Catholicism, fails to conform to reason; both of them are inventions of the human mind, impostures that have distorted the natural law to which all religious men should now return.

Such was the work that Lessing disinterred, and, so doing, stirred up a scandal which went on for years. Melchior Goetze took up the gauntlet: narrow-mindedness and obstinacy personified, a man who had impeached his own colleagues on a charge of impiety, and not his colleagues only, but his friends; in short a tough antagonist for whom, however, Lessing had conceived a certain esteem, because the man was intransigence itself. Goetze called down on him the condemnation of the Christian world, and demanded chastisement for the blasphemer. But Lessing kept on his way. Sermons, petitions, pamphlets, books, insults, threats did but excite him the more: "I have published these Fragments and I shall go on publishing them, let all the Goetzes in the world consign me to the lowest pit of Hell."

Nevertheless, even when he took up this attitude of bitter opposition, he did not regard himself as an adversary of religion as such. He did not cease to contemn those misguided triflers who held sacred things up to ridicule. The habit of some philosophers of talking about superstition when they wanted to attack religious belief struck him as a contemptible device. He did not believe that from the dawn of time men had deluded themselves when they worshipped and prayed. He was no supporter of the facile theory that the Church of God was the outcome of some rude conspiracy hatched by the priesthood and their royal confederates. Since the craving for religion was a fact, a reality that had always existed from the earliest ages, they were fools who continued to deny it. All that needed to be done was to save it from that which was not itself, and to give it its true meaning.

With this object in view, Lessing reverted to certain ideas that had been expressed to him, and round about him, not, however, without imparting to them the impress of his own personality. There was the idea that religion proceeded from something divinely dictated, from a Bible, or a Koran; or that it was an indwelling truth; that God was the presence within our souls of a universal and eternal reason, to which no one could refuse to adhere. Faith was a reality of the conscience, anterior to theology, and independent of it. Religion existed before there had been any such thing as theology; and even if theology should cease to be, religion would go on existing.

He dealt with the idea that morality was religion. As his friend Nicolai, the publisher, said in his novel *Das Leben und die Meinungen des Herrn Magister Sebaldus Nothanker* (1773–1776), "The Life and Opinions of Master Sebaldus Nothanker," a pastor who adheres to dogma in its most strictly orthodox sense, who is punctual in all pious observances, who collects money to build new chapels, is nevertheless a bad pastor if he is hard on the poor, and pitiless towards the unfortunate, and if he consigns to eternal punishment all who do not think as he does. On the other hand, even if you are a recognized heretic and schismatic, so long as you live a virtuous life, and show kindness to those around you, you will be dear to the heart of God, who is at once the God of Reason and the God of Humanity. The Collegians of Amsterdam, who belong to no special church, but who give free admission to all men in their fraternal assemblies, because, they say, you may enter the City of God by more gates than one, and who do not ask a starving man for his certificate of baptism before giving him something to eat, are nearer to what true religion is than the most orthodox of Lutherans.

Lessing took up the idea of a progressive intellectual ascent, after the manner of that set forth by another of his close associates during his Berlin days, by Moses Mendelssohn in his *Phaedo* (1767). This was a Phaedo who had read Leibniz and Spinoza and put into the mouth of Socrates such things as this: "We have good grounds for believing, in the light of this resistless reaching out of reasoning beings toward an ever more and more perfect state, that their perfection is the supreme aim and purpose of Creation. We may put it that this vast universe was brought into existence in order that there might be reasoning beings that could rise step by step, increase little by little in perfection, and find, in this ever growing progress, their joy and felicity."

Finally there was Semler, whose theory was that in every religion there was a local, national and transitory element not to be confounded with its permanent substance. But Semler did not go all the way with Lessing; he was indeed among those who condemned him, because he, Lessing, had the hardihood to wind up all these preliminary considerations, and utterly to transform the character of the whole, by imposing on it the philosophy which looked on all things as "becoming", evolving.

What, in point of fact, did revelation mean for him? Nothing more nor less than the progressive education of the human race. That, indeed, was the title of the outstanding work which he brought out in the year 1780: *Die Erziehung des Menschengeschlechts*. What education is for the individual, revelation is for mankind as a whole. Just as education gives a man nothing that he has not already within him, but merely brings it to light more easily and rapidly, so does revelation give mankind nothing that it cannot of itself attain, but aids it to set free and bring out treasures as yet obscure and undefined. Revelation is no sudden lightning flash; it takes its time. Although the first man was endowed with the notion of a one and only God, it was not possible that this idea, imparted and not discovered, should continue to retain its original purity, and man gave himself up to idolatry, to polytheism, which things, however, are not to be despised, which have their significance, provided they are considered against the background of their time, and in their proper perspective, and as the rude and imperfect adumbration of things to come. Such aberrations might have gone on occurring for millions of years, if God had not interposed, and given them a fresh direction. He chose a race—the most ignorant race of all, the Israelitish people—in which to implant the idea of a single supreme God, and this marked a considerable advance. Yet how far were they, even yet, from the transcendental concept of unity! A race in its infancy was capable of receiving only the education suited to children. Meanwhile, the other races had held on their way towards the light of reason; many lagged a long way behind, a few were well ahead. The Israelites learned in their servitude among the wise people of Persia to measure their belief against the idea of a single Supreme Being, as a better trained reason had conceived and honoured him. Revelation had guided their reason, now it was the turn of reason to contribute to the progress of revelation; the first reciprocal service which these two powers had exchanged; in the eyes of the Creator such a mutual influence is so far from being improper that, without it, one of the two, revelation or reason, would be ineffective. It was through this contact, that the Jews came nearer to a knowledge of God. There were, in their sacred writings, certain allusions and references to the subject of the immortality of the soul, but this article of belief was too lofty for the general run of people and remained the appanage of a few individuals. It was in this sort of preparatory work that the value of the Bible consisted; it was an elementary work, and destined to be superseded.

Superseded it was. Christ came; the New Testament was the second book, more advanced than the first. It served its turn, it occupied the human mind for centuries; but it could not go on forever. The onward march would continue. We should get new and more accurate ideas, ideas closer to the truth, concerning the Divine Essence, our own nature, and our relations with God; we should come nearer and nearer to that selfless morality which would lead us to prize virtue for its own sake. Lessing waxes lyrical, and he speaks with the voice of the prophets as he reveals to us the vistas of the distant future. It will come, yea it will surely come, that day of fulfilment, of the great consummation, when man will do right for right's sake, regardless of the reward that was at one time dangled before his eyes, a necessary expedient, it used to be thought, for keeping his eyes fixed on the goal. It will surely come, that day, when a new Gospel shall be vouchsafed to us, that new Gospel of which the promise was already implicit in the earlier book. March on, march on with thy imperceptible step, O Providence, but grant that because thy step is imperceptible I may not despair of thee, even though thou seem to go retrograde. It is not true that the shortest line is the straight line; so many are the things thou hast to drag along with thee upon thine everlasting road!

If he takes on this exalted tone, the hard, unbending Lessing, the reason doubtless is that he counts himself one of those apostles who toil and suffer amid ingratitude, misunderstanding, and open hosility, to extend to civil society those benefits which the present holds in embryo, and which the future will gather in in their maturity. In his soul, the God of Revelation is at work, and likewise the God of Reason, both commingled in one sole God. As we may readily imagine, he presented his own part of the work in a Dialogue[1] which begins as a riddle and ends as a declaration of faith in the moral destiny of man. One of the two interlocutors declares himself a freemason, not because he belongs to a lodge, but precisely because he has undergone no initiation, taken no oath, and participated in no rite. What was it he had in mind? Human societies, set up in order to ensure the happiness of mankind, miss their goal; they are familiar with dissensions and wars, they set nation against nation, French, English, German, Spanish, Italian, Russian. In the very heart of every nation it is easy to discover flaws, long-standing abuses, privileged classes, the glaring contrast between rich and poor. It was, therefore, all important that there should be men of wisdom free from the prejudices of their tribe, and of their times. They would cure the ills from which the citizen, however fortunate he might seem to be, could not be exempt. Their progress would be slow; it might continue for century upon century; they would go on working for peace, justice and love, until such time as good deeds became spontaneous, and men would do what was right without hope of reward, or fear of punishment.

Such was how Lessing saw himself in the closing years of his life.

Lessing, a deist; a deist, yes; but in a sense very different from the one ordinarily put upon the word; a sense which retained for the positive forms of religion, and for Christianity in particular, both gratitude and respect; beholding in them a touching endeavour to reach the truth, an episode, a stage, in one long spiritual conquest. Voltaire, in the third conversation in the *Dîner du comte de Boulainvilliers*, wrote, "In the matter of religion,

[1]Ernst und Falk, *Gespräche für Freimaürer,* 1778; *Fortsetzung,* 1780. Lessing died on the 15th February, 1781.

people have taken a line diametrically opposed to what they have done with regard to clothing, housing and food. We started with cave-life, huts, skins of wild animals for clothes, and acorns for food. Later on we had bread, nourishing dishes, clothes of wool and woven silk, clean and comfortable dwellings; but, so far as religion is concerned, we have gone back to mast, caves and the hides of animals." A specious, but superficial, idea, against which one of the loftiest theories ever conceived to explain the march of mankind now comes into being.

Lessing an apostle of reason; but of a reason at once immanent and transcendent; a reason which, in its task, sometimes turns to intuition for assistance, a reason which does not disdain the ethereal visions of certain mystics, taking them to be merely forerunners who have hurried on and outstripped their times. In this way, he reinstated forces whose value, and whose very reality, had been denied by his predecessors.

Lessing, one of the leaders of the Aufklärung, and not the least glorious of them! But his was an Aufklärung with a difference. For other men it was the pride of the age, the age of light; for Lessing it was a light which had been shining, albeit feebly, from the remotest times. What the present age had done had been to strengthen it, and it would go on still gaining in purity and brilliance throughout an illimitable future. For the rest it was a fact, by them made clear, by them established; a thing fixed and definite, once for all. For Lessing it was a becoming. For the others it was a rejection of what was not *their* truth; for Lessing it was an acceptance and an interpretation of the whole. For the others it meant the irretrievable defeat of metaphysics and religion; for Lessing it was a metaphysic in itself, and almost a religion.

Before this, the Reformation had completely shattered the unity of belief, shattered it so utterly that all efforts to repair it, no matter how determined, had been in vain. But now it was quite a different matter. Religious unity could never be anything now but a memory of the distant past. Every thoughtful man formed his own idea of the nature of the kind of God whom he still longed to retain. When these various doctrines fell into the minds of the multitude, they began to dwindle away, to melt, till they finally disappeared altogether. It was no longer a case of the great mass of the faithful, with a few rebels among them. There was only one army now, the army of the indifferent. Not only, now, was Christendom rent asunder; it began to crumble, to dissolve. All that remained was a herd that looked for happiness in this mortal life, and with no very high standard of happiness at that. It was now no more to them than worldly well-being, material comforts and, sometimes, just pleasure. They were not even atheists, for that would have meant that they denied something. They were now, just nothing, nothing at all. It was everyone according to his conscience, and conscience there was none. Over and beyond the duties imposed upon them by the fact that they were part of a society, they were not conscious of any others. All they thought about now were, not duties, but rights. Tens of thousands, hundreds of thousands, millions, unvisited by any of the agonies of mind that tormented men like Pope, seeing in Voltaire only the destroyer, and utterly incapable of following Lessing in his speculations, or of soaring with him to the heights, lost all notion of the Divine, whether as a starting point or a goal. Such was the final phase of deism; its ultimate expression.

CONCLUSION

CONCLUSION

EUROPE: THE TRUE AND THE FALSE

WHAT exactly was meant by Europe? None could say. To the eastward its limits were indeterminate; and, within, it had not always been divided up in the same way among the peoples who inhabited it. Even of its name there was no very satisfactory explanation. Jupiter, disguised as a bull, had carried off Europa, the daughter of Agenor, as she was walking with her companions along the shore of Phoenicia. In honour of the fair one, he gave the name Europa to one of the quarters of the globe. A fabulous story in which even Herodotus declined to believe. But if precision was somewhat lacking in people's ideas about Europe, there was a very strong European feeling: "Europe is superior in every way to all the other quarters of the globe. It is not so extensive, of course, as Asia, Africa or America, and that, no doubt, was a little annoying, but, people hastened to add, this inferiority in actual size was made up for by a host of causes for pride. Uncertain its limits doubtless were, that was freely granted, but it formed none the less *ein bewunderswürtiges Ganze*, a marvellous whole."[1] It had laws in common, and a common religion, which had won it the name of Christendom; a proud memory, now, which had not been banished even from rebellious hearts. It constituted "a kind of great republic, embracing several States, some monarchical, some not, the former aristocratic, the others democratic, but all in relationship one with another, all having one and the same religious basis, the same principles of public law, the same political ideas, all of them unknown in the other parts of the world."[2] And just as the Greeks might

[1]Joh. Chr. Adelung, *Pragmatische Staatsgeschichte Europens*. . . . Gotha, 1762. *Vorlaüfige Einleitung,* p. 4.

[2]Voltaire, *Siècle de Louis XIV, Introduction,* chap. II.

quarrel among themselves while maintaining mutual relations of seemliness and polite behaviour, as though inhabitants of one and the same city, so Europeans might fight and rend each other, and yet remain united at heart. In a word, "it is not from one country alone, nor from one race, that the eighteenth century derives its celebrity. It owes it to all the peoples, and to all the countries, of Europe; and that is what renders it so great, so full of significance, and so real. . . ."[1]

People continued to belaud the virtuous Chinese, and the sage Egyptians, but it had to be confessed that neither China nor Egypt had fulfilled its long-standing promises. They had remained inert, whereas the Western mind had been characterized by an eager and unwearying curiosity. It had never stood still, so that the Greeks and Romans themselves had been surpassed by the present generation. Before now, there had been centres of light, but they were few in number; nothing eclipsed Athens and Rome, but in the age of their splendour "Paris was but a little barbarous city, Amsterdam but a marsh, Madrid a desert, and from the right bank of the Rhine to the Gulf of Bothnia, all was wild and uncivilized." Thus modern Europe was of greater worth than ancient Europe. What wonderful advantages have accrued to her: military power, vast expenditure, mighty battles, enormous quantities of troops, and the ceaseless maintenance thereof. Agricultural development, a temperate climate, fertile soil, except for the lands situated in the far North. Thriving trade, assisted by the abundance of means of communication. Numerous inhabitants, opulent cities. But above all, intellectual superiority: the sciences, the fine arts, the mechanical arts and the increase in production resulting from them; the rule of a reason which tended to become universal, which checked all foolish national pride, which did away with the *ingenium glebae*. The philosophical and intellectual arsenal of the world. This is not to say that these modern Europeans did not have their faults. Restless spirits, their history was one of ceaseless revolutions, and their annals a tissue of misfortunes, follies and crimes. Corrupted by luxury, they cruelly exploited the natives of the colonies they had conquered. Nevertheless, they retained the right to hold their heads high. How was it

[1]*Esprit et Génie des écrivains du XVIIIe siècle.* Amsterdam. Voltaire, *L'A.B.C.*, 1768. *Septième Entretien.*

that the peoples of Asia and Africa had not landed in their ports, conquered their territories, and imposed their yoke on the rulers thereof? Because the Europeans were too strong for them. And they were the stronger because they excelled in wisdom, and by the same token, they represented a higher grade of civilization.[1]

They travelled as people anxious to gain a surer hold on their estate, their unrivalled estate. Travelling took on a new character. It was no longer the craze of some "curious impertinent" with an itch for roaming about and idly gaping at things; it was now an apprenticeship to life, a serious undertaking, the finishing touch to one's education. It was in fact the school for Europeans. The English did what they called the *Grand Tour* under the eye of a tutor; the Germans knew very well that they were not properly licked into shape till they had had a little polish applied to them by foreign travel; Italians and French people were to be met with everywhere. Russians, nowadays, were not the sort of outlandish Muscovites that had filled the preceding generation with amazement; they came blithely to unload their roubles in the big western cities and notably in Paris. When you said good-bye to the village pump, it was not as if you were going off on some sort of perilous expedition, where your life might be in danger. Roads were improving and communications getting easier. Town gates were no longer closed at curfew, and postilions whipped up their horses boldly along the dim highways. Time was saved by a half. Wealthy folk had big carriages specially built for them. The Duc de Richelieu had a bed in his, as well as a meat-safe to hold three *entrées*. The story goes that in 1742, just as he was starting off from Choisy-le-Roi, he ordered the sheets to be warmed and "went to bed with thirty people looking on, and said he was to be called at Lyons". All those actors we have brought on the stage, ought to be shown again in mobility. Hardly a single man of letters in the eighteenth century but was bitten by the travel bug. Even Samuel Johnson, the most massive of writers, left his home, his easy-chair and his seat at the Cheshire Cheese, friendliest of taverns, to go and travel on the Continent; even Diderot at last consented to leave his Paris and betake himself to St.

[1]Samuel Johnson, *Rasselas,* 1759, Chap. XI. Montesquieu, *Cahiers,* Ed. Grasset, pp. 65 *et sqq.*

Petersburg. Even princes, for all their attachments to the hereditary domain, took to travelling abroad. The Crown Prince of Sweden was in his box at the Paris Opera when news was brought him that his father was dead, and he, King Gustavus the Third.

They went about inspecting all the well-known Natural History collections, and all the things of curious interest; they went into ecstasies over stones that had water inside them, over fossils, and those monstrous creatures, strange and disquieting jests of Creation. They called on the scientists and scholars in their modest abodes, and attended meetings of the learned societies. They went about taking the measurements of churches and counting the steps of the towers. They crowded into the theatres, and never missed an opera, especially in Italy; for they delighted in music, and nothing pleased them better than to stow away in their baggage the score of the latest thing by Pergolese, so as to be able to get it played in their own country when they got back. They made their way into the studios of artists and sculptors, bought pictures, statues and collected ancient medals. There were capitals that were specially European in character. There was Paris, where they felt strangely free, where you could put in an appearance as and when you liked, and where you could disappear without anyone being any the wiser. A home of marvels; here was every country's best and choicest; there was a grace and charm about the people and their ways that made the place attractive beyond all others; a meeting-place for foreigners who put up in the hotels; Paris, light of lights. And then there was Venice, sweet city of pleasure, seductiveness and charm; the carnival, the masques, the gondolas, gaming-tables, theatres named after churches, concerts everywhere, even in nunneries, the trestle-stage in the square of St. Mark; the courtesans and their palace-like abodes; Venice, the modern Sybaris. Then, Rome and its Holy Week; Naples, and the springtime. Vienna, half-Latin, half-Teuton, a gate opening on the Orient.

Guide-books, descriptions, itineraries, nay, whole libraries of travel-literature, bore witness to this ever-growing fashion. More than that, the foreigner became a sort of comedy-figure, and Lord Runebil, the Chevalier Le Bleau, Don Alvaro of Castile, and the Count de Bosco Nero all confronted one another on the stage. There were performances of *Le Français à Londres*, and *L'Anglais à Bordeaux*. Rough and ready pictures, in which people were pleased to represent the inhabitants of other countries, sometimes true enough, but more often false, became so stereotyped in men's minds that time was powerless to efface them. No need to say good-bye to the Faubourg Saint-Antoine, or the rue Saint-Denis; you could see on the stage the Englishman, taciturn, philosophical, solemn, always rich and always generous; the Italian, unfailing lover of the fine-arts; the Spaniard, invariably noble and proud; and you had the idea that you were one of a strange company, indeed, but an indissoluble one. Customs, institutions, travelled too; the Italian opera, the English tea, and even the *matinée à l'anglaise*; so that in time people came to talk about "European habits", "the European mode of life".

In their private correspondence, people talked, not so much about their personal concerns, their own interests, their love-affairs, as of what was going on in the intellectual world; such and such a book had just come out, such and such a play had been a flop. Learned societies also corresponded. There were paid writers whose business it was to give the German princes the earliest news of what came out in Paris. Newspapers, once the repositories of purely native talent, were now invaded by reviews of books from beyond the mountains or beyond the seas. New journals were started for the express purpose of facilitating literary exchanges, such as the *Bibliothèque anglaise*, the *Bibliothèque germanique*, the *Journal des nouveautés littéraires d'Italie*, the *Journal étranger*. Others, by their very title, proclaimed their European character. Such were *L'Europe savante*, *Histoire littéraire de l'Europe*, *Bibliothèque raisonnée des savants de l'Europe*, *Biblioteca universale o gran Giornal d'Europa*, *Estratto della letteratura europea*, *L'Europa letteraria*, *Giornale letterario d'Europa*, *Correo general historico, literario y económico de la Europa*; reading them, as an Italian paper put it, "men who were once Romans, Florentines, Genoese or Lombards, were all becoming more or less Europeans."[1]

If, in the schools, foreign languages were almost totally neglected, they began to be taken up when it was perceived that, in after life, they were necessary for the interchange of mind with mind. A grammar came out; edition after edition was

[1] *Il Caffè*, 1764. First Article.

published and it had a long run, till another compiler, picking out the faults of his predecessor, the ignorant fellow, came along with another grammar still more of a money-maker than the first. In the end, the rivals, instead of cutting each other's throats, thought it best to combine their separate grammars into one; a good thing for the buyer and a good thing for the sellers, too. And then there were dictionaries, numbers of them. And selections, and anthologies. The language-masters were a mixed crowd, including, at one end of the scale, the most shady adventurers, and, at the other, some of the most illustrious men of letters; Bareti was a teacher of Italian in London, and Goldoni in Paris.

And those translations! If we regard them carefully, we shall see how they rose in status during the seventeenth and eighteenth centuries. Translations, in which blunders, misunderstandings and positive howlers bore eloquent testimony to the ignorance of the bold people who had undertaken them, ignorance not only of the foreign language, but of their own; commercial enterprises, factory-produced goods, turned out by needy workmen for rapacious publishers; masterpieces treated "like those unlucky individuals who were stripped by a pirate of their sumptuous attire to be put up for sale, all rags and wretchedness, in some place far from their native land".[1]

Insolent fellows, these translators, who call themselves plenipotentiaries, and even think themselves superior to the original authors whose defects they remove and whose virtues they accentuate without a blush. Faithless, some, and necessarily so, because one had to go, without too much of a jolt, from the unknown to the known, and to get something with an exotic flavour swallowed without any marked dislike. Such as they were, they passed muster, and as time went on, they contributed to build up an international literature.

The more numerous these interchanges became, the greater grew the need for some kind of order, some sort of hierarchy of values, and, at the top of it, an agreed authority. For a time it looked as if the Power chosen by Europe to fulfil this lofty function was France. Because she possessed political power, without which literature feels that it is rather in the air; because

[1]La Barre de Beaumarchais, *Lettres sérieuses et badines,* 1729, Vol. II, Part II, Letter 19.

she had the advantage of numbers and a teeming population; because she had a long cultural tradition at the back of her; and finally because she had just emerged from the age of Louis XIV with its constellation of brilliant geniuses, she it was who, from the last century onward, had offered herself as a model. And, instead of her light growing dim, as generally happens after the Pleiads have set, behold she took on a new lustre. Corneille and Racine, Bossuet and Fénelon had not yet given all they had, when other stars appeared in her firmament. The upward trend went on, and the writers who now brought honour to her name had the requisite quality for exciting emulation, they were in the ranks of modernity. There were none more eager, more daring or more prompt in formulating, defending and disseminating the ideas which were then so much engrossing the contemporary mind. Thus France still retained the literary supremacy which had come to her as a heritage, and she vindicated her title to the distinction by bringing a substantial contribution. Pretty well all the other races had an impression of being behind-hand when they compared themselves with her, and in their anxiety to catch up, the first thing that occurred to them was to take her for their guide. A rare privilege for a country to supply at once both rule and inspiration, to represent at once the firmness that gives confidence, and the mobility which betokens life. They sought to get level with her in those classical forms wherein she had excelled and still continued to excel, and together with all that, they aimed at thinking as she did, that is to say, with daring and with speed. This was the age when French modes of expression, gallicisms, were making their way into the vocabularies of other nations, a fact of which those other nations were not only unashamed, but positively proud. For the French tongue, so pure, so clear, so refined, had now become the very organ of the reason. What kind of out-of-date puristic pedantry, or narrow nationalistic prejudice could have stood in the way, or led people to refuse to draw on her vocabulary or to adopt her analytical tone? Those were the days when French as spoken at Versailles was heard also on the banks of the Neva; the days when many an author, discarding his native idiom, adopted the tongue that was dear alike to the Graces and the Philosophers, and enabled a writer to be read and understood in every land. It was at this time that the Berlin Academy, as the subject for the prize competition for 1784, proposed the following questions: "What is it that has made French the universal language of Europe? What merits entitle it to this distinction? Is it probable that it will retain it?" Now, too, it was that she bestowed her crown, not only on the discourse of the German, Schwab, but also on that of Rivarol, which set the seal on French intellectual hegemony.

"The French have been for more than a hundred and fifty years the race best acquainted with the art of social life, the first to free it from all constraint. . . ."[1] Another prerogative which explained the same pre-eminence—It Europe was destined to form a single society, France again would present it with an ideal. Paris was like a great drawing-room, a great *salon*, in which it was a delight to talk, to shine, or merely to listen. Those who had experienced the charm of living there, but had had to leave it, felt a sort of homesickness, a longing as for some lost Paradise. Such was the Abbé Galiani who, when he had, much against his will, to leave it and go back to Naples, was never able to console himself. A way of life was adopted there, better, it would seem, than any of which the past had offered an example; a *commercio umano*,[2] a more humane mode of intercourse, and it had been well if the rest of the world had followed the example. The aristocracy, the upper middle-classes of the various countries were doing their best to attract to their own abodes the spirit of the people who had had the skill to erect this auspicious edifice. A start was made with furnishing the house, and with the adornment of the person, with the culinary art, with the services of the butler, the wig-maker and the tailor. With French hair-dressing and French clothes came the French tone and the French manner. When the dressmakers of the rue Saint-Honoré sent their dolls, attired in the latest Paris fashion, to be exhibited in the shop fronts of the foreign capitals, they were playing their part in moulding social life. So were the dancing-masters; so were the milliners. The process was carried on by the stage-players who performed to royalty at foreign courts, and toured the capitals and even established themselves there sometimes. "If you saw our theatre, you

[1]Voltaire, *Dictionnaire philosophique,* Article *Langues.*

[2]Letter from Frugoni to Algarotti, from Parma, 13th Oct., 1758.

would see something very funny; you would see a school for little children. Everybody's got his book in front of him, his head well down, never looking up to see what is taking place on the stage. It seems that all they want to do is to learn French."[1] The good work was carried on by artists of every sort. They too did their best to construct a French Europe in this age of enlightenment.[2] If, by way of experiment, we were to arrange in their several categories the various gallicisms which, at this time, had obtained official recognition in foreign countries, we should find that they had to do with the art of eating well, dressing well, cutting an attractive figure, polished behaviour, and conversing like a well-bred man of the world. We should also note further that they conveyed those subtle nuances, psychological and moral, which play their part in intellectual refinement; they formed a coherent whole, when the disturbance caused by their first arrival had subsided. They implied the notion of art, military art, the art of conversation, the art of painting or sculpture; the art of thinking, the art of life.

There even came about this singular phenomenon—the meaning of the word "cosmopolitan" was misconceived. Strange to say, the cosmopolitan, though he may not have recognized as much, had come to signify someone who thought *à la française*; he became one of a tribe, or species; yes, he was the citizen of a nation, a nation which included the civilized members of all the other nations, a nation whose members felt themselves united by a common language and a common outlook on life. The type, in its ultimate perfection, is represented by a man who was the most brilliant of them all, the Prince de Ligne. The Prince de Ligne declared that he had so many countries that he did not know with certainty to which of them all he properly belonged. He felt as perfectly at home in Vienna as he did in St. Petersburg. Forever on the move, Europe for him was one great highway, with a succession of inns, and through it he drove at full speed. The fact was that the language he spoke, and wrote, the tone and texture of his mind, his habits, his whole way of life, made him one with the *élite*, wherever he encountered them, people who made it seem to him that he was among friends, people who identified Paris with Cosmopolis.

[1] L'abbé Galiani to Mme d'Epinay, from Naples, 16th Jan., 1773.

[2] Louis Réau, *L'Europe française au siècle des lumières*, 1938.

"A single, identical current of ideas in those days permeated the whole of western Europe, bringing about a spiritual unity comparable to that of the Renaissance, to humanism and, later on, to romanticism."[1] At least such a unity did tentatively come about. An attempt was made to re-create a European mind. Even the peoples on the outer limits, whose remoteness, whose very distinct kind of language and whose marked individualism seemed to exclude them from the general movement, gradually came to throw in their lot with it. Sweden, after the death of Charles XII, was obliged to draw in her horns. To begin with, she entered on a phase which strongly resembled inertia, but which was in reality merely a sort of stock-taking. Before long, she contributed her quota to the work of science, then engrossing the whole of Europe, by giving it Linnaeus; Olaf Dalin, the court poet, treated of fashionable themes in the fashionable kinds of versification; and in 1750, Mme Nordenflycht started the first salon Stockholm had ever known. Hungary, through the Dutch universities, which were attended by a considerable number of her students, and through the German universities, where others of her young men were imbibing the philosophy of Wolff; through the Jesuits and the Piarists; through Vienna; through her direct relations with Paris; through all these divers representatives of that Reason which was becoming the inspiring force of the new era—in all these ways, and by all these means, Hungary was putting on modernity. Poland, torn by domestic strife, a prey to anarchy, powerless to resist the cupidity of her neighbours, and doomed to perish, had, ever since the accession of Stanislas Augustus, been carrying on a pathetically hopeless task; she would set herself to renounce that Sarmatic heritage which had led her for so long to acquiesce with complacency in her ancient defects; she would obtain from the foreigner the secret of those social reforms which should be her salvation; she would change her system of education; she would get herself a philosophy from the Encyclopaedia; logic she would learn from Condillac; she would recover her vital force; a tremendous effort, yet all the time the process of dismemberment went on which, before long, was to cause her to disappear from among the nations. It was

[1]Rudolf Mertz, *Les amitiés françaises de Hume et le mouvement des idées*. *Revue de Litt. comparée*, 1929.

a race, a test of speed, and she hoped to win it; and if she lost, well, she would at least have given assurance of a will to endure for a future generation to profit by. Russia, though her gaze was towards the East, at least turned to Europe to aid her with her artists, her scholars, her scientists, her engineers, and her philosophers, reviving thus the tradition of Peter the Great.

So it was that an ideal map began to take shape. In the centre, was the country that gave more than it received, the country whose language provided the several nations with the means of communication they needed, the land of dazzling ideas, namely France. By her side, as though to lend her aid, was Holland, with her bookshops and her news-sheets, and Switzerland, *Helvetia mediatrix*. At varying distances away, according to the worth of what they produced but constantly revolving about this same centre on the planetary chart, were all the other nations. And permeating the whole, one spiritual order, and that, European.

This was not mere appearance, mere outward seeming; it was one of the aspects of the reality of things; one, but not the only one. Europe was seeking unity; the fact is certain; but not less certain than the fact that she was rending herself asunder. And, as was her wont, she was doing so with might and main. Writers who made mention of the Swiss or the Poles, of the Portuguese or the Muscovites, never failed to tack on some uncomplimentary epithet to their description; they would always introduce a "but" to qualify the recital of their worthier qualities, as though they wanted to modify or destroy the effect of their encomiums. Take Moreri's *Dictionnaire historique* and turn up the article on Europe, and you will at once have an example of a *parti pris*, a prejudice which is universal. "The French are described as polite, skilful, generous, but hasty and inconstant; the Germans are said to be sincere, good workers, but heavy, and too much addicted to wine; the Italians are agreeable, sensitive and soft-spoken, but jealous and treacherous; while the Spaniards are secretive, cautious, but blustering, and too much given to outward display. As for the English, they are brave to the point of recklessness, but haughty, scornful and almost truculently proud. . . ." Everyone is served with his portion. Turn up some of Boissy's plays; Boissy, who was one of those who had a taste for bringing foreign, outlandish sorts of people into his comedies.

> J'ai parcouru sans faire résidence,
> L'Allemagne, la Suisse, où l'on m'a forcément
> Enseigné l'art de boire alternativement
> En même pot qui fait la ronde,
> Et de m'enivrer proprement
> Pêle-mêle avec tout le monde.
> Puis j'ai vu la Hollande où l'esprit, l'agrément,
> Où le plaisir paraît un être imaginaire;
> Où le vrai savoir-vivre, où le grand art de plaire,
> Est l'art de commercer toujours utilement.
> J'ai fait le tour de l'Italie;
> La j'ai, pendant dix mois, subsisté de concert,
> Ou n'ai vécu que de dessert. . . .[1]

Just look at Caraccioli's *Voyage de la raison en Europe* (1772). Caraccioli was a francophile of the kind that made French their principal language. "'Come now', says Reason, 'let us see whether the enlightenment that I distributed among the Europeans has been dimmed, and whether they still revere my laws'." Reason, in the person of a good-natured philosopher, is disappointed, for Holland, though still retaining some eminent virtues, is declining; commerce excites too sordid an interest there; the Portuguese are clever, but too obstinately engrossed in scholasticism; the Spaniards have a few rare and exalted spirits among them, but on the whole they are brutalized by their sloth.

Since the French look on themselves as a superior race, the critic handles them with peculiar severity. Out on "Jean France", that lover of good food, wine and women; on the "Mossoo" who gets on your nerves with his compliments, his pirouettes, and his supercilious disdain for anything that doesn't bear the Paris trade-mark. Out on the "Mamselle" the heartless

[1]Without making my home there, I have travelled all over Germany and Switzerland where I had to learn the art of drinking in my turn after others out of the same cup as it went the round, and getting properly drunk with all the rest. Then I saw Holland where wit, pleasure seemed to be something imaginary; where the real *savoir-faire,* and the art of pleasing was to do a useful bit of business. Then I did Italy, and for ten months lived on concerts and only had dessert to eat. *Le mari garçon,* 1742.

little flirt; out on M. de Fatencourt and M. Lebhaft, on the "fripon francese", on the adventurer who assumes a sham title of nobility and worms his way into decent families, and then swindles them; out on M. Ricaut de la Marlinière! "Often a Frenchman, when he has run through all his money, says good-bye to Paris as there's no fortune to be made there, leaving his tailor's bill unpaid, and goes and teaches languages at a couple of florins a month somewhere in Germany."[1] To put it in a nutshell, these stuck-up French people are the "Graeculi" of the modern world.

Quarrels break out, and bring these animosities to light. Paris made a huge jest of Rostbeef the Englishman; London retaliated by putting the Parisian dandy into a farce and making him a figure of fun. Look at him, when his finery is laid aside; look at his sackcloth shirt, look at his head, now that his wig has fallen off, all scabs and plaster; and in his pockets a crust of half-gnawed bread, a few onions he's been nibbling at, a filthy comb with half its teeth gone.[2] Walpole kept a strict control over the London theatres, but he did allow a French company to come and pit themselves against the Londoners. They opened up in October, 1738. The mob broke down the doors, rushed all the seats, booed the intruders, threw all sorts of missiles at them, knives included; outside, they smashed window-panes and lamps and wrecked the façade. When the trouble extended to the thing about which a country is probably most sensitive of all, namely music, the dispute looked as if it would go on for ever. In 1752 an Italian company came and took up its quarters at the Paris opera. French music deemed itself attacked in its innermost sanctuary. The adversaries stand face to face, in battle array. On the King's side are ranged the officials, the conservatives, the supporters of Rameau. On the Queen's, the philosophers, the innovators, the supporters of the Bouffons. Follows a war of taunting rhymes, pamphlets and lampoons. A dummy, supposed to be Jean Jacques Rousseau, who backed the Italians, was burnt in the courtyard of the Opera. Even when the Italians were obliged to give in and depart, passions were

[1] *Il fripon francese colla dama alla moda,* commedia del marchese Gioseffo Gorini Corio, Milan, 1730.

[2] Zacharie, *Le Mouchoir, Poème heroï-comique,* Chant III. In *Choix de Poésies allemandes,* by Huber, 1766.

not appeased, the quarrels still went on. The whole business began again in 1773, with the Gluckists against the Piccinists. There was only one thing to put an end to the squabbles, and that was the Revolution.[1]

After all, one rubs along pretty well in the family circle, even though there may be a little bickering sometimes; but now it was the family itself that was changing. On that map, the one which we were talking about just now, we have got to write in some new intellectual centres. Berlin looks like eclipsing Leipzig, the city of books; then there is Dresden, the home of the fine arts; Hamburg, the great commercial city; London bids fair to outshine Paris, and that's the plain truth of the matter. For a long time literary Germany had been regarded as something that did not count. Science, Law, if you will, but Poetry, no! What! these Barbarians of the North, claiming a place in the running? Dull wits and an unpronounceable language! They had not a single writer who had made any sort of stir in Europe; if they had, we should have heard of him. "Tell me of one creative spirit on that Parnassus of yours, I mean name a single German poet that has produced an original work of any note. I tell you, you cannot."[2] The challenge was taken up and we may see, step by step, how the awakening came about. Here is what Grimm says in 1750: "For thirty years or more now, Germany has been an aviary of little birds, only waiting for the propitious season to begin their song. Perhaps the time of glory for the Muses of my native land is not so far away." In 1752, the Baron de Bielefeld gives us his *Progrès des Allemands dans les belles-lettres et les arts*. Then, in 1753, Grimm again: "The demand for translations from the German seems to be growing every day. . . ." In 1762, "German poetry and German literature in general are now all the fashion in Paris. . . . A dozen years ago, if anyone had spoken of a German poet, he would have been laughed at. Times have changed." In 1766, Dorat, *Idée de la poésie allemande,* "O Germany, our heyday is over, yours is about to begin." In 1766, Huber with his *Choix de poésies allemandes*, a Summa presenting the public with the work of a number of authors bearing some curious names, Uz, Gellert, Rabener, Hagedorn, Lichtwer, and others not to be

[1]Abbé Prévost, *Pour et Contre,* No. 80.

[2]Mauvillon, *Lettres françaises et germaniques,* 1740.

overlooked. "Hardly sixteen years ago", wrote Huber, "German poetry was still quite unknown in France." That brief span marked the transition from ignorance to infatuation.

What it amounted to was a change in kind. The Swiss shepherd, Gessner, stood for the simple as opposed to the elaborate, the natural to the artificial, real warm-heartedness to a shallow gallantry. Klopstock stood for the songs of the Bards, and for the poetry of religion; Winckelmann for a new conception of Beauty. The *Werther* of the youthful Goethe offered for the admiration and imitation of his innumerable readers a new human type. The German output, so profoundly different from what France had to offer, called for some discrimination; some selection was necessary. In his *Discorso sulle vicende della letteratura,* published in 1761, Denina, a Piedmontese, has only a few lines to spare for the Germans; the only poet, it seemed to him, they had to boast of was Haller, and he was a Swiss. In 1763, a second edition of his *Discorso* came out in Glasgow, which subsequently, in 1767, appeared in Paris in a French translation bearing the title, *Tableau des Révolutions de la littérature ancienne et moderne.* This time full amends were made. In the distant past, the Germans had written all their learned works in Latin; only twenty years since, all they had in the vernacular were a few wholly extravagant poetical compositions; "Now, however, it seems that they intend to keep abreast of the most learned peoples of Europe, especially those most noted for their literary production." They ran one risk, and that was an excessive imitation of the French and English.

For it was a fact; people *did* copy the English, now. The English were not content with having given to the world the most illustrious of philosophers, an army of deists, ingenious apologists, a liberal supply of moralists, and even some latter-day classics, like Dryden and Pope; they were now setting out to lead people along unfamiliar paths. Among their exports were the works of such people as Defoe and Swift, Richardson, Fielding, Smollett, Sterne, Young, Gray, Hervey, Ossian; a whole school of original literature. Quality and quantity, both were theirs. From that inexhaustibly fertile island came a ceaseless flow of novel ideas eagerly devoured on the Continent. It was the English whom the Germans, beginning now to forsake the French, were taking as their masters. Like a docile pupil, Germany took in all she was told by the English freethinkers, moralizing journalists, romantic writers, playwrights and poets. As was remarked by Uz, picturing the poets as they climbed up the Parnassus of the day, the Germans, rather than pursue the usual highway fragrant with flowers and ending with the statue of Homer, were taking a rough and stony track with an English statue of black marble at the end of it. "English ideas seem to be having the same influence today on the German Parnassus as the wealth and military strength of England have on the political equilibrium of Europe; London *is* what Paris *was*."[1]

Restraint, good taste, balance, observance of the sainted rules —no, these hampering formalities were not for the English, only too happy to get back to their native freedom. The apprehension of the concrete, feasts of imagination, be they never so melancholy, so funereal; forebodings of the sensitive mind; pangs of the heart, these were the things they opposed to the dominance of the abstract, and the discipline of logic and philosophy. But what was France doing, in view of the progress this rival of hers was making? France welcomed her with open arms, she encouraged her, she made much of her. Her curiosity, her sympathy, her favour, she bestowed them freely on merits which were pretty nearly in exact opposition to her own. More than that, she contracted the fashionable epidemic; she became herself an anglo-maniac. Nay, more even than that, she made herself the intermediary between England and the rest of Europe. English books were apt to be somewhat ponderous, she gave them lightness; they were ill-constructed, she put that right; they were over-long, she abridged them; all this she did in her translations. She saw to their toilet, saw that they were properly dressed, so that they should not scare away her customers. After a brief stay in Paris, they would set out for the Latin countries, and even for the German ones, for Italians, Spanish and Portuguese, and, at least till the middle of the century, the Germans too were indebted to France for their knowledge of English literature. So it looked as though the very people who claimed hegemony in these matters were blithely doing their utmost to discard it. And the two neighbours we have cited

[1]In *Choix de poésies allemandes*, Huber, Vol. IV; *Épitres morales*, pp. 202 *et sqq.*: *A M. le Conseiller C.*

as propagandists of their fame, altered their attitude accordingly. Highly characteristic was the work carried out by Justus Van Effen, a Dutchman. Making use of the French language for his purpose, he introduced English journals, and notable English works to his public. And then Switzerland; from Berne, also in French, Béat de Muralt proclaimed the coming ascendancy of England over France. At Zurich, Bodmer and Breitinger assume the office of introducers of the new German literature. Haller starts a school of philosophic poetry on the English model; Geneva, like Paris, is seized with anglo-mania.

The wheels had run full circle. Because she was under a charm; because she felt she must renew her spirit; because, being purveyor-in-ordinary to her foreign clientèle, she felt she must put in her basket the goods that were in demand; because there was a touch of proselytism in all her undertakings—for all these reasons, France proceeded to assist Europe to free itself from the intellectual supremacy of France! Now and again, she realized how, by extolling these new ideas, she was cutting the ground from under her own feet. "Young's 'Night Thoughts' have made a fortune here", wrote Mme Riccoboni in a letter to Garrick; "no one can deny that that implies a complete change in the French mentality." More often than not, she seemed to be unaware of any essential difference. She had apparently no idea that England had pulled up short in her advocacy of the new philosophy. While she was all enthusiasm for Bolingbroke, Hume and Gibbon, recognizing in them her comrades in arms, she never guessed that British opinion had decided on a return to Puritanism. William Law, a mystic who, back in 1723, had published *A Serious Call to a Devout and Holy Life*, and, later on, in 1731, *The Case of Reason*, was a name almost unknown in eighteenth-century France. According to Law, the Man of Nature and the Man of Reason were alike to be condemned; Nature was blood, and the flesh and sin; Reason was a factitious light, coming from without; only the Christian, illumined by the inward light of Divine Grace, could win through to the Truth and the Light. Whenever by chance she happened to hear of him, France showed but very little respect for John Wesley, who, about the year 1738, had been visited by a sudden illumination of the spirit. Regularly, every day of his life, he went forth preaching the Gospel to the miners of Newcastle, or the weavers of Bristol, or the poor of London, or making his way from town to town, from village to village, bringing back belief in the Saviour to those who had lost it, and giving new hope to the poor and the oppressed, bidding them, in their depths of desolation, never to despair; and all this in the name of Christ. A crusade among the lowly; but the result of it was that, through Methodism, England found its moral basis once again.

Thus, after noting the forces which tended to unite Europe in one common attitude of mind, we are beginning to get a glimpse of others, working in an opposite direction. And here are a few more of them.

Of course we are all aware that nationalism, the jealously nationalistic spirit, was a product of the nineteenth century. But it was already brewing a century before. And how deep-rooted, how vigorous was the hidden instinct which preceded the actual idea, how quick to discern, among the various foreign influences which impinged upon it, those which it would keep as germane to its purpose, and those which it would discard as irrelevant. It seemed that each separate country was an organism persisting in its own being and early or late adhering exclusively to its own proper law. Among all those which we have instanced, there was not one, not a single one, whose chief and primary aim was not to ensure its own individual existence; not one but looked upon whatever it gained from France, whether it appertained to the intellectual, or to the outward and visible, as a temporary expedient to enable it to become, in due time, more firmly and definitely itself; not one but submitted to an intellectual hegemony for the time being, as a means of securing its own independence in the end.

Let us take as an example a country which had long been a compact and unified whole, namely Spain. For the first time in the history of the modern world, it looked as if Spain was being influenced by France, by the French spirit. She must needs have an academy similar to the one that held its sessions at the Louvre, and it did in fact come about that, through the active intervention of a man who was in close touch with foreign scholars, the Marquis de Villena, the *Real Academia española* was founded in 1714 and started work on a Dictionary, the first volume of which appeared in 1726. It must also have a journal on the lines of the *Journal des Savants*, and so the *Diario de los Literatos de España* began to appear in 1737. Several others followed it. Spain, too, must of course submit her genius to the restraints imposed by good taste. She, too, would have a classic drama, she, too, would have high tragedy on the classic model, strictly governed by the law of the three unities. There were Spaniards who repudiated Calderon and Lope de Vega; there were Spaniards who demanded, and successfully demanded, that the *autos sacramentales*, one of the treasures of their heritage, should be excluded from all stage representation. A royal decree to this effect was promulgated on the 11th June, 1765. French fashions in dress were proudly displayed, not only by the women, but by men, the *petimetres* as they were called. The language was belarded with French turns of speech; ministers of state were imbued with French ideas. It looked like a triumph for the *afrancesados*.

But was it? Or was it all superficial, all a matter of appearance? The precarious victories of the francophils were not scored without a prolonged struggle, and, even so, they had no morrow, no sequel. However extravagant some might be in their praise of Paris, others there were who had some harsh things to say about the French people and who came down pretty heavily on Spaniards who were foolish enough to ape them. What it all amounted to was that the only productions that had any lasting quality about them were those that brought out the genuine national spirit, such as the short dramatic sketches of Ramon de la Cruz, and the comedies of Nicolas Fernandez de Moratin. Those foreign influences had no effect whatever on the mass of the people, nor on the lower middle classes, nor on the aristocracy in general, nor even on all the literary people, not by any means. They stopped short at a level which is very easily influenced. Let anyone speak disparagingly of Spain and forthwith her defenders are up in arms. A highly significant episode is the quarrel that took place between certain Italian critics and the Spanish Jesuits. The Jesuits had been expelled from their country, with what brutality we have already seen, and the greater number of them had sought refuge in Italy. The Italians took up the old story, alleging that Seneca and Martial in their day had infected Rome with that virus of bad taste which had spelt the ultimate corruption of Latin literature; and that, in later times, Gongora had gone on with the same ill-omened work. At this, the Spanish Jesuits took up the pen. There were Fr. Juan Andres, Fr. Tomas Serrano, and Fr. Javier Lampillas. Oblivious of the wrong their country had done them, they vehemently defended the national honour. Another banished Jesuit, Fr. Juan Francisco de Masdeu, began to bring out in 1783 a monumental *Historia critica de España*, in the first volume of which he set forth the renown of his native country, showing that it owed its merits entirely to itself, and to no foreign source. The fact is it was not so easy to handle old Spain; her features were too strongly marked to be obscured by any transient fashion of the day. That she was determined to remain herself, to retain her grim, unapproachable independence, she was soon to make clear in her struggle with Napoleon.

In the eighteenth century, there was a nationalistic spirit abroad in England which had taken root there some time before. There was a similar spirit in France, which revealed itself conspicuously, when de Belloy staged his *Siège de Calais* in 1765. The public shouted applause, wept, and proclaimed it a masterpiece; not so much from the intrinsic merits of the play as from the emotions it called forth. "Here we have perhaps the first French tragedy to awaken the country's interest with a plot concerning its own history." "Good-bye to those pallid ideas about cosmopolitanism where a country, a native land, is no longer identical with the actual kingdom:

> Je haïs ces coeurs glacés et morts pour leur pays
> Qui, voyant ses malheurs dans une paix profonde,
> S'honorent du grand nom de citoyen du monde.[1]

But nowhere was this sentiment more active than in two great countries that were still split up, but where a national literature was voicing its appeal to the national spirit. To what an extent Italy was partitioned we know full well. Pretty well every kind of government was represented within her borders; from end to end of her provinces it was one long succession of frontiers and

[1] I hate those icy hearts that are dead to the love of their country and who, beholding her misfortunes in the profoundest peace, proudly describe themselves as citizens of the world.

customs posts; she seemed to be made up of a quantity of miscellaneous fragments that would never be put together again. Howbeit, she knew her political weakness well enough; she took it to heart, she was filled with longing, and already a vague hope was stirring dimly within her. Thoroughly gallicized though she was, a pang went through her every time the French, or any other nation for that matter, took her to task. It was not true that her drama, her poetry, her philosophy, or her science were in any respect second-rate; her supremacy in art, if nothing else, should suffice to assure her a place in the sun. It was not true that she was reduced to servile imitation. Nor was it correct to say that in any of her capitals, Milan for example, an Italian that was not a Milanese was looked on as a foreigner. An Italian was at home anywhere in Italy, as much at home as an Englishman was in England, or a Dutchman in Holland.[1] The poets returned again and again to the familiar theme, common to all Europe, namely, the decadence of present-day Italy, compared with the majesty of imperial Rome. However, they treated that splendid memory in a way of their own, they referred to it as a patent of nobility that was valid still.

Even if we made the grave error of disregarding these appeals, these claims put forward through the printed word, these summary demands, one psychological landmark would stand out clear and certain. Those who have made an intimate study of the deeper characteristics of the Italian race have never failed to remark on a certain strain of practical common sense which they regard as one of the dominant features of the Latin character. It shows itself impenetrable to any and every ideology. Liberty, Equality, Progress—fine, high-sounding words these, and they stood for some valuable ideas, but what Italy was concerned with was their practical and specific application to her own case. It was her business to set her own house in order before concerning herself with the affairs of the world at large. She was not so terribly smitten with liberal ideas as not to be able to come to an understanding with other governments, even autocratic, if they were disposed to further her interests. Whether Naples was a republic or an absolute monarchy, the essential thing was effectively to combat those feudal abuses which weighed so

[1]G. Rinaldo Carli, *Della patria degli Italiani*. In *Il Caffè*, 1764–1765, semestre terzo, pp. 12–17.

crushingly on the people. For her, equality was not reducing everyone to one dead level, but a better organization of the classes. Progress, to her, meant a more equitable distribution of taxes, the establishment of a valuation board, measures to stimulate trade and agriculture. The absolute mind was a rarity with her, and one would have looked in vain there for the like of a Baron d'Holbach. She felt no call to abolish her ancestral religion, whether because of a mild sceptical tendency which kept her from going too far in any direction, that of unbelief included; or because she revered her traditions; or because she was content to remedy abuses in ecclesiastical administration, while refraining from tampering with religion itself. Her great works—Parini's, Pietro Verri's, Beccaria's—were social or economic. In Italy, the new philosophy did not take the shape of revolution but of evolution, of measures which offered a quick return. If it would be incorrect to credit her at so early a date as this with any definite plan for bringing about national unity, we must nevertheless recognize the existence of a lively sentiment of *Italianitas*, which was at the root of her political resurrection. The Risorgimento was stirring, even in the eighteenth century.

The second of the two countries which made *il gran rifiuto* was Germany. There was the same sensitiveness in her writers to all unfavourable judgments passed on them by foreigners. The same bitterness, the same anger at the idea that they were receiving less than justice; the claim to be assigned a high place, perhaps even the highest. But over and above it all, an output of such vigour that it embodied an answer to all the attacks; and this brings us again to Lessing.

Hamburg had long been wanting to have a theatre of its own; and some enthusiasts had come forward, who undertook to relieve the manager of what generally brings about the undoing of such enterprises from the artistic point of view; that is to say, financial problems, money worries. They wished him to have at his side an inspirer, someone who, not having any material preoccupations to take up his time, having nothing to do with getting casts together, or with stage-management, or with administrative details of any kind, should have, as his sole function, to act as the spiritual and intellectual guide, as it were, of the undertaking. No one was better fitted for such a post than

Lessing, and so he was duly appointed. On the 22nd April, 1767, he published the first feuilleton of his *Dramaturgie*. "It will be a critical review of every play put on; it will take note, step by step, of whatever progress in poetry and dramatic art may be made here."

And that was precisely what he did. He dealt with all the plays that were given a performance, one by one, saying, for example, why Cronegk's *Olinte et Sophronie* was not a good play, and explaining why it was that Johann Elias Schlegel's *Le Triomphe des Honnêtes femmes* gave him pleasure. The trouble was that there were scarcely any German comedies worth putting on, and no tragedies at all. The result was that they were obliged to have recourse to the French repertory, so that, very surprisingly, the Hamburg national theatre would have become a symbol of French supremacy, had it not been for Lessing. He had kindly feelings for Regnard and Dancourt, he was sympathetic enough towards Diderot, and his plays about bourgeois life, but he was pitilessly down on the classic tragedy. To that he gave no quarter. Would the proud, the puffed-up thing, never die out? Every time the people applauded it, he demonstrated why their applause was misplaced. Whenever someone vaunted its merits, he insisted on its faults; frigid, conventional, artificial, powerless to bring its characters to life. There were rules, rules that were valid for all time, as being based on the immutable dictates of reason. These rules Aristotle had formulated with the same certitude with which Euclid set forth his propositions. To these rules the French flattered themselves they had conformed; but they hadn't, not a bit of it; they had made a mockery of them. Their whole drama was based on a false conception; strictly speaking, they had no drama at all.

Lessing was obliged to listen, more often than he would have wished, to the tragedies of Voltaire. No matter whether it was *Sémiramis*, or *Alzire*, or *Mérope* (incomparably inferior to Maffei's), they were all bad, every one of them. How now! More Voltaire! but it's always Voltaire, everlasting Voltaire! And Lessing explains the reason: "It seems to me that there is no better way for a critic than to adopt this course: let him pick out some adversary to attack; in this way he will sooner or later come to his subject, and the rest will follow of its own accord. That is why, in the present work—I frankly admit it—I have made

French writers the main object of attack, and in particular M. de Voltaire. So here again, a faint salute, and then, '*En garde!*' " But not satisfied with doing that piece of execution, he must needs bring down another writer, greater still, no less a person than the creator of French tragedy himself, Pierre Corneille. Lessing could not bear to hear him called "the great Corneille". The huge, the monstrous Corneille, if you will; but there is no greatness where truth is not. Not only are his tragedies bad, but he wanted to make people believe that he had been true to the Aristotelian rules, in order to try and put himself in the right after the event. In the *Discours* which followed his work as a playwright, he, with calculated perfidy "put a completely false construction" on the Greek philosopher's words. He, then, Corneille, was the prime offender, the real culprit, the man who gave people the illusory notion that the French had a school of drama, whereas in fact they had nothing of the kind. "I will here go so far as to make a proposal which you may take or leave at your pleasure; let anyone tell me of a play by the great Corneille which I could not make into something better than he ever could. Who will take on the bet?"

No one took it on. The Hamburg theatre had a short life; the final feuilleton of the *Dramaturgie* is dated 19th April, 1769. Acrimonious, pedantic, unjust, all this it was; that we freely grant; yet it was so impassioned in tone, it spoke with such deep conviction, it was so original in its ideas, that it remains, and must remain, among the great works of criticism. It marked an epoch in history; it was an open and declared revolt against the genius of France, flouting it in the very temple of its glory, the Drama. In the place occupied by Corneille, Racine, Voltaire, Lessing would put Shakespeare, the "giant", who, compared with the French school, was as a fresco to a miniature. He even called to his aid the Spanish *Comedia*, because it was not conventional, and because it gave utterance to an indomitable spirit. So sore was the need of the indignant Lessing for comrades, English, and Spanish, to fight with him, alongside the Germans, to lower the prestige of France!

Another thing, too, that Italy had not, was one in whom the nation's spirit, the nation's soul was incarnate. Such an one was that great man whom someone defined as "an intelligence and a will which direct a force"; such an one was Frederick II.

Anyone who, not having been warned beforehand, sets himself to read the great output of German lyrical poetry which blossomed forth in such profusion towards the middle of the century, is amazed to come across, among the many odes, Bacchic, Anacreontic, edifying, or simply vapid, allusions to the proud Germans of bygone days, to their strength, their courage, their independent spirit, together with laments for Germany now so sorely oppressed; passionate appeals for unity. Unskilled they may be, these bards, but they all express the same national sentiment, which was everywhere gathering strength, a sentiment which was to concentrate, to crystallize, so to speak, about the person of Frederick II. The *Chants d'un grenadier prussien* by Gleim, which were collected and published in 1758, are no masterpiece, but they clearly reflect the change-over from the Prussian to the German point of view. Gleim pretends to be a soldier, a fighting-man, declaring that he is something very different from a Pindar or a Horace; he is a modern Tyrtaeus. He exalts war, belauds heroic deeds and sings the praises of those brave men who give their lives for their country and deservedly live for ever in the memory of their compatriots; he sings the glory of Frederick the Great. "Victoria! God is with us!" Prussia has brought Austria to her knees, she has given Germany her freedom:

> Wenn Friedrich, oder Gott durch ihn
> Das grosse Werk vollgebracht
> Gesandigt hat das stolze Wien,
> Und Deutschland frei gemacht. . . .

But this great conqueror, this German, in what language does he choose to express himself, if not in French? In what language does he compose his written works? Again, in French. Here then is a matter—the final one—that also calls for explanation.

1779. Frederick II, *Lettres sur l'amour de la patrie, ou correspondance d'Anapistémon et de Philopatros.*

The King is a little uneasy in his mind about where some of the ideas of those allies of his, the philosophers, are going to lead them. He proceeds to explain what he means, without any room for ambiguity. Anapistemon has been visiting his friend Philopatros. Back home again, he writes to thank him for his pleasant stay. The night before he came away, he had a talk with him about society and its ties, and about the mutual obligations of its members. He had never given much thought to this important matter; would Philopatros be so good as to let him have a letter giving him some more information?

So here we have Philopatros playing the schoolmaster to Anapistemon the sceptic, the Epicurean, the *cosmopolite*. He has recourse to the usual arguments, designed to show that the welfare of the bee cannot be considered apart from that of the hive as a whole; but the crux of the matter, from our point of view, is that for society, a more or less vague idea, he substitutes something much more precise, the idea of one's country. "Is it really possible for a man to love his country?" asks Anapistemon. "Would it not be truer to say that this alleged love was invented by some philosopher, or some woolgathering legislator to try to get from men an ideal of conduct of which they are not really capable. How do you suppose one is going to love the common people? How can you expect a man to sacrifice himself for the good of some province of the kingdom which he has never even seen? In short, what I want you to tell me is how can one possibly love with fervour and enthusiasm something one knows nothing whatever about?" And Philopatros, that is, Frederick II, gives him the answer:

The good of society is your own good. You are so closely linked with your country, though you know it not, that you cannot isolate yourself, or cut yourself off from her, without yourself becoming aware that you have done wrong. If the nation is flourishing, you will prosper; if it is in a bad way, the nature of its evil plight will react on you. Love of country is not something evolved by the reason, it actually exists, it is a reality.

Anapistemon is not convinced. He has heard tell of an Encyclopaedist who taught that the earth was the common habitation of all the beings of our species, that the enlightened man was a citizen of the world, and that wherever he was, he was equally well off. Some man of letters had said the same thing in his hearing, and the idea had carried him away. Is it not a fine thing, instead of continuing to be an obscure member of some little state, to become a part of the Universe?

At this Philopatros waxes hot. These Encyclopaedists, and the writing men who take their cue from them, sometimes talk a lot of nonsense. The earth as a whole is the habitation of the race; of course it is, we all know that; no need to dwell on so commonplace a truth. The wise man is a citizen of the world; quite so; but that does not mean that he has got to go wandering about, at a loose end, out of mere boredom, like some resourceless vagrant. What would those Encyclopaedists have to say if their Native Land personified were to come to them and address them in words like these: "Children, unnatural and ungrateful children, to whom I gave the light of day, will you always be insensible to the good things which I lavish upon you? Whence came the ancestors from whom you spring? 'Twas I who brought them forth. Whence did they win the food that nourished them? From my inexhaustible fertility. And their upbringing, their education? That, too, they owe to me; all their possessions, all they call their own. My soil it was that produced them. You, you yourselves, are the children of my womb." If thus his Country were to speak to him, these are the words in which he would make reply: "My heart, deeply moved by love and gratitude, needed not to see you and to hear your voice, to pour forth its affection for you. Yes, I confess, I owe you all; therefore it is that to you I am attached by bonds as tender as they are indissoluble; my love and gratitude will last as long as my life endures; and this life of mine, even that is yours; and when you call upon me to give it back to you, gladly will I lay it down for your sake. To die for you, is to live for ever in the minds of men; to serve you is to bring inevitable glory on my name." Philopatros asks pardon for these lyrical outpourings. "Pardon me," he says, "pardon me this wave of enthusiasm on which my zeal bears me irresistibly away. You behold my very soul all naked before you."

1780. *Of the German literature, of the defects that may be alleged against it; of the causes thereof and of the means whereby they may be corrected.*

Now this same Frederick II knew well enough that the Germans were greatly astonished at his fondness for another country's literature. He will explain matters, we might almost say, excuse himself. Let us examine the matter in the light of reason: this Germany of ours has not yet arrived at the point of maturity; so far, she still lacks a common language; how then could she be expected to produce masterpieces? Our ancestors performed their task well and truly when they made the fatherland strong and prosperous; that was the first thing that had to be done; the finishing touches, the adornments were for a later day. Nowadays, the general taste is set so decidedly on whatever is calculated to shed a lustre on this glorious land of ours, that we too are anxious to have our place in Memory's shrine; but we have yet to merit this crowning glory. Therefore, let our writers set themselves to learn at the school of the ancient classics, and at the school of their modern successors, the French; but let them not take for their model any such person as Shakespeare, whose tragedies are but "sorry travesties, worthy of the wild men of Canada". What is this *Goetz von Berlichingen* which is now appearing on the stage but a detestable imitation of bad English plays? However, the pit applauded it enthusiastically and wants more of these "disgusting platitudes". In these terms Frederick II, dissociating himself from the new German literature, explains his attitude. He does not waver; he is as staunch as ever in his love for his country; but, in so far as great literary achievements are concerned, he considers that there is still much preparatory work to be done; for the masterpieces, we must wait till the morrow. As things are at present, to write in German is to shut oneself up in a prison; to write in French is to have all Europe for an audience.

1781. Justus Möser, *Ueber die deutsche Sprache und Literatur.*

Of the various writings that give an idea of the feeling aroused by the King's expression of his views, this is the best. Justus Möser, the historian of Osnabrück, is full of deference, indeed of respect, in what he says. He knows how far to go. While he laments that the Germans have as yet only a literary fatherland common to them all, and whereas the very voicing of this lament implies an allusion to a political unification as yet unachieved, he keeps strictly within the bounds of discretion. For all that, his tone is unmistakable; he points out very firmly where it seems to him the great Frederick went astray. If the Germans are behindhand, it is not for lack of assiduity in imitating the French models; the real reason is that they have not had the courage to rely for inspiration on their own genius. It is a mistake to value the formal French garden more than the great oaks of the Teutonic forests. Never would the sickly products of foreign hothouses grow successfully on German soil. *Goetz von Berlichingen* draws its inspiration from the nation's history, and that is what makes it so fine a play. The usual French tragedy is characterized by a factitious simplicity; it is the outcome of successive subtractions; and of abstractions as well; whereas the German drama of the youthful Goethe mirrors life in all its infinite variety. Thus we have two distinct conceptions of art, of which the latter is unquestionably to be preferred; and two conceptions of the world. It is also wrong to suppose that German literature will blossom only in the promised land, for it has blossomed already, and Klopstock, Bürger, Goethe are the proof thereof. The language itself, impoverished by ill-advised "purifications", is regaining its pristine richness by bringing in popular words and turns of speech. Lessing and Goethe have drawn on this source with the happiest results. Thus, if the King is mistaken, the reason doubtless is that he composed his statement some time ago, when the changes that have since come about in Germany were still wrapt in uncertainty, and at a time when he was still the pupil of Algarotti and Voltaire. How great he is as often as he puts his trust in that German strength which gives us the pledge that it will never fail! What a noble German heart he displays! But when he sets himself to compete with foreign nations, imitating the models set up by them, then he yields his pride of place, then he takes but the second rank, and great is the pity thereof.

Resistance here; rebellion there; fierce endeavours to bring down France from her envied throne; different languages, literatures and philosophies all directed to the task of giving utterance to an upsurge of national feeling that gathers strength with every day that passes: States that voice their determination to live their own particular way of life; Spain impenetrable to outside influences; Italy bent on restoring the ancient Roman unity; Germany becoming a great moral force in the world; England with ideas that are taking the Continent by storm; here then, to mention only those countries that directed the trend of public opinion throughout Europe, are a few of the factors overlooked by Rivarol when, with serene complacency, he proclaimed that the time was come when we might speak of "the French world".

There was to be no spiritual concord inspired by one living nation, and even such cultural community as did exist was threatened with extinction. All through the great classical period, all children of good family had lived in the company of Caesar, Livy, Virgil; they had hardly known whether to choose Hannibal or Scipio for their favourite; they had dreamed of imitating the great men portrayed by Plutarch; and the Urbs was their city. When these youngsters were no longer together, when they had grown to man's estate, they were not wholly adrift; there remained a moment in time, an interval in space, when they had all held ideas in common; and now they had memories that were shared by them all, and a common standard or canon by which they judged the present; once on a time they had dwelt together on a Happy Isle, and of those bygone days they still retained the recollection. But now this new sort of education, this craze for being modern, this hankering after some new state of things which each one imagined as his own particular dream-vision depicted it, tended to wipe out those bygone days in which they had once been so united.

Nor would there be any political concord; but, at the most, mere temporary coalitions which would always be breaking up as soon as they were made. It was not those men of wisdom, the philosophers, who would govern the various States, but much rather Machiavelli, stubborn and triumphant. There would be no such thing as universal peace, only a truce now and again for the time being, so as to give people a chance of preparing for the next war with still more effective means for mutual annihilation. For Science, as had been hoped, would increase man's power, but it would, by the same token, increase his power to destroy. The eighteenth century was to go out amid the wars of the Revolution, the nineteenth was to be ushered in by the campaigns of Napoleon.

And so it would go on; wars, revolutions, catastrophes on an amplified scale. To a Europe, a geographical entity not easy to define, to its vague agreements, its vague longings for a unified whole, its ideological projects, its aspirations for some future when the ills that were now so cruelly felt would be mitigated by a genuine agreement among the nations—to all this, to all these hopes, ideas and projects, would be opposed a false Europe, a chaos of rival interests and warring passions. In the end the whole would go down in ruin.

Is there nothing else to record, nothing in the intellectual order? Nothing but this tumult and disorder, these rancours, these everlasting struggles? Nothing but these storms and tempests, these shipwrecks, these drifting spars? Must despair be the end of it all? Europe indeed must have some indestructible vital principle within her since, amid unimaginable disasters and catastrophes, she still lives on.

We did indeed propound this question when we were examining Europe's intellectual history during the period that extends from 1680 to 1715, and, having declared that she was, to start with, a mob of nations for ever at war with one another, we went on, "What is this Europe? A spirit that is for ever seeking. Unsparing of herself, she is ceaselessly pursuing two goals; one of them is Happiness; the other—and this she holds the more vital, the more dear—is Truth. No sooner does she make some discovery that seems to her to satisfy her twofold need, than she suspects, nay, she knows, that what she grasps, all too precariously, is, after all, but a makeshift, an imperfect thing. And so she sets forth once more on her eternal quest, at once her glory and her endless pain." Yes, that indeed is how it was; and that, too, is how it is for this eighteenth century, and so, without doubt, it will continue; through all her failures, all her disappointments, the lasting vigour of a principle that saves.

Her unquenchable thirst for truth! Therein, however pitiable her plight, lies her greatness; therein it is that, above all other continents, she personifies the lot of human kind. She will not have it that what is, must be so of necessity. She puts not her trust in those mechanical devices which, while they add to our material comfort, lull our higher faculties to sleep. She is not faint-hearted; she holds her head high, she will not give in. The stone has rolled all down the mountain, it has fallen back again to the plain from whence it started; well, once more it must be heaved up again towards the peaks. So back to her task Europe betakes herself. She will never deem the price too high if only she fulfils her mission at last. She creates, but even then she is seeking. She rails against God, yet she is a believer still. Her discouragements know no morrow.

Europeans, for ever restless, says Voltaire.[1] "A spirit of freedom which makes each part of it very difficult to subjugate and to bring under a foreign power", says Montesquieu.[2] And Lessing: "What constitutes man's worth is not the truth he

[1]*Œeuvres*, Ed. Garnier, Vol. XXII, p. 491.
[2]*Esprit de Lois,* Book XVII, Chap. VI.

possesses, or thinks he possesses; it is the sincerity of the effort he makes to approach it. For it is not the possession of, but the search for, truth which strengthens the forces that contribute to his ever-growing perfection. Possession makes a man easy in his mind, inert and self-satisfied. If God held the whole truth in his right hand, and in his left, the eternal longing for truth . . . and if he were to bid me choose, humbly I should choose the left, saying 'Give me that, Father, for perfect truth is for thee alone'."[1]

Or to express the matter differently, in the words of a twentieth-century writer:[2]

"*He had begun to understand what Europe really meant to him. It stood not only for his own past, but for the past of three hundred millions of men, together with what he knew of it, and carried with him in his blood; not only the particular region which had produced him, but also the image and outline of all the countries between the North Sea and the Mediterranean, their atmosphere, their history, their development, not merely in connexion with this, that, or the other town in which he had stayed, but with hundreds of others, and in them, the churches, the palaces, the mansions, the works of art, the libraries, and all the traces their great men had left behind them Was there a single event in his life with which the memories of several generations were not linked up, memories born at the same time as himself? Europe was—the idea was inconceivable and filled him with awe—a single whole that had existed for thousands of years, Pericles and Nostradamus, Theodoric and Voltaire, Ovid and Erasmus, Archimedes and Gauss, Calderon and Dürer, Phidias and Mozart, Petrarch and Napoleon, Galileo and Nietzsche, a countless host of radiant spirits, and another host, equally innumerable, of demons, light always finding its counterpart in an equal mass of darkness, but shining bright in the midst of it, creating a vase of gold from the black dross around—catastrophes, noble inspirations, revolutions, eras of darkness, manners and fashions, the common weal, its fluctuations, its inter-relations, its gradual evolution; the Mind, such was Europe.*"

[1]G. E. Lessing, *Eine Duplik*, Werke, Ed. Hempel, Vol. XVI, 26.

[2]J. Wassermann, *Der Fall Maurizius. L'Affaire Maurizius*, translated from the German by J. G. Guidau, 1930.

INDEX

Paul Hazard was born on August 30, 1878. A literary historian and long a professor at the Sorbonne and Collège de France, he founded, with Fernand Baldensperger, the *Revue de littérature comparée* in 1921. Hazard is the author of the famous Ph.D. dissertation *La révolution française et les lettres italiennes, The European Mind* (Meridian Books—M152), and *European Thought in the Eighteenth Century*. Professor Hazard was elected to the French Academy in 1939 and in 1941 he was nominated as president of the Sorbonne but was rejected by the Nazis as unacceptable. He died in Paris on April 13, 1944.

MERIDIAN BOOKS

Art, Architecture, and Music

BARZUN, JACQUES *Berlioz and His Century.* M30
BERENSON, BERNARD *The Italian Painters of the Renaissance.* M40
BIKEL, THEODORE *Folksongs and Footnotes.* MG27
FRY, ROGER *Vision and Design.* M33
GILSON, ETIENNE *Painting and Reality.* M79
HUXLEY, ALDOUS *On Art and Artists.* M99
KAUFMANN, EDGAR, AND RAEBURN, BEN (EDS.) *Frank Lloyd Wright: Writings and Buildings.* MG22
NOSS, LUTHER (ED.) *Christian Hymns.* LA38
PACK, ROBERT, AND LELASH, MARJORIE (TRS.) *Mozart's Librettos.* M80
PANOFSKY, ERWIN *Gothic Architecture and Scholasticism.* M44
PATER, WALTER *The Renaissance.* M124
PHILIPSON, MORRIS (ED.) *Aesthetics Today.* M112
READ, HERBERT *The Grass Roots of Art.* M108
READ, HERBERT *The Philosophy of Modern Art.* M7
SMITH, G. E. KIDDER *The New Architecture of Europe.* MG33
STEINBERG, SAUL *The Catalogue.* M147
TOVEY, DONALD FRANCIS *The Forms of Music.* M36
TOVEY, DONALD FRANCIS *The Main Stream of Music and Other Essays.* M74

Fiction

BABEL, ISAAC *The Collected Stories.* MF3
BEDFORD, SYBILLE *A Legacy.* MF4
BELLOW, SAUL *Dangling Man.* MF9
BUECHNER, FREDERICK *A Long Day's Dying.* MF7
CURVERS, ALEXIS *Tempo di Roma.* MF15
DE BEAUVOIR, SIMONE *The Mandarins.* MF1
DENNIS, NIGEL *Cards of Identity.* MF13
DREISER, THEODORE *An American Tragedy.* MF21
GADDIS, WILLIAM *The Recognitions.* MF20
GASCAR, PIERRE *Beasts and Men* and *The Seed.* MF10
GOLD, HERBERT *Love and Like.* MF16
HOWE, IRVING, AND GREENBERG, ELIEZER (EDS.) *A Treasury of Yiddish Stories.* MG13
JARRELL, RANDALL *Pictures from an Institution.* MF2
MACAULAY, ROSE *The Towers of Trebizond.* MF8
PALEY, GRACE *The Little Disturbances of Man.* MF14

POWELL, ANTHONY *The Acceptance World.* MF11
RENAULT, MARY *The Charioteer.* MF19
ROSENFELD, ISAAC *Passage from Home.* MF18
ROTH, PHILIP *Goodbye, Columbus.* MF5
SPARK, MURIEL *Memento Mori.* MF12
STERN, RICHARD G. *Golk.* MF17
WILSON, ANGUS *The Middle Age of Mrs. Eliot.* MF6

Literature, Criticism, Drama, and Poetry

AIKEN, CONRAD *Ushant.* M148
AUBERBACH, ERICH *Scenes from the Drama of European Literature.* M63
BELLOW, SAUL; BOTSFORD, KEITH; AND LUDWIG, JACK (EDS.) *The Noble Savage 1.* M88
BELLOW, SAUL; BOTSFORD, KEITH; AND LUDWIG, JACK (EDS.) *The Noble Savage 2.* M102
BELLOW, SAUL, AND BOTSFORD, KEITH (EDS.) *The Noble Savage 3.* M113
BELLOW, SAUL, AND BOTSFORD, KEITH (EDS.) *The Noble Savage 4.* M125
BELLOW, SAUL, AND BOTSFORD, KEITH (EDS.) *The Noble Savage 5.* M136
BERDYAEV, NICHOLAS *Dostoevsky.* LA15
BERRYMAN, JOHN *Stephen Crane.* M131
BRADLEY, A. C. *Shakespearean Tragedy.* M20
BRENAN, GERALD *The Literature of the Spanish People.* MG9
BROOKS, VAN WYCK *The Ordeal of Mark Twain.* M14
BROWNE, E. MARTIN (ED.) *Religious Drama 2: Mystery and Morality Plays.* LA20
BURNSHAW, STANLEY (ED.) *The Poem Itself.* M142
EISENSTEIN, SERGEI *Film Form* and *The Film Sense.* MG10
EMPSON, WILLIAM *Seven Types of Ambiguity.* M11
FIEDLER, LESLIE A. *Love and Death in the American Novel* MG43
FOWLIE, WALLACE *Dionysus in Paris: A Guide to Contemporary French Theater.* M92
FOWLIE, WALLACE *A Guide to Contemporary French Literature.* M48
GRIGSON, GEOFFREY (ED.) *The Romantics.* M132
HALL, DONALD, AND PACK, ROBERT (EDS.) *New Poets of England and America: Second Selection.* M135
HALL, DONALD; PACK, ROBERT; AND SIMPSON, LOUIS (EDS.) *New Poets of England and America.* M50

HALVERSON, MARVIN (ED.) *Religious Drama 1: Five Plays.* LA10
HALVERSON, MARVIN (ED.) *Religious Drama 3.* LA27
HELLER, ERICH *The Disinherited Mind.* M66
HELLER, ERICH *Thomas Mann: The Ironic German.* M118
HIGHET, GILBERT *Talents and Geniuses.* M77
HOWE, IRVING *Politics and the Novel.* M46
HUXLEY, ALDOUS *Grey Eminence.* M70
KIRSCHBAUM, LEO *Clear Writing.* MG38
KIRSCHBAUM, LEO (ED.) *The Plays of Christopher Marlowe.* MG42
KNIGHT, G. WILSON *The Wheel of Fire.* M43
LOWELL, ROBERT *Lord Weary's Castle* and *The Mills of the Kavanaughs.* M107
MAUROIS, ANDRÉ *Proust: A Biography.* M54
MAYAKOVSKY, VLADIMIR *The Bedbug and Selected Poetry.* M94
New Directions 15: International Issue. M18
O'BRIEN, JUSTIN (ED.) *From the N.R.F.* MG20
PACIFICI, SERGIO *A Guide to Contemporary Italian Literature.* M122
PASTERNAK, BORIS *I Remember.* M100
PRAZ, MARIO *The Romantic Agony.* MG5
RAHV, PHILIP (ED.) *Literature in America.* MG11
RIVIERE, JACQUES *The Ideal Reader.* M103
ROSE, H. J. *Outlines of Classical Literature.* M119
STANISLAVSKI, CONSTANTIN *My Life in Art.* MG4
TATE, ALLEN *The Man of Letters in the Modern World.* M13
TRILLING, LIONEL *Matthew Arnold.* M19
WINTERS, YVOR *On Modern Poets.* M73

Social Sciences, Psychology, and Anthropology

ACTON, LORD *Essays on Freedom and Power.* M12
AICHHORN, AUGUST *Wayward Youth.* M5
ARENDT, HANNAH *The Origins of Totalitarianism.* MG15
COOKE, JACOB E. (ED.) *The Federalist.* MG39
CRAWLEY, ERNEST *The Mystic Rose.* MG24
FREUND, PAUL A. *The Supreme Court of the United States.* M123
FROBENIUS, LEO *The Childhood of Man.* MG23
GLOVER, EDWARD *Freud or Jung?* M34
HARRISON, JANE ELLEN *Prolegomena to the Study of Greek Religion.* MG3
HARRISON, JANE ELLEN *Themis: A Study of the Social Origins of Greek Religion.* M145

HUTCHINS, ROBERT M. *Freedom, Education, and the Fund.* M31
JUNG, C. G. *Answer to Job.* M86
JUNG, C. G. *Two Essays on Analytical Psychology.* M28
KARDINER, ABRAM, AND OVESEY, LIONEL *The Mark of Oppression: Explorations in the Personality of the American Negro.* M141
LASSWELL, HAROLD *Politics: Who Gets What, When, How.* M58
LEKACHMAN, ROBERT (ED.) *The Varieties of Economics, Vol. I.* MG46A
LEKACHMAN, ROBERT (ED.) *The Varieties of Economics, Vol. II.* MG46B
LERNER, DANIEL (ED.) *The Human Meaning of the Social Sciences.* M64
MACDONALD, DWIGHT *Memoirs of a Revolutionist.* M56
MALINOWSKI, BRONISLAW *Sex and Repression in Savage Society.* M15
NELSON, BENJAMIN (ED.) *Freud and the 20th Century.* M45
PIAGET, JEAN *The Language and Thought of the Child.* M10
ROSE, H. J. *Gods and Heroes of the Greeks.* M59
ROVERE, RICHARD H. *Senator Joe McCarthy.* M98
SCHUMPETER, JOSEPH *Imperialism and Social Classes.* M4
SWADOS, HARVEY (ED.) *Years of Conscience: The Muckrakers.* M129
WILLIAMS, CHARLES *Witchcraft.* M62
WILSON, WOODROW *Congressional Government.* M27
ZIMMER, HEINRICH *The King and the Corpse.* M93

History

ACTON, LORD *Lectures on Modern History.* M109
BOORSTIN, DANIEL J. *America and the Image of Europe.* M89
COULTON, G. G. *Medieval Panorama.* MG2
D'ARCY, M. C. *The Meaning and Matter of History.* M110
DAWSON, CHRISTOPHER *The Making of Europe.* M35
DILL, SAMUEL *Roman Society in the Last Century of the Western Empire.* MG31
DILL, SAMUEL *Roman Society from Nero to Marcus Aurelius.* MG48
FINLEY, M. I. *The World of Odysseus.* M68
GEYL, PIETER *Debates with Historians.* M57
GEYL, PIETER *Encounters in History.* M114
GLATZER, NAHUM N. (ED.) *Jerusalem and Rome: The Writings of Josephus.* M106

GRANET, MARCEL *Chinese Civilization.* MG14
HASKINS, C. H. *The Renaissance of the 12th Century.* M49
History 1. M72
History 2. M83
History 3. M95
History 4. M117
HUIZINGA, JOHAN *Men and Ideas.* M61
KIRKPATRICK, F. A. *The Spanish Conquistadores.* M146
LUETHY, HERBERT *France Against Herself.* MG8
MAYER, J. P. (ED.) *The Recollections of Alexis de Tocqueville.* M82
MOMMSEN, THEODOR *The History of Rome.* MG32
PIRENNE, HENRI *Mohammed and Charlemagne.* M42
ROEDER, RALPH *The Man of the Renaissance.* MG17
RUNCIMAN, STEVEN *Byzantine Civilization.* M23
SAUNDERS, DERO A. (ED.) *The Autobiography of Edward Gibbon.* M111
SEYFERT, OSCAR *Dictionary of Classical Antiquities.* MG34
STERN, FRITZ (ED.) *The Varieties of History.* M37
TARN, W. W. *Hellenistic Civilisation.* M121
TOYNBEE, ARNOLD *Civilization on Trial* and *The World and the West.* M52
WOODCOCK, GEORGE *Anarchism: A History of Libertarian Ideas and Movements.* M133

Meridian Documents of American History

BARCK, OSCAR THEODORE, JR. (ED.) *America in the World.* M127
DIVINE, ROBERT A. (ED.) *American Foreign Policy.* M91
KIRWAN, ALBERT D. (ED.) *The Confederacy.* M76
KLINGBERG, FRANK W. (ED.) *A History of the United States: From 1865 to the Present.* M115
LEFLER, HUGH T. (ED.) *A History of the United States: From the Age of Exploration to 1865.* M101

Philosophy

BABBITT, IRVING *Rousseau and Romanticism.* M3
BOSANQUET, BERNARD *A History of Aesthetic.* MG36
BURKE, KENNETH *A Grammar of Motives* and *A Rhetoric of Motives.* M143
BURNET, JOHN *Early Greek Philosophy.* MG30
CLIVE, GEOFFREY *The Romantic Enlightenment.* M85

COHEN, MORRIS R. *A Preface to Logic.* M32
GUARDINI, ROMANO *The Death of Socrates.* M138
HERBERG, WILL (ED.) *The Writings of Martin Buber.* M29
HUME, DAVID *A Treatise of Human Nature, Book 1: Of the Understanding.* M139
HUXLEY, ALDOUS *The Perennial Philosophy.* M144
JAMES, WILLIAM *Essays on Faith and Morals.* M130
JAMES, WILLIAM *Pragmatism.* M16
KAUFMANN, WALTER (ED.) *Existentialism from Dostoevsky to Sartre.* M39
KAUFMANN, WALTER *Nietzsche.* M25
KONVITZ, MILTON R., AND KENNEDY, GAIL (EDS.) *The American Pragmatists.* M105
MARITAIN, JACQUES *Creative Intuition in Art and Poetry.* M8
MARSAK, LEONARD (ED.) *French Philosophers from Descartes to Sartre.* MG40
MILL, JOHN STUART *Utilitarianism, On Liberty, Essay on Bentham.* M140
MOLNAR, THOMAS *The Decline of the Intellectual.* M128
MONTESQUIEU *The Persian Letters.* M104
ORTEGA Y GASSET, JOSÉ *On Love.* M84
ROSS, W. D. *Aristotle.* M65
RUSSELL, BERTRAND *An Outline of Philosophy.* M97
SALOMON, ALBERT *In Praise of Enlightenment.* M137
TAYLOR, A. E. *Plato: The Man and His Work.* MG7
VIGNAUX, PAUL *Philosophy in the Middle Ages.* M81
WOLFSON, HARRY AUSTRYN *The Philosophy of Spinoza.* MG16
ZELLER, EDWARD *Outlines of the History of Greek Philosophy.* M9
ZIMMER, HEINRICH *Philosophies of India.* MG6

Religion (General)

BARTH, KARL *Anselm: Fides Quaerens Intellectum (Faith in Search of Understanding).* LA39
BOUYER, LOUIS *Newman.* M87
CAMPBELL, JOSEPH *The Hero with a Thousand Faces.* M22
COGLEY, JOHN (ED.) *Religion in America.* M60
DANIÉLOU, JEAN *God and the Ways of Knowing.* M96
D'ARCY, M. C. *The Mind and Heart of Love.* M26
D'ARCY, M. C., GILSON, ETIENNE, ET AL. *St. Augustine: His Age, Life, and Thought.* M51

DAWSON, CHRISTOPHER *Religion and Culture.* M53

DRIVER, S. R. *An Introduction to the Literature of the Old Testament.* MG29

DUPONT-SOMMER, A. *The Essene Writings from Qumran.* MG44

HAZELTON, ROGER (ED.) *Selected Writings of St. Augustine.* LA37

LIETZMANN, HANS *A History of the Early Church, Vol. I.* MG26A

LIETZMANN, HANS *A History of the Early Church, Vol. II.* MG26B

MARITAIN, JACQUES *St. Thomas Aquinas.* M55

MILLER, PERRY *Jonathan Edwards.* M75

PIKE, E. ROYSTON *Encyclopaedia of Religion and Religions.* MG37

REINHOLD, H. A. (ED.) *The Soul Afire.* MG28

SMITH, W. ROBERTSON *The Religion of the Semites.* ML4

UNDERHILL, EVELYN *Mysticism.* MG1

WELLHAUSEN, JULIUS *Prolegomena to the History of Ancient Israel.* MG35

WHITE, VICTOR *God and the Unconscious.* M120

WHITEHEAD, ALFRED NORTH *Religion in the Making.* LA28

WILSON, EDMUND *The Scrolls from the Dead Sea.* M69

Of Catholic Interest

BOUYER, LOUIS *Newman.* M87

BROWNE, E. MARTIN (ED.) *Religious Drama 2: Mystery and Morality Plays.* LA20

COGLEY, JOHN (ED.) *Religion in America.* M60

DANIÉLOU, JEAN *God and the Ways of Knowing.* M96

D'ARCY, M. C. *The Meaning and Matter of History.* M110

D'ARCY, M. C. *The Mind and Heart of Love.* M26

D'ARCY, M. C., GILSON, ETIENNE, ET AL. *St. Augustine: His Age, Life, and Thought.* M51

DAWSON, CHRISTOPHER *The Making of Europe.* M35

DAWSON, CHRISTOPHER *Religion and Culture.* M53

GUARDINI, ROMANO *The Death of Socrates.* M138

HASKINS, C. H. *The Renaissance of the 12th Century.* M49

HAZELTON, ROGER (ED.) *Selected Writings of St. Augustine.* LA37

MARITAIN, JACQUES *Creative Intuition in Art and Poetry.* M8

MARITAIN, JACQUES *St. Thomas Aquinas.* M55

MARTY, MARTIN E. *A Short History of Christianity.* LA24

REINHOLD, H. A. *The Soul Afire.* MG28

VIGNAUX, PAUL *Philosophy in the Middle Ages.* M81

WHITE, VICTOR *God and the Unconscious.* M120

Of Protestant Interest (Living Age Books)

BARTH, KARL *Anselm: Fides Quaerens Intellectum (Faith in Search of Understanding).* LA39

BARTH, KARL *The Faith of the Church.* LA22

BERDYAEV, NICHOLAS *Dostoevsky.* LA15

BERDYAEV, NICHOLAS *The Meaning of History.* LA36

BOEHMER, HEINRICH *Martin Luther: Road to Reformation.* LA9

BRIGHTMAN, F. E. (ED.) *The Private Devotions of Lancelot Andrewes.* LA32

BROWNE, E. MARTIN *Religious Drama 2: Mystery and Morality Plays.* LA20

BULTMANN, RUDOLF *Primitive Christianity in Its Contemporary Setting.* LA4

BURROWS, MILLAR *What Mean These Stones?* LA7

CULLMANN, OSCAR *Peter: Disciple, Apostle, Martyr.* LA21

DODD, C. H. *The Meaning of Paul for Today.* LA8

FEY, HAROLD E. (ED.) *How My Mind Has Changed.* LA33

GILL, THEODORE (ED.) *The Sermons of John Donne.* LA17

HALVERSON, MARVIN (ED.) *Religious Drama 1: Five Plays.* LA10

HALVERSON, MARVIN (ED.) *Religious Drama 3.* LA27

HALVERSON, MARVIN, AND COHEN, ARTHUR A. (EDS.) *A Handbook of Christian Theology.* LA18

HAZELTON, ROGER (ED.) *Selected Writings of St. Augustine.* LA37

HOLL, KARL *The Cultural Significance of the Reformation.* LA25

INGE, W. R. *Christian Mysticism.* LA3

LEFEVER, ERNEST; MORGENTHAU, HANS (INTRO.) *Ethics and United States Foreign Policy.* LA19

MARTY, MARTIN E. *The Infidel: Freethought and American Religion.* LA34

MARTY, MARTIN E. *A Short History of Christianity.* LA24

NIEBUHR, H. RICHARD *The Social Sources of Denominationalism.* LA11

NIEBUHR, REINHOLD *An Interpretation of Christian Ethics.* LA1

NIEBUHR, REINHOLD *Essays in Applied Christianity.* LA26

NIEBUHR, REINHOLD *Leaves from the Notebooks of a Tamed Cynic.* LA13

NOSS, LUTHER (ED.) *Christian Hymns.* LA38

OESTERLEY, W. O. E., AND ROBINSON, THEODORE H. *An Introduction to the Books of the Old Testament.* LA23

OGDEN, SCHUBERT M. (ED.) *Existence and Faith: Shorter Writings of Rudolf Bultmann.* LA29

OTTO, RUDOLF *Mysticism East and West.* LA14
ROWLEY, H. H. *The Unity of the Bible.* LA16
SAYERS, DOROTHY L. *The Mind of the Maker.* LA2
TALON, HENRI A. *God's Knotty Log: Selected Writings of John Bunyan.* LA31
THOMPSON, BARD (ED.) *Liturgies of the Western Church.* LA35
TILLICH, PAUL *The Religious Situation.* LA6
TROELTSCH, ERNEST *Christian Thought.* LA12
VISSER 'T HOOFT, W. A. *Rembrandt and the Gospel.* LA30
WHITEHEAD, ALFRED NORTH *Religion in the Making.* LA28
WILLIAMS, CHARLES *The Descent of the Dove.* LA5

Of Jewish Interest (Jewish Publication Society Series)

ABRAHAMS, ISRAEL *Jewish Life in the Middle Ages.* JP4
ASCH, SHOLEM *Kiddush Ha-Shem* and *Sabbatai Zevi.* JP9
BAECK, LEO *Judaism and Christianity.* JP23
BARON, SALO W. *Modern Nationalism and Religion.* JP18
BEIN, ALEX *Theodore Herzl.* JP30
BUBER, MARTIN *For the Sake of Heaven.* JP1
DUBNOW, SIMON *Nationalism and History: Essays on Old and New Judaism.* JP20
FINKELSTEIN, LOUIS *Akiba: Scholar, Saint and Martyr.* JP25
GINZBERG, LOUIS *On Jewish Law and Lore.* JP26
GINZBERG, LOUIS *Students, Scholars and Saints.* JP2
GRAYZEL, SOLOMON *A History of the Contemporary Jews.* JP16
HA-'AM, AHAD *Selected Essays.* JP29
HERBERG, WILL *Judaism and Modern Man.* JP10
HERTZBERG, ARTHUR (ED.) *The Zionist Idea.* JP17
HESCHEL, ABRAHAM JOSHUA *God in Search of Man.* JP7
HESCHEL, ABRAHAM JOSHUA *The Earth Is the Lord's* and *The Sabbath.* JP28
HUSIK, ISAAC *A History of Mediaeval Jewish Philosophy.* JP3
KORN, BERTRAM W. *American Jewry and the Civil War.* JP24
LEWY, HANS; ALTMANN, ALEXANDER; AND HEINEMANN, ISAAK (EDS.) *Three Jewish Philosophers.* JP13
LIPTZIN, SOLOMON *Germany's Stepchildren.* JP19
MARCUS, JACOB R. *The Jew in the Medieval World.* JP14
MARGOLIS, MAX, AND MARX, ALEXANDER *A History of the Jewish People.* JP6

MODDER, MONTAGU FRANK *The Jew in the Literature of England.* JP15

PARKES, JAMES *The Conflict of the Church and the Synagogue.* JP21

ROTH, CECIL *A History of the Marranos.* JP12

SAMUEL, MAURICE *Prince of the Ghetto.* JP11

SCHECHTER, SOLOMON *Studies in Judaism.* JP5

SPIEGEL, SHALOM *Hebrew Reborn.* JP27

STRACK, HERMANN L. *Introduction to the Talmud and Midrash.* JP8

TRACHTENBERG, JOSHUA *The Devil and the Jews.* JP22

Natural Sciences

DANTO, ARTHUR, AND MORGENBESSER, SIDNEY (EDS.) *Philosophy of Science.* M90

DAMPIER, WILLIAM CECIL *A Shorter History of Science.* M47

GALTON, FRANCIS *Hereditary Genius.* M134

IRVINE, WILLIAM *Apes, Angels, and Victorians.* M78

KÖHLER, WOLFGANG *The Place of Value in a World of Facts.* MG19

NORTHROP, F. S. C. *The Logic of the Sciences and the Humanities.* M71

PEARSON, KARL *The Grammar of Science.* ML7

General and Reference

BOLTIN, LEE *Jail Keys Made Here and Other Signs.* MG21

ELAM, SAMUEL MILTON *Hornbook for the Double Damned.* MG47

JEFFERY, GRANT *Science & Technology Stocks: A Guide for Investors.* MG41

KIRSCHBAUM, LEO *Clear Writing.* MG38

The Meridian Compact Atlas of the World. M126

SEYFFERT, OSCAR *Dictionary of Classical Antiquities.* MG34

SIMON, KATE *New York Places & Pleasures: Revised Edition.* MG18R

Webster's New World Dictionary of the American Language (Concise Edition). MG25

Meridian Books are published by The World Publishing Company, Cleveland and New York. For a free Meridian catalogue please write to Department AM, Meridian Books, 119 West 57th Street, New York 19, New York.